W9-CCQ-753

FREEDOM, VIRTUE, AND
THE COMMON GOOD

American Maritain Association Publications

General Editor: Anthony O. Simon

———————————

Jacques Maritain: The Man and His Metaphysics
Edited by John F. X. Knasas, 1988
ISBN 0-268-01205-9 (out of print)

Freedom in the Modern World: Jacques Maritain, Yves R. Simon,
Mortimer J. Adler
Edited by Michael D. Torre, 1989, Second Printing 1990
ISBN 0-268-00978-3

From Twilight to Dawn: The Cultural Vision of Jacques Maritain
Edited by Peter Redpath, 1990
ISBN 0-268-00979-1

The Future of Thomism
Edited by Deal W. Hudson and Dennis Wm. Moran, 1992
ISBN 0-268-00986-4

Jacques Maritain and the Jews
Edited by Robert Royal, 1994
ISBN 0-268-01193-1

Freedom, Virtue, and the Common Good
Edited by Curtis L. Hancock and Anthony O. Simon, 1995
ISBN 0-268-00991-0

FREEDOM, VIRTUE, AND THE COMMON GOOD

Curtis L. Hancock

&

Anthony O. Simon

Editors

With Epilogue by

Michael Novak

American Maritain Association
Distributed by University of Notre Dame Press

Copyright © 1995 by

American Maritain Association

All Rights Reserved

Manufactured in the
United States of America

Library of Congress Cataloging-in-Publication-Data

Freedom, virtue, and the common good / Curtis L. Hancock & Anthony O.
    Simon, editors ; with epilogue by Michael Novak.
        p.   cm. — (American Maritain Association publications)
    Includes bibliographical references and index.
    ISBN 0-268-00991-0 (cl.)   0-268-00992-9 (pb.)
    1. Virtue. 2. Comon good. 3. Man. 4. Natural law. 5. Human
rights. 6. Christian ethics. 7. Sociology, Christian (Catholic)
I. Hancock, Curtis L., 1950–   . II. Simon, Anthony O.
III. Series.
BJ1531.F74 1995   95-686
170—dc20   CIP

∞ *The paper used in this publication meets the minimum requirements of the American
National Standard for Information Sciences—Permanence of Paper for Printed Library
Materials, ANSI Z39.48-1984.*

American Maritain Association
Anthony O. Simon, Secretary
508 Travers Circle
Mishawaka, Indiana 46545

Distributed by University of Notre Dame Press
Notre Dame, Indiana 46556

IN MEMORIAM:

PATRIS WILLIAM L. ROSSNER, S.J.,
AMATOR SAPIENTIAE

Contents

Acknowledgments

While compiling and editing this collection of essays, many friends and colleagues have counseled and encouraged us. We would like to thank Raymond Dennehy, Deal W. Hudson, and Peter Redpath for their availability and moral support throughout the editing of this volume.

In addition, we would like to thank John Ehmann, James Langford, and Jeffrey Gainey of the University of Notre Dame Press for their help in coordinating schedules for publication. Thanks also must go to Fred Schoerner of Photo Composition Service, Grand Rapids, Michigan, who supplied the camera-ready manuscript.

We are also grateful to Jules Brady, S. J., and Joseph Freeman, S. J., Professors of Philosophy at Rockhurst College, who provided financial support for preparing this publication. They have also inspired us by their deep appreciation for Maritain and Simon and the Perennial Philosophy.

Three other members of the Rockhurst College Community must also be thanked. Rodney Yarnal was of invaluable assistance in providing the computer skills necessary to compile the initial set of essays. Renee McGautha also helped in this regard. Dr. Charles Kovich, Chair of the Department of English, carefully read the penultimate manuscript.

Further, we express our gratitude to Ralph McInerny, Director of the Jacques Maritain Center at the University of Notre Dame, for his advice and his commitment to the aims of the American Maritain Association. Also we must thank Michael Novak of the American Enterprise Institute for graciously accepting our invitation to write the Epilogue to this volume.

Lastly, a tribute must be paid to our wives, Sandra Hancock and Judith Simon, who endured and encouraged us during these seasons of work.

Introduction:
Lessons and Reminders

It has become something of a commonplace to declare that modern moral philosophy has bankrupted itself on account of numerous confusions and errant assumptions. What was once the occasional complaint of certain Catholic intellectuals, such as Jacques Maritain and Yves R. Simon, who argued forcefully that the Enlightenment project had borne little fruit to nourish either speculative or practical understanding, has now been sounded even by thinkers prominent in the "mainstream" Anglo-American philosophical community. In a work that snapped many ethicists out of their modernist slumbers, Alasdair MacIntyre argued that the Enlightenment vision of ethics has left us either with the empty formalism of deontology or the sterile quantification of utilitarianism. Sadly, these are, it turns out, the only "accepted" alternatives available to those thinkers still brazen enough to maintain that there is an ethics at all, for a great many philosophers have dismissed the very possibility of such a discipline, embracing instead emotivism or nihilism. These latter, MacIntyre says in *After Virtue*, are live options for descendants of the Enlightenment view of ethics given that neither Kantianism nor utilitarianism commit to a definite view of the good, leaving it ultimately to be defined as a matter of preference. Hence, by the late twentieth-century moral life has been reduced by the philosophers to so many arbitrary choices. Attendant on this is the prevailing "malaise" which has produced many commentaries by those of an "existentialist" persuasion.

The present volume is an examination of the philosophical errors that have pushed moral philosophy into its narrow and uncomfortable corner. Indeed, MacIntyre's work influences several articles that contribute to this examination (Loughran, Ramos, Hibbs). Yet this book is

1

not just a polemical exercise. It is also constructive, aiming to restore an ethics that puts moral philosophy back on a sound footing.

One might say that this work is an effort at "recovering" a *virtue ethics*, broadly understood as a moral philosophy giving primacy to character-formation and to the development of individual and social habits that reflect the attainment of a life lived in a fully human sense. By its appeal to a standard of human actualization, virtue ethics may alternatively be called a "natural law" morality insofar as the latter refers to norms in human nature requisite for determining how a human being ought to live; that is to say, natural law identifies those natural potentialities which, by means of prescribed habits and actions, must be actualized in order for a human life to be meaningfully lived.

Natural law and virtue supply the foundations not just for ethics as it is individually realized but as it is communally lived as well, a point indicated by our reference above to social habits as well as individual ones. Accordingly, in addition to outlining the nature of a virtue ethics in general, this volume will discuss prescriptions for how the human person ought to live as a social and political creature. After all, it is in our communal life that the wayward ethics of modernist philosophy has produced its signal failures, sometimes spawning monstrous ideologies regarding the social condition and role of the human being. Perverse theories of the common good and of political authority have emerged because of failed philosophical anthropology, for as one's philosophy of the human person goes so goes one's ethics. This point is reiterated at the end of this book as Michael Novak explains that the common good is often a pretext for tyranny. His remarks echo Yves R. Simon.

> In all periods of history, voluminous facts signify that under the name of common good, republic, fatherland, empire, what is actually pursued may not be a good state of human affairs but a work of art designed to provide its creator with the inebriating experience of creation. The joy of the creator assumes unique intensity when the thing out of which the work of art is made is human flesh and soul. The artist's rapture is greatest when he uses as matter of his own creation not marble and brass but beings made after the image of God.[1]

---

[1] Yves R. Simon, *A General Theory of Authority* (Notre Dame, Indiana: University of Notre Dame Press, 1980), p. 27.

The common good has to *respect* the human person, not merely use her or him as a means to political ends. This check on the abuses of the common good requires a sensitive philosophy of the human person so as to understand what sort of individual and communal life truly and fully befits human beings.

As a group of "recoverists" (as Russell Hittinger has named contemporary champions of natural law ethics), the contributors to this volume are serious about retrieving an intelligent philosophy of human nature as a necessary condition for setting ethics aright. These contributors also provide a warning, for much of what passes as natural law ethics has often been merely its counterfeit. "Natural law" is an expression fraught with dangers when used in philosophical discourse. It is subject to serious misinterpretations which undermine the value of its recovery. History records these misinterpretations, many of which continue to make it suspect in the eyes of contemporary thinkers, even among those who in principle would be sympathetic with its recovery.

Error and falsification crept in as Renaissance thinkers, such as Grotius, began, perhaps unwittingly, to divorce natural law from the virtues.[2] Matters only worsened as Renaissance rationalism began to absolutize natural law into fixed rules and prohibitions, a tendency that even many Thomists later, certainly of the "manual" variety, demonstrated to their shame. This, combined with a deductive methodology so dear to the rationalists, turned natural law ethics into a caricature of morality, making it more like geometry than a philosophical discipline. What took place ultimately was a confusion of the speculative with the practical reason, an error endemic to deontological "solutions." Such an ethics reduces moral experience to a matter of rules and fails to affirm moral choice and action as principally a matter of actual, lived existence, where the human being is often situated in ambivalent circumstances; where prudence, not categorical imperatives, must govern choice and action. Maritain salutes the existentialism of thinkers like Kierkegaard, Marcel, and Berdyaev, however many limits their philosophy may suffer otherwise, for at least averting the error of rationalistic and formalistic accounts of moral life—accounts which

---

[2]See Jacques Maritain, *Man and the State* (Chicago: The University of Chicago Press, 1971), p. 84.

ignore the inductive bases of ethics and which overlook the need to situate ethics on existence rather than essence.

This last remark demands clarification as it is central to an intelligent and successful recovery of natural law ethics. Natural law has often been interpreted along essentialistic lines, reducing human nature—the cornerstone of natural law—to an anemic abstraction or even to a Platonic Form, neither of which expresses the existential circumstances of the human person, which are *lived* and *individual*. As with philosophical anthropology, the lessons of one's metaphysics will radically influence the development of one's ethics. Averting the error of essentialism will keep ethics from devolving into apriorism, with its idolatry of deductive inference and abstractions. Instead, the kind of recovery Maritain and Simon envision is based on an "authentic existentialism," an expression serving to remind us that moral agents are not essences but individual subjects, actual *existents*. According to this metaphysics, existence has primacy over essence in that existence, as a real intrinsic principle of a being, actuates that being's very nature. Things do not exist as universals, or as abstract essences, but as *this* or *that* real existent, having been actuated by a distinct intrinsic principle, *esse*, the act of existence. Human beings indeed have natures, and the expression "human nature" has objective meaning, separating effectively this metaphysics from the contemporary philosophies of Sartre's variety which claim such a phrase is empty. Still, it is necessary to appreciate that our human nature is *existential*; in other words, it always exists in *particular* social and historical situations—a truth Sartre understood, but he erred by making it the premiss to deny that there are essences. Hence, the principle of existence radically individuates and circumstantializes moral life, a point so often overlooked by natural lawyers as they draw their conclusions *more geometrico demonstrata*.

In spite of the fact that many Thomists in the past were victims of an encroaching apriorism and essentialism, some members of that tradition did escape these errors and should be honored for understanding the deeper anthropological and metaphysical foundations. Listening to their words now will forewarn us as we begin to commission a natural law ethics for a new age.

Michael Bertram Crowe spoke specifically of the *anthropological* foundations when he published the following words in 1981:

> To begin with, we have a basic anthropology, a conception of human nature which is the underpinning of morality. The phrase "human nature"

can be highly ambiguous: and Thomas' appeal to it has been presented in a simplistic way. In reality his concept of human nature is far more complex and far more flexible than is often assumed. It should not be forgotten that he did say, upon occasion, that human nature is changeable (*natura humana mutabilis est*). He also had a good deal to say about the flexibility and variability of moral reasonings, which would belie the rigid conclusions often foisted upon him in the name of human nature. As a good Aristotelian, he recognized that in moral matters one cannot look for the kind of demonstrations and certainty appropriate to the speculative sciences. (*In negotiis humanis non potest haberi demonstrativa probatio et infallibilis; sed sufficit aliqua conjecturalis probabilitas.*) These assertions are less startling when seen in their context. For Aquinas is not talking about unchanging abstract nature, but about human nature concretely exemplified in the individual, who finds himself in a particular historical and cultural situation in which his fellow-men play an inescapable part. Aquinas would hardly accept Sartre's suggestion that human nature is what we make ourselves; but he might have considerable sympathy for . . . [the] notion of man's nature in a process of development to which man himself contributes.[3]

A second counsel heard from the Thomistic tradition is that of Leo Sweeney, who reminds us that, since our existence actuates our relationships as well as other aspects of our essence, and since these relationships may be uniquely ours, the circumstances of one agent's choices and actions may be quite different from and only analogous to another's. In making this important point, Sweeney speaks to the *metaphysical* foundations of a sound natural law ethics.

The fact that Aquinas' existentialism is authentic can also profit contemporary radical existentialists, as well even as non-existentialists. "Natural law" is anathema to radical existentialists who accept Sartre's dictum, "Existence precedes essence or nature," where the verb "precedes" is equivalent to "eliminates." On the other hand, "natural law" can be taken in too rigid and narrow a sense by traditionalists and essentialists. What better interpretation does Thomas himself offer? In his existentialism "essence" or "nature" includes absolutely everything in someone except existence;

---

[3]Michael Bertram Crowe, "Thomism and Today's Crisis in Moral Values," in *One Hundred Years of Thomism*, ed. Victor B. Brezik (Houston, Texas: Center for Thomistic Studies, 1981), pp. 83–84.

therefore, it comprises not only a man's soul and matter (his substantial being), his faculties and their operations, the operative habits (both moral and
intellectual) which perfect them, his skills; but also all his relationships—
spatial, temporal, ecological, familial, civic, cultural, environmental: all
these are the actual situations in which he lives, all these help constitute
his *nature* (see S.T., I, 84, 7 resp.). But the natural law is founded directly
upon nature; therefore, natural law is founded upon and must express all
those actual and intrinsic perfections, including, yes, his substantial being
(which he has in common with other people), his operative powers, habits
and skills, but also his relationships (which may be uniquely his).

Thus existentially conceived, natural law remains an objective norm,
based not only on the accidental but also on the substantial aspects of his
being (thus it would be better than the often arbitrary and entirely subjective set of values a radical existentialist such as Sartre might elaborate for
himself). But it is more concrete and flexible than more traditional and
abstract conceptions of natural law because it takes into account the entire
actual person—not only in his substantial being and properties but also
in all his individual circumstances and situations (hence, it may offer a
greater opening to individual morally justified choices . . .).[4]

What these observations mean is not lost on Maritain, who in *Existence and The Existent* boldly describes their implications, especially
in light of the fact that a human being's relationships include God
and that God's revelation and grace put into final perspective human
existence.

St. Thomas teaches that the standard of the gifts of the Holy Ghost is
higher than that of the moral virtues; that of the gift of counsel is higher
than that of prudence. The saints always amaze us. Their virtues are freer
than those of a merely virtuous man. Now and again, in circumstances
outwardly alike, they act quite differently from the way in which a merely
virtuous man acts. They are indulgent where he would be severe, severe
where he would be indulgent. When a saint deserts her children or exposes
them to rebellion in order to enter into religion; when another saint allows
her brother to be assassinated at the monastery gate in order that there be
no violation of the cloister; when a saint strips himself naked before his
bishop out of love of poverty; when another chooses to be a beggar and
shocks people by his vermin; when another abandons the duties of his

---

4Leo Sweeney, "Can St. Thomas Speak to The Modern World," *ibid.*, pp. 133–134.

status in society and becomes a galley slave out of love of the captives; when still another allows himself to be unjustly condemned rather than defend himself against a dishonorable accusation—they go beyond the mean. What does that signify? They have their own kind of mean, their own kinds of standards. But they are valid only for each one of them. Although their standards are higher than those of reason, it is not because of the object taken in itself that the act measured by their standards is better than an act measured by the mere moral virtues; rather it is so by the inner impetus which the saints receive from the Spirit of God in the depths of their incommunicable subjectivity, which impetus goes beyond the measure of reason to a higher good discerned by them alone, and to which they are called to bear witness.[5]

Does this mean that there is no natural law? Does this mean that Maritain's existentialist ethics has brought us to a pure subjectivism? No, for the exception proves the rule: there is a human nature, but since it is always *this* or *that* human nature, characterized in part by unique relationships, natural law requires a healthy sense of analogous application; what is more, in the case of the saints, its application may be so strained as to appear equivocal because commands of their conscience are now mediated by natural law that is informed and elevated by their intimate relationship with God Himself, the author of natural law. It is now a natural law stamped by grace that rules their lives. The point is that natural law ethics fails if it loses sight of the fact that human persons, by virtue of their unique relationships to the world around them, to other persons, and to the Person of God, can accommodate and respond to remarkably divergent—indeed, seemingly equivocal—callings.

This is why there would be no saintliness in the world if all excess and all that reason judges insensate were removed from the world. This is why we utter something deeper than we realise when we say of such acts that they are admirable but not imitable. They are not generalisable, universalisable. They are good; indeed, they are the best of all moral acts. But they are good only for him who does them. We are here very far from the Kantian universal with its morality defined by the possibility of making the maxim of an act into a law for all men.[6]

---

[5]Jacques Maritain, *Existence and the Existent* (New York: Pantheon Books, 1964), pp. 55–56.
[6]*Ibid.*, 56.

We are also here very far from an abstract, deductive, *a priori* natural law morality.

These are chastening words that tell us of the conditions and parameters for a satisfactory recovery of a natural law and virtue ethics tradition. In short, Maritain is saying that natural law must suit the *Perennial Philosophy*, which is open to truths discovered anywhere, including the truths which radiate from the Gospel and which illuminate the community of saints. Thus, the Perennial Philosophy must foreswear a rigid, narrow, abstract, *a priori*, essentialistic, ahistorical, asocial view of the natural law. In other words, if a natural law philosophy is to be satisfactory, it must not be just a theoretical construction but an ethics emerging out of reflection on the concrete, practical, living circumstances of free, human existents.

Taking these words to heart, the articles contained herein elaborate the central elements of a natural law and virtue ethics, showing, first, how such an ethics applies to our individual and communal existence and, secondly, how it satisfies the demands of the Perennial Philosophy. To express this twofold aim, the contents are divided into three parts: Part I: "First Principles and The Human Person"; Part II: "Moral Directives: Principles, Habits, and Judgments"; and Part III: "The Moral Agent and The Common Good." The volume closes with a timely epilogue by Michael Novak.

In Part I Don Asselin, Mary Carmen Rose, and Brendan Sweetman make a contribution to the prefatory discourse necessary for rooting moral philosophy in the deeper anthropological foundations. Don Asselin provides a penetrating discussion of human nature, entertaining an analysis and criticism about evidence for the soul's immortality. Mary Carmen Rose amplifies on man's spiritual nature by discussing alternative accounts of the good—accounts which focus on competing arguments about the nature of human appetite and our inclination to the highest good, God. Brendan Sweetman boldly compares Maritain and Marcel on the question of primitive, pre-conceptual, non-rational human inclinations—connaturality, if you will—toward the goods which rightly orient moral life, and which philosophy as an intellectual discipline seeks to make formally and explicitly intelligible. The interface between Maritain and Marcel on connatural understanding is often mentioned in passing but seldom studied in depth. Sweetman has remedied this deficiency in the literature by contributing here a lucid analysis.

Having set the scene with these articles on philosophical anthropology, Asselin, Rose, and Sweetman have now prepared us to take up a formal examination of how one should live his life. Part II provides a detailed inquiry into the moral principles necessary for making sense of the moral aims of an individual life well-lived. Since human beings are social and political animals, no study of ethics is satisfactory which does not explain how the common good gives moral content to the individual's existence. The task of Part III, of course, is to show how a philosophy of the common good supplies specific prescriptions for our political choices and actions.

Part II opens with an informative and acutely reasoned article by Donald DeMarco who defends Maritain's explanation of duty and who attempts to rescue the notion from the deontologists, who for too long have held it prisoner. In Maritain's philosophy DeMarco finds a clearer and more satisfactory explanation of value, personality, and freedom. The integration of these three principles is necessary to make sense of obligation, and is likewise necessary to relate successfully rights and freedom to duty.

There next appears a lively essay written by Ralph McInerny. Like DeMarco he shows how a philosophy, such as Simon's and Maritain's, having its roots in an ancient and medieval tradition, contrasts with the deontological and utilitarian tendencies of modernist alternatives. His essay is instructive in the way it shows how Simon took over key elements in St. Thomas's philosophy of prudence and practical knowledge and drew out of them surprising and fruitful implications for a contemporary moral philosophy.

John Killoran also examines the moral thought of Yves R. Simon. In particular, he takes up the principle of *habitus*, a special feature of Simon's ethics, which again shows the powerful influence of St. Thomas's ethics on his position. Closely connected with the formation of habit is the medieval principle of *synderesis*, a notion which captures (and much more besides) our modern idea of "conscience." Mark McGovern discusses this subject at length in the subsequent article. His analysis is thorough and historically sensitive, showing, moreover, that the principle of *synderesis* is not just a medieval oddity but is still serviceable for a sound ethics today.

Conscience turns to moral rules to give it direction. One such rule, which has been given a prominent place in traditional moral discourse, is the Principle of the Double Effect. Wilfred LaCroix asks whether this Principle is still useful for the contemporary ethicist, especially in light of the fact that it has drifted out of fashion in the past few decades. He argues that, while the traditional analysis and defense of the principle (an apologetics which goes back to ancient times) is problematic, the Principle still has value given that its source, after all, is the actual moral judgments of ordinary people.

Like LaCroix, John Trapani is interested in how moral principles and judgments can carefully direct moral action. He presents this discussion against the backdrop of a study by William L. Rossner, S. J., to whom this book is dedicated. Complementing Rossner's observations on the nature of moral choice and action with Maritain's analysis of the types of moral judgments, Trapani reaches provocative conclusions about the limits to sound moral choice, carrying with them suggestions of a peculiarly theological kind.

Just as Trapani compares Rossner and Maritain, Joseph Pappin takes up a comparison between Rahner's ethics and Maritain's, labeling them both representatives of an "existential" ethics. For Rahner and Maritain, in spite of their many differences, which Pappin takes pains to catalogue, human freedom constitutes the beginning of ethics. A sound moral philosophy must do justice to this first principle, while at the same time acknowledging that human existence is situated socially and historically. In short, philosophical reflection on freedom and the human condition generates all the issues that give ethics its special focus and that make it an important discipline. Rahner's and Maritain's ethics are both rich in an appreciation of this truth.

Yet individual and social freedom requires specific aims, and diverse moralities compete to offer the human person an account of the nonmoral good to satisfy this need for direction. Thomas Loughran inquires into the various reasons for choosing one version of the nonmoral good over another. Analyzing the natural law, the communitarian, and the informed-desire approaches, and employing the convictions of Alasdair MacIntyre's appeal to narrative in ethics, Loughran aims to defend a position known as "Ideal Tradition Theory." This position borrows strong elements from the natural law philosophy but transcends it, Loughran argues, by drawing on other perspectives which help make moral explanation more specific. After all, it is lack of specificity in moral explanation and prescription that constitutes the most nagging criticism of natural law philosophy.

Alice Ramos's essay is an explicit study of the writings of Alasdair MacIntyre. Specifically, she comments on his argument that a sound moral philosophy is informed by a tradition which, having borne the wisdom of past generations, provides a legacy of truths which assist in the further deepening and cultivating of the habit of rational moral discourse. While elaborating this view, she finds parallels between MacIntyre's regard for philosophical tradition and authority and Augustine's position that philosophy is rightly anchored in faith—faith seeking understanding.

Thomas Hibbs's article is also interested in the "narrative" trend in ethics made fashionable by MacIntyre, Nussbaum, Taylor, Hauerwas and others. In his opening paragraph, Hibbs tells us that in "the wake of the critique of academic moral philosophy, terms such as 'experience' and 'narrative' have become pervasive. The emphasis has shifted from analysis to stories, the stories of individuals and communities, even stories of the history of moral philosophy." Is this fascination for narrative something that a philosopher working primarily under the influence of St. Thomas can respect and accommodate? It may come as a surprise, Hibbs claims, that a Thomist can find much in narrative ethics that is "congenial"; this in spite of the fact that narrative ethics suffers certain pitfalls that the Thomist must skirt.

While an appreciation of narrative is well-and-good, Roger Duncan's polemic stresses that ethics must ultimately turn on a non-negotiable core of objective prescriptions, all of which are inductively defensible in light of a comprehension of human nature. No narrative can be intelligent that obscures these principles and truths. Specifically, Duncan argues that the human mind can become confused in its pursuit of the good and that error can put apparent goods at cross purposes with our real goods. This means that we might be in pursuit of things contrary to what fulfills human nature, leading us to engage in "unnatural acts," an expression he admits is quaint and unfashionable. Nevertheless, it has value in reminding us of what vice does to the human person, confusing her moral judgment, and thereby creating a kind of moral war within her character. Duncan, relying on clear and clever illustrations, applies these observations to an analysis of contraception.

Traditionally, virtue ethics has argued that the cultivation of vice undermines happiness. Accordingly, no study of virtue ethics would be complete without some discussion of the formal and final causality that happiness is supposed to exercise in moral life. William Bush in a provocative essay suggests that philosophers, especially those of a teleological and natural law persuasion, have wrongly given happiness centrality in their writings. A broader understanding of man's moral life and aims could take into account a more disinterested love of God, which certainly transcends happiness, with its egocentric associations. Bush's essay serves to provoke a response from Deal Hudson, who defends the natural law conception of happiness, charging that Bush has not sufficiently captured its subtlety.

While Bush and Hudson may disagree about the primacy of happiness in a moral philosophy, both agree that a meaningful human life must find God as its object. This is a truth central to the evaluations of human life found in Scripture. Whether we think of the human person's moral life from the vantage point of natural reason or from the standpoint of reason elevated by revelation, God, Scripture tells us, is the Alpha and Omega of our existence. To express the continuity between our philosophical and revealed understanding of the natural law, Joseph Koterski comments on the book of *Wisdom*. Like other books of the Bible, *Wisdom* contains references to natural law in the form of prescriptions which, if observed, put one in proper obedience to God and the law of one's own happiness. Father Joseph de Torre completes this discussion by arguing how it is that, from the vantage point of the Perennial Philosophy, philosophical ethics is not disconnected from theological morality.

This brings us to Part III, where the focus is on the relationship of the individual human person to the common good. To open this discussion, Joseph Califano explains that to be human is to be in community. That as a free, rational, self-reflective agent, the human person reflects the community unto himself. We are made for community and find our destiny in it.

Diane Caplin explains how the natural law basis of Yves R. Simon's account of the common good effectively defends democratic government against anti-democratic ideologies. In short, the human person's goods on a multiplicity of levels are best realized in the kind of community of free, yet social, persons that democracy provides.

Clarke E. Cochran and Thomas Rourke appeal to the thought of Yves R. Simon to show how certain views of political economy are problematic, especially, they charge, from the standpoint of a Christian morality. They describe in lucid and engaging detail what a satisfactory political economy must look like according to Simon.

These discussions of Simon, democracy, and the common good highlight the issue of the separation between autonomy and communal obligation, one aspect of which is the private space in which a citizen is allowed to make choices and act before he or she runs against limits set by political obligation. This issue confronts the "private morality versus public enforcement" debate which appears commonly today in political discourse. Peter Redpath explains that the distinction between these two borders is sometimes artificial and frequently camouflages moral confusions.

Redpath's essay makes the point that the custodians of the common good can easily overstep their bounds and perpetrate injustices against their citizens. Redpath appreciates clearly that an intelligent philosophy of the common good must coordinate with a convincing theory of justice. Ralph Nelson finds such a theory in the work of Yves R. Simon, although the task of distilling Simon's formulations on the subject are a challenge since he wrote no specific essays, much less a monograph, on justice alone. Nelson is especially interested in capturing Simon's sense of the "scope" of justice, which includes commutative and distributive senses of justice but also issues bearing on the limits of the exercise of rightful authority and the extent of obligations even beyond a nation's borders. Nelson's essay is biographically informative, taking stock of the influence of Proudhon on Simon's thought and making reference to many of the events and issues to which Simon responded as a French citizen and a student of international politics. Nelson also goes out of his way to furnish timely illustrations which relate Simon's philosophy of justice and the common good to our own contemporary political challenges.

Lastly, Michael Novak has written an eloquent capstone to our study. His essay reminds us that, if our vision of a "recovered" ethics is not to be yet again marginalized, it must remain grounded in a common-sense awareness of actual moral and political events. In this regard Simon and Maritain are again our models. "Both of these masters," Novak asserts, "understood quite well the nobility and limits of the philosophical vocation, its 'poverty and misery,' and its high moral demands. But they also knew themselves to be incarnated historical creatures, called to master the maelstrom of their own time (surely even more confusing and desperate than our own) and responsible in their time and place for speaking to the needs of their fellow voyagers through that time." Like Maritain and Simon, we face our own moral challenges: a world still checkered with too many authoritarian regimes, where constitutionally limited democratic government and free economics are held in low esteem, and where failed and even crackpot anthropologies give license to autocrats to trammel under their feet the personal rights of their subjects. Novak calls for a diaspora of moral and philosophical reformers who, now equipped with an ethics based on common-sense intuitions and defensible principles, can be apologists for a vision of social order that is paradoxically fresh because it abjures recent bromides—all the while cherishing what is right and true in modern contributions—and restores our moral judgment with a tonic prescribed by the wisdom of the ancients. These combined sources—which form the Perennial Philosophy—supply the rationale for championing the dignity of the human person. This is the charter which *Freedom, Virtue, and The Common Good* commissions for the next generation of moral and philosophical reformers.

Curtis L. Hancock, Rockhurst College

Anthony O. Simon, Yves R. Simon Institute

PART I

FIRST PRINCIPLES
AND THE HUMAN PERSON

A Weakness in the
"Standard Argument"
for Natural Immortality

Don T. Asselin

Not so long ago, gangster films, pirate films, and westerns climaxed
when the executioner said, "May God have mercy on your immortal
soul." Today, alienation from the eternal forms a crisis in moral
philosophy. By eternal, I mean both the eternal, intelligible world of
truth and the eternal being who is God. But in our age, the possibility
of communion with eternal truth, whether in knowing truth in the arts
and sciences or in resurrected life in God, is roundly dismissed. To
the Catholic mind, this attitude bespeaks man robbed of the dignity of
supernatural life. It shows revelation and right philosophy, divorced.
Opposing divorce, Catholic philosophers have long fought this attitude
by demonstrating the immortality of the soul.

Laudable as this is, problems remain. This paper urges a reconstruction of one Thomistic demonstration of the natural immortality
of the soul. It is the argument from the immateriality of intellectual
functions and from the principle, *agere sequitur esse* (ASE), to the
natural incorruptibility of the soul. I do not deny any premise in the
demonstration, nor again its conclusion. Rather, I urge that the ASE
principle, in this argument, does not explain why the human soul, of
itself, must survive what we call bodily death. More thinking needs to
be done, if the standard argument is to be made both purely philosophical and demonstrative. One over-all motive, then, is polemical. It is to
get us to study our opponents, following the example of St. Thomas.

To speak of his precept, two problems afflict the standard argument.
The first, stated here in only one of several ways, is that immaterial

17

functions do not entail that the human intellect is subsistent and must survive bodily death. The second problem, discussed in passing, is that extra-philosophic appeal to bodily resurrection is required to demonstrate immortality in the broader, more interesting sense: vital activity, natural to the soul, after bodily death. For the most part I shall use "natural immortality" loosely, to indicate necessary survival of bodily dissolution, or natural incorruptibility, alone.

The Immaterial Function Argument

As presented in the *Summa Theologiae*, incorruptibility of the human soul follows its subsistence, in this manner: It is impossible that a subsistent form cease to exist, because being belongs to a form, which is an act, in virtue of itself; and what belongs to something, in virtue of itself, is inseparable from it. But being belongs to a subsistent form of itself, which is to say that being cannot be separated from a subsistent form; and the human soul is a subsistent form.[1] On whether the human soul is subsistent, St. Thomas notes that its knowledge of all corporeal things means that the soul cannot itself be corporeal. And:

> Therefore the intellectual principle which we call the mind or the intellect has an operation *per se* apart from the body. Now only that which subsists can have an operation *per se*. For nothing can operate but what is actual: *wherefore a thing operates according as it is.* . . . We must conclude, therefore, that the human soul, which is called the intellect or mind, is something incorporeal and subsistent.[2]

The natural immortality of the soul, its necessary *per se* existence, and so its incorruptibility, follows from subsistence. Behind this, Premise 1 affirms that intellection is an incorporeal function, and Premise 2 that as something acts, so it is. Thus, if the soul acts in an incorporeal manner, it must be incorporeal; if incorporeal, it is not subject to corporeal dissolution, and so survives corporeal dissolution, which the death of a man is. And Premise 3, the subsistence premise, says that only what exists of itself (subsists) can operate of itself, because only what is actual can operate. But to operate means to exist, and to operate *per se* means to exist *per se*; thus nothing that operates *per se* can lose its existence, because its existence is

---

[1] *ST.*, I, 75, 6.
[2] *ST.*, I, 75, 2.

inseparable from it. In itself the human soul is directly ordered to existence; it is naturally immortal.

Prominent Thomists regard this argument as the superior philosophical demonstration.[3] Gilson claimed that of the several arguments St. Thomas collected to demonstrate natural immortality, "Most . . . stress the incorporeal nature of understanding and its act, and rightly so." He also wrote that "if it is agreed that the soul exercises such an incorporeal operation, its existence as an incorporeal nature is thereby established and its immortality possible; but its immortality is more than possible, it is certain, if this immaterial substance is actuated by an act of being of its own."[4]

Now let us grant the second consequence just quoted from Gilson. Natural immortality is certain, if this immaterial substance is actuated by an act of being of its own. This consequence depends upon the soul being an incorporeal nature, from which its immortality is possible. What is the evidence that the soul is an incorporeal nature? It is that the soul has a *per se* intellectual operation, and the ASE principle. But here the cogency of the argument reduces to the ASE principle, to its own intelligibility and cogency. Accordingly, belief in the natural immortality of the soul lies open to an objection, namely, that the ASE principle cannot be demonstrated against one who would deny it in this case; and if not, then plainly the natural immortality of the soul may be demonstrated only as a possibility, not as a necessary philosophical result.

But why might someone deny the ASE principle in this case? Why, if not because something that has an immaterial intellectual operation is not *ipso facto* an immaterial subsistent entity? Indeed, in our own time this is precisely the position of the substance monist/property dualist. Such thinkers concede that mind-brain identity theories need to be substantially qualified, in order to explain the property differentiation between electro-chemical brain states and the apparently immaterial properties of sensation and intellection. They concede that brain and mind states are not identical in every respect, namely, that they are virtually identical, but that mind properties are immaterial.

---

[3]See, for example, George P. Klubertanz, S. J., *The Philosophy of Human Nature* (New York: Appleton, 1953), pp. 307–09, 312–13; Etienne Gilson, *Elements of Christian Philosophy* (Garden City, New York: Doubleday, 1960 and the reprint edition (Westport, Connecticut: Greenwood Press, Publishers, 1978), pp. 205–11; and Joseph Owens, *An Elementary Christian Metaphysics* (Houston, Texas: Center for Thomistic Studies, 1985), pp. 323–24.

[4]Etienne Gilson, *ibid.*, p. 211.

They argue that mind properties immaterially supervene on brain properties.[5] Let us call this the supervenience thesis. It says that immateriality of the intellect supervenes on immaterial functions, part of intellect's structure, insofar as this structure's containing immaterial functions constitutes the intellect's being immaterial.[6] From the thesis nothing follows about the mind as an independent substance that is immaterial. On the contrary, the only consequence that must follow is that certain intellectual beings have immaterial properties; we need not conclude that they are subsistent intellects.[7]

The Thomist in us rises to counter-punch. Has not the substance monist/property dualist made out the Thomistic position to be a substance dualism, whereas it is no such thing? But is this punch well aimed? The objection itself says only that the ASE principle does not necessarily hold in this case. Substance monism/property dualism is not an absurd or unintelligible position on the mind-brain question. More, even if it cannot finally silence its critics, it affects our problem. For example, if the human soul has immaterial functions, by extension of substance monism/property dualism logic, it is possible that the soul is an immaterial subject. In other words, substance monism is not the only necessary result of admitting property dualism. Its proponents usually maintain that it is the best position, citing what to them is massive evidence for physicalism. But just as something that is

---

[5]For a recent exposition, see William Seager, *Metaphysics of Consciousness* (London: Routledge, 1991), pp. 136, 174–88, and 197–201. Seager aims to develop a theory of mind-brain relation that is quite minimally physicalist (p. 201) and that is neither (i) an identity theory, nor (ii) a creeping dualism (epiphenomenalism), nor again (iii) a stout dualism, (parallelism). Seager regards the general evidence of physicalism overwhelming. Simultaneously, he thinks that differentiation between psychological (intentional) states and physical (motivating-sensation) states is undeniable. Given the general evidence of physicalism and the evident weaknesses of both identity theory and dualism, Seager proposes that mind-states constitutively supervene upon brain-states (pp. 198–201; for his general definition of constitutive supervenience, see following note). My point is not that Seager's or any similar view is intrinsically more defensible than the Thomistic view needed to make natural immortality a necessary philosophical conclusion. It is that without an adequate defense of the ASE principle, or without something equivalent to it, objections that arise from a position like Seager's cannot be answered.

[6]Thus Seager: "property P of X constitutively supervenes on a set of properties, Z, of X's constituent structure, S, just in case S's having Z constitutes X's having P", *ibid.*, p. 177.

[7]Nor does Richard J. Connell's position on mind-brain identity answer objections that arise from supervenience-theories of mind-brain relation; see Connell, *Substance and Modern Science* (Houston, Texas: Center for Thomistic Studies, 1988), pp. 122–38. Connell demonstrates a real distinction between brain properties and sensation, but he does not demonstrate the non-corporeality or virtual immateriality of sensation against the supervenience thesis.

material might have an immaterial function, so something that has an immaterial function might itself be immaterial; and thus it might survive death. But in outlasting the body, it is not necessarily, naturally immortal; and even if it were, the result is not necessarily linked to immateriality.

Parallel issues in Plato's *Phaedo* indicate as much. Plato finally appeals to the nature of the soul as an absolute that, as absolute, cannot admit its opposite.[8] That is, if the soul's nature is to live, then it cannot admit death. The soul's causing the body to live (as in the discourse on causation, 100b–107a) is stated as a brute fact. Nothing of the earlier argument about the indissolubility of what lacks physical parts enters the later statement; immateriality is not necessary to this final appeal. Accordingly, the objection that the soul might not forever outlive body (87d–e) remains unanswered. Therefore, by parity of reason it remains possible that the soul is not naturally immortal simply because it is immaterial.

Without resolving the problem about the ASE principle itself, we have an impasse between our objector's position and the Thomistic immaterial function argument. Immaterial function does not entail natural immortality, if the ASE principle does not apply here.

The Cogency of the ASE Principle Directly Considered

Of course, only a fool would deny the principle outright. The Toronto Blue Jays won the World Series. Their playing baseball and not hockey partly states the cause. Everyday causal explanations resemble this. Shovels dig better than rakes, being for removing and not gathering. Fire heats, being hot; ice does not, not being hot. Brisk air is cool and dry. It refreshes. St. Thomas and Thomists deploy the ASE principle frequently in philosophical psychology, metaphysics, and theology. It functions as a conceptual foundation of the many *quia* argumentations from visible effects to invisible causes; it is invaluable in the Thomistic panoply.

Does this global utility transfer to the case at hand? When St. Thomas demonstrates the unity of the divine attributes, for example, he uses the ASE principle in the following fashion: Everything that is truly predicated of God is God. For if something acts in a

---

[8]Cp. *ST.*, I, 75, 5.

certain manner (as God), it must be in a certain manner (God). Let us suppose that at this extreme, the ASE principle is unassailable. At another extreme, for example, with the everyday causal relationships just mentioned, it is equally unassailable. But let us note something about these extremes. With the unity of the divine attributes, we make an entailment about a being that by (nearly?) universal admission is immaterial and naturally immortal. The inference goes from a mode of being to a being the same in kind. The same is true of the everyday causal relationships. At each extreme the ASE principle is perfectly intelligible. The attribute in question and the being in which it inheres naturally befit one another. Accordingly, the ASE principle functions as a necessary principle at each extreme.

With the attribute or property of immateriality of the soul, it need not function this way. The principle is only possible here, where two acts of the soul are critical: the soul animates and rules the body and it has its own immaterial operations of knowing. On neither account must we find the fitness between property and entity that we found before. The natural immortality of God is directly, necessarily intelligible to us in light of there being in Him certain—no, all—perfections without His being a body. From countless experiences, we know the connection between fire being hot and its heating something. Natural science only confirms the point with its more polished explanations. The problem, obviously, is that there is no necessary, natural connection between something's having these two critical acts, animating/ruling a body and having subsistence-grade immaterial knowing operations. In our case the ASE principle permits a possible inference from the latter property to subsistent, immaterial being; so it permits a possible inference to natural immortality. But it does not compel the conclusion.

Cajetan Redivivus?

In 1513, Seventh Session of the Fifth Lateran Council, Cajetan refused to affirm Pope Leo X's (then reiterated) condemnation of those who taught that the human soul is mortal.

Cajetan himself intended to teach nothing of the sort. Instead, he urged that no purely philosophical demonstration of the contradictory can be regarded as indubitable.[9] To this, Leo said that demonstrating

---

[9]Cajetan's position evolved in this manner. His first formal writings (1503 and 1507) on the topic agreed with St. Thomas; Cajetan demonstrated immortality by appeal to the spirituality

the immortality of the soul taught by the Catholic faith ought to be possible.[10] Agreed. So the position taken here is not exactly like Cajetan's. The point remains that the immaterial function argument does not require the conclusion that the soul must be immortal of its nature. But perhaps it is small beer so to disavow Cajetan. A favored authority in general, his position on this question has been rejected by the majority of Thomists. The dependence of the immaterial function argument upon the subsistence premise is the reason.

The Subsistence Premise

The subsistence premise again says that only what exists of itself (subsists) can operate of itself, because only what is actual can operate. But the human soul operates of itself; it must exist of itself. And if it does, then its existence cannot be separated from it, i.e., it cannot pass out of existence. Joseph Owens says that "the force of the argument lies in the impossibility of separating being from itself.[11]

Two evidences are necessary for this reading of the subsistence premise. One is a general appeal to the direct existence of immaterial form, its independence of matter for existence[12] so that, as in *De*

---

of intellectual and volitional functions. By 1509, when preparing his *De Anima*, he agreed with Averroës that dependence on phantasms indicates that only active intellect is immortal. Besides the incident at the Lateran Council, three times later (1527, 1528, and 1534), he denied that immortality can be demonstrated in a purely philosophical manner. Each occasion was commentary on Scripture. If "[t]he reason for Cajetan's change of view is still far from certain," *New Catholic Encyclopedia* (New York: McGraw, 1967), 2:1054B, it is reasonable to probe concepts such as supervenience to illustrate the non-necessary force of the philosophical proof.

[10]For a brief account, see Etienne Gilson, *Elements of Christian Philosophy*, p. 217.

[11]Joseph Owens, *An Elementary Christian Metaphysics*, p. 324, n. 4. It is necessary to note the specific reasoning, according to which it is impossible to separate existence from the soul (as subsistent form). At least as Owens presents it, this argument explains spirits as necessary beings. It yields inseparability via substantial incompositeness. The perspective is a metaphysics of existence, wherein existing is the immanent, substantial act of the spiritual being. As Owens elsewhere admits, this line of inference does not entail immortality of the soul: "What the [inseparability] argument demonstrates with metaphysical cogency is only the soul's indestructibility. . . . But Aquinas seems to have kept this demonstration strictly in the order of substance. He gives no satisfactory indication of extending it to vital activity in his own reasoning", Owens "The Inseparability of the Soul from Existence," *The New Scholasticism*, 61 (1987), pp. 249–70, 269–70. I do not here take up the separate question, suggested by Owens, whether Aquinas himself studiously avoided making a direct application of the inseparability argument to immortality. The point remains that the majority in the Thomist tradition would have made such a direct application, thinking that Aquinas would warrant the move.

[12]Vd. *De Ente et Essentia*, c. VI, 4.

Potentia: "Where the form itself subsists in being, in no way will it be able not to be, just as being cannot be separated from itself."[13] Here, incompositeness provides the link. The other is that individual soul is precisely such an immaterial form directly ordered to existence. Only this can yield natural immortality of the individual soul as a necessary conclusion of philosophy.

Nor does this second evidence lack foundation. Developing it St. Thomas turns the tables on the Averroists. He notes that it is precisely the individual man who knows; thus by implication, it is precisely the individual soul that itself has operations independent of the body. The Averroists do not want anything like an unqualified denial that the individual man knows. With St. Thomas they would understand the truth, and the truth is as Aristotle said: "This man understands, because the intellectual principle is his form."[14] With the second statement, however, St. Thomas asserts an essential, irreversible dependence of the act of understanding upon the soul's being the form of the body. The soul, he reasons, is the form of the body. Otherwise, we must deny an obvious truth, namely, that "each one is conscious that it is himself who understands."[15] For the soul is the knowing power, and if bodily it would not do what it can do: know all bodies.

But without independent evidence of the soul's subsistence, the Thomist's opponent is free to make a move such as pleading supervenience to explain the immaterial process of knowing all bodies. This, he might say, is what some bodies are able to do, and to do it, they must have an immaterial property. But, he might continue, it is not absolutely necessary to the individual's knowing all bodies that the specific knowing power be both a subsistent intellect and the form of the body; only the latter is necessary, and it is compatible with supervenience. In Question 76, article 1 of the *Summa*, St. Thomas undertakes to demonstrate both relations. That is, if the man is to know all bodies, his knowing power must be both the form of the body and a subsistent intellect. Yet the arguments in article 1 expressly demonstrate only the necessity of the first relationship. The demonstration of the subsistence of the intellect there is an analogous one. It goes

---

[13]*De Potentia*, V, 3c; quotation from Joseph Owens, *An Elementary Christian Metaphysics*, p. 324, n. 6.

[14]*ST.*, I, 76, 1.

[15]*Ibid.*

from comparison between corporeal forms to the conclusion that the noblest form of body must have an operation and a power in which corporeal matter has no share whatever.[16] Nor will it suffice to appeal to Question 75, article 2: this again had demonstrated subsistence from immaterial functions. These latter the Thomist's opponent concedes without necessarily conceding subsistence.

In other words, the cogency of the subsistence premise reduces to the cogency of the ASE principle. But the necessity of the ASE principle in reference to this hylomorphic composite remains as questionable here as it did in the earlier analysis. True, it remains possible that the whole man knows, because his individual soul of itself is a subsistent form, as it must be if it knows all bodies. But natural immortality remains a necessary philosophical conclusion only on condition of the necessity in this case of the ASE principle.

Two Objections Answered

To all this defenders of the standard argument might reply that they do not focus any link whatever between something's everlasting life and its existence being inseparable from itself. In other words, they might concede the purely logical possibility that the demonstration does not yield a necessarily true philosophical principle. On the other hand, they might continue, the question before us is not the necessity of things from a purely logical standpoint—or to put it similarly, but in St. Thomas's own words, the question is not what God can do, but what belongs to the nature of things as they actually are.[17] Accordingly, St. Thomas is talking about the sorts of beings and operations that we know. I mean ourselves and our souls, insofar as their operations make them known to us. In this locale, it is inconceivable that, if something acts of itself in a non-corporeal manner, it be anything but a necessary existent, and thus naturally immortal. There are no other spaces in created reality for such beings to be, except that left open for the human soul. The human soul does everything that such a being needs to do; and no other being does. But we have already exposed the weakness of this objection, by noting St. Thomas's appeal to the nobility of the human soul. This explains the fitness of

---

[16]*Ibid.*
[17]*ST.*, I, 76, 5, ad 1.

the individual soul's having what it takes to be naturally immortal. It does not demonstrate the cause.

Secondly, someone might object that in doubting the absolute necessity of the link between the individual soul's knowing and its existence being inseparable from itself, we are implying that the soul owes its existence to something besides itself. We might imply, for example, that the body is what makes the soul exist and act. With Aristotle I have assumed that the relation goes in the other direction. But there is no incompatibility between defining the soul as the first act of a potentially living body and denying that one of individual soul's processes entails that it is a subsistent form. Nor is denying this entailment the same as denying that the individual soul is a subsistent form. It is only to deny the necessary implication between exercising immaterial functions and being a subsistent form. Nor is any of this to deny that existence is inseparable from the individual soul. It is to concede the real possibility; it is to point to a logical flaw in the standard proof; and it is to invite rebuttal, or reconsideration and reconstruction.

Reconstructing the Argument

The standard argument wants the operations of the intellect to explain both a) that the intellectual principle is united to the body as its form and b) that the soul must be a subsistent form, having operations in no way shared by corporeal matter. Neither by itself nor alongside the subsistence premise does the ASE principle require the link, though it permits the link. One possible reconstruction is to present a knockdown demonstration of the falsity or incoherence of the supervenience thesis. This would be to demonstrate that nothing bodily can give rise to immaterial operations that are not themselves necessarily the product of an individual subsistent form. Here the virtual immateriality of sensation is evidence, but it forms a double-edged sword. One edge cuts toward making subsistence credible; the other, toward making the immateriality of intellect only a high degree of virtual immateriality. Success in this option would reconstruct the standard argument fully. But it would be difficult to achieve, because, as just noted, concluding to an individual intellectual form is much easier than manifesting individual intellectual form as subsistent.

A second reconstruction, partial but more promising, is of the ASE principle itself. It comprises two phases. In one, the initial exaggerated use of the ASE principle in metaphysics is granted, but then the principle is amplified with evidence from natural philosophy, accumulated especially around the relation between cognition and becoming.[18] In the second and converse phase, the denial of the ASE principle becomes less and less plausible. In this reconstruction, natural-philosophical evidence builds up to the ASE principle and makes objections to it rebuttable. But Cajetan-like reserve must be included in this picture. Unless countermoves are made, the initial concession removes the standard argument from the category of necessary and purely philosophical proofs, where Thomists since Cajetan have assigned it. Equally important, appeal to the resurrection probably remains necessary to demonstrate immortality as vital activity natural to the separated soul.

This suggests a tacit ambiguity that affects the whole problem of natural immortality. Doubtless, the primitive expectation we have of the argument is proof of life, not mere existence, of the separated soul. Thus, a third reconstruction suggests itself. It begins with the premise that for a living being, to be *is* to live.[19] But the arguments presented and analyzed so far seem to imply, erroneously, that this is not so. That is, they imply that one can demonstrate natural immortality, but that one does not thereby demonstrate anything more than post-mortem existence of the soul; and this is absurd, because the soul exists simply to live. But where immortal life itself is concerned, the reconstruction might continue, everyday knowing in the arts and sciences, not to mention the pious desire for a holy life, present themselves as undeniable instances. They are only continued after body/soul separation. The soul continues to live simply as the living principle. One item immediately removes this third reconstruction from the main arguments considered so far: it jettisons Aristotelian hylomorphism. This may be a sound move. But it is one that many Thomists would be loathe to make. Notice, too, that Thomists now ally themselves with Plato. In this case, they lie open to the Phaedo-objection already mentioned: that something that is living principle is not *ipso facto* everlasting.

This all suggests a set of questions: Supposing that a valid, purely philosophical demonstration of personal immortality were to be produced, what difference would Thomists think it should make? Would we use it independently of revelation? Should we?[20]

---

[18]The natural philosophy part of this reconstruction was suggested to me by Ralph McInerny.

[19]Marc Griesbach suggested this element of the third reconstruction.

[20]In addition to those mentioned in notes 18 and 19, thanks go to Thomas J. Burke, Jr., James Stephens, and Donald Westblade for helpful discussion and criticism of this paper.

Eros and Christianity

Mary Carmen Rose

Eros Interpreted As The Individual's Longing
For Spiritual and Intellectual Fulfillment

In Western thought *eros* has been a perennially useful concept and
has been given diverse interpretations. Thus, from *eros* comes "erotic,"
which is used to name feelings, desires, satisfactions, and interests
arising from the stirring of genital sexuality. It is, however, unwise to
conclude (as some have done) that the erotic encompasses the whole
of the meaning of *eros*—i.e., that *eros* is properly understood as the
"sexual, passional, sensual aspect of love."[1] In this essay I shall take
the point of view that *eros* names the individual's seeking and, I
suggest, finding and sustaining his relation to whatever objects of
love satisfy his longing for fundamental, lasting spiritual as well as
intellectual fulfillment. Each of the great world religions provides its
own distinctive view or views of *eros* and its own answers to questions
pertaining to the relation between *eros* and sexuality. A Christian
understanding of *eros* is given us by Augustine in his remark that
"Thou hast made us for thyself and our hearts are restless until they
find their rest in thee."[2]

The Traditional and the "Pansexual View"
of the Christian Understanding of Eros

Within Christianity, then, there has been what I will call the
"traditional" view of *eros* for which Christian spirituality basically

---

[1]Wilkie Au, *By Way of the Heart* (Mahwah, New Jersey: Paulist Press, 1989), p. 142.
[2]St. Augustine, *Confessions.* Book I, Section 1.

fosters some "asexual" experiences, though—ideally—without den-
igrating the sexual experiences which are at the heart of Christian
marriage. This view is fundamental to Augustine's *Confessions*, which
I will discuss below.

At present, however, this traditional view is challenged by a number
of contemporary revisionist views of *eros* which, although they differ
among themselves, share the belief that expressions of the individual's
sexual nature are desirable components in all his experiences, interests,
concerns, relations with all other persons, and relations with other-
than-human forms of life and non-living entities. This view is to be
found in the thought of Rosemary Haughton,[3] Matthew Fox,[4] and
Richard Chillson;[5] and is also presupposed in *Human Sexuality*, by
Anthony Kosnik, *et al.*[6] "Sexuality" here stresses genital sexuality and
the "sexual feelings [to which it gives rise but] which need not always
be fully expressed."[7] Hereafter, I shall refer to this as the "pansexual
view." In this essay I wish to criticize and reject the pansexual view
and to defend the traditional view.[8]

Fundamental Unclarities In The Pansexual View

When in conversation I have criticized the claim that sexuality is
relevant to virtually all aspects of the Christian's life, I have often been
told that the pansexual view "pertains to gender"—i.e., that the view
means that women should express their femininity, rather than repress
it, and that *mutatis mutandis* this is also true of men. This interpretation
of the pansexual view, however, questions the wisdom of sustaining
and expressing all the subjective states that originate in arousal of
sexuality. On the other hand, the pansexual view is sometimes said
to mean (in ways that are not specified) that genital sexuality is the

---

[3]Rosemary Haughton, "Sexuality, Women, and Contemplation." Lecture given summer, 1990
in Baltimore, Maryland under the auspices of the Baltimore Carmelite Community.

[4]Matthew Fox, *The Cosmic Christ* (San Francisco,: Harper and Row, 1988).

[5]Richard Chillson, *Prayer Making* (Minneapolis, Minnesota: Winston, 1977).

[6]*Human Sexuality : New Directions in American Catholic Thought* (A Study Commissioned
by the Catholic Theological Society of America) by Anthony Kosnick, William Carroll, Agnes
Cunningham, Ronald Modras, and James Schulte (Mahwah, New Jersey: Paulist Press, 1977).

[7]Richard Chillson, *Prayer Making* (Mineapolis, Minnesota: Winston, 1977), p. 133.

[8]For a contemporary interpretation of eros which is different from that of the pansexual view
but also different from the traditional Christian view which I am defending here, see Ginette
Paris, *Pagan Meditations* (Dallas, Texas: Spring Publications, 1986. Chapter six.

basis of all the needs and satisfactions of *eros*, although in some of these needs and satisfactions the sexual origin is transfigured and so not recognized. This second interpretation of the pansexual view is sometimes a result of an undeveloped, undefended borrowing from Hindu, Buddhist, or Taoist accounts of *eros*. Both of these interpretations of the pansexual view merit examination; but neither is a necessary component of, nor identical with the interpretation of the pansexual view which accompanies them, and which I wish to critique in this essay.

The Bases of Some Revisionist Views of Christian
Sexuality Which Include the Pansexual View

Some thinkers have grounded their revisionist view of Christian spirituality and their acceptance of the pansexual view in the speculative use of conclusions of the human sciences. Thus,

> The experience of people today supported by contemporary behavioral and theological sciences understands sexuality much more broadly [than it was formerly understood]. Sex is seen as a force that permeates, influences, and affects every act of a person's being at every moment of existence. It is not operative in one restricted area of life but is rather at the core and center of our total life response.[9]

Another experientially based source of a revisionist view of Christian sexuality which includes the pansexual view may be said to be "quasi-scientific." The use of the word "science" is justified here because the view is offered as deriving from the thinker's personal experiences and interpretations of the experiences of other persons. But this inquiry differs from what we usually call "science" because it is not presented as the result of systematic investigation; it is not offered to an appropriate investigative community for on-going verification; and (unlike the best of science) it is asserted with finality. An example is Rosemary Haughton's appeal to "quasi-sexual" components in everyday experiences which serve as evidence for the pansexual view: e.g., she speaks of a sexual element in our enjoyment of food which combines textures, tastes, and smells and our enjoyment of the feel and color of fabrics; in the longing that "can never be satisfied"; in the art

---

[9]*Human Sexuality : New Directions in American Catholic Thought* (Mahwah, New Jersey: Paulist Press, 1977, p. 81.

lover's enjoyment of color and form in pictures; in the care we give to babies and young children; in the "ambiguities of our feelings toward babies"; and "in the satisfaction that physicists and mathematicians take in their work."[10]

Some pansexual views result, at least in part, from selected aspects of Eastern (and at present usually Indian) views of sexuality. Thus, Chillson regrets that Christianity does not have a Hatha yoga.[11] Matthew Fox's thought is a prime example of the deriving of a revisionist view of Christian sexuality along with the pansexual view from a philosophy of nature which, in turn is derived from a partial metaphysics supported by an emphasis on the "cosmic Christ" and creation spirituality.[12]

Rosemary Haughton seeks additional ground for her urging of the pansexual view in her interpretation of Julian of Norwich's *Showings*. Though Haughton asserts that Julian "never used the word *sexuality*," she concludes that Julian is making sexuality an important component of our sensuality, while in this sensuality which "is our substance, . . . we are oned with God."[13] All of these grounds on which the pansexual view is argued are complex, and assessment of any one of them would require interpretation and criticism. It suffices here, however, to point out that each presupposes that "we are our bodies" and sees sexual components as *desiderata* in all our experiences and concerns. Thus, no one of them recognizes the important roles of asexual experiences in Christian spirituality.

Critique of the Pansexual Interpretation of Sexual Experience

Proponents of the pansexual view seem to presuppose that whether sexual interests are directly or indirectly expressed, or fully or partially expressed, in all sexual intentions and experiences, loving appreciation

---

[10]Rosemary Haughton, "Sexuality, Women, and Contemplation." This investigative approach to the pansexual view would also yield to a phenomenalistic analysis.

[11]Richard Chillson, *Prayer Making* (Minneapolis, Minnesota: Winston), p. 100, 133. Also, Philip St. Romain, *Kundalini Energy and Christian Spirituality* (New York: Crossroad, 1991).

[12]Matthew Fox, *The Cosmic Christ* (San Francisco: Harper and Row, 1988).

[13]Rosemary Haughton, "Sexuality, Women, and Contemplation," Lecture 1990, Baltimore, Maryland. In the source from which I have taken Haughton's view it is not clear whether or not she is using two arguments for the pansexual view—i.e., whether she both argues from experience and appeals to the authority of Julian of Norwich. Another interpretation would be that she is using one of these (the experiences or the writing of Julian) as evidence for the other.

of other persons arises easily and that no attention needs to be given to the frequency and ease with which unsatisfactory, self-seeking, and evendestructive sexuality also arises. Thus, Haughton asserts, "we have to find a way . . . to feel and to believe that sexuality and contemplation are words expressing aspects of the same spiritual energy, which enables men and women to be healed and become whole and to be themselves healers. . . ."[14]

Sexuality, however, can be completely self-serving. So far as subjective states are concerned, sexual intentions and experiences which in some sense involve another person can nonetheless be a variety of autosexuality and thus devoid of any reaching out to another. But even though the reaching out to another person is present, it need not include an intention of fostering the well-being of the other. Also the cultivating of a sexual component in virtually all experiences may be a way of coping with emotional problems; a way of relating to others in an effort to gain their acceptance; a spirit of aggression or hostility toward others; or, a will toward dominance over others. Again, the welcoming of sexuality in one's relations with others can endanger the sincerity and wholesomeness of those relations; can be an inconsiderate interference with the spiritual development of the person whose views on sexuality are not yet formed or who does not have sufficient strength of character to resist that interference; can be a way of making demands on others which they would rather not have in their lives; or can be a way of taking advantage of the emotional needs of another. But in this context what matters most is that the pansexual view does not encompass the asexual experience in one's relation to others.[15]

Eros and Embodiment

Are there aspects of the self that contribute to virtually all of the individual's experiences? Yes, there is at least one aspect of the self which is present, sometimes centrally and sometimes peripherally, in all our conscious moments. This is our sense of embodiment, the

---

[14]Rosemary Haughton, *ibid.*

[15]Cf. Paris, *Pagan Meditations* (Dallas, Texas: Spring Publications, 1986). Paris accepts the importance of what I have called the asexual experience within spirituality, but she argues on secular or naturalistic grounds, rejecting the traditional Christian view of the asexual.

"withness of the body." Does sexuality either necessarily or ideally have a role in all experiences of embodiment? There may be some persons for whom every experience has a sexual component. As we have seen, there are some who deem the presence of sexuality in all situations to be an ideal. What of a Christian view of the roles of sexuality in the experience of embodiment? It is true that in a context of Christian thought it is sometimes asserted that the human being "is his body."[16] But it is doubtful whether identification of the self with the physical body does justice to the Christian view of the spiritual aspects of man. Furthermore, the assertion "I am my body" need not be interpreted as having as a corollary the assertion that all my experiences have a sexual component. The embodied human being may have beneficent experiences that are not sexual. Also, we have noted that sexuality is not always beneficent, a *desideratum*, or welcome. And as I will emphasize in what immediately follows, many Christians have spiritual experiences which they prize very highly and which have no sexual component.

Eros and The Asexual Experience

For the traditional Christian view, the characteristics of beneficent sexuality are not co-extensive with all spiritually significant human experiences. Thus, in the experience of beneficent sexuality there is a self-consciousness which includes some degree of awareness of one's own body. At the heart of this experience is the shared pleasure of two persons who have a mutual love which legitimately gives rise to shared psychological and spiritual as well as to physical attraction. Certainly for Christians, and I suggest for numerous non-Christians, some of the most significant human experiences lack these characteristics. There are experiences in which we are not involved self-consciously with our own subjective states and in which our awareness of our own bodies is decidedly peripheral and may be virtually non-existent. And apart from sexuality, most of us have had experiences of a wholesome self-forgetfulness in which we are free from demands of our subjective states of frustration, confusion, anger or fear for our personal

---

[16]*Human Sexuality: New Directions in Catholic Thought* (Mahaw, New Jersey: Paulist Press, 1977), p. 83.

affairs. In these experiences we get outside ourselves in compassion for, admiration of, simple enjoyment in, profound involvement with, interest in, or sense of mystery and awe before what is not ourselves, but to which we respond with respect, love, or a desire to care for or to protect.

Examples of these spiritually significant experiences which for some of us have no sexual component are not hard to find. There is the intellectuality and spirituality by virtue of which some persons lose themselves in the very great fulfillment they find in mathematical, scientific, or philosophical inquiry.[17] There is the getting free of our self-consciousness in an outgoing delight of beauty in nature; the beauty which divine grace gives to the human spirit; the loving, caring response to human infants; and, the pleasure in the playful companionship of animals. There is the aesthetic delight in the sound of well-made bells, the fragrance and structure of blossoms, or the contemplation of the sky on a cloudless night when city lights do not interfere with our seeing the stars. There is the experience of wonder before the complexity of nature and of the mystery which surrounds us everywhere in the physical world, in other persons, and in our own spiritual and intellectual potentialities which the traditional Christian believes can be realized only through grace. There is the Christian hope for stability and peace in his life and in the lives of others, a hope which he cultivates in the midst of fear and unrest. There is compassion for the suffering of a sentient being, whether human or non-human, and the voluntary self-giving required to alleviate that suffering. And there is the Christian's gratitude to Jesus for his redemptive suffering and death.

In current studies of the roles of sexuality in the Christian life, how shall we determine the most adequate interpretation of the nature and value of experiences which are spiritual and asexual? I have suggested that interpretations of human sexuality which include the pansexual view are shaped by a confused set of presuppositions and investigative procedures. This view appeals to experiences of those contemporary Christians, for whom sexuality is that whereby "we are present and

---

[17]The pleasure and fulfillment to be found in these activities are well known to me, and I cannot agree with Haughton that these have a sexual component or that such a component would be a desideratum.

open to that which is not ourselves. . . ."[18] And it is not clear whether the pansexual view is an inductive or speculative conclusion derived from experience or a deduction from the assertion "we are our fleshy bodies" together with the presupposition that to be "fleshy" is to possess a pervasive sexuality.

In any event, inquiry into the significance of spiritual asexual experiences and concerns requires the inclusion of personal experiences of Christians. The pansexual view draws on these personal experiences but stresses only those which seem to admit sexuality. The traditionalists, however, have their supporting experiences too. On these matters, then, among present-day Christians there is diversity; and some of us, without being alienated from our sexuality, are in agreement with Augustine that an ever-present sexuality resulting from our necessary embodiment would make impossible the attainment of some of our most prized experiences and the cultivation of some of our most valued concerns.

Asexual Experiences and the
Christian's Relation to The Divine

In the foregoing I have emphasized the asexual nature of the Christian's experiences with other persons, with truth-seeking, and with visible and tangible aspects of creation; and I suggested that the Christian's meditation on his relation to Jesus is ideally an asexual experience. It is sometimes claimed, however, that sexual elements are *desiderata* in Christian meditation and mysticism.[19] In what immediately follows I will argue that both of these aspects of Christian spirituality are ideally asexual experiences.

At the present time the nature of meditation and mysticism and the relation between them are controversial subjects.[20] In this context

---

[18]*Human Sexuality: New Directions in Catholic Thought* (Mahaw, New Jersey: Paulist Press), p. 83.

[19]Richard Chillson, *Prayer Making* (Minneapolis, Minnesota: Winston, 1977), p. 132.

[20]Fox gives a list of "experiential definitions of mysticism" which include "experience itself,", "affirmation of the world as a whole," [the being] "self critical", etc. This definition, however, leaves out the experience of the encounter with the transcendent God who is also immeasurably close and who must be conceived in personal terms. See Matthew Fox, *The Cosmic Christ* (San Francisco: Harper and Row, 1988), Part II: 13.

by Christian meditation I mean a spiritual/intellectual effort in which a Christian initiates, sustains, and draws to a close his reflections on issues which are of some moment within his life of faith and thus may be either directly or indirectly related to the divine. By mystical encounter with the divine I mean experiences in which the individual has been enabled to encounter one of the three divine Persons, and notably God, the Father. Of course, Christian meditation and mystical encounter with God are interrelated. Thus, the Christian believes that in at least some of his meditations he is guided, supported, and illumined by the Holy Spirit. He might be given new insights or courage, even though he is not conscious of the presence of the Holy Spirit. Nonetheless, as I use the terms here, Christian mysticism is fundamentally a passive experience, while Christian meditation is consciously carried on by the Christian himself.

Sexual elements are, I suggest, not compatible with Christian meditation and mystical experiences. In Christian meditation we are concerned with, and in mystical experience we receive, what is spiritual: "God is spirit, and those who worship him must worship in spirit and in truth." Moreover, in mystical experience and in some meditation we are given what other humans cannot give us and what we cannot generate for ourselves: namely, spiritual development, increase in our faith, and deepened conviction that we are cared for, regardless of the roles the Cross may have in our lives. Moreover, the meditation which the Christian chooses and whatever of mystical experience is given him always have two foci. Their chief focus is awareness of God's love for the mystic and for all men. And their second focus is the divine gift of encouragement for the Christian to deepen his love for his neighbors and assurance that he will have further divine assistance in his endeavors to give that love. But only in the Christian's relation to his human spouse is his sexual nature invited.

Sometimes religious interpretations of the meaning of art objects are used as support for a revisionist view of Christian sexuality. The use of art objects for this purpose, however, is easily criticized. First, any art object is merely one artist's expression of his way of seeing his subject, while the use of an art object as evidence supporting any one view of Christian spirituality is an appeal to one viewer's or reader's interpretation of the artist's view, which is more revelatory of the spiritual and intellectual nature of the interpreter than of the nature of the artist's creation. I can illustrate this point with references to the "Song of Songs," John Donne's poem addressed to the "three-personed

God," in which the poet declares that he "cannot be free, Nor ever chaste, except you [i.e., God] ravish me"; and Bernini's statue of St. Teresa in ecstacy.

That the language of the "Song of Songs" is to be taken literally is one hypothetical interpretation. But it is important to consider the possibility that the poem uses figures of speech to express the soul's relation to God. Today, of course, we urge the poet to create his own idiosyncratic "images," quite apart from any philosophy of sources and roles of figures of speech. Given the ancient wide-spread interest in correspondences, archetypes, and analogies of metaphysical truth, however, we do well to reflect on the alternative hypothesis that this poem is explained by the view that human sexual nature repeats patterns which are also found in nonsexual realities, and specifically in the soul's relation to God and its longing for God. *Mutatis mutandis*, the same is true of John Donne's poetic line.

Again, mystical experiences are pre-eminently private experiences. The argument that, since mysticism involves the body, it necessarily has a sexual component (being a "holistic experience") requires extensive examination. Such an argument perhaps fails to suitably illumine the *de facto* subjective content of Christian mystical union with God. And *a propos* of Bernini's statue of St. Teresa, investigation of Christian sexuality and mysticism requires emphasis on reports of the subjective content of the Christian's experience with both sexuality and mysticism rather than on an interpretation of merely an artistic depiction of behavioral aspects of the Christian mystic's experience of God.

Finally, there are reports of Christians whose sexuality is a component in their meditation and mystical experience. I suggest that the presence of sexual elements in these circumstances derives either from psychological and spiritual immaturity or from non-Christian (probably Eastern) elements which are improperly assimilated into Christian spirituality.

Augustine's View of Sexuality

A contemporary study of ideal as well as actual roles of sexuality in the Christian life of faith will need to encompass both traditional and contemporary revisionist views on this topic. In part this is true because the inquiry must be based on well-grounded conclusions concerning the traditional view rather than on superficial opinion or unexamined bias. But it is also true because, although in our day some Christians have denigrated Augustine's views on sexuality, others find Augustine a satisfactory spiritual guide in this matter. At the present time Augustine's view of sexuality requires more development and defense than he gave it; Augustine could not enjoy our extensive, diverse, and "enlightened" modern explanations of sexuality. As we know, many psychological, sociological, theological, and medical conclusions concerning sexuality are incompatible with his view. Of course, Augustine could not be expected to have answered challenges to his views on sexuality which had not yet become topics for discussion within Christendom. In light of this, Christians should suspect the perspective from which, and the spirit in which, current work on Augustine is carried on. Thus, Matthew Fox writes, "Augustine basically regrets the fact that we are sexual, sensual creatures."[21] But Friederich von Hügel had a different perspective. He wrote that Augustine did not "censure the sex instinct as such . . . he declared a moderate, readily controllable sex instinct to be right. . . ."[22]

Augustine emphasizes asexual spiritual experiences which are opportunities for self-giving, for self-forgetful praise of God, and for maintaining faith during times of spiritual dryness, anxiety, or intense psychological and spiritual suffering. I suggest that Augustine has not recommended that Christians become alienated from their sexuality, but rather has called attention to the fact that without Christian discipline, our sexual nature can become tyrannous over us, thus preventing our discovery of the beneficent spiritual experiences which are high points in our lives of faith and in which sexuality is neither a necessity nor a *desideratum*.

Conclusion

The contemporary pansexual view of Christian sexuality is offered as factual. These reports of real or imagined pervasive sexual interests and experiences probably have a multiplicity of sources. Some of the emphases may be semantic because of a tendency today to define

---

[21]*Ibid.*, p. 183.

[22]*Spiritual Counsel and Letters of Baron Friederich von Hügel*, ed. by D. V. Steere (New York: Harper and Row, 1964) p. 116.

all beneficent experiences in terms of mysticism; all mysticism in terms of creativity; and all creativity in terms of sexuality.[23] This, of course, is a revisionist rather than traditional understanding of Christian sexuality as well as of Christian mysticism, which may in some of its contemporary occurrences have Taoist, Buddhist, or Hindu components.[24] Also the phenomenon of some Christians finding that sexuality is pervasive in their lives may be the product of sexual, psychological, and spiritual immaturity which is exacerbated by the contemporary widespread urge to cultivate a sexual component in almost all of our interests.

I have suggested, however, that within the Christian life there are numerous opportunities to seek and to love asexual spiritual experiences and that there are contemporary Christians who know and cherish the self-forgetfulness, courage, and strength which derive from the spiritual experience that is asexual. This experience is shaped by the divine urging (to paraphrase Augustine) to satisfy *eros* through love for and service to the creatures of God, for the sake of God, with God, and in God.

---

[23]Matthew Fox, *The Cosmic Christ* (San Francisco: Harper and Row, 1988), Part II: 13.

[24]The combining of Christian and non-Christian elements in a particular spiritual path, which might prove rewarding, is also beset with pitfalls. This important topic lies outside the scope of this essay.

Non-Conceptual Knowledge in Jacques Maritain and Gabriel Marcel

Brendan Sweetman

Jacques Maritain (1882–1973) and Gabriel Marcel (1889–1973) are two of the most significant Catholic philosophers of the twentieth-century. They are also both converts to the Catholic faith, each finding it more intellectually and religiously congenial to their respective philosophies of life than alternative systems of meaning. Yet the two French philosophers are usually not seen as intellectually sympathetic to each other, are not generally regarded as like-minded, and are seldom studied side by side by Catholic philosophers. One of the main reasons for this is the fact that Maritain is a Thomist philosopher, and Marcel is a Christian existentialist philosopher.

It is true that Maritain occasionally calls himself an existentialist, even sometimes describes his metaphysics as "existentialist," and yet he does not use the term in the same way Marcel would use it. Maritain employs the word "existentialist" to focus on the notion of *existence* in all its manifestations, and, through this, on being, which is the proper and central subject of metaphysics.[1] For Marcel, on the other hand, the term "existentialist" refers to the view that philosophical

---

[1] See Jacques Maritain, *Existence and the Existent: An Essay on Christian Existentialism*, trans. Lewis Galantiere and Gerald B. Phelan (Garden City, New York: Image, 1956), pp. 11ff.

enquiry must properly begin with the concrete lived experience of the individual subject in his or her concrete situation in existence. This starting point will turn out to have important implications for human knowledge and meaning.[2]

Indeed, I think it is fair to say that it is this issue of the significance of human subjectivity for philosophical enquiry that has been largely responsible for the discrete distance the two philosophers maintained from each other throughout their own lifetimes. Maritain believed that the emphasis Marcel placed on human subjectivity and on existentialist philosophy in general led inevitably to an irresponsible neglect of the proper subject matter of metaphysics, *being* as such. Marcel, on the other hand, and existentialist philosophers in general, were motivated, at least in part, by the belief that traditional metaphysics had led to the predominance of abstract systems of philosophy, systems which were in danger of losing touch with, and rendering even more inaccessible, the philosophical issues they were supposed to illuminate. (Although this was a criticism the existentialists aimed primarily at Cartesianism, more than at other philosophical systems.)

Throughout the period Maritain and Marcel were contemporaries, during which time they often met and discussed philosophical issues, there was a general distrust of existentialism by Thomists and a corresponding distrust of traditional philosophy by existentialists.[3] This mutual distrust was another reason which prevented these philosophers

---

[2]Of course, the existentialists differed among themselves over the meaning of the term. Marcel clearly disagrees with Sartre. In his well known essay "Existentialism is a Humanism", Sartre defines existentialists (in whose number he explicitly includes Marcel) as holding that "existence precedes essense, or, if you prefer, that subjectivity must be the starting point." [J.P. Sartre, *Existentialism and Human Emotions*, trans. by H. Barnes (New York: Citadel, 1990 ed.), p. 13.]. However, Sartre is mistaken in thinking that these alternatives are the same, for Marcel accepts that subjectivity must be the starting point for philosophical enquiry but he does *not* accept that existence precedes essense. [See Marcel's "Reply to John D. Glenn, Jr" in P.A. Schilpp and L.E. Hahn (eds.), *The Philosophy of Gabriel Marcel* (LaSalle, Illinois: Open Court, 1984), p. 552]. For Marcel's critical essay on the philosophy of Sartre, see his *The Philosophy of Existentialism*, trans. M. Harari (New York: Citadel, 1991 ed.), pp. 47–89.

[3]In his "Autobiographical Essay" in P.A. Schilpp and L.E. Hahn (eds.), *The Philosophy of Gabriel Marcel*, Marcel says, " . . . Charles Du Bos and I had weekly meetings with Jacques Maritain, who took great pains to help us understand Thomist thought better and to appreciate it more. All three of us showed good will, but the result was meager indeed." (p. 30). See also H. Stuart Hughes, "Marcel, Maritain and the Secular World," *The American Scholar*, Autumn 1966, pp. 728–749, especially p. 746.

from focusing in their own lifetimes on what they had in *common* rather than on what separated them. For Maritain and Marcel share several key philosophical meeting points, and now, in retrospect, I believe these meeting points are much more significant than the issues over which they differed.

One obvious difference between Marcel and Maritain—obvious to anybody who takes even a passing glance at their respective works—is their style of philosophizing. Seldom have two styles been more opposed. Where Marcel is unsystematic, cursory, and often cryptic, Maritain is systematic, focused, exhaustive in detail, and generally quite clear. Whereas Maritain has a clear project in mind and does all in his power to realize that project, Marcel is suspicious of system-building in philosophy and prefers instead to offer fragmentary and often scattered points aimed not very clearly at a more distant philosophical endpoint. Marcel, of course, wishes to make a philosophical point by adopting his particular style of philosophizing; and, in a sense, one might say that this is true of Maritian also. Nevertheless, I draw attention to their differences in style here simply to emphasize that we should not let such differences become a barrier to our recognition of the many similar themes and concerns to be found in their respective works.

The points of *similarity* between Maritain and Marcel are many and very deep. The most important are: a) a dissatisfaction with the philosophies of Cartesianism, idealism and empiricism, and a determination to offer a realist alternative to them; b) the key role each allows for non-conceptual knowledge in their work; c) their recognition of the importance of art and other creative works for illumining philosophical truths; and d) their similar concern with the structure and development of modern society—culturally, socially, and politically. The crucial *difference* between them, which kept them apart in their own lifetimes, was the respective roles they each assigned to conceptual knowledge in their thought.

My focus in the rest of this chapter will be on the second issue mentioned above, the nature and importance of *non-conceptual knowledge* in the respective philosophies of Maritain and Marcel. This, it seems to me, is the most significant point of agreement between the two philosophers. And the fact that each philosopher attached great significance to pre-conceptual knowledge is a further indication of a deeper affinity between them, an affinity which neither of them was quite prepared to acknowledge in his own lifetime. In the next two sections I will provide a brief exposition of the nature of non-conceptual knowledge in the work of each philosopher, and also briefly discuss the role non-conceptual knowledge plays in the overall philosophical position of each. In the third section, I will briefly compare and contrast the main points of agreement and disagreement which have emerged from our analysis of the work of both thinkers, and also suggest a way both philosophers might respond to a contemporary objection often made concerning the possibility of non-conceptual knowledge in human experience.

I

Although Maritain's principal aim is the development of an adequate and complete metaphysics, which would serve as both an alternative to, and as a critique of, Cartesianism and empiricism, he recognises that an adequate epistemology is a necessary and integral part of this task. Maritain's major work in epistemology is *The Degrees of Knowledge*, and, as the title indicates, his aim is to identify and describe the different types of knowledge in human experience. In the book as a whole he distinguishes two realms of knowledge, natural and supernatural (suprarational) knowledge. Natural knowledge pertains to the things of the natural world, which are known in a variety of ways, whereas supernatural knowledge pertains to the realm of the supernatural. Within the realm of natural knowledge, Maritain further distinguishes three main kinds of knowing—the scientific, the philosophical, and the connatural—of which the third will be our main concern here.

The key datum for Maritain in all three types of knowledge is the chief insight of his whole metaphysics: the realization that the human mind in all genuine knowledge *conforms to the object*. Truth emerges for Maritain in natural knowledge when the mind lies in "conformity to *what is* outside of it and independent of it."[4] The object dictates the way in which it shall be known; according to Maritain the object is master and the intellect is at once passive in the face of it (it does not modify the object), and yet active too in coming to receive or have *knowledge* of the object. Yet scientific and philosophical knowledge differ fundamentally from connatural

---

[4]Jacques Maritain, *The Range of Reason* (New York: Charles Scribner's Sons, 1942), p. 12.

knowledge. This is because the former types of knowledge occur by means of and require the employment of *concepts*, whereas connatural knowledge is *pre-conceptual*. According to Maritain, in scientific and philosophical knowledge, the concept is a *formal sign*, which means that the concept itself is not what is grasped by the mind in knowledge; rather the object is grasped or made known *by means of the concept*. Concepts, therefore, are not the objects of thought, but that by which we come to know the objects of thought. Knowledge in either of these forms issues in explicit and basically accurate judgments, judgments which can then form the basis of further reasoning and argumentation. Further, scientific and philosophical knowledge arise mainly through observation, empirical evidence, experience, etc., and by means of deductive and inductive reasoning from the evidence.

In contrast to these two types of natural knowledge, Maritain places knowledge by connaturality, which is discussed briefly in *The Degrees of Knowledge*, and in a little more detail in *The Range of Reason*.[5] According to Maritain, connaturality is "a kind of knowledge which is produced in the intellect but not by virtue of conceptual connections and by way of demonstration." This negative definition is about as close as Maritain comes to providing a philosophical description of the nature of knowledge by connaturality. This is not surprising, however, given that such knowledge is non-conceptual. It may be possible to give some account of connatural knowledge by means of concepts (i.e., it may be possible to approach a *theoretical* analysis of that which is essentially non-theoretical). This is what Maritain, the philosopher, is attempting in his philosophical work. However, since this kind of knowledge is essentially non-conceptual, one should not expect a precise conceptual account of its nature.

Maritain, of course, is not the first philosopher to draw attention to the presence of this kind of knowledge in human experience. He himself believes that this kind of knowledge has a long history in human thought, and he suggests that Aristotle makes appeal to it in the *Ethics* in his discussion of the virtuous man. The virtuous man is "co-natured" with virtue, and therefore behaves virtuously. Something very similar to connaturality, although obviously expressed in different terminology, can also be found in St. Thomas Aquinas, in some Indian

---

[5]Jacques Maritain, *The Degrees of Knowledge*, trans. Gerald B. Phelan (New York: Charles Scribner's Sons, 1959), pp. 280–283; and *The Range of Reason*, pp. 3–29.

philosophers, and in the work of more recent philosophers such as William James, Henri Bergson, Martin Buber and Marcel, to name only a few.[6]

By the term "connatural knowledge," Maritain refers to knowledge which occurs when the individual subject becomes "co-natured" with the object of knowledge. In such knowledge the intellect does not operate alone or primarily by means of concepts, but operates also with "the affective inclinations and the dispositions of the will, and is guided and directed by them."[7] So strictly speaking, connatural knowledge is not *rational* knowledge, i.e., it is not knowledge arrived at *by means of concepts alone*. Nevertheless, it is a real and genuine knowledge, even if a little obscure; certainly it resists the attempt to make it fully accessible in conceptual terms. Despite the difficulty in bringing precision to our *philosophical understanding* of the nature of connatural knowledge, such knowledge, according to Maritain, plays an important, and indeed indispensable, role in human experience. It is to be found in particular in "that knowing of the singular [the concrete] which comes about in everyday life and in our relationship person to person."[8] Connatural knowledge is particularly important in the areas of morality, art, and mystical experience. To illustrate the notion further, Maritain focuses on an example taken from moral experience.

Moral experience offers the most widespread instance of knowledge through connaturality. This is due to the central significance of morality in human experience. Moral knowledge, according to Maritain, is gained in an *experiential* way for most people, and such experiential knowledge is nearly always adequate for the regulation of one's moral behavior. In short, moral knowledge is usually knowledge by connaturality. The individual usually has a non-conceptual insight, or realization, of how a particular virtue, for example, is to be understood and applied in human experience. Yet the individual may not be able to, and usually cannot, articulate this knowledge, nor provide a conceptual account of it.

An example Maritain discusses is the virtue, *fortitude*. On the one hand we may possess in our minds conceptual and rational knowledge of this virtue: knowing how to explain and describe it; how it is

---

[6]Jacques Maritain, *The Range of Reason*, p. 22.
[7]*Ibid.*, p. 22, and Maritain, *The Degrees of Knowledge*, pp. 280–283.
[8]Jacques Maritain, *The Range of Reason*, p. 23.

to be applied in experience; which experiences display it, require it, lack it; etc. In this case, our intellect would be in conformity with various truths which pertain to this particular virtue.[9] We would be in a position to answer any question about fortitude by simply identifying the appropriate truth involved. In this way, a moral philosopher could know a great deal about virtue, but still not be virtuous. Conversely, we may know none of these truths conceptually, yet we may "possess the virtue in question in our own powers of will and desire, have it embodied in ourselves, and thus be in accordance with it, or co-natured with it, in our very being."[10] In this second case the individual possesses the virtue, and when asked a question about it, will answer it through inclination, or through the will, by consulting his or her own being, by consulting what he or she is. A virtuous person may therefore be totally ignorant of moral philosophy. This example illustrates clearly the distinction between knowledge of fortitude by connaturality and knowledge of the same virtue through concepts. In the former case we experience, possess in our being, what the virtue is, whereas in the latter case we do not possess experiential knowledge of fortitude, but we do have an abstract, theoretical understanding of the virtue.

The analysis of moral knowledge as connatural knowledge is also used by Maritain to discuss and elaborate on the nature of natural moral law. The natural law is known by all in a pre-conceptual, non-rational, non-cognitive, and non-propositional way. Natural law is not natural simply because it expresses the normality of functioning of human nature, but also because it is *naturally known*.[11] Natural law is then made explicit in conceptual judgments, but these judgments proceed, not from prior conceptual knowledge, but from "that *connaturality or congeniality* through which what is consonant with the essential inclinations of human nature is grasped by the intellect as good; what is dissonant, as bad."[12] It is important to realize that the word "inclinations" does not merely refer to animal-like inclinations (although these are also possessed by humans), i.e., to biological impulses of one sort or another. Rather, the word is intended to convey what is *essentially human*. These inclinations are,

[9]*Ibid.*, p. 23.
[10]*Ibid.*, p. 23.
[11]*Ibid.*, p. 23.
[12]*Ibid.*, p. 26.

according to Maritain, *reason-permeated* inclinations; they are inclinations refracted through the crystal of reason in its unconscious or pre-conscious life.[13] Maritain's point is that human beings have a pre-conscious, but reason-permeated, connatural knowledge of moral experience, which is known to all, and which is progressively revealed in the conceptual development of the natural law.

Maritain makes a further relevant and important point about the natural law. Since the fundamental principles of morality are known by inclination, or by connaturality, they are known in an *undemonstrable* manner. This is why human beings are unable to fully justify *in conceptual terms* their most fundamental and cherished moral beliefs. This fact is a further indication of their essential naturality. In this sense moral philosophy is truly a *reflective* knowledge. It does not create or discover the natural law; all it does is critically analyze and rationally elucidate moral standards and rules of conduct whose validity was previously discovered in a non-conceptual and non-rational way.[14]

Analogous to Maritain's explanation of our "connatural knowledge" of morality is his account of connatural knowledge of art and of connatural knowledge of God in mystical experience.[15] The artist and the poet have their own special way of knowing the world, which is clearly neither philosophical nor scientific, i.e., it is non-conceptual. Art does not generally communicate on the level of the conceptual, and this is true even of literature or poetry. Art is rather a type of experience not only for the artist but also for the audience. Poetic experience too, Maritain holds, is born in the pre-conscious life of the intellect, and is essentially an obscure revelation both of the subjectivity of the poet and of some flash of reality coming together out of sleep in one single awakening.[16] Art also very often *communicates* to the spectator in a *non-conceptual* way. Mystical experience, however, is the highest form of knowledge by connaturality because its object is God, and also because, unlike art which gives us only indirect knowledge of God, mystical experience issues in *direct* knowledge of God.

It is important to consider briefly the relationship between connatural knowledge and conceptual knowledge in Maritain's thought.

---

[13]*Ibid.*, p. 27.
[14]*Ibid.*, p. 27.
[15]*Ibid.*, pp. 27–28.
[16]*Ibid.*, pp. 24–26.

One question to consider is whether or not connatural knowledge is a kind of foreknowledge of the principles which later emerge in abstract metaphysics? In other words, is the intuition of being, which is central to Maritain's metaphysical system, a type of connatural knowledge? This is a crucial question and reflection on it will help us clarify further the notion of connaturality in Maritain's thought. Maritain emphatically rejects the idea that the principles of metaphysics might be principles which are initially known in connatural knowledge, and which then become explicit in the intellectual knowledge typical of abstract metaphysics.[17]

The first point Maritain makes is that the critique of knowledge—i.e., the philosophical investigation of the origin, nature and types of knowledge—is part of metaphysics. This is also true of the investigation of knowledge by connaturality; its recognition and analysis belong to metaphysics. However, he further holds that connatural knowledge has nothing to do with metaphysics itself. This is because metaphysics proceeds purely by way of conceptual and rational knowledge, while connaturality proceeds in an essentially non-conceptual and non-rational way. So Maritain's position is that while the actual knowledge one gains by connaturality (e.g. of fortitude) has nothing to do with metaphysics (because it is non-conceptual), the identification and analysis of *the nature of connaturality itself* as a type of knowing does belong to metaphysics. The identification and analysis belong to metaphysics at least to the extent that one can give a partial, though always inadequate, philosophical account of this type of knowledge.

Maritain further points out that metaphysics requires the intuition of being, and that the intuition of being is *not* a kind of connatural knowledge. Rather, the intuition of being is an intellectual intuition; insofar as it is an intellectual intuition, it is *objective*—which means that it can be known and expressed *conceptually*. The intuition of being is not, therefore, a "co-naturing" with any object, a co-naturing which could only be hinted at, but not fully captured, in conceptual knowledge. Maritain further adds that it is very important not to confuse the two types of knowledge, for any attempt to make connatural knowledge a type of philosophical knowledge (i.e., a type of conceptual knowledge), and similarly any attempt to express those principles

---

[17]*Ibid.*, p. 26.

proper to philosophical knowledge in terms of connaturality, will have the effect of spoiling both types of knowledge and their objects.[18] So Maritain is careful to keep the two types of knowledge—philosophical and connatural—clearly distinct, while at the same time maintaining that the task of the identification and elucidation of connaturality as a way of knowing belongs to philosophy.

II

Gabriel Marcel is also very concerned in his work with the distinction between conceptual and non-conceptual knowledge, or to use Marcel's special terms, with the distinction between primary reflection and secondary reflection, and with the corresponding realms of problem and mystery. In fact, the distinction between conceptual and non-conceptual knowledge forms the basis for Marcel's Christian existentialist account of the human person. One of Marcel's primary aims is to explore the role and limits of conceptual or abstract knowledge in human life. He is concerned with this issue because he holds that conceptual knowledge is unable to give an adequate account of what he calls the "being-in-a-situation," or what I call the "situated involvement", of the subject in his or her world.

According to Marcel, the subject is fundamentally an *embodied being-in-a-situation*, and is not solely a thinking or knowing subject.[19] The subject is always located in a *specific context* by virtue of its particular embodied situation in the world. This *embodied situation* is defined by the subject's particular spatial and temporal location, general and personal history, cultural and economic context, etc.[20] This realm is ontologically basic; it is the realm where the subject's experiences take place at the level of existential contact, not at the level of abstraction. In short, the various experiences of the individual subject *are what they are* because of the subject's involvement in a *particular concrete situation*. The (conceptual) meanings of the subject's experiences at the basic level of being-in-a-situation can later, and then only partially and with great difficulty, be abstracted by the

---

[18]*Ibid.*, p. 29.

[19]*Ibid.*, p. 29.

[20]Gabriel Marcel, *The Mystery of Being*, Vol. I, trans. by G. S. Fraser (Chicago: Regnery, 1951), pp. 154–181.

intellect and presented as "objects" of knowledge available for all to consider. However, this basic level of being-in-a-situation, Marcel holds, is not *fully* accessible to conceptual or theoretical thinking, nor are the higher levels of being,[21] of moral experience, human relationships, the subject's relationship to God, and other profound human experiences. This is a crucial point because one of the great abuses of modern thought has been its tendency to try to objectify all human experience in concepts, and failing this, to judge that any experience which cannot be so objectified is not worthy of serious philosophical consideration. Marcel wishes to challenge and correct this contemporary dogma and in so doing to preserve and defend the integrity and dignity of the human person.

Marcel's initial characterization of reflection is especially significant. He situates it as occurring *after* our *pre-reflective* lived experience. According to him, reflection is "nothing other than attention"[22] to our pre-reflective lived experiences, which are habitual and primary. However, it is possible to distinguish between primary and secondary reflection. According to Marcel, "we can say that where primary reflection tends to dissolve the unity of experience which is first put before it, the function of secondary reflection is essentially recuperative; it restores that unity."[23] Primary reflection then is "ordinary" reflection which relies upon, as an essential aspect of its operation, conceptual generalizations and the use of abstract thinking. This is the kind of reflection which seeks functional connections and which is operative in the sciences, mathematics, and "theoretical thinking" of any kind. It involves a "standing back" from, or *abstraction* from, our fundamental involvement with things, and engages in an enquiry which proceeds by means of *disinterested* concepts, which have shareable, public, and, therefore, universal content.

This type of reflection typically deals with *problems* of various kinds. Problems of any kind, according to Marcel, require a solution which is available for *everybody*.[24] This in fact is what is meant by a

---

[21]S. Kruks, *Situation and Human Existence* (London: Unwin, 1990), p. 12.

[22]The "levels" of Being which can be distinguished in Marcel's thought are identified in E. L. Strauss and M. Machado's, "Gabriel Marcel's Notion of Incarnate Being" in P. A. Schilpp and L. E. Hahn, eds., *The Philosophy of Gabriel Marcel* (LaSalle, Illinois: Open Court, 1984), p. 129.

[23]Gabriel Marcel, *The Mystery of Being* (Vol I), p. 78.

[24]*Ibid.*, p. 83.

"problem." A problem presupposes a community of enquiry in which the problem can be publicly formulated, discussed and, hopefully, solved. But features of experience can only be presented as "problems" for the mind if the individual first *abstracts from* the "situated involvement" which defines the lived experience of the enquirer, and these features can only be maintained and discussed as problems if everyone involved in their appraisal does likewise. Suppose, for example, that a person is watching TV when the TV set suddenly stops working. In this instance, the individual will "abstract" from his or her "situated involvement" of watching TV and focus on the problem, i.e., on the broken TV set itself. Perhaps the individual will notice that the electrical connection is damaged, and will set about repairing it. This problem, however, is one which could, in principle, be identified and solved by *any* person. Primary reflection is, therefore, the means by which it is possible for the community of human beings to collectively formulate and discuss problems, and to attempt to arrive at solutions to them. Characterized in this way, primary reflection is obviously a very important feature of the ontological structure of human beings, a fact which Marcel does not wish to deny.

One of Marcel's most significant claims, however, is that primary reflection, understood in his sense, cannot give an adequate account of the actual "situated involvement" of the individual in his or her particular situation in the world, nor should it be required to. This is because the individual subject's personal experience, in his or her unique situation in existence, cannot be fully captured in concepts, which, after all, are supposed to be *disinterested* and have sharable, public content. Indeed, the process of abstraction requires that we set aside and ignore what is *personal* in our experiences. Marcel points out that a strong tendency of the mental activity characterized as primary reflection is to sever permanently the human subject itself from the immediacy and unity of its experiences, so that the subject too is now treated as an object and therefore becomes an object among objects.[25] This tendency, for him, is evident in modern thought, particularly in modern scientific thought and in modern bureaucracies; consequently it is prominent in much of modern life. Yet primary reflection, according to Marcel, cannot deal adequately with the human subject

---

[25]*Ibid.*, pp. 4ff.

because many of the subject's most profound experiences simply will not submit to the categories and specifications peculiar to primary reflection. In short, Marcel argues that there can be no "scientific" or "theoretical" account of human life *in its fullness*. This fundamental involvement of human beings in the world is often called by Marcel a *mystery*, not because it is unknowable but because it *cannot* be *fully* captured in functional concepts (that is, in primary reflection).

The realm of mystery, for Marcel, is a realm where the distinction between subject and object breaks down: "A mystery is something in which I am myself involved, and it can therefore only be thought of as a sphere where the distinction between subject and object, between what is in me and what is before me, loses its meaning and its initial validity."[26] The most basic level of human existence, being-in-a-situation, or situated involvement, is the level at which the subject is immersed in a context, a level where the subject does not experience "objects" (in the abstract sense of "object"). This realm of human existence is best described as "mysterious," from the philosophical point of view, because it cannot be fully captured and presented in concepts. It is even difficult to reveal or evoke in phenomenological descriptions. Some of the other "mysteries" of Being, according to Marcel, are our experience of our own embodiment, the unity of body and mind, the nature of sensation, and the higher levels of Being: the "concrete approaches" of love, hope, fidelity and faith. These experiences are all *mysterious* because they intimately and essentially *involve the questioner* in such a way that the meaning of the experience cannot be *fully* conveyed by means of abstract conceptual thinking, i.e., by cutting the individual subject off from the experience.

If the realm of mystery is non-conceptual, how is it known? It is at this point that Marcel introduces the notion of *secondary reflection*, or of non-conceptual knowledge. He argues that it is by secondary reflection that access to the realm of mystery is gained. What is common to the above mentioned experiences, including the experience of embodiment, is that they resist being made wholly objective to the mind and cannot be fully captured in concepts. They cannot retain their identity and character apart from the individual(s) involved. According to Marcel, secondary reflection helps us to *recover* these experiences.

---

[26]*Ibid.*, pp. 22–47.

Yet he also describes it as a "second reflection" on primary reflection.[27] That is, he indicates that secondary reflection is both the *act* of critical reflection on primary reflection *and* the *process* of recovery of the "mysteries of being."

Therefore, secondary reflection, it seems to me, is best characterized in the following way: secondary reflection begins as a) the *act* of critical reflection (a "second" reflection) on ordinary conceptual thinking (primary reflection). This "second," or critical, reflection enables the philosopher to discover that the categories of primary reflection are not adequate to provide a true account of the nature of the self or of the self's most profound experiences. Here secondary reflection involves ordinary reflection but with the crucial difference that, unlike ordinary reflection, it is a critical reflection directed at *the nature of thought itself.*[28] The act of secondary reflection then b) culminates in a *realization*, a *discovery*, or an *assurance* of the realm of mystery, and motivates human actions appropriate to this realm. This discovery is a kind of intuitive grasp or experiential insight into various experiences which are non-conceptual and which conceptual knowledge can never *fully* express. "Secondary reflection" is a general term which refers to both *the act* of critical reflection on primary reflection and the *realization* or *assurance* of the realm of mystery, which lies beyond primary reflection. Since secondary reflection has this dual meaning, it is easy to understand why the term has often been misleading, a point which Marcel himself has recognized.[29]

Marcel gives many examples throughout his work, several of which we have already mentioned. One of the most interesting concerns the experience of fidelity. Marcel illustrates that a complete and precise conceptual analysis of the meaning of the experience of fidelity is not possible. However, one can *recognize* and appreciate the experience quite easily when one is in the presence of fidelity. Marcel argues that when one reflects philosophically on the meaning of the experience of fidelity one is led to two insights: first, that the meaning of the experience eludes conceptual analysis, and secondly, that nevertheless

---

[27]Gabriel Marcel, *Being and Having*, trans. K. Farrer (Boston: Beacon Press, 1951), p. 117.

[28]Gabriel Marcel, *Creative Fidelity*, trans. by R. Rosthall (New York: Farrar, Strauss, 1964), p. 22.

[29]Gabriel Marcel, *Creative Fidelity*, p. 22. See also Clyde Pax, "Philosophical Reflection: Gabriel Marcel," *The New Scholasticism*, Vol. XXXVIII, (1964), p. 170.

one can be assured of its meaning in experience or at the level of existential contact. This example nicely illustrates the dual movement of secondary reflection. The meaning of fidelity can be partially known in conceptual knowledge, yet in the end it exhausts and eludes conceptual knowledge and must ultimately be experienced to be fully "known", for it is fundamentally non-conceptual. Marcel provides a similar analysis of those other areas of experience which resist conceptual explanation, such as the experience of embodiment, the unity of body and mind, and the "concrete approaches" of faith, hope, and love.[30]

This new dimension to which secondary reflection allows us access is what Marcel refers to as the realm of *Being*, or of the unity of experience. This realm, as we have seen, cannot be deduced in the logical sense from the structure of thought,[31] and, as Marcel points out, this realm is itself the *guide* (the "intuition") of reflective thought.[32] So, like Maritain, Marcel agrees that conceptual knowledge is a vital aspect of experience, but as philosophers we must identify its place and its limits. We must also be aware of the possibility of non-conceptual knowedge, and he agrees with Maritain that the identification and elucidation of this realm belongs to philosophy.

III

It is obvious that the realm of non-conceptual knowledge not only plays a very important role in the respective philosophies of Maritain and Marcel, but also that their respective explications converge at many points. For Maritain, non-conceptual knowledge, or connaturality, is one of the main routes by which we gain knowledge of morality, art, and the deepest human relationships. It is also a way in which one can express one's relationship with God. Marcel too believes that some of the deepest human experiences, such as human relationships, including their moral dimension (as manifested in the

---

[30]See "Conversation 2" between Marcel and Paul Recoeur in Marcel's *Tragic Wisdom and Beyond*, trans. by S. Jolin and P. McCormack (Evanston, Illinois: Northwestern University Press, 1973), pp. 223–229.

[31]For a good summary of Marcel's account of fidelity, see *Creative Fidelity*, Ch. VIII.

[32]Kenneth Gallagher, *The Philosophy of Gabriel Marcel* (New York: Fordham University Press, 1975 edition), p. 83. See also Gabriel Marcel, *The Existential Background of Human Dignity* (Cambridge, Massachusetts: Harvard University Press, 1963), p. 68.

concrete approaches of fidelity, hope and love), as well as our relationship with God, are all essentially non-conceptual. He even suggests that the absolute and unconditional commitment which is the defining feature of the most profound human relationships must be ultimately grounded in the Absolute Thou, that is, in the existence of God.[33]

Maritain allows for more conceptual labor in moral philosophy than Marcel would be happy with; however, both philosophers accept some version of the theory of natural law, although Marcel does not use the term. But Marcel clearly accepts that there are important and profound human experiences which are objective to all, and which, to use Maritain's phrase, are *naturally known*. They may also be said to be *reason-permeated* (to use another phrase of Maritain's) in the sense that they are rational and can be made philosophically explicit, at least to some degree. Like Maritain, Marcel also recognizes that artistic expression, especially in drama and music, helps us to convey some features of those crucial human experiences which are not fully accessible to conceptual knowledge. So both philosophers agree that any adequate epistemology must take account of non-conceptual knowledge because such knowledge plays a crucial role in human experience.

The strongest disagreement between the two thinkers arises, I believe, over the notions of existence and Being.[34] In fact, more generally, disagreement over the understanding of these two notions defines to a large extent the fundamental difference between Thomism and existentialism. For Thomists, the concept of existence is applied to whatever exists, and Thomistic philosophers focus on what exists precisely in so far as it exists or is actual. But for the existentialists, the concept of existence refers primarily to *human* existence (although the existentialists differed individually over the correct account of human existence). Moreover, the term "being," for Maritain, refers to the object of knowledge which is initially known in an intellectual intuition and which is later made explicit in metaphysical reflection. For Marcel, on the other hand, "Being" refers to all of those areas of experience which are inaccessible to conceptual knowledge and which must be approached *non-conceptually*, by means of secondary reflection, and which can be lost if they become the exclusive focus of conceptual knowledge. It is important to emphasize that the term

---

[33]Gabriel Marcel, *The Mystery of Being*, Vol. I, p. 38.
[34]Gabriel Marcel, *Creative Fidelity*, p. 166.

"Being" has this different meaning, or different application, in the thought of each philosopher, for once we realize that Maritain and Marcel are not talking about the same issue, we begin to suspect that their disagreement is not perhaps as great as it might initially appear.

The differences between Maritain and Marcel have their roots in the issue over which both philosophers disagreed most sharply, and which ultimately divided them in their own lifetimes. This is the issue of the right approach to, and the correct subject matter of, philosophy. Marcel, the existentialist, regarded abstract metaphysics with suspicion because in his view it was too speculative, was divorced from experience, and relied too heavily on conceptual knowledge. Maritain, the Thomist, looked on existentialism with suspicion and saw it as relativizing the key notions of being and existence to human experience and of irresponsibly downplaying or ignoring reason and conceptual knowledge in favor of individual subjectivity and freedom. Yet even on this issue, I suggest that neither philosopher is committed to the view that the other position is untenable.[35] There is room for some accommodation by each philosopher, at least for the concerns of the other.

While Maritain believes that conceptual knowledge is essential to attain knowledge of being, and therefore of all reality, still, like Marcel, he emphasizes the role of experience in philosophy and even in metaphysics. He often reminds us that reality overflows concepts, and that metaphysics itself initially requires an experience of being, or of the fact that the world is there.[36] It is not stretching the matter too much to suggest that, like Marcel, he would also agree that there is an irreducible quality about this experience, and that it is only open to minds disposed to receive it. Marcel, on the other hand, clearly does not wish to deny the objectivity of knowledge nor to denigrate the importance of conceptual knowledge in human experience.[37] He explicitly agrees with Maritain that "thought is made for being as the eye is made for light."[38] But while the objectivity of knowledge

---

[35]Jacques Maritain, *The Range of Reason*, p. 9. See also James Collins, *The Existentialists* (Chicago: Regnery, 1952), pp. 143ff.

[36]For a more detailed discussion of this issue, see Leo Sweeney, "Existentialism: Authentic and Unauthentic," *The New Scholasticism*, Vol. XL, (1956), pp. 36–61.

[37]Jacques Maritain, *A Preface to Metaphysics* (New York: Mentor, 1962), pp. 9–19.

[38]For a more detailed discussion of this topic, see my "Gabriel Marcel and the Problem of Knowledge," forthcoming in the *Bulletin de la Société Américaine de Philosophie de Langue Française*.

is maintained precisely in the move to abstraction, Marcel is keen to define both the role and the limits of conceptual knowledge in human experience. Maritain, on the other hand, holds that an adequate conceptual analysis of what it means to exist in general is essential in metaphysics and epistemology, and he consequently provides a much richer account of intentionality and of the objectivity of knowledge than Marcel, who provides little or no account of these crucial matters.

Marcel is not comfortable with the project of conceptual system-building in philosophy to the extent that Maritain is, and Maritain is not prepared to emphasize experience to the extent that Marcel is; herein lies their fundamental disagreement. Moreover, if Marcel had provided a detailed account of intentionality and of the realm of conceptual knowledge, one can also be sure that it would differ significantly from Maritain's analysis of these matters. However, from our vantage point I am surely right in suggesting that the differences between the two philosophers are not as significant as they themselves seemed to regard them. For we have seen in this chapter that Maritain and Marcel have many substantive points in common, and both thinkers are on the same side in their philosophy of the human person, in their epistemologies, and, of course, in their overall world-views.

In closing I want to consider briefly one objection often made against the notion of non-conceptual knowledge and suggest a way both philosophers might commonly respond. This objection is: how can the realm of non-conceptual knowledge be known and communciated at a philosophical level if it is truly non-conceptual? Contemporary philosophers are often uneasy with the suggestion that a type of non-conceptual knowledge allows us access to a realm that is beyond conceptual thinking. Some might object that it is not possible to discuss this realm of non-conceptual knowledge without objectifying it. And if we cannot objectify it, then how can we know it? More generally, this kind of objection is often motivated by the view that if the experiences to which Maritain and Marcel appeal cannot be discussed at a conceptual level, then we cannot really know anything about them at all.

Neither Maritain nor Marcel has explicitly addressed this criticism, but I believe their work provides the basis for an adequate response. If connaturality or secondary reflection is ultimately beyond the knowledge given in concepts, i.e., goes beyond the knowledge given in objectivity, then it must be "thought," "inadequately conceptualized," "approached" in *conceptual* knowledge (i.e., in metaphysics or primary reflection). The point is that to *describe* non-conceptual knowledge we require conceptual knowledge. To put it more accurately, we can employ conceptual knowledge to describe or conceptualize certain experiences which must ultimately be *experienced* to be fully known, "known," that is, at a level which is beyond the distinction between the self and the concept it grasps.[39] Both Maritain and Marcel are attempting such a description of non-conceptual knowledge in their *philosophical* work. Marcel also illustrates in his plays that it is in dramatic work that we best see the "mysteries of being" manifested, i.e., manifested at a level beyond mere thinking. In this way, art complements philosophy in attempting to understand and communicate some insight into the nature of the knowledge which is non-conceptual. Marcel and Maritain are in full agreement on this point. In drama, for example, various experiences are portrayed in the dramatic action such that we can recognize, not just as spectators but also as *participants*, the profundity of the experiences the characters undergo in the dramatic action. This recognition should at least make us *open* to the fact that such experiences are *possible* and *valuable*.[40]

Both these thinkers have shown us that it *is* possible to form at least an inadequate *concept* of the realm of non-conceptual knowledge to the extent that it can be identified and discussed on a *philosophical* level. Therefore, neither philosopher holds that this is a *totally* private realm to which *no* objective, collective access is possible. Critics may still insist that it is a private realm in the sense that it cannot be made *fully* objective and cannot be fully presented in conceptual knowledge. The reply to this charge is that it is true that the realm of non-conceptual knowledge cannot be made fully objective. Yet it is fallacious to claim that it must be *fully* private if it cannot be made *fully* objective, and, even more importantly, that it can have no philosophical or epistemological significance unless it can be made fully objective.[41] It is this philosophical point which both Maritain and Marcel expound most convincingly in their defense of the realm of non-conceptual knowledge.[42]

---

[39] *Being and Having*, p. 38.
[40] Gabriel Marcel, *The Mystery of Being*, Vol. I, p. 66, where Marcel argues that realities which are not represented can nevertheless be experienced. See also Marcel, *Creative Fidelity*, p. 6.
[41] Gabriel Marcel, *Creative Fidelity*, p. 92.
[42] *Ibid.*, pp. 6ff.

PART II

Moral Directives:
Principles, Habits, and Judgments

The Fundamental Role of Duty in Jacques Maritain's Moral Philosophy

Donald De Marco

Jacques Maritain, notwithstanding the immense contribution he has made to Catholic philosophical thought in general, has not made a major contribution to the specific field of moral philosophy.[1] He has not added any discoveries or original insights to the extant corpus of moral thought. Nonetheless, he has made an important contribution in the order of clarification by shedding light on a number of fundamental moral notions that modern philosophy frequently misrepresents, and the modern world commonly misunderstands. Among these notions is that of duty, which is especially misrepresented and misunderstood in the contemporary climate.

Clarification in the area of moral philosophy is of particular importance because our age, as many of its prominent critics have pointed out, has little comprehension of what morality is, even in its most general features, nor a grasp of more specific and problematic notions such as duty.[2] The modern world has fallen prey to a tendency toward moral and intellectual fragmentation, something Maritain refers to as "a sad

---

[1]Charles A. Fecher, *The Philosophy of Jacques Maritain* (Westminster, Maryland: Newman Press, 1953), p. 186.

[2]Alasdair MacIntyre, for example, states that "we have—very largely, if not entirely—lost our comprehension, both theoretical and practical, of morality." See *After Virtue* (Notre Dame, Indiana: University of Notre Dame Press, 1981), p. 2.

law of human nature."[3] It has taken its Judeo-Christian patrimony and reduced it to an assortment of unrelatable elements. As Maritain himself has explained, "you need only lessen and corrupt Christianity to hurl into the world half-truths and maddened virtues . . . which once kissed but will now forever hate each other."[4] Thus, the modern world views rights apart from duties, ethics as divorced from objective value, freedom uprooted from reason, reason in opposition to faith, and faith as incompatible with science. In this way, as Maritain continues, "the modern world abounds in debased analogies of Catholic mysticism and shreds of laicized Christianity."[5]

Our treatment of Maritain's contribution clarifying the notion of duty will be developed in three parts, in accordance with three distinct sources in Maritain's writings. The first source is a general one, reflecting material derived from several of his works, while the next two are restricted to his only two specifically moral works. In several of his books, Maritain repeatedly opposes two modern and erroneous positions concerning duty: first, that it is not nearly as important as rights; secondly, that it is an obstacle to liberty. The second source is based on a collection of lecture notes which he prepared for a graduate seminar at Princeton University, now published in English under the title, *An Introduction to the Basic Problems of Moral Philosophy*.[6] Although he regarded this work as merely a "fragment" of a more fully developed, systematic examination of the fundamental problems of moral philosophy, which he intended to but did not produce, it does contain a great deal of important material on the notion of duty. The final source is Maritain's longest work on morality, *Moral Philosophy: An Historical and Critical Survey of the Great Systems*.[7] While Maritain does not provide a specific treatment of duty in this work, he does provide invaluable insights on the subject, particularly in his criticisms of the concepts of duty developed by Immanuel Kant, Auguste Comte, and Henri Bergson. Maritain wants to preserve for duty three essential factors that these three philosophers fail to

---

[3]Jacques Maritain, *Man and the State* (Chicago: University of Chicago Press, 1966), p. 94.

[4]Jacques Maritain, *Three Reformers: Luther, Descartes, Rousseau* (New York: Thomas Crowell, 1970), p. 143.

[5]*Ibid.*

[6]*Neuf leçons sur les notions premières de la philosophie morale* (Paris: Téqui, 1950).

[7]French language edition, Paris: Librarie Gallimard, 1960.

incorporate: *objective moral value, the subjectivity of the person,* and *freedom of the will.*

Two Modern and Erroneous Positions Concerning Duty

The first position concerns the widely held contention that duty is not nearly as important as rights. For Maritain the most dangerous implication of modern philosophies concerning human rights is their tendency to emphasize the rights of people in the absence of any proper concern for their concomitant duties or obligations.[8] In ancient and medieval times, more attention was paid to duties and obligations than to rights. The eighteenth-century, however, due to progress in moral and social experience, brought into full light the importance of human rights. But the achievement on the level of rights was paid for by a loss of the importance of duty. Epochs are invariably one-sided; philosophy strives for a more integrated and balanced view of things. A more authentic and comprehensive view, needless to say, would set rights and duties in their proper relationship with each other.

Because both rights and duties are based on the natural law, they are derived from a common source. Here, "the notion of right and the notion of moral obligation are correlative."[9] If one is morally bound to the things that are necessary to fulfill his destiny, he has the right to fulfill that destiny. As Maritain states, "natural law deals with the rights and duties which are connected in a necessary manner with the first principle: 'Do good and avoid evil'."[10] Just as one person has a right not to be a victim of evil, so, too, another has the duty not to be its perpetrator. Moreover, the right to be treated in accord with one's dignity as a person implies the corresponding duty to treat people in the same way. Concerning the question of how one comes to know what the natural law duties are, Maritain advises that the answer lie in a knowledge by connaturality or inclination which everyone possesses,

---

[8]Jacques Maritain, *The Rights of Man and Natural Law*, trans. Doris Anson (New York: Charles Scribner's Sons, 1947), pp. 65–66.

[9]Jacques Maritain, *Man and the State* (Chicago: University of Chicago Press, 1966) p. 94. See also John Dunaway, *Jacques Maritain* (Boston, Massachusetts: Twayne, 1978), p. 81 and Jacques Maritain, *The Rights of Man and Natural Law* (New York: Charles Scribner's Sons, 1947), pp. 80–81.

[10]Jacques Maritain, *Man and the State* (Chicago: University of Chicago Press, 1966), pp. 97–98.

even if it is not cultivated in everyone. Through such knowledge, one becomes better attuned to who he is in his nature and what proper actions and ends he should pursue. In Maritain's words, one "consults and listens to the inner melody that the vibrating strings of abiding tendencies make present in the subject."[11]

The second position concerns the commonly held belief that duty is an obstacle to liberty. Those who regard duty as an obstacle (if not an enemy) to liberty—Rousseau, Nietzsche, and Sartre, in particular—conceive freedom as an absolute, independent of any limitation and all objective measure. Such a conception, lacking as it does any foundation in being, represents for Maritain a form of metaphysical nihilism. When Rousseau states that man is subject to no other law than that of his own will and freedom, and that he must "obey only himself," he is actually disavowing the world of nature, with its laws and regulations which provide the very basis for his freedom. Rousseau is trying to fulfill himself upon the refusal to be himself in any real and substantial way.[12] He plants himself in an existential vacuum which prevents him from drawing even the first breath of freedom. Freedom, in the deepest moral meaning of the term, is not absolution from all restrictions, but the opportunity to be who one is, that is to say, to make choices that are consonant with the nature and inclinations of one's being.

Sartre holds that, since existence precedes essence, there can be no model or basis for any duty to conform to any particular form or nature. Existence functions independently of essence. Thus, authentic existence demands total freedom or emancipation from any essence. Essences by their nature constrict freedom. Maritain argues that Sartre's existentialism is apocryphal, for without essence, which is what existence posits, there can be no existence. Essence and existence are correlative and inseparable; by abolishing essence, one abolishes existence at the same stroke.[13] Existence without essence is "unthinkable," since in the absence of essence, there is nothing for existence

---

[11]*Ibid.*, p. 92.

[12]Jacques Maritain, *Man and the State* (Chicago: University of Chicago Press, 1966), p. 67; Jacques Maritain, *Three Reformers: Luther, Descartes, Rousseau* (New York: Thomas Crowell, 1970), p. 129; Jacques Maritain, *Scholasticism and Politics*, translation ed. by Mortimer J. Adler (Garden City, New York: Doubleday, 1960), p. 95. See also Joseph Pappin III, "Maritain's Ethics for an Age in Crisis," in *Understanding Maritain: Philosopher and Friend*, ed. Deal W. Hudson and Matthew J. Mancini (Macon, Georgia: Mercer University Press, 1987), p. 306.

[13]Jacques Maritain, *Existence and the Existent*, trans. Lewis G. Galantiere and Gerald B. Phelan (Garden City, New York: Doubleday, 1957), p. 3.

to actuate.[14] Sartre's position does not secure freedom but removes its basis and therefore its possibility.

Similarly, Nietzsche maintains that a man can have no obligation to truth because, in fact, such truth would hold him in bondage and smother his freedom. Maritain regards such a position, which represents the absolute isolation of the self from the world of intelligibility as not only unthinkable, but as a disposition that would inevitably lead to insanity.[15] For Maritain the ground for establishing the existence of duty is the fact that the formal constitutive element of human morality is not liberty, but reason. And it is in the relationship between reason and the good that we find the basis for duty, a duty that is fully compatible with liberty. Liberty itself cannot be the basis of liberty. Without reason and all the counsels it provides, liberty is singularly fragile. Knowledge, advice, and the like are not incompatible with freedom; in fact, they support it and supply the context in which it can operate. The only way to preserve liberty is to ground it in reason, for as Aquinas stated, "the whole root of liberty is established in reason."[16] When reason is suppressed, liberty is suppressed along with it. Liberty without a rational ground that would give it meaning "is nothing but that amorphous impulse surging out of the night which is but a false image of liberty."[17]

Other modern philosophers, Soren Kierkegaard and Karol Wojtyla in particular, clearly understand how freedom becomes impotent in the absence of reason. In *Works of Love* Kierkegaard discusses the unbreakable relationship that exists between freedom and reason (or law as an expression of reason), and how this relationship provides the basis for duty:

> By coming into existence, by becoming a self, he [man] becomes free, but in the next moment he is dependent on this self. Duty, however, makes

---

[14]*Ibid.*, p. 15. See also Jacques Maritain, *A Preface to Metaphysics* (New York: New American Library, 1962), p. 27: "Therefore Cajetan can say in a phrase full of meaning for the metaphysician that it is not contradictory to say *existentia non existit*, existence does not exist. For the term *existentia*, the concept and the term existence designates existence itself from the standpoint of essence, inasmuch as it is an intelligible concretion, a focus of intelligible determination, *existentia ut significata*, as apprehended by a concept."

[15]Jacques Maritain, *An Introduction to Philosophy*, trans. E. I. Watkin (London: Sheed and Ward, 1937), p. 180.

[16]Aquinas, *De Veritate*, 24, 2: *Totius libertatis radix est in ratione constituta.*

[17]Jacques Maritain, *Existence and the Existent* trans. Lewis G. Galantiere and Gerald B. Phelan (Garden City, New York: Doubleday, 1957), p. 69.

a man dependent and, at the same moment eternally independent. "Only law can give freedom." Alas, we often think that freedom exists and that it is law which binds freedom. Yet it is the opposite: without law freedom does not exist at all, and it is law which gives freedom.[18]

In another modern work about love, *Love and Responsibility*, Karol Wojtyla reaffirms the indispensable relationship between freedom and norms (i.e., objective norms which the mind can grasp) in the establishment of duty. He writes that

freedom of the will is possible only if it rests on truth in cognition. This is where the concept of duty comes in. For it is a man's duty to choose the true good. It is, indeed, duty that most fully displays the freedom of the human will. The will "ought" to follow the true good, but this "ought to" implies that it "may" equally well not do so. Situationism and existentialism, which reject duty allegedly in the name of freedom, thereby deny themselves any real understanding of free will, or at any rate of that which most fully reveals it. For the freedom of the human will is most fully displayed in morality through duty. But duty always grows out of the contact of the will with some norm.[19]

These statements of Kierkegaard and Wojtyla are fully in accord with Maritain's view of duty. Rousseau, Sartre, and Nietzsche all fail to grasp how reason, because it is the formal constitutive element of morality, links the moral subject to a world of values which not only gives meaning and direction to liberty, but provides the very condition which makes liberty possible. Moreover, the proper exercise of informed liberty is the very essence of duty.

An Introduction to the Basic Problems of Moral Philosophy

Maritain's only systematic treatment of duty appears in the work, *An Introduction to the Basic Problems of Moral Philosophy*. The first point he makes concerning *duty* or *moral obligation* (he uses the terms interchangeably) is that it depends immediately on value.[20] By

---

[18]Sören Kierkegaard, *Works of Love*, trans. Howard and Edna Hong (New York: Harper and Row, 1962), p. 53.

[19]Karol Wojtyla, *Love and Responsibility*, trans. H. T. Willetts (New York: Farrar, Straus, Giroux, 1981), pp. 119–120.

[20]Jacques Maritain, *An Introduction to the Basic Problems of Moral Philosophy*, trans. Cornelia N. Borgerhoff (Albany, New York: Magi Books, 1990), p. 92.

"value" Maritain refers to moral good in the perspective of formal causality, that is, the good as signifying the intrinsically good quality of a human act. Aquinas refers to this good (as did the ancients) as the *bonum honestum*, the honorable good, or value, or the good in and for itself.[21] One has an obligation with regard to this good because of the *value* it possesses. The first duty is to choose God because He represents infinite value. Every duty depends on the value of the act that is performed: if it is morally good, then it must be done; or if it is morally evil, it must not be done. Duty, therefore, is based on value, by virtue of the first practical principle: *the good is to be done and evil is to be avoided.*[22]

A person has a duty to respect the life of his neighbor not because it is a means for attaining his ultimate end, but because it is of itself a morally good act that responds to a value. One does not exercise an honorably good act (*bonum honestum*) as a means of attaining one's ultimate end. This would disregard the value inherent in such good acts. Rather, one attains one's end because he has responded to his duties in performing honorably good acts. Ordination to one's final end does not establish obligation; it presupposes it.[23]

Value, as it is described here, is not related to taboos, external social constraints, or the psychological transference of fears, but to the natural law. Maritain cites the example of Sophocles's heroine, Antigone, who, by insisting that her brother be buried, is unswervingly faithful to the unwritten natural law. Antigone is prepared to obey her obligation even at the price of her own life. Her obligation seems to be independent of any concern for happiness. As Maritain states, moral obligation "imposes itself on our consciousness without the slightest consideration either for life or for happiness, simply by the compelling force of what is seen as beautiful and good (thus to be done) or as evil (thus not to be done)."[24]

Nonetheless, value alone does not suffice as the motive of moral action. There must be a bond or level of identification between the moral act and the moral subject. The value of the act provides the *formal* cause for which it is chosen. There still remains, however,

---

[21]*Ibid.*, p. 20.
[22]*Ibid.*, pp. 92–93.
[23]*Ibid.*, p. 94.
[24]*Ibid.*, p. 103.

the *final* cause that explains how the act can be exercised and passed into existence. The order of *specification*, then, is distinguishable from the order of *exercise*. In the case of Antigone, her fraternal piety appears to her not only as better in itself (the *formal* cause), but also as better for herself (the *final* cause). She acts as she does, in part, because she must protect something precious in herself. Moreover, the correlation between the formal aspect of a good with the good for the individual person, that is, the act as specified with the act as exercised, implies a broader correlation between the person's total good and the absolute Good which is God.

Concerning the correspondence between duties and rights in different moral agents, Maritain contends that there can be duties for which there are not corresponding rights. He offers the example of our relationship with animals. We truly have duties *to* them even though, because animals are not moral agents or persons, they can possess no corresponding rights. One has a duty to feed a particular dog, for example, without that animal being the possessor of any corresponding rights.

In addition to such kinds of duty, which are based on what Maritain calls "respect for life," are the "duties of charity."[25] These latter duties are indeed duties and are not superogatory, even though they presuppose no corresponding rights in the individual for whose benefit they are exercised. A disabled person does not have a right to some particular thing I may give him. But I have a duty in charity to him based on the law of superabundance, which is at the heart of being. The exercise of such duties manifests a certain generosity that goes beyond justice. This generosity springs from the "deepest requirements of being, those through which beings resemble God."[26] Duties that correspond to a right are centered in the other. "Duties of charity," on the other hand, are centered beyond or above the other, in the very center of being.

Duty, therefore, has a certain primacy over rights inasmuch as it is directed toward *the good* (or to avoid *evil*). Primarily, a person is obliged to do *the good* and to avoid *evil*. It is only secondarily that duty corresponds to a possessor of rights. In the final analysis, duty

---

[25]*Ibid.*, pp. 168–169.
[26]*Ibid.*, p. 170.

to the good culminates in an obligation to the Subsisting Good, who is God.

Finally, moral obligation implies a *free* act that excludes any coercion, external or internal. The binding force of obligation comes from reason. Here, Maritain quotes Cajetan, who states that "The binding power of moral obligation comes from right reason alone as the constraining power."[27] The only pressure brought to bear on the will is intellectual. Yet this intellectual pressure in no way violates the freedom of the will, because the faculty of desire is naturally ordinated to the good which right reason is able to identify and clarify. Moral obligation appears as a constraint to people only when they are rebellious to reason. It loses that aspect of constraint, according to Maritain, to the extent that we are transformed by love and are willing to do the good which reason illuminates, of our own accord.[28]

Moral Philosophy: An Historical and Critical Survey of the Great Systems

Maritain's systematic treatment of duty, though incomplete, does provide a good working basis from which he is able to criticize the views on moral obligation propounded by a variety of modern thinkers. In his critical survey of moral systems, Maritain directs his energies to three modern views of duty in particular. In assessing these views—represented by Kant, Comte, and Bergson—Maritain is able to clarify further the shape and substance of his own position on the subject.

The essential weakness in the concept of duty according to Immanuel Kant is the elimination of value. In the speculative order, Kant establishes knowledge not on being but on the knowing subject and its *a priori* forms. In the practical order, he establishes the whole moral life not on the good (the *bonum honestum*) but on the pure form of duty. Maritain's fundamental criticism of Kant's philosophy, then, is that inasmuch as it is a form of "acosmic idealism," it withdraws from the real world of being and takes refuge in the ideal world of pure

---

[27]*Ibid.*, p. 182, from Cajetan's *De obligatione et observatione praeceptorum*, p. 2: *Vis obligativa in debito morali ex sola ratione ut a coactiva cirtute proficiscitur.*
[28]*Ibid.*, p. 180.

thought.[29] His particular criticism of Kant's ethics is that it is severed from the world of objects and hence from a world of real value.

Given this separation from a world of objective good, Kant can state that "A person is subject to no other laws than those which he (either alone or jointly with others) gives to himself."[30] In other words, as Jean-Jacques Rousseau had declared, man must "obey only himself" because every measure or regulation originating from the world of nature would destroy his autonomy as well as his dignity.

Maritain states emphatically that obeying a law established by another (particularly the natural law established by God) does not violate autonomy and dignity, because the law we are speaking of is the law of our own nature and created for our own good. Therefore, when one understands through reason that the law he obeys is just and good, it is his own reason that he is obeying. For Maritain "[t]he only authentic autonomy for the human being is to fulfill the law—the law of another—which he has made his own through reason and love."[31]

For Kant one's duty is to obey the categorical imperative, which, detached from objective value, is justified on the purely formal plane of universalizability and freedom from inherent contradiction. The Kantian "you ought," according to Maritain, is like an eruption from the heaven of Pure Reason, imposing itself on the empirical world. It has no content. It is the manifestation of Pure Reason's rule over us "without the least reference to intrinsic goodness, to the *good as value*."[32]

Just as Kant rejected the "thing-in-itself" from the world of knowledge, he rejects the "good-in-itself" from the sphere of ethics. In the same way that knowledge is subsumed under *a priori* forms, value is subsumed under a rational maxim that is legitimized because it can be universalized without contradiction. Duty, then, is not a response to a value that is extramental and identifiable with one's own good. Rather, it is an acquiescence to a purely formal law which is imposed by the categorical imperative under the authority of a Pure Practical Reason. Maritain concludes that "in this ethics the specification of moral acts

---

[29]Jacques Maritain, *Moral Philosophy: An Historical and Critical Survey of the Great Systems* (New York: Charles Scribner's Sons, 1964), p. 97.

[30]Quoted in Jacques Maritain, *Man and the State* (Chicago: University of Chicago Press, 1966), pp. 83–84 from Immanuel Kant, *Introduction to the Metaphysics of Morals*, IV, 24.

[31]Jacques Maritain, *Moral Philosophy : An Historical and Critical Survey of the Great Systems* (New York: Charles Scribner's Sons, 1964), p. 105.

[32]*Ibid.*, p. 107.

is freed from any consideration of the good, of the goodness-in-itself of the object (that is to say, of its conformity with reason in virtue of the nature of things); and this is logical enough, since things in themselves cannot be reached in Kant's system."[33]

The major problem in the notion of duty for Auguste Comte is the extinction of personality. The positivism of Comte is a direct reaction to the formalism of Kant. He believed fiercely that Christianity was too much caught up in abstractions and too little concerned about the good of others, or, in Comte's language, "positivist altruism." He accused Christianity of being essentially anti-social for several reasons: a) because seeking personal salvation exemplifies pure egoism; b) because loving others for the love of God excludes "human sympathy"; and c) because Christianity's emphasis on "purely interior observations" profoundly isolates the individual person from Humanity.[34] For Comte the man who believes that he is in touch with Absolute Being can only be a ferment of social disintegration. To live for others, then, becomes each individual's paramount and enduring duty.[35] Humanity, conceived sociologically as a collective whole, is the true human reality, whereas the individual is an abstraction because he exists, lives, and had value and dignity only as a part of this whole.[36]

The obligation of everyone toward Humanity, the "new Supreme Being," as Maritain states, is the only relation of justice which finds a place in Comte's thought.[37] At the same time, any inclination to personal good—that is to say, to the good of the self—is held to be essentially egoistic and nonintegratable with the pure, disinterested love of others. Love for others is presumed to be a total repudiation of every kind of love for oneself.

Maritain rejects such a pure form of disinterested love as metaphysically impossible. Since, as he maintains, "the one whom I love is another myself, my natural love for myself is the matrix in which

---

[33]*Ibid.*, p. 116.

[34]*Catchisme positiviste* (Paris: 10 Monsieur-le-Prince St., 1890), pp. 277–278. See also Henri de Lubac, S. J., *The Drama of Atheist Humanism*, trans. Edith Riley (New York: The World Publishing Co., 1966), p. 106.

[35]*Ibid.*, pp. 166–167.

[36]Jacques Maritain *Moral Philosophy: An Historical and Critical Survey of the Great Systems* (New York: Charles Scribner's Sons, 1964), p. 330.

[37]*Ibid.*, p. 331.

a new love, utterly different, takes form, loving another not for my sake, but for his sake."[38] Natural love for oneself, therefore, serves as an ontological support for love of others.

Comte, in advocating a love superior to Christian charity, conceives a love that excludes the lover's own being and his proper perfection. The tender adoration of the Great Being—Society—leaves no room for the good of the individual's own personality. One is truly a man, according to Comte, if, when he is confronted with the needs of society, every claim of his individual personality fades away.

The fundamental problem with Comte's positivist altruism in Maritain's view is that, properly speaking, there simply are no others.[39] If there is no good present in the subjectivities of individual persons, there is nothing for them to give to others, no basis for any love or sympathy, and no ground even for any positive identification with others. With the extinguishing of personality, what remains is a false and abortive love, merely a feeling, a form of sentimental hedonism. The "I-Thou" relationships of Christianity give way to "I-It" relationships in the illusory perspective of Comte, cut off from the ontological density that characterizes the absolute of personal subjectivity.[40]

For Maritain knowledge of self becomes ontological when it gains an intuition of the basic generosity of existence that is inscribed in one's being. Subjectivity superexists through knowledge and love, existing because of its inner law of generosity, simultaneously for self and others: "self-mastery for the purpose of self-giving."[41]

But for Comte there is not only no knowledge of self but no self in any substantive sense that could be subject for self-knowledge. In stating that Positivism never admits anything but duties, of all to all—that "Each has duties, and towards all; but no one has a right properly speaking,"—Comte is effectively destroying any basis for individual personality.[42] Because Comte, true to his Positivism, could not ascribe any intangible dignity to the person, he could not grant him

---

[38]*Ibid.*, p. 335.

[39]*Ibid.*, p. 336.

[40]*Ibid.*, p. 337.

[41]Jacques Maritain, *Existence and the Existent*, trans. Lewis G. Galantiere and Gerald B. Phelan (Garden City, New York: Doubleday, 1957), p. 89.

[42]*Catchisme positiviste*, pp. 298–300.

any rights. "Our young disciples," Comte writes, "will be accustomed, from childhood, to look on the triumph of sociability over personality as the grand object of man."[43]

By emphasizing duties to the exclusion of rights and even to the exclusion of personality, Comte made morality submit completely to the world, to *"nothing but the earth,"* as Maritain remarks.[44] In so doing he failed to see that man has a moral duty to transcend the order of the world in keeping with his duty to be himself. A society of self-less automatons, whatever one may call it, is not a human society.

The central error in Henri Bergson's understanding of duty is the submersion of freedom. In Bergson's *Two Sources of Morality and Religion*, he speaks of moral obligation in the "closed society" as "a force of unvarying direction, which is to the soul what force of gravity is to the body." This force "ensures the cohesion of the group by bending all individual wills to the same end. Man was made for such a society, Bergson goes on to say, "as the ant was made for the antheap."[45]

Maritain does not recognize this as moral obligation at all, but rather as a purely factual force of the same order as cosmic and organic energies.[46] Moral obligation binds a person's conscience to do good and avoid evil even though all of society brings pressure to bear on him in the opposite direction.

In Bergson's treatment of the "open society," he speaks of obligation as the force of an "aspiration" or an impetus which bears a resemblance more or less to instinct.[47] Here obligation is not so much "attenuated compulsion" as it is "irresistible attraction."[48] Therefore,

---

[43]*Ibid.*, p. 263.

[44]Jacques Maritain, *Moral Philosophy: An Historical and Critical Survey of the Great Systems* (New York: Charles Scribner's Sons, 1964), p. 347.

[45]Henri Bergson, *The Two Sources of Morality and Religion*, trans. R. Audra et al. (Garden City, New York: Doubleday, 1954), p. 166. See also the University of Notre Dame Press reprint, 1986.

[46]Jacques Maritain, *Moral Philosophy: An Historical and Critical Survey of the Great Systems* (New York: Charles Scribner's Sons, 1964), p. 429. See also Jacques Maritain, *Ransoming the Time*, trans. H. L. Binsse (New York: Charles Scribner's Sons, 1946), p. 92.

[47]Henri Bergson, *The Two Sources of Morality and Religion*, (Garden City, New York: Doubleday, 1954), p. 55.

[48]*Ibid.*, p. 96.

his obligation to aspiration in the open society is fundamentally as coercive as is his notion of obligation in the closed society. Although obligation associated with aspiration originates from a higher source, interior to the soul, it, like the obligation of the closed society, remains essentially incompatible with freedom in the truest sense of the term.

Authentic obligation, as Maritain explains, is a paradox because it binds free will, and yet allows it to retain all its spontaneity. The binding force of obligation has nothing to do with anything physical; nor can it be identified with pressure or aspiration, the constraints of society, or the attraction of love. The force of obligation is purely intellectual. It relates not to efficient or final causality but to formal causality alone. Obligation is freely accepted by the will whose natural ordination is to the good as formally recognized. Obligation does not impose itself on the will as an efficient cause, since such force would be contrary to the free nature of the will as a power that is not determined to choose this or that particular good.

The free will, according to Maritain, is so constituted that it is natural for it to be formed by the light of the intellect. At the same time it is necessary that the will be directed to that which is morally good. The will is obliged by virtue of what the intellect sees as good. Thus, it is possible to speak of moral obligation as a constraint naturally undergone, one that does not impede the will from remaining master of its action or from operating in accord with its nature. Obligation has nothing to do with coercion but is merely a vision made known by the intellect of what is good or bad, which permits the will to operate freely and in full accord with its nature.[49]

Bergson, as far as Maritain is concerned, attaches too much coercive weight to his notion of obligation. He does this with respect to both his open and closed societies. As a result, he submerges freedom and replaces authentic obligation with various forms of compulsion.

Conclusion

Maritain's evaluations of duty according to Kant, Comte, and Bergson reveal three essential ingredients of duty that these modern philosophers lose sight of, namely: *value*, *personality*, and *freedom*.

---

[49]Jacques Maritain, *Moral Philosophy* (New York: Charles Scribner's Sons, 1964), p. 434.

Maritain's view of duty is an intricate and carefully reasoned integration of these three factors. A positive side-effect of his critique is the further clarification of an earlier position stated in his more systematic work, *Introduction to the Basic Problems of Moral Philosophy*. In other words, Maritain shows how duty can be brought into better balance with rights and how it is not in any way an obstacle to freedom.

Maritain argues that duty is more comprehensive than rights, touches the heart of one's moral being, and represents a generosity of existence that is not found in rights.[50] He also argues, however, that the notion of rights is more profound than that of duty because God has a sovereign right over His creatures, and yet has no moral obligation towards them (although He owes it to Himself to give them what is required by their nature).[51] We may resolve this paradox by understanding that from the viewpoint of man, duties are more profound than rights because duties more faithfully characterize the human being as the initiator of moral action. On the other hand, and indeed from God's standpoint, rights are more profound because they more accurately characterize God as exercising his Divine prerogative as Creator. God has His rights, and man, his duties. The correspondence between Divine right and human duty captures the essential drama of the creation of man and his return to God.

---

[50]Jacques Maritain, *An Introduction to the Basic Problems of Moral Philosophy* (Albany, New York: Magi Books, 1990), p. 170.

[51]Jacques Maritain, *The Rights of Man and Natural Law* (New York: Charles Scribner's Sons, 1947), p. 65.

On Yves R. Simon as a Moral Philosopher

Ralph McInerny

The work of Yves R. Simon fascinates in many ways. There is first of all an encounter with a powerful mind, but it is ever the mind of a thinker whose feet are planted solidly on the ground. And this thinker thinks, not *ab ovo*, but within a tradition. Simon is a Thomist and this in several ways. We find in his writings exegetical passages in which he turns his close attention on the text of Thomas and seeks to display its meaning. In this quest he un-self-consciously makes use of the great commentators. References to Cajetan and John of St. Thomas stud his work. In this he is like Jacques Maritain, and the similarity is by no means accidental. Simon is a grateful student who on crucial occasions rose to the defense of Maritain. First, then, Simon is a Thomist working in a tradition of interpretation that culminates in Maritain. But, secondly, he is all the more a Thomist in that, having assimilated that tradition, he carries it forward into hitherto uncharted territory.

The Jacques Maritain Center at the University of Notre Dame is the custodian of the papers of Yves R. Simon. The gift came in 144 folders that represented the topics or categories of the great encyclopedic task in which Simon was engaged when his life came to an end. We retained his categories as we transferred the papers to acid-free archival boxes, separating the pages with preserving sheets of paper. The material, including tapes, is now catalogued, computerized, and available for perusal and study.

I mention this in order to explain the diffidence I feel before the task I have been given here. Any student of Simon will be aware of the published books, including, of course, the growing list of posthumously published material. Impressive as the published output is, quantitatively it fades to insignificance in comparison with the unpublished material. As I think of all that, I am struck by the impertinence of discussing Simon as a moral philosopher in a paper the length of this one. Our understanding of Simon will deepen as scholars make greater use of his papers. I do not foresee any radical alteration in the interpretation of his thought but rather an enrichment of understanding. Even so, I think that too ambitious a summary statement would be at present premature.

Ergo, I propose to go back to his famous little book *Critique de la Connaissance Morale*,[1] published in 1934 and thus just shy of its 60th birthday. It is hoped that an English version will be published by the University of Notre Dame Press, perhaps in the year of the book's sixtieth anniversary. Not only does this work put us at the dawn of Simon's career, it is a fundamental work. It starts at the beginning and goes on from there, and if it does not attempt to reach the end—something possible only in Wonderland anyway—we are struck by the clarity and order of the discussion. An understanding of this little book is essential for an orientation in Simon's work in moral and political philosophy.[2]

Practical Knowledge

How to lay before his reader the notion of practical knowledge? Simon's discussion in his opening chapter is chiefly based on two texts: one from Aristotle and the other from Thomas. Practical knowledge

---

[1] Cf. Yves R. Simon, *Critique de la connaissance morale* (Paris: Desclée de Brouwer, 1934) Pp. 167. The first nine chapters of this volume appeared preliminarily in the *Revue de Philosophie* (Paris) N.S. Tome III, 1932, pp. 449–473 and 531–555; chapter ten appeared in *La Vie Intellectuelle* (Paris) N.S. 5e année, Tome XXV, No. 1, 1933, pp. 55–65.

[2] Here are the chapter headings of this little book of some 160 pages.
   1. The Concept of Practical Knowledge
   2. Prudence
   3. Intelligence the Disciple of Love
   4. The First Principles of the Practical Order
   5. The Movement of Practical Thought
   6. Moral Philosophy
   7. Practically Practical Science
   8. Christian Ethics
   9. Moral Philosophy and the Science of Moral Facts
   10. Political Science: A Proposal

is distinguished from theoretical knowledge in the way set forth in the *locus classicus* in the *De anima* of Aristotle.

> Both of these are capable of originating local movement, thought and appetite: thought, that is, which calculates means to an end, i.e., practical thought (it differs from speculative thought in the character of its end); while appetite is in every form of it relative to an end; for that which is the object of appetite is the stimulant of practical thought; and that which is last in the process of thinking is the beginning of the action (III. 10, 433a13–18).

Every act of thinking is for the sake of an end, but when that end is simply truth, the thinking is called speculative. Practical thinking bears on an end *extra genus notitiae*, beyond thought; it does not seek the perfecting of thinking as such, truth, but the bringing into being of the thing thought. In the strong sense of speculative thinking, the objects are such that truth about them is the only possible end in view: they are not make-able or do-able by us. Thinking about coming down stairs or descending in an elevator, to say nothing of shaping an image of your mother-in-law with Play-Dough, is to think about what may be done or made. Yet there you are, supine in your Barcalounger, the picture of contemplation, thinking such thoughts. You might just as well be pondering the parallel postulate. Obviously, more distinctions are required.

Simon finds them in the *Summa Theologiae*, Ia, q. 14, a. 16, where Thomas asks whether God has speculative knowledge of creatures. Thinking can be simply speculative or simply practical, or partly speculative and partly practical. In short, there are degrees of practical thinking. This is possible because there are several criteria in play—something Simon saw rising out of the text of Aristotle with which he began. Thomas gives three criteria:

> Knowledge may be speculative study only, or practical only, or in one respect speculative, in another practical. This will be evident if we observe that knowledge may be called speculative on three accounts: (i) from the nature of things known, when they are not producible by the knower, e.g., man's knowledge of natural things or of divine things; (ii) with respect to the mode of knowing, e g., if an architect defines, analyses and examines the qualities proper to *house* in general. This is to consider producible things but in a speculative way not *qua* producible. A thing is producible by way of application of the form to the matter, not by way of the resolution of the composite into its formal principles considered

universally. (iii) Knowledge can be speculative with regard to the end or purpose: *the practical intellect differs from the speculative in the end it looks to* as we read in *On the Soul.* The aim of the practical intellect is production, that of the speculative intellect the consideration of truth. Thus if a builder considers how some house could be built, not with a view to building it but merely for the sake of knowing, his consideration, so far as concerns the end he looks to, will be speculative, though still about what could be produced (*ST.* I. 14, 16).

In discussing this passage (pp. 17–19), Simon relies on Cajetan. That there are degrees of practical knowing is the clear meaning of the text. *Completely practical knowledge* is had when the thing known (or the object), the way of knowing, and the end of the knower are all practical. But one can think about an operable object, and in a practical way one can think of the steps to be taken if the artifact is to be realized—and yet one need not actually be engaged in producing it. And, of course, one can think of an operable object in the same way one thinks about natural things, defining it, citing subtypes of it, etc.

The analysis of this passage from the *Summa* functions as the fundamental text to be explained and developed in the chapters that follow. But Simon turns in his second chapter to the discussion of prudence, whose act will provide an instance of completely practical knowledge. He begins with this interesting remark:

> Whatever the sense, or senses, of the term "practical science" that we shall arrive at, one thing is certain from the start: it is not in practical *science* that the idea of practical knowledge is realized in all its purity.[3]

Moral science will not exemplify what is meant by completely practical knowledge. To define virtue and species of virtues is to be thinking of things we can bring about or acquire by action, but this way of thinking of them is quite remote from particular actions. Such knowledge can be called practical in only the minimal sense: its object is operable, but its mode and end are speculative. That kind of *minimally practical knowledge* shows up in moral science, but it is not perhaps characteristic of it. To think of operable objects in a manner that takes into account how they are brought about by our

---

[3]Yves R. Simon, *Critique de la connaissance morale* (Paris: Desclée de Brouwer, 1934) p. 21.

acts has been called *virtually practical knowledge*. Thinking of how justice might be served in certain circumstances is not as such an instance of the kind of just action being thought about by the moral philosopher. Jacques Maritain, as is known, suggested four and not simply three degrees of practical knowledge,[4] and Simon defends the proposed addition, *la science pratiquement pratique*, in chapter VII of his *Critique*.

Practical Truth

Completely practical knowledge is exemplified in singular actions. A singular act of prudence, of practical wisdom, counts as completely practical knowledge. In his discussion of prudence and its act, Simon is of course guided by Aristotle. Art and prudence are virtues of practical intellect, the former being "identical with a state or capacity to make, involving a true course of reasoning," (*NE* VI. 4. 1140a20), the latter "a reasoned and true state of capacity to act with regard to human goods." (1140b20) As a habit of intellect, prudence's truth might seem to present no difficulty. Is not any thinking true when it puts together what is together in reality, and separates what is separate in reality? But that would make practical thinking indistinguishable from theoretical thought. Simon seeks further light from Aristotle.

> What affirmation and negation are in thinking, pursuit and avoidance are in desire; so that since moral virtue is a state of character concerned with choice, and choice is deliberate desire, therefore both the reasoning must be true and the desire right, if the choice is to be good, and the latter must pursue just what the former asserts. Now this kind of intellect and of truth is practical; of the intellect which is contemplative, not practical, not productive, the good and the bad state are truth and falsity respectively (for this is the work of everything intellectual); while the part which is practical and intellectual the good state is truth in agreement with right desire. (1139a21–31)

---

[4]Jacques Maritain, *Distinguer pour unir: ou Les Degrés du savoir*, 4th edition (Paris: Desclée de Brouwer, 1946) pp. 647–649; see now *Jacques et Raïssa Maritain: Oeuvres Complètes*, Volume IV (Paris: Editions Saint-Paul, 1983), pp. 847–850. See also the excellent English translation *Distinguish to Unite or The Degrees of Knowledge* trans. Gerald B. Phelan (New York: Charles Scribner's Sons, 1959).

Prudence, as a *virtue* of practical intellect, must assure unfailing rectitude in the singular judgment of what I ought to do and sure guidance as director of appetite. But actions are singular, contingent occurrences in contingent settings. A virtuous habit of intellect must govern the attainment of the proper aim of intellectual judgment. That is true. But this, in turn, suggests necessity, not contingency.[5] Simon works up this conflict, so that when he cites the text from the *Nicomachean Ethics*, which comes earlier than the definition of prudence he quoted, the Aristotelian text seems to provide the answer. But what kind of an answer is it?

To wheel in a new kind of truth might seem an *ad hoc* device to hurry past the difficulty. The demands of truth in the usual sense can obviously not be met. The mind's conformity with the contingent must be as fleeting as the corresponding fact. It is not that we cannot form and utter judgments about singular occurrences: "I am seated"; "you are seated"; "they are seated"; "it's snowing outside"; "the frost is on the pumpkin"; and "the needle reads '80' ". We do it all the time. There is a problem for two reasons. First, we are talking about a virtue which would ensure that the mind always makes true judgments; secondly, practical reason is not dedicated simply to the amassing of more or less accurate assessments of fleeting facts.

From the point of view of action, we seem advised to remain at a level of generality if we want certitude, knowledge that stands a chance of being unaffected by the kaleidoscope of contingency. Thus, natural law principles are distinguished from those general guides and rules which express what by and large, *ut in pluribus*, is the way to act. Already at the level of generality, there is a falling away from certitude and necessity and a growing reflection of the contingency of the order of action which practical reason would direct. It would seem to follow that, when mind is engaged with the singular and contingent as such, truth must be attenuated indeed, and that it makes little sense to speak here of certainty and unerring direction on the part of reason. But

---

[5]Cf. Aquinas, *ST.*, I–II, 57, 5, obj. 3. "Moreover, thanks to intellectual virtue one is able always to say what is true and never what is false. But this seems not to be the case with prudence: it is not given to humans never to err in taking counsel about things to be done, since what humans do are contingent matters which can be otherwise. Thus we read in Wisdom 9,14: 'The thoughts of mortals are apprehensive and uncertain is our foresight'. It seems then that prudence ought not be numbered among the intellectual virtues".

that is just what prudence is taken to provide. The question follows: is this assurance made simply by changing the meaning of the key terms so that what might seem to be reassuring is actually a linguistic shell game? "Of course, the judgment of prudence is certainly true! By 'true' and 'certain', however, I mean what elsewhere would be called 'false' and 'unsure'." Is that what is going on?

Simon cites St. Thomas's expression of the proposed distinction between speculative truth and practical truth.

> Truth is not quite the same for the practical and for the speculative intellect. The speculative intellect is true when it conforms to objective reality. Since it cannot unerringly conform to things in contingent matters, but only in necessary matters, no theoretical habit of mind about contingent things is an intellectual virtue, but only such as is engaged with necessary things. On the other hand, the practical intellect is true when it conforms to a right appetite. This conformity has no place in regard to necessary matters, which are not dependent upon the human will, but only in contingent matters which can be effected by us, whether they are internal activities or external works. Hence it is only about contingent matters that intellectual virtues are appointed for the practical intellect, namely, art as regards products, and prudence as regards deeds (*ST.*, I–II, 57, 5, ad 3).

Simon likes Cajetan's statement of the difficulty. "Si la prudence est une vertu intellectuelle, elle dit toujours le vrai, mais dès lors il semble qu'elle ne puisse avoir pour objet le contingent, car la contingence est mère de multiples erreurs . . . elle ne dit pas toujours le vrai, mais alors ce n'est pas une vertu intellectuelle."[6] We translate: "If prudence is an intellectual virtue and always tells the truth it cannot have the contingent for its object; but if it does not always tell the truth, it cannot be an intellectual virtue." Clearly, if prudence is to be a sure deliverer of truth, this requires a different conception of truth. Speculative truth is had when the mind's judgment is in conformity with the way things are. Practical truth is had when the mind's judgment is in conformity with right appetite. The prudent man is sure when he acts; his practical guiding judgment of his contingent circumstances directs him unerringly to the good. Now this sounds alarmingly like saying that our particular practical judgments are true if they serve

---

[6]Yves R. Simon, *Critique de la connaissance morale* (Paris: Desclée de Brouwer, 1934), p. 29.

our appetites. Simon takes up two questions at this point. The first has to do with what might be called the virtuous circle; the second, more pressing, with the way false judgments about contingent facts are compatible with practical truth.

The practical judgment is said to be true when it is in conformity with *rectified* appetite—i.e., with a good will—and not simply when it is at the service of any desire whatsoever. The latter possibility would void "true" of any meaning whatsoever, since then no practical judgment could fail to be true. If the practical judgment of prudence cannot fail to be true, this is because it is in conformity with right appetite. Aristotle suggested that pursuit and avoidance are appetitive analogues to affirmation and denial.

The Circle. Will is an intellectual appetite whose movement is informed by mind. Only the known good moves the will. Thus, if the will is rectified, this must be due to mind. If now we say that the mind's judgment is true when it is in conformity with rectified appetite, we seem to be moving in a circle. The mind's direction rectifies will's orientation, and the mind's judgment is rendered true because it is in conformity with rectified appetite. "Pour sortir de ce cercle apparent, il suffit d'observer que la bonne direction de la volonté s'entend par rapport aux fins de celle-ci, et que le jugement prudentiel concerne les moyens" (p. 35). Prudence presupposes that will is ordered to the true good, the true end; its judgments bear on the means, on the way to achieve that end here and now, and its judgments will be true thanks to the appetite's firm fix on the true good. Judgments about that real good are not subject to the same variability as are those bearing on the here and now demands of the good in contingent circumstances.

Truth and Error. The arguments advanced against prudence being a virtue, capable of delivering certain and true judgments in the contingent order, are meant to be answered by the concept of practical truth. But what generated those objections is not thereby altered. Let us take an example from *Aquinas on Human Action.*

> Valence Quirk enters the building in which he lives and sees at his feet an envelope on which is printed in large letters: For Patricia Parlous. Valence picks it up, glances at the unmarked mail boxes in the lobby, then decides to slip the envelope under the door of Patricia's apartment as it has apparently been slipped under the entry door. He knocks on her door, hears the sound of a shower within, and does indeed complete the delivery, slipping the envelope under the door. He ascends whistling the whistle of

the righteous to the floor above. Five minutes later a tremendous explosion rocks the building. Subsequent investigation discloses that Patricia Parlous, the *nom de guerre* of an IRA agent, was killed when a letter bomb slipped under her door went off. A horrified Valence Quirk thinks, "My God, I did that."

In what sense can Valence Quirk be said to have brought about the death of Patricia Parlous? That he did in some sense is clear enough. If he had not done what he did the letter bomb would have gone off in the lobby and whatever destruction it did or did not do would not have led him to say, "I did that." Our question is: does what Valence did count as a human act?

That Valence was engaged in a plurality of human acts in the little scenario is clear enough. He delivers to Patricia Parlous an envelope addressed to her and clearly intended for her. He means to do a good deed, to do a favor, to perform an act of kindness. That is the act he thinks he is performing. To that degree we are describing a human act. But in so doing, Valence delivers the bomb that ends the life of Patricia Parlous. That is a true statement. Is it a statement of a human act? It does not seem to describe an act of man.

It is clear enough that we must know how to identify the human act here in order to find out what Valence is answerable for and whether his action is morally good or not. The example is of someone who brought about what he did not intend but which would not have happened if he had not intentionally done what he did.[7]

In this little episode we have by definition an agent whose character is such that he is inclined to do helpful things for others. The act of delivering the letter to the right address is one he judges to fall under what guides his actions in such matters. He slips the envelope under the door with disastrous results.

Such examples, which can easily be multiplied, are usually employed to illustrate involuntary action, as indeed they do. But let's look at it now from the angle of the problem Simon is discussing. Has the helpful tenant performed a good action? It was certainly no intention of his to blow up Patricia and one would have to be paranoid indeed, or a resident of Belfast, to suspect every letter in the mail. Implicit in his

---

[7]Ralph McInerny, *Aquinas on Human Action : A Theory of Practice* (Washington, D.C.: The Catholic University of America Press, 1992), pp. 14–15.

deed is the judgment that this envelope, addressed to Patricia Parlous, contains some communication or other—a bill, a *billet doux*, another breathtaking offer to purchase a platinum credit card—and so he acts. That is not the only judgment he makes about the circumstances, but it is certainly one, and, in the event, a highly relevant one. And yet, it is a false judgment. Does this vitiate his action?

If we took it to be the promise of prudence that we would never mistake our circumstances in this way, we would of course be sorely disappointed. But then of two things, one. Either this is not the kind of judgment that is said always to be rendered true by its conformity with right will, or prudence sometimes fails, and then it is not a virtue.

Characteristically, Simon looks to the great commentators, and this time he cites John of St. Thomas (or Jean Poinsot, as John Deely would have us call him, which I shall be happy to do whenever Deely agrees to call St. Bonaventure "Giovanni Fidanza").

> John of St. Thomas illustrates this point as follows. A man suspects his title to a fortune. He does everything he can to ascertain the facts but does not succeed in eliminating all doubt. Very well, even though doubt persists concerning the truth of the matter, there is one point that is not doubtful, namely, that he has done all that he could and should have done. *There is certitude that the will is good*, and the judgement which regulates action in conformity with this good will is infallible in its pure function of direction, even if possibly not with regard to the facts of the case.[8]

This is still a fairly benign example. If such a man, having made the inquiries suggested and having acted on them, eventually finds that his claim is *not* grounded, what is the status of the acts he performed up to this time? They were based on what he now knows to be a false judgment of the validity of his claim. What we want to know is not simply whether a practical judgment may be made on the basis of *fallible* assessments of the facts, the deficiency being made up by the will's adherence to the true good, but whether *false* judgments of the facts vitiate the judgment of prudence.

It all depends. The example Simon takes from John of St. Thomas makes it clear that there are two sorts of judgment made by prudence

---

[8]Yves R. Simon, *Critique de la connaissance morale* (Paris: Desclée de Brouwer, 1934), pp. 32–33.

that are relevant here. Actually, Thomas speaks of other virtues joined to prudence—*eubulia*, *synesis*, and *gnome*, which together signify taking counsel and judging. There are three acts of reason *circa agibilia*—taking counsel, judging, and commanding. The first two, Thomas says (*Ia IIae*, q. 57, a. 6, c.) are analogous to acts of speculative intellect, but the third, *praecipere* (to command) is proper to practical intellect.

The judgment of the circumstances is fallible as bearing on the singular and contingent. The directing and commanding act of prudence can be *true* and *certain*, if it is in conformity with rectified appetite. This is not to say that the assessment of the circumstances is expressive of more than opinion. Simon owes this distinction between the two judgments to Cajetan and John of St. Thomas (cf. p. 33, n. 1). He cites as well *IIa IIae*, q. 47, a. 3, ad 2: *Utrum prudentia sit cognoscitiva singularium?* Our knowledge of singulars never surpasses *ut in pluribus* knowledge. Cajetan, commenting on this article, writes:

> Note that the certitude of prudence is twofold, *one consisting of knowledge alone*, and this taken universally is the same as the certitude of moral science, whose universals are true for the most part. Taken particularly however it does not exceed the certitude of *opinion*, since it deals with future and absent things. *And this is not proper to prudence.* The other is the certitude of practical truth, which consists in conformity with rectified appetite (*quae consistit in confesse se habere appetitui recto*). This is proper to prudence, which does not consist in reason alone.[9]

And if after careful consideration of the circumstances one judges falsely and acts on false factual judgments, the judgment of prudence is nonetheless true because it is in conformity with right will.

I apologize for dwelling at such length on such elementary matters. My excuse is a desire to underscore the patient attention Yves R. Simon accorded such matters. A good beginning is half the journey.

As we all know, Simon and Maritain saw the connection between what Thomas says of the prudential judgment and the *judicium per modum connaturalitatis*, of which Thomas speaks in the very first question of the *Summa Theologiae* when he asks whether *sacra doctrina* is wisdom. He distinguishes two kinds of judgments, one *per modum cognitionis*, the other *per modum connaturalitatis*, and he

---

[9]*Ibid.*, 33, note 1.

illustrates them by contrasting the judgment of moral science with the judgment of a good man on the subject of chastity.

Both Kierkegaard and Newman seem to echo Aquinas's view. When confronting the objection that faith is based on insufficient evidence, they suggest the analogue of moral judgment. "The reason we have forgotten what it is to be a Christian is that we have forgotten what it is to be a man." Sören Kierkegaard lampooned the suggestion that Euclidean certitude is needed at all times. (See the unfinished novel, *Johannes Climacus, or De omnibus dubitandum est*.) No one could ever act, if such a requirement had to be met; for that matter, no one could *not* act either. The tenth and eleventh *Sermons Preached Before the University* deal with faith and reason. Both were given in January, 1839, when Newman was still an Anglican. Like Kierkegaard, Newman suggests that the complaint against faith would have to be turned against any moral decision. We simply do not have time to arrive at an exhaustive appraisal of our circumstances and, if we took the time, the circumstances would change even as we inquire. If, as the rationalist said, it is immoral to accept anything as true on insufficient evidence, then it would always be immoral to act and all acts would be immoral.

Kierkegaard and Newman invoke Aristotle on the matter. Both suggest an analogy between moral action and religious belief. It is interesting to note that Thomas Aquinas draws exactly the same analogy when he considered Augustine's *Nemo credit nisi volens*. In *Q. D. de virtutibus in communi*, a. 7, Thomas likens faith to prudence: both depend on right will in order to function. It is the will, moved by grace, that prompts the mind to assent to truths beyond its comprehension.

My moral is simple. The great Thomists teach us two things: first, that we must immerse ourselves in the texts of Thomas, of Aristotle, and of the great commentators; and secondly, that we must ever put the assimilated doctrine to new uses. In this dual sense, we should make Maritain's motto our own: "Woe to me if I do not Thomisticize."

A Moral Realist Perspective on Yves R. Simon's Interpretation of Habitus

John Killoran

Introduction

One of the most notable aspects of recent moral philosophy is a renewed interest in moral realism—the view that moral truths exist independently of ourselves. Prior to the 1980s many moral philosophers in the analytic tradition took as their primary task distinguishing ethical discourse from discourse about the world. Moral truth, it was argued, depends upon the use of language, not the nature of the world. Gradually, though, moral philosophers have begun to realize that this rather sterile conception of moral philosophy cannot do justice to the richness of the moral life. The consequence is a greater willingness to admit the objective existence of moral truth. At first blush this trend appears salutary since "contemporary moral realism" seems to promise an antidote to the moral anti-realism which has been the staple of moral philosophy for most of this century. Closer study, however, reveals that it fails to deliver on this promise. In this paper I will argue that Yves R. Simon's interpretation of the Thomistic concept of *habitus* yields a moral realism that is not only an effective antidote to moral anti-realism but also to the spiritual malaise spawned by misguided moral philosophies.

My discussion will begin with a critique of a version of contemporary moral realism I consider exceptional for its sophistication and originality, namely, that proffered by legal and moral theorist, Michael

Moore.[1] Next I will show how the concept of *habitus*, as interpreted by Simon, enables the moral theorist to resolve the difficulties encountered by contemporary moral realism. Then, I will examine the theory of goodness which, in my view, underwrites the effectiveness of Simon's Thomistic moral realism. I will conclude with some brief remarks on how a Thomistic moral realism might respond to the "present crisis in moral philosophy."

Critique of Contemporary Moral Realism

The crucial problem for the contemporary moral realist is explaining the metaphysical status of moral properties. This problem can be cast in the form of a dilemma. On the one hand, the moral realist can argue that moral properties are simple, non-natural properties which are grasped by a special faculty of moral intuition sometimes referred to as "moral sense."[2] But this horn of the dilemma requires that he adopt an ontology that contains entities "utterly different from anything else in the universe,"[3] as well as an epistemology that countenances mysterious faculties such as intuition. On the other hand, the moral realist can hold that moral properties can be explained naturalistically. This horn of the dilemma, however, proposes a reductionist analysis of moral properties, an alternative which is unacceptable because it identifies certain natural properties with moral properties, resulting in an impoverished understanding of the latter.[4] A viable moral realism, then, will cut through this dilemma, eschewing non-naturalism and naturalism alike. Michael Moore proposes such a moral realism.

Moore's moral realism draws its inspiration from the "realist" theory of meaning formulated by Saul Kripke and Hilary Putnam, which

---

[1]See Michael Moore, "Moral Reality," *Wisconsin Law Review*, No. 6 (1982), pp. 1061–1156; Moore, "A Natural Law Theory of Interpretation," *Southern California Law Review* 58 (1985), pp. 277–398 and Moore, "Metaphysics, Epistemology, and Legal Theory," *Southern California Law Review* 60 (1987), pp. 453–506. For a discussion of Moore's moral realism as it relates to legal theory, see Graham Walker, *Moral Foundations of Constitutional Thought: Current Problems, Augustinian Prospects* (Princeton, New Jersey: Princeton University Press, 1990), pp. 47–57.

[2]A classic defense of this view, which may be considered a form of intuitionism, is found in Francis Hutcheson, *Inquiry into the Original of Our Ideas of Beauty and Virtue* (London, 1725).

[3]J.L. Mackie, *Ethics: Inventing Right and Wrong* (London: Penguin Books, 1977), p. 38.

[4]Some moral realists, however, do defend versions of naturalism. See, for example, Richard Boyd, "How to be a Moral Realist" in Geoffrey Sayre-McCord, ed., *Essays on Moral Realism* (Ithaca, New York: Cornell University Press, 1988), pp. 181–228.

argues that the meanings of terms depend upon the nature of things.[5] Kripke and Putnam see their theory of meaning as an alternative to the traditional "conventionalist" view, which holds that meaning is a matter of linguistic practices. Conventionalist theories of meaning maintain a) that the meaning of a term is the set of descriptions typically associated with it, and b) that the extension of a term is determined by these descriptions. Thus, the meaning of the proper name 'Shakespeare' is the 'the man who wrote *Hamlet*'; 'the man who lived in Stratford-upon-Avon'; etc.[6] But surely it is possible that someone else satisfies these descriptions, perhaps Francis Bacon. Conceivably, the individual referred to by the proper name 'Shakespeare' was a stage-hand at the Globe Theater who allowed his name to be used by the author of the plays we now recognize as "Shakespearean." The point is that the descriptions associated with the proper name 'Shakespeare' may fail to designate the individual to whom it purportedly refers. Coventionalist theories of meaning, it is argued, cannot accommodate such failures of reference.

The realist theory of meaning, on the other hand, holds that the meaning of a term is its reference. In other words, for the realist, the meaning of a proper name, for instance, is determined, not by any set of descriptions or conventions, but by the individual the proper name designates. So, to employ Kripke's nomenclature, a proper name is a "rigid designator," since it necessarily refers to or rigidly designates the same individual regardless of whether the individual satisfies or fails to satisfy some set of descriptions.[7] Kripke and Putnam then extend their analysis to so-called "natural kind" terms, e.g., 'gold,' 'water,' arguing that a natural kind term necessarily refers to the same substance independently of whatever descriptions the substance may satisfy.[8] So, for example, although properties like yellowness,

---

[5]See Saul Kripke, "Naming and Necessity" in Donald Davidson and Gilbert Harman, eds., *Semantics of Natural Language* (Dordrecht: D. Reidel, 1972), pp. 253–355 and Hilary Putnam, "The Meaning of 'Meaning'" in Hilary Putnam, *Mind, Language and Reality: Philosophical Papers*, Vol. 2 (Cambridge: Cambridge University Press, 1975), pp. 215–271.

[6]John Searle's essay "Proper Names" is the classic source for this position. See John Searle, "Proper Names" in P. F. Strawson, ed., *Philosophical Logic* (Oxford: Oxford University Press, 1967), pp. 89–96. See also Ludwig Wittgenstein, *Philosophical Investigations*, second edition, trans. G. E. M. Anscombe (New York: The Macmillan Company, 1958), pp. 36–37 (#39).

[7]See Saul Kripke, "Naming and Necessity," p. 269.

[8]*Ibid.*, p. 314–331. See also Putnam's "Is Semantics Possible?" in Hilary Putnam, *Mind, Language and Reality: Philosophical Papers*, Vol. 2 (Cambridge: Cambridge University Press, 1975), pp. 139–152.

friability, etc. are typically associated with gold, the meaning of 'gold' consists in having the atomic number 79, since the best available scientific theory informs us that gold uniquely possesses this quality. Or, as Moore puts it, "The realist theory asserts that the meaning of a word is to be found only by developing a theory about the kind of thing to which the word refers."[9] The upshot is that because science reveals the necessary qualities of natural kinds, statements about natural kinds are empirically established necessary truths, a position which contrasts with the traditional view that all necessary truths are *a priori*. From the perspective of the realist theory of meaning, then, linguistic conventions, formerly the key to meaning, become merely guides to usage.[10]

Following a suggestion of Putnam's, the realist theory of reference has also been extended to moral terms.[11] So Moore argues that moral kind terms refer, not according to conventions or social practices, but rather according to the "best theory" about the nature of such kinds, for "it is the nature of things . . . that determines the extension of a moral word."[12] But Moore, for one, is careful to point out that his moral realism is not committed to providing a naturalist account of moral kinds. As he remarks, the moral realist "need not argue that there is a hidden nature of a physical sort to generosity, courage, or injustice."[13] But if this is so, how can moral kind terms have a realist application? Moore replies:

> To justify the application of a realist theory of meaning to moral words, it is enough to show that they, like the namesof natural kinds, betray our commitment to the necessity of theory. One need only show that moral words have a kind of "semantic depth" akin to that possessed by natural kind words. . . . [14]

By the claim that both moral and natural kind terms have "semantic

---

[9]Michael Moore, "Moral Reality," p. 1144.

[10]Putnam makes a distinction between the use of a term and its meaning. Conventions, social practices, etc., may have a role in establishing how a word is used—i.e., in fixing its paradigmatic use or "stereotype"—but meaning is determined by the entity to which it refers. See Hilary Putnam, "Is Semantics Possible?" See also "The Meaning of 'Meaning,' in *Mind, Language and Reality: Philosophical Papers*, Vol. 2, pp. 247–252.

[11]Hilary Putnam, "Language and Reality," *Ibid.*, p. 290.

[12]Michael Moore, "Moral Reality," p. 1144.

[13]*Ibid.*

[14]*Ibid.*

depth," Moore means that they can have no exhaustive explanation.[15] Just as in science, theoretical improvement in our understanding of moral concepts is an ongoing effort, since moral language is continually coming to grips with a world that, given its complexity, often proves quite recalcitrant to our investigative efforts. So, although we may commence our inquiries with a grasp of the truth-conditions for applying these concepts, we will nonetheless remain unable to provide a complete analysis of them because it is characteristic of theories to undergo periodic revision. Consequently, any theoretical explanation of moral as well as of natural kind terms will exhibit semantic depth. For the contemporary moral realist, then, what these terms have in common is not that they refer to similar sorts of qualities but that they share the important feature of semantic depth. So, presumably, the concept of semantic depth enables the contemporary moral realist to provide an account of moral properties that is neither naturalist (since moral kinds are not identified with natural kinds) nor non-naturalist (since moral kinds are, like natural kinds, theoretically explicable and hence not entirely *sui generis*).

Nevertheless, what the contemporary moral realist has to say about the role of semantic depth in determining the reference of moral terms is somewhat unsatisfactory. To begin with, although contemporary moral realism holds that science and morals appeal to the "best theory" to settle questions of reference in their respective domains, reference in the former is resolved by determinate features of the world, namely, natural kinds, while reference in the latter is determined solely through the articulation of the best moral theory. The key claim is that, for Moore, moral concepts are theoretically constructed rather than empirically discovered.[16] Thus, the anti-realist can argue that if the reference of moral terms is established by theoretical considerations only, the moral realist's position collapses into conventionalism, since agreement about the use of terms rather than some feature of the world becomes the ultimate arbiter of meaning. On the other hand, if the moral realist accepts the position that moral kind terms refer in much the same way that natural kind terms do,

---

[15]The concept of semantic depth originates in the moral realism of Mark Platts. See his Ways of Meaning (London: Routledge and Kegan Paul, 1979), ch. 10.

[16]Stephen Munzer proposes this understanding of Moore in his essay "Realistic Limits on Realist Interpretation," *Southern California Law Review* 58 (1985), p. 465.

i.e., by designating physical natures, then his position becomes indistinguishable from naturalism. Once more the contemporary moral realist's use of the notion of semantic depth is not really helpful because it does not account for the differences between these two sorts of terms. The dilemma faced by the contemporary moral realist unhappily remains, for he is unable to provide an explanation of moral properties that escapes the unacceptable alternatives of naturalism and non-naturalism.

Simon's Thomistic Moral Realism

The failure of contemporary moral realism (as formulated by Moore) to account for the metaphysical status of moral properties suggests that an adequate moral realism has a dual task; that is, it must explain a) the sense in which moral and natural kind terms identify features of the world, as well as b) the sense in which they differ from each other. In Yves R. Simon's interpretation of *habitus* we have the means for addressing these two points. In his book *The Definition of Moral Virtue*, Simon suggests that *habitus* resembles the natures of physical things—indeed, the similarities between the realm of nature and that of morality underwrite his Thomistic moral realism.[17]

But he also recognizes the important differences between the two realms. He claims, for instance, that free choice distinguishes *habitus*. Let us, then, with Simon's guidance take a closer look at the concept of *habitus*.

English editions of St. Thomas's writings usually (and misleadingly) translate *habitus* as "habit."[18] In standard English, of course, 'habit' refers to a disposition to perform certain acts repeatedly and unreflectively. Habits "cause" us, as it were, to act in these ways. So the acts that habits occasion lack the cognitive direction characteristic of genuine human actions. (In Thomistic terms, habits may

---

[17]Yves R. Simon, *The Definition of Moral Virtue*, ed. Vukan Kuic (New York: Fordham University Press, 1989), pp. 69–79.

[18]Reviewing Anton C. Pegis's edited translation of St. Thomas, *Basic Writings of St. Thomas Aquinas* (New York: Random House, 1945), Simon notes: "After many others, Professor Pegis translates *habitus* by *habit*, thus making the concept of *habitus* unintelligible to those who do not know that *habit*, in his translation, stands for *habitus*. *Habit* simply does not signify the same thing as *habitus*. Science is a *habitus*, it would be ridiculous to say that it is a habit; an infused virtue is a *habitus*, it would be contradictory to say that it is a habit." *The Commonweal*, July 13 (1945), p. 314.

be characterized as so-called "acts of man" [*actiones hominis*].)[19] Because habitual acts have no purpose or end, "The necessity of habit is subjective."[20] But the concept of *habitus*, particularly as it is found in the works of St. Thomas, has a quite different meaning.[21] To put it baldly, *habitus* (unlike habit) exhibits intelligence. Consider the following example. Learning how to play the piano, or learning any other complex skill for that matter, requires the direction of reason. Although the skills of a gifted pianist, like habits, are acquired through a good deal of repetitive practice, they are nonetheless characterized by an *essential* steadiness, that is, "a steadiness which is guaranteed by the necessity in the object,"[22] namely, the requirements of the musical score, rather than by subjective necessity, as in the case of habit.

Simon's point is that *habitus* reveals an "objective necessity" in the sense that it rationally orders or "dis-poses" one's skills, potentialities, and possibilities.[23] This point receives support from John of St. Thomas:

> So wherever a certain multiplicity is to be arranged in some order or reduced in some way, there is need for a disposition. . . . Consequently,

---

[19]*ST.*, I-II, Q. 1, a. 1.

[20]Yves R. Simon, *The Definition of Moral Virtue*, p. 78. See also *ibid.*, p. 53: "Brought about by repetition of acts, then, the necessity of habit, despite appearances, remains forever subjective."

[21]See *ibid.*, pp. 57–58. In *ST.*, I-II, Q. 49, a. 3 and in *ST.*, I-II, Q. 54, a. 1, St. Thomas considers two kinds of *habitus*: *habitus* in relation to act (*habitus in ordine ad actum*) and *habitus* in relation to nature (*habitus in ordine ad naturam rei*). This distinction is derived, in turn, from a more fundamental distinction, namely, that repectively between power in reference to act (*potentia ad agere*) and power in reference to being (*potentia ad esse*). See, for example, *ST.*, I-II, Q. 55, a. 2, where St. Thomas says: "Unde, cum duplex sit potentia, scilicet potentia ad esse et potentia ad agere." *Potentia ad esse* provides the subject for entitative *habitus*—in particular, the entitative *habitus* of sanctifying grace, for it is through grace that the *being* of the soul is brought to perfection. *Potentia ad agere*, on the other hand, provides the subject for operative *habitus*, which brings *human acts* to perfection. My concern in this essay is the latter. For a discussion of the distinction between the two kinds of potency, see Vernon Bourke, "The Role of Habitus in the Thomistic Metaphysics of Potency and Act," in *Essays in Thomism*, ed. Robert E. Brennan (Freeport, New York: Books for Libraries Press, 1972), pp. 103–109. For some historical background on the *habitus* doctrine, see Cary Nederman, "Nature, Ethics, and the Doctrine of 'Habitus': Aristotelian Moral Psychology in the Twelfth Century," *Traditio* 45 (1990), pp. 87–109.

[22]Yves R. Simon, *An Introduction to Metaphysics of Knowledge*, trans. Vukan Kuic and Richard J. Thompson (New York: Fordham University Press, 1990), p. 159.

[23]Yves R. Simon, *The Definition of Moral Virtue*, pp. 79–87.

disposition is called an order among parts, that is, their fitting or correct positioning.[24]

This disposition or ordering constitutes a "dynamic whole,"[25] a structure which has a reality of its own and is therefore irreducible to its constituent parts. The development of piano skills involves integrating knowledge of musical scores, emotional expressiveness, and manual dexterity. The resulting *habitus* is a dynamic whole in which all of these elements are ordered to constitute an effortless, virtuoso performance at the piano keyboard. So, once a person has acquired considerable skills at the piano, he is able to perform by "second nature," so to speak. A gifted pianist, for instance, knows certain scores through and through, so much so that he can "play them in his sleep."

Nevertheless, proficiency in a discipline or art is no guarantee that a person will develop his talents. Our gifted pianist could decline concert engagements, choosing instead to waste his talents playing in seedy saloons. He has the qualifications or abilities but refrains from using them. Much the same can be said about scholars and scientists. A scientist or scholar may be qualitatively ready to practice his discipline but, for one reason or another, may choose not to do so. According to Simon, this sort of readiness—"qualitative" *habitus*, as he terms it— must be carefully distinguished from the readiness of moral *habitus*.[26] The morally virtuous person is not only properly disposed but always prepared to act rightly. As Simon remarks:

> By a man's disposition we mean precisely the unique arrangement of all his moral traits. And when this arrangement makes him totally reliable

---

[24]Quoted in Simon, *An Introduction to Metaphysics of Knowledge*, p. 69, n. 32. For John of St. Thomas, the objective necessity of *habitus* is founded in principles: "Thus science, so far as its intrinsic principles are concerned, is a habitus, for it proceeds from evident causes, which are firm, and the same holds for virtues, which proceed from practical principles known and directed by the synderesis." *The Material Logic of John of St. Thomas*, ed. and trans. Yves. R. Simon, John J. Glanville, and G. Donald Hollenhorst (Chicago: The University of Chicago Press, 1965), p. 380.

[25]Concerning *habitus* as a "dynamic whole," Simon states: "I would like to designate [the disposition of a person] as 'dynamic.' Perhaps we could also call it a functional whole with functional parts, but dynamic is better: the 'psychological totality' which represents a person's moral character is a dynamic whole with dynamic parts." Simon, *The Definition of Moral Virtue*, p. 81. Robert Nozick's account of value in his book *Philosophical Explanations* (Cambridge, Mass: Harvard University Press, 1981), p. 416, parallels Simon's. Nozick explains intrinsic value as expressing "organic unity," that is, "unity in diversity."

[26]Yves R. Simon, *The Definition of Moral Virtue*, p. 71.

and dependable in human affairs, we call both the man and his disposition [morally] virtuous.[27]

His readiness to act virtuously is thus "existential," since it betokens a propensity "to do the right thing at the right time."[28] So scientific and artistic *habitus* exhibit just qualitative readiness, but moral *habitus* exhibits both qualitative and existential readiness, for the morally virtuous person not only possesses virtue but also practices it. Interestingly enough, Simon contends that some of the clearest examples of "existential readiness" occur within nature, particularly in the "finality" of organisms.[29] Of course, many natural scientists are reluctant to employ the notion of finality to explain natural regularities, since teleological explanations rely upon unverifiable concepts like 'goal' and 'purpose'. Yet in many instances the teleological character of natural events is undeniable. In his book *The Cosmic Blueprint*, cosmologist Paul Davies maintains that "the steady unfolding of organized complexity in the universe is a fundamental property of nature."[30] While Davies rules out the existence of vitalistic principles such as "entelechies," he notes that the sort of complexity and novelty found in the natural realm cannot be explained in reductionist terms. Thus, he holds that in nature there is "the possibility of *self-organization*, in which [natural] systems suddenly and spontaneously leap into more elaborate forms."[31] Indeed, the evidence for such processes is abundant:

> Research in areas as diverse as fluid turbulence, crystal growth and neural networks is revealing the extraordinary propensity for physical systems to generate newer states or order spontaneously. It is clear that there exists *self-organizing* processes in every branch of science.[32]

The "propensity" for self-organization to which Davies refers in the passage above captures, I believe, what Simon means by "existential readiness." There is, as Simon suggests, a tendency, an existential readiness, in things to combine and "self-organize" into more complex

---

[27]*Ibid.*, p. 84.

[28]*Ibid.*, p. 71.

[29]*Ibid.*, p. 72.

[30]Paul Davies, *The Cosmic Blueprint: New Discoveries in Nature's Creative Ability to Order the Universe* (New York: Simon and Schuster, 1988), p. 142.

[31]*Ibid.*, p. 198.

[32]*Ibid.*, p. 1, Preface.

structures. These newly emergent structures are (to borrow a term from the discussion of *habitus*) "dynamic wholes" which cannot be reduced to their constituent parts. Their irreducibility originates in the fact that each is ordered in a determinate way, exhibiting a "finality" specific to the kind of thing that it is. In this rather Aristotelian sense, each of these structures exhibits existential readiness. So, to use Simon's own example,[33] the elements silver and chlorine manifest an existential readiness to form the molecular structure silver chloride, a compound whose complexity and behavior cannot be explained simply in terms of its constituent elements, silver and chlorine. It is a new dynamic whole which manifests an existential readiness of its own, that is, a finality specific to its nature as silver chloride.

The implications of the preceding are far-reaching, particularly with respect to the relation between science and morals. Simon aptly notes that, prior to the seventeenth century, the term 'virtue' was used to refer to the presence of existential readiness in natural things.[34] He then goes on to assert that existential readiness is found in morality as well as in science. Thus:

> there is a continuity between the laws of nature and the laws of morality, and the 'virtue' of a physical thing is so-called because of perceived resemblance to moral virtue. They are both seen as instances of existential readiness, which makes for trust, confidence, dependability, reliability, and indeed predictability.[35]

As Simon suggests in this passage, the natures of physical things resemble moral kinds. For just as existential readiness is exhibited by a natural kind, so it is likewise to be found in moral virtue, which, as *habitus*, is a sort of "second nature."[36] The importance of this analogy is paramount. In a mechanistic universe, say that described in Lucretius's Epicurean poem *De Rerum Natura*, "things including man, have no ends and have, therefore, to be assigned 'values' from the outside."[37] The upshot is that "In a world devoid of finality, all values

---

[33]Yves R. Simon, *The Definition of Moral Virtue*, p. 73.

[34]*Ibid.*, p. 74.

[35]*Ibid.*, p. 75.

[36]On *habitus* as a "second nature," see *ST.*, I-II, 53, 1 ad 1; *ST.*, I-II, 56, a. 5; *ST.*, I-II, Q. 58, a. 1; and *ST.*, I-II, Q. 60, a. 4 ad 2. On *habitus* as a "sort of nature," see St. Thomas's *Commentary on the Nicomachean Ethics*, II, lec. 3, no. 265.

[37]Yves R. Simon, *The Definition of Moral Virtue*, p. 107.

must of necessity be both subjective and artificial; and when these 'values' collapse, despair is all that is left."[38] The finalism of Simon's Thomistic realism presents a stark contrast to the preceding, since "in a world of natures, values reside in the nature of things. Thus if man has a nature, he also has a destiny, and we can relate what is right and wrong for him to do to his nature and to his end objectively."[39]

Simon's universe, as we see, is one in which values are *in rerum natura* rather than merely being projections of human attitudes, as in the moral philosophies of those modern epigones of Epicurus, the anti-realists. Thus, the meanings of moral kind words like 'courage' and 'temperance' are based upon clearly objective, identifiable features of human nature, to wit, moral virtues such as courage and temperance. Reality, rather than the best available moral theory, becomes the benchmark of meaning. Indeed, for Simon, moral virtue can be the object of scientific inquiry, for "any moral philosopher should be able to handle scientifically questions pertaining to moral essence and tell you what is right and what is wrong in general."[40] This point is reinforced by the fact that moral *habitus* or moral essence exhibits an existential readiness toward "self-organization," just as natural systems do. The practice of moral virtue, which involves doing the right thing at the right time, requires that the various potentialities and abilities which go into a person's character be rightly ordered or disposed. Moral virtue is a "dynamic whole" which emerges from the integration or self-organization of the elements that constitute a person's character. The study of how this integration occurs, moreover, yields knowledge that is just as legitimate as that acquired in the investigation of nature.

But if *habitus* resembles natural processes, how are we to explain the freedom and voluntariness that characterize virtuous action? To begin with, Simon contends that free choice is oftentimes associated with indeterminism, most notably in the philosophy of Epicurus. Epicureanism "places the principle of all free choice in an act of contingency boldly conceived apart from any cause, any nature, and any intelligible ground."[41] In Simon's thought, contrastingly, free

---

[38]*Ibid.*

[39]*Ibid.*

[40]*Ibid.*, p. 101.

[41]Yves R. Simon, *Freedom of Choice*, ed. Peter Wolff (New York: Fordham University Press, 1992), p. 11.

choice has its source in the integration of character occasioned by the acquisition of moral virtue, for it is through moral virtue that a person achieves mastery over himself. Free choice is thus a matter of "superdetermination" rather than "indetermination."[42] Simon intimates, moreover, that free choice is revealed most eminently in the self-mastery and directiveness that is found when one acts with a purpose. Hence, freedom does not proceed, as many believe, from indeterminism, irrationality, formlessness, and the like. Quite the contrary, it proceeds "from a particular excellence in power, from a plentitude of being and an abundance of determination, from an ability to achieve mastery over diverse possibilities, from a strength of constitution which makes it possible to attain one's end in a variety of ways."[43]

In Simon's thought, then, the very same features which enable us to identify *habitus* also explain the sense in which morally virtuous actions are free and voluntary. Indeed, it is Simon's contention that the existential readiness of moral virtue finds its expression in free choice. So, while freedom and voluntariness distinguish the moral virtues from other aspects of reality, their nature as *habitus* explains why the moral virtues should be considered, not as theoretical constructions (à la Moore), but as determinate features of reality. Accordingly, Simon's Thomistic moral realism explains how moral kinds are identifiable features of the world, as well as how they differ from natural kinds, thus yielding an account of the metaphysical status of moral properties that escapes the dilemma encountered by contemporary moral realism.

Theories of Goodness

The success of Simon's Thomistic moral realism is due in large measure to its implicit rejection of an assumption which underlies most of contemporary moral philosophy, namely, that goodness cannot be present in the natural order. Of course, there are exceptions to this generalization;[44] nevertheless most moral philosophers—contemporary moral realists included—restrict the use of the concept of

---

[42]*Ibid.*, p. 152.

[43]*Ibid.*, p. 153.

[44]One thinks, perhaps, of A. N. Whitehead for whom "Goodness is a qualification belonging to the constitution of reality . . . Good and evil lie in depths and distances below and beyond appearance. They solely concern inter-relations within the real world." *Adventures in Ideas* (New York: The Free Press, 1961), p. 268; see also his essay, "Mathematics and the Good," *The*

goodness to human actions, traits, choices, and desires. The suggestion, of course, is that there is a hiatus between the moral and the natural order, since nothing in nature can rightly be called "good." Accordingly, if the concept of goodness is confined to the moral realm, it becomes difficult to explain how moral kind terms can have a realist application, since their semantical function will diverge widely from that of natural kind terms. Rather, it becomes more plausible to say that natural kind terms *refer* to entities in the world, while moral terms *express* our desires, choices, or perhaps our agreements. Simon, however, rejects the assumption that value cannot be present in the natural order; to the contrary, he holds that natural systems and structures can exhibit goodness, a position not to be confused with naturalism which *identifies* goodness with natural properties. Simon's contention is that the concept of goodness has many senses, some of which are non-moral. The doctrine of *habitus*, as we will see presently, illustrates this analogical understanding of goodness.

The moral philosophy of Simon presupposes a non-reductionist view of reality, a philosophical perspective that puts his thought at odds with the prevailing tenor of contemporary philosophy. If one were to canvass contemporary philosophical opinion, one would probably discover that the dominant view is a reductionist naturalism. For the naturalist, values, and things of the spirit generally, are "nothing but" desires and interests. Ironically, however, naturalism has its origins, not in the materialism of Epicurus and Lucretius, but in the "spiritualism" of Descartes. In his book *The Great Dialogue of Nature and Space*, Simon points out that Descartes sought to mathematicize nature by ridding it of unquantifiable entities such as natural kinds.[45] So, instead of comprising a multiplicity of natures, reality, for Descartes, is just geometrical space configured by vortical motion. The Cartesian conception of reality, evidently, is reductionist, in the sense that material things are understood as "nothing but" specific configurations of geometrical space. Consequently, the world of Descartes has no place

---

Philosophy of Alfred North Whitehead, Paul Arthur Schilpp, ed. (New York: Tudor Publishing Co., 1951), pp. 666–668.

[45]Yves R. Simon, *The Great Dialogue of Nature and Space* (Albany, New York: Magi Books, 1970), p. 10. For a discussion of how Cartesianism expunged finality from the natural order, see also Yves R. Simon, *Practical Knowledge*, ed. Robert J. Mulvaney (New York: Fordham University Press, 1991), p. 122.

for finality. But, as Simon notes, where finality is ruled-out, there can be no goodness, for the notion of finality embodies that of something being ordered to another, of each thing being in the right place, indeed of a "good state of affairs."[46]

Descartes's reduction of physical reality to a single plane of intelligibility devoid of value and goodness, namely, geometrical space, set the foundation for a similar reduction in ethics. After Descartes values are to be found, not in the world, but rather in the passions, specifically in what human beings desire. In the words of an English philosopher who was profoundly influenced by Descartes:

> But whatever is the object of any man's Appetite or Desire; that is it, which he for his part calleth *Good*; And the object of his Hate and Aversion, *Evil*. . . . [47]

It is easy to see, then, why the *habitus* doctrine dropped out of sight in the seventeenth-century. The Cartesian emphasis on the univocity of being (and the concomitant denial of the Thomistic analogy of being) ineluctably led to the naturalistic doctrine that goodness and desire are one and the same. So goodness no longer consisted in order within nature or order within the human soul, but simply in what human beings desire. To be sure, many post-Cartesian philosophers denied naturalism, and yet they typically concurred with the central Cartesian claim, to wit, values are not part of the world. Such is the legacy Descartes's "spiritualism" has bequeathed to modern moral philosophy.

The contemporary moral realist's claim that moral properties are part of the world may be considered an attempt to escape this unfortunate Cartesian legacy, albeit an attempt which, as I have argued, ultimately fails. Significantly, the assumption upon which this failure rests—that goodness and value cannot be present in the natural order—has its roots in Cartesian reductionism, for it suggests that the concept of goodness has a single, determinate meaning, i.e., the good is what people desire or want. Eliminate this assumption, as Simon does, and an entirely different conception of goodness comes to the fore, namely, one that is analogical. Viewing goodness analogically enables the moral theorist to hold that, just as the goodness of a natural kind

---

[46]Yves R. Simon, *The Great Dialogue of Nature and Space*, p. 9.

[47]Thomas Hobbes, *Leviathan* (New York: E. P. Dutton and Co.), p. 41.

consists in having a specific finality, so likewise the goodness of *habitus* consists in the purposiveness of free choice. Thus, in its own way, each kind of goodness, whether moral or natural, encapsulates what is essential to the concept of goodness, namely, the integral unity and the consequent perfection of the subject of goodness.

The Present Crisis in Moral Philosophy

For the contemporary person, goodness is, perhaps, the most elusive of concepts. Of course, our sophisticates inform us quite authoritatively that goodness really consists in what we, either individually or collectively, rationally desire. The masses take the "wise" at their word, with the result that the common understanding of goodness becomes whatever a person happens to prefer.[48] After all, who among us is in a position to determine what is rationally desirable for others? Morality, thus, becomes a purely subjective affair. But the social and psychological consequences of this reduction of goodness to preference are enormous because one loses sight of the fact that genuine happiness is achieved, not by dispersing one's psychic energies into the pursuit of fleeting satisfactions, but by integrating the elements of one's personality into an ordered unity. Unfortunately, the intellectual marketplace is crowded with hucksters of all persuasions promising "wholeness," "self-respect," and other kinds of ersatz salvation— provided one is able to pay the price, financial as well as psychological. Yet what is being offered, is a spurious form of happiness. The tragedy, however, is that it is not recognized as such. The explanation for this ready embrace of falsehood lies in a failure to recognize what is essential to moral goodness, that, in the words of George Mora, "the law governing the human personality is to integrate all its constituent parts with reason, so as to achieve unity of action and intent."

It is to the understanding of goodness embodied in the concept of *habitus* that we must turn in order to confront the present crisis in moral philosophy. As interpreted by Simon, *habitus* expresses within

---

[48]What Manzoni said about seventeenth-century Milan is probably applicable today: "From the inventions of the ignorant, the educated took whatever they could fit into their own ideas; from the inventions of the educated, the ignorant took whatever they could understand; and the result of both was a vast and confused mass of public folly." Allesandro Manzoni, *The Betrothed*, trans. Archibald Colquhoun (London: The Reprint Society, 1952), p. 444.

the human personality a dynamic wholeness that has its analogues throughout nature. So, rather than being separate from nature, the moral order is continuous with it. The foundation for the unity of the natural and the moral orders is the independent reality of created things. We do not create or construct our reality (as idealism maintains); instead reality is already present for us to behold. Accordingly, moral judgments, far from being expressions of attitude or prescriptions, are, in fact, judgments about reality itself. Contemporary moral thought, however, is blind to the important insights that a realist metaphysics can provide moral inquiry. The result is that, for many moral thinkers and their disciples, "so-called value-judgments are not supposed to express what things are: they spring from within [oneself]." Eventually, all that remains is the "existentialistic despair" that accompanies every effort to create values. The way out of this despair, Simon suggests, is to embrace a metaphysics that discovers goodness in the order of being. From the perspective of the moral realist, then, the achievement of Simon's interpretation of *habitus* is its recognition that moral reality is a genuine part of the order of being. For this accomplishment, all of us, philosophers and non-philosophers alike, remain indebted to the moral thought of Yves R. Simon.

Synderesis: *A Key to Understanding Natural Law in Aquinas*

Mark McGovern

Not only is *synderesis* a key to Aquinas's conception of natural law, as the title of this article suggests, but also is, in my judgment, an antidote to the modern malaise (largely engendered by the positivists) that any ethical statement is correctly reduced to a matter of feeling. Commenting on *synderesis* and its connection with natural law should clear away a number of moral confusions, even some held by contemporary Christian ethicians.

St. Thomas's account of *synderesis* can be ascertained by a simple analogy which he himself employs. There is a natural *habitus* in the order of speculative knowledge, namely, *intellectus*, by which the human mind (or soul, if you will) is enabled to recognize immediately the truth of first principles in the speculative sphere. Likewise, there is in the order of practical knowledge a natural *habitus*, namely, *synderesis*, by which the human soul immediately recognizes the truth of first principles in the moral order. In both cases it is not the first principles which are implanted in the soul, but rather what is present in the soul from birth is a natural *habitus* by which the human soul recognizes the truth of first principles. If it were true, as unfortunately some theologians and philosophers in seminary lead me and other students to believe, that the first principles are implanted in the soul, then it would indeed be difficult to explain why there is not unanimous agreement on the first principles in the moral order. But in fact, as Aquinas himself explains, some are hindered from applying the primary principles of the natural law as a result of bad training in the moral life or as a result of the lack of the development of the virtues in their upbringing. This is why Aquinas will say, basing his remarks on St. Paul, that it is the virtuous man who is the judge of all and judged by no one.[1] Unfortunately, in our society we have arrived at the position that everyone's opinion is of equal value in judging of the moral order.

These are the issues I intend to investigate in this article: first, I will give a synopsis of Aquinas's view on *synderesis*; secondly, I will compare Aquinas and Jacques Maritain on the subject, to show to what extent Maritain has elucidated this point for contemporary followers of the Angelic Doctor. For the sake of brevity, I will be selective in my references to Maritain's works.

History of the Term, "Synderesis"

Since others have treated fully the source of *synderesis*,[2] suffice it to say that the term seems to have been introduced to Latin writers of the West by Saint Jerome. Aquinas himself is aware of Jerome's reference to *synderesis* in the latter's commentary on *Ezekiel* 1:7. Jerome identifies what the Greeks call *sunteresin* with the "spark of conscience" in the heart of Adam, which remained even after he was ejected from paradise.[3] But how *synderesis* functions and how it is a part of the very nature of the human mind is a question about which philosophers have disagreed both before and after Aquinas. In this article I will limit my attention mainly to what Aquinas means by the term.

It is my contention that much of the disagreement, at least in modern times, about what Aquinas intends by *synderesis* and its relation to the natural law can be overcome by close attention to his own presentation. It is one thing to disagree about what Aquinas means and another thing to know what he means and nevertheless disagree with him. In this

---

[1] See *ST.*, I-II, 94, 6. Cf. Odon Lottin, "La synderese chez Albert le Grand et saint Thomas," *Revue Néo-scolastique de Philosophie* 30 (1928), p. 38. See also 1 *Cor.* 2:15. Cf. *Super epistolas s. Pauli lectura*, cura Raphaelis Cai, 3rd ed., vol. 1 (Marietti, 1953), cp. 2, lect. 3.

[2] A very thorough treatment is given by Odon Lottin, *Problemes de morale*, Vol. 2, part 1 of *Psychologie et morale aux 12e et 13e siecles* (Louvain: Abbaye du Mont Cesar, 1948), pp. 101–349.

[3] Cf. *De Veritate*, 16, 2 obj. 1; 3 obj. 4.

discussion I do not address my remarks to those who fall into the latter category, however few or many they may be. Personally, I think that group is small indeed; rather, I address the former category.[4]

Synderesis in Early and Late Works of Aquinas

Odon Lottin argues that a primary development in Aquinas's moral thought occurs with regard to the question of whether *synderesis* is a power or a habit. In the early works he calls *synderesis* a power with a habit. It is only in the later works that it becomes clear that *synderesis* is basically a habit. Lottin argues that Aquinas calls *synderesis* a habit with a power only because of his respect for the received tradition.[5]

Powers, Habits, and Synderesis

For Aquinas *synderesis* is a habit of the possible intellect. But it is not an acquired or infused habit. Rather, it is innate, i.e., a natural habit.

It is well to bear in mind the context of the writing of Aquinas on any given topic; I shall do so here in discussing the nature and function of habits. For Aquinas the end of man is happiness. This is obviously achieved through human acts. So it is necessary not only to consider human acts but also their principles if one is to determine how man is to achieve happiness. Some human acts are proper to man, such as acts of reason and will. Other human acts are proper to man and animals, such as the passions. After studying human acts, St. Thomas then proceeds to study the principles of human acts, namely, powers and habits. He follows Aristotle in defining a habit as "a disposition whereby that which is disposed is disposed well or ill, and this either in regard to itself or in regard to another. . . ." For Aquinas *synderesis* as a natural habit (a habit that is neither infused nor

---

[4]For the disagreement before Aquinas see Odon Lottin, *Problemes de morale*, pp. 101–210. I once attended at a prominent Midwestern university a lecture on Aquinas' natural law theory in which *synderesis* was never mentioned. Two articles which do give some attention the the relationship of *synderesis* and the natural law are (1) *The New Catholic Encyclopedia*, s. v. "Synderesis"; (2) Vernon Bourke, "El principio de la sinderesis: fuentes y función in la Etica de Tomas de Aquino," *Sapientia* 34 (1980) pp. 615–626.

[5]Odon Lottin, "La synderesis chez Albert le Grand et saint Thomas," p. 36, 40. *De Veritate*, 16, 1; *ST.*, I-II, 79, 12.

acquired) resembles natural dispositions, such as those possessed by a person who is irascible by nature or who is a natural runner, wrestler, etc. Some natural dispositions describe a characteristic of the body, e.g., a person who is naturally healthy in appearance. Others describe a characteristic of the soul, e.g., a person who is naturally irascible. Likewise, habits as the first species of quality describe a disposition related to the very nature of the subject either on the level of the soul: as *synderesis* describes a disposition to know first principles in the practical order; or on the level of the body: as health or beauty describes a disposition of the physical body.[6] Moreover, habits are necessary for some beings but not for others. For a thing to need to be disposed to something else, i.e., to need a habit, three conditions are necessary. First, that to which it is disposed must be something other than itself; thus God does not need habits. Secondly, that which is in potency to another is capable of being determined in many and diverse ways; thus the celestial body has no need for habit, since it is disposed only to one thing, a determined motion. "The third condition is that in disposing the subject to one of those things to which it is in potentiality, several things should occur, capable of being adjusted in various ways so as to dispose the subject well or ill to its form or to its operation." In short, if a being has only one operation by which it achieves its end, then that being has no need for habits to achieve its end.[7]

While the same power is capable of both good and evil, this is not the case with habit. For example, by the power of sight we can do good or evil, but the habit of *sapientia* directs us always to the good decision.

Habits are primarily in the soul and secondarily in bodies. They can be said to be in the body only insofar as the soul acts through the body.[8] Since the soul is the principle of operations through its powers, habits are in the soul according to its powers. The exception is the habit of grace which is in the soul according to the essence of the soul.

---

[6]*Ibid.*, 16, 1 ad 1; 16, 1 ad 13. *ST.*, I-II, 1, 6 & 49 prefaces. *ST.*, I-II, 49, 1; Aristotle's *Metaph.* 5, 20 (1022b10). *ST.*, I-II, 49, 2. *ST.*, I-II, 49, 3 & 4. Cf. also 50, 1.

[7]*ST.*, I-II, 49, 4; ad 1 & 2.

[8]*ST.*, I-II, ad 3 & 55, 3. *ST.*, I-II, 50, 1; 50, 2.

It seems, then, that habit is present in the body only in an accommo-dated sense. In this sense Aquinas maintains that habit is not present in the sensitive powers which act from the instinct of nature, but only in those sensitive powers which act by the command of reason. Accordingly, there is no habit present in the power of sight or hearing, but habit can be present in the sensitive appetitive powers and even in the sensitive apprehensive powers such as imagination and sense memory. As to the question of whether there is any virtue or habit in us by nature, Aquinas says that

> virtue is natural to man according to a kind of beginning . . . insofar as in man's reason are to be found instilled by nature certain naturally known principles of both knowledge and action which are the nurseries of intellectual and moral virtues, and insofar as there is in the will a natural appetite for good in accordance with reason.[9]

The point is that we are born with the first principles of both the speculative and practical order already present in the soul. Now, the primary principle in the practical order is "do good and avoid evil." Is Aquinas saying that this principle is already present at birth? This is a problem of interpretation and moral philosophy that I will discuss later. How is it that both the habit of *synderesis* and the principle known by *synderesis* are already present in the soul at birth? If the principle is already present, why is a habit necessary to know it?

As we have seen above, Aquinas considers powers and habits as the intrinsic principles of human acts. The Devil and God are the extrinsic principles.[10] Let us now consider the relation between powers, habits, and *synderesis*.

For Aquinas the speculative and practical intellect are not distinct powers of the soul. Rather, the speculative intellect directs what is apprehended to consideration of truth, while the practical intellect directs what is apprehended to operation. The speculative intellect by extension becomes the practical intellect. It would seem, then, that if there is a natural habit by which the speculative intellect immedi-ately recognizes the first principles of truth, such as the principle of noncontradiction, there needs to be a natural habit, namely, *synderesis*, by which the practical intellect immediately recognizes first principles

---

[9]*ST.*, I-II, 50, 3 & ad 3; 63, 1. Partly my translation.
[10]*ST.*, I-II, 49 & 90 preface.

of operation, such as that the good ought to be done and evil avoided. I would say that this is confirmed by experience because once a child grasps the concept of good and evil, he or she immediately, without discursive thought, knows that the good ought to be done and evil avoided.[11] Thus, *synderesis* is not an acquired or infused habit but rather is innate or natural.

Moreover, Aquinas says

> The act of *synderesis* is not an act of a power simply but a preparatory thing to the act of a power just as natural things [e.g., natural talents] are preparatory things to the freely given and acquired virtues.[12]

Synderesis and Conscience

Conscience is the application of the knowledge of *synderesis* as well as of superior and inferior reason to a particular act to consider whether it should be done or avoided. Aquinas supplies the following illustration: suppose I am considering whether or not to commit an act of fornication. How does conscience operate in this situation? Here is the syllogism Aquinas uses to sum it up:

> Nothing prohibited by God is to be done (the judgment of *synderesis*). Fornication with this person is against the law of God (the judgment of superior reason). Fornication is to be avoided (the application of conscience).[13]

Obviously, neither Aquinas nor I would argue that each time a person makes a moral choice the process is this simple. Many other factors can enter into a moral choice, such as compulsive and sinful habits. Nonetheless, if one guards against over-simplification, the above mentioned can be useful as an analytical tool.

Errors occur not in the judgment of *synderesis* but in the superior reason or in the application of conscience. Conscience, "which applies the universal judgment of *synderesis* to particular works" can err,

---

[11]*ST.*, I, 79, 11; *ibid.*, s. c. Helen Keller, at age 8, is a test case. Once she had the first concept, i.e., that the water her teacher, Miss Sullivan, pumped over her hand was representd by the letters, W-A-T-E-R, which the teacher traced on the other hand, she then realized, when Miss Sullivan traced D-O-L-L in her hand, that it was wrong for her earlier to have thrown down the doll in a fit of anger. She reports that she experienced remorse for the first time in her life and wept bitterly. Cf. *The Catholic World Report*, June 1992, p. 1.

[12]3 *Sent.* d. 33, q. 2, a. 4; cf. *De Veritate* 16, 1, 14; 16, 2, 5.

[13]*De Veritate*, 17, 2. Cf. also 2 *Sent.* d. 39. q. 3 a. 2 & *Quodl.* 3, 12, 1. *De Veritate*, 17, 2.

but not *synderesis* itself. However, in immediate conclusions from
the judgment of *synderesis* conscience never errs. Moreover, it is
synderesis which exposes a false conscience.

In commenting on *John* 16:2, Aquinas gives an example of how
the false judgment can come from superior reason. In this case the
syllogism is as follows:

> God is to be obeyed (the universal judgment of *synderesis*). The killing
> of Apostles is pleasing to God (the false judgment of the superior reason).
> Therefore, God commands the killing of Apostles (the application of
> conscience).[14]

This reasoning describes the thinking of St. Paul before his experience
on the road to Damascus. Beforehand, his mind operated not from
a false application of conscience but from a false judgment of the
superior reason.

Synderesis and Passion

Although it is true, absolutely speaking, that *synderesis* as a habitual
light can never be extinguished, nevertheless as an act it can be. Because of bad habits it is possible for a person to extinguish *synderesis*
by sinful choices. In speaking of this Aquinas distinguishes two ways
of referring to *synderesis*:

> that *synderesis* can be extinguished can be understood in two ways. In
> one way insofar as it is a habitual light. In this way it is impossible that
> *synderesis* be extinguished. . . . In another way insofar as it is an act and
> this in two ways. In one way when it is said that the act of *synderesis*
> is extinguished inasmuch as the act of *synderesis* is totally taken away.
> And thus it occurs that the act of *synderesis* is extinguished in not having
> the use of free choice nor any use of reason. . . . In another way when the
> act of *synderesis* is drawn to the contrary. In this way it is impossible for
> *synderesis* to be extinguished in a universal judgment. But in a particular
> thing to be done it is extinguished whenever one sins in choosing. . . . But
> here *synderesis* is not extinguished absolutely but only in a certain way
> [*secundum quid*]. Wherefore absolutely speaking we must concede that
> *synderesis* is never extinguished.[15]

---

[14]*De Veritate*, 16, 2 ad 1; 17, 2; 16, 3, 6; 16, 2 ad 2.

[15]*De Veritate*, 16, 3. A recent example of how *synderesis* as an habitual light can be
extinguished by passions, in this case by contrary customs, is the case of women in Siberia

Another instance of the same phenomenon occurs in the case of heretics. Since heresy is a sin and heretics seem not to have remorse concerning their infidelity, it may appear that *synderesis* is extinguished in their moral character. In answering this question Aquinas again shows that the error lies in the application to the particular act rather than in the universal judgment of *synderesis*. For he remarks that

> with regard to heretics, on account of the error which is in their superior reason from which it happens that the judgment of reason is not applied to this particular case, their conscience does not murmur against infidelity. For the judgment of *synderesis* remains in them with regard to the universal case since they judge that it is evil not to believe those things which God has revealed. But they err in this, i.e., in superior reason because they do not believe that this thing is revealed by God.[16]

Synderesis and Fomes

In speaking of whether *synderesis* is absent from the souls in Hell, Aquinas says that the connaturality of *synderesis* even defines the life of the damned. This becomes evident when he contrasts *synderesis* with *fomes*, defined as the inclination within us to evil.

> [E]vil is outside of nature and so nothing prohibits the inclination to evil [i.e., *fomes*] from being removed from the blessed. But good and the inclination to good follows upon nature itself. Wherefore, since nature remains [in them] the inclination to good cannot be taken away even in the damned.

While *fomes*, the inclination to evil, can be removed after death, the inclination to good is so much a part of our nature that it remains after death, even in those who pursued evil as a way of life and died unrepentant. But if that is the case—namely, that *synderesis* is present even in demons—could one not argue that some of their acts are good? The answer is that while *synderesis* is not extinct in them it is thwarted by a perverse will. St. Thomas puts it this way:

> In *synderesis* . . . there are the universal principles of the natural law. Wherefore it is necessary that it murmur against everything in them [the

---

who have had up to 20 abortions and were not aware that it was wrong until told so. But when told so they became alarmed. Cf. *The Witness*, July 19, 1992, p. 10.

[16]*De Veritate*, 16, 3 obj. 2; 16, 3 ad 2. My translation.

demons] which occurs contrary to the natural law. But, for all that, this murmur is the act of nature. For a perverse will in the demons resists insofar as they close their perceiving powers from the consideration of good.[17]

Synderesis and Its Relation to Natural Law

I have already briefly considered the relationship between the speculative and practical intellect. In order to consider the connection of *synderesis* to the natural law, I think it will be helpful to consider more fully the relationship between knowledge in the speculative and the practical intellect.

1. Discovering Truth in the Speculative Order

According to Aquinas one discovers truth in the speculative order in the following manner: there are certain propositions which the human mind immediately recognizes as true once the terms of the proposition are known. Thus, for example, once one understands the meaning of "whole" and "part," one also recognizes immediately the truth of the proposition: "the whole is greater than its part." It is important to note here that this first principle and other such first principles are not impressed upon the mind. Rather, it is the case that there is present in the human mind or soul a natural habit, which Aquinas calls *intellectus*, by which one immediately recognizes the truth of the first principles. Thus, what is innate in the human mind is not truth but a habit, i.e., a capacity or disposition to recognize the truth. That which is the case with regard to first principles in the speculative order is also the case with regard to truths which are not first principles; that is to say, one arrives at certitude concerning their truth or falsity because of the presence in the speculative intellect of the intellectual virtues or habits. The habit of *scientia*, an acquired and not a natural habit, as is the case with *intellectus*, enables one to correctly recognize truths which are deduced from the first principles. The same is the case with the acquired intellectual virtue of *sapientia*, the presence of which, according to Aquinas, is necessary for achieving certitude in metaphysics. It should be noted that these intellectual virtues are distinct from the same intellectual virtues which are gifts of the Holy

---

[17]*De Veritate*, 16, 3 ad 5. 2 *Sent.* 2, 1, 2, obj. 3, 2 *Sent.* 2, 1, 2 ad 3. My translation.

Spirit because knowing with certitude becomes connatural for the one who has these gifts.[18] Thus, that one will make a correct judgment in the speculative order depends upon the presence of the intellectual virtues. Everyone correctly judges the truth of first principles because everyone—i.e., each person who understands the terms of the proposition of a given first principle—has present in his mind from birth the habit of *intellectus*. But not everyone equally recognizes the truths deduced from first principles or the truths of metaphysics because not all persons have acquired the habits of *scientia* and *sapientia*, the habits of mind necessary for these two disciplines. Thus, for example, what might be clearly evident to a mathematician will be obscurely seen, if seen at all, by a non-mathematician. The latter simply lacks the proper habit of mind, *scientia*. Aquinas indicates how these three virtues of the speculative intellect are related and how they function:

> Now, truth can be considered in a twofold manner: in one way as known in itself; in another way as known through another. On the one hand, what is known in itself is a principle and is understood immediately by the intellect. And so the habit perfecting the intellect for the consideration of such truth is called *intellectus* which is the habit of principles. On the other hand, what is known through another is not immediately understood by the intellect, but rather is known through reason's inquiry and is as a term.[19]

But in order to understand the role of *sapientia*, one must realize, further, that the term of reason's inquiry can be either the ultimate term in any given genus or the ultimate term in the whole of human knowledge. And it is the latter which is the domain of *sapientia*. For it considers the highest causes, that is to say, the first causes of all things. This is why *sapientia* "judges and orders all things because perfect and universal judgment cannot be had except through resolution to first causes."[20] In my opinion, the role played by *caritas* in the practical intellect is similar to the role played by *sapientia* in the speculative

---

[18]Aquinas (*ST.*, I-II, 57, 1) says that the habits of the speculative intellect are virtues. They are three: *sapientia*, *scientia*, and *intellectus*. Rectitude of judgment "propter connaturalitatem quandam ad ea de quibus iam est iudicandum" is described at *ST.*, II-II, 45, 2.

[19]*ST.*, I-II, 57, 2.

[20]*ST.*, I-II, 57, 2.

order, a very important point which I hope to make apparent by the
end of this article.

2. *Discovering Truth in Ethical Matters*

What is the case in the speculative order is also the case in the
moral order, the order of the practical reason. Just as intellectual
virtues of the speculative intellect are present in the human mind
either naturally or by way of acquisition or infusion, and just as they
make it possible for the mind to judge with certitude in the order
of speculative knowledge, so also in the practical intellect there are
natural, acquired, and infused virtues which make it possible for the
mind to judge with certitude in the moral order, the domain of ethics.
In practical reason there is a natural habit, *synderesis*, by which the
mind knows first principles, and an acquired habit, *prudentia*, by which
the mind more effectively makes decisions in practical matters. Thus,
prudence in the practical intellect corresponds to the role of *scientia*
in the speculative intellect. But without the perfection of *caritas*, there
is no true virtue. For example, if one is prudent in being avaricious,
this is not true virtue.[21] At this point someone may object: are there
not cases of those who do some good acts without love? May they
not yet feed the hungry or clothe the naked? The answer, as Aquinas
says, is that

> The act of one lacking charity [*caritas*] may be of two kinds. One is
> in accordance with his lack of charity, as when he does something that
> is referred to that whereby he lacks charity. Such an act is always evil.
> Thus, Augustine says that the actions which an unbeliever performs as an
> unbeliever are always sinful even when he clothes the naked or does any
> like thing and directs it to his unbelief as end. There is, however, another
> act of one lacking charity, not in accordance with his lack of charity, but
> in accordance with his possession of some other gift of God, whether faith
> or hope or even his natural good [*bonum naturae*] which is not completely
> taken away by sin . . . In this way it is possible for an act without charity
> to be generically good, but not perfectly good because it lacks its due
> order to the last end.[22]

---

[21]The relation between acquired and infused moral virtues is discussed among other places
at *ST.*, I-II, 65, 2. Cf. *ST.*, II-II, 47, 6; *ST.*, II-II, 23, 7. Cf. Marianne Childress, "The Prudential
Judgment," *Proceedings of the American Catholic Philosophical Association*, 22 (1947), p. 142.

[22]*ST.*, II-II, 23, 7, obj. 1 and ad 1.

Furthermore, even if we accept that *caritas* is not possible without faith, is it still not the case that even among unbelievers there can be true chastity and true justice so long as they curb their sensual desires and judge rightly? In short, it seems that in these cases true virtue is possible without *caritas*. Aquinas answers that whether true virtue is present depends on the end for which one acts.

> Since the end is in practical matters what the principle is in speculative matters, just as there can be no strictly true science [*scientia*] if a right estimate of the first indemonstrable principle be lacking, so there can be no strictly true justice or chastity without that due ordering to the end which is effected by charity, however rightly a man may be affected about other matters.[23]

It seems, then, that one cannot act with perfect virtue unless one performs the action for the sake of the ultimate end, that is to say, for the love of God. And this is not possible without the virtue of *caritas*.

This is not to say that the parallel between the speculative and practical reason is exact. It would be foolish, for instance, to expect the same degree of certitude in an argument about the morality of nuclear war as in an argument about the certitude of a particular conclusion in geometry. This is perhaps where some ethicians have gone astray: in their desire that the same kind of certitude be possible in both the moral and the speculative order. And when they find that this is impossible, they conclude that all ethical claims are either tautologies or mere expressions of feeling.[24] Aquinas's ethical theory provides an antidote to such a sceptical conclusion. Although absolute certitude cannot be achieved in every domain of the moral order, this does not imply the triumph of scepticism. The moral philosopher can still

---

[23]*ST.*, II-II, 23, 7, obj. 2 and ad 2.

[24]Aquinas follows Aristotle's *Nicomachean Ethics*, Bk. I, ch. 3 (1094 b 13–28) in his view on degrees of certitude. Cf. *In decem libros Ethicorum Aristotelis ad Nicomachum expositio*, ed. tertio, cura et studio Raymundi Spiazzi (Marietti, 1964), lec. 3, n. 36, p. 10. For morality as an expression of feelings, see A. J. Ayer in *Language, Truth, and Logic* (New York: Dover Publications, Inc., 1946), pp. 107–110. A brief review of the attempt in Western philosophy to apply logic and the dialectical process in order to solve ethical problems is presented by Howard P. Kainz, "The Use of Dialectic and Dialogue in Ethics: A Reflection on Methodology," *The New Scholasticism*, Vol. 56, n. 2 (1982), pp. 250–257. For examples of such attempts, see Michael V. Murray, S.J., *Problems in Ethics* (New York: Henry Holt and Company, Inc., 1960), pp. 238–239, and Austin Fagothey, S.J., *Right and Reason: Ethics in Theory and Practice* (St. Louis: The C. V. Mosby Company, 1976), p. 119.

appeal to the starting point of the practical reason and afterward to arguments that preclude arbitrariness, arguments that are known either by the ethician or by the virtuous person, as we shall see. And that starting point makes for solid ground because, just as there is a natural habit (*intellectus*) of the speculative intellect, which enables one to judge with certitude about first principles in the speculative order, likewise there is a natural habit of the practical intellect (*synderesis*) which enables one to judge with certitude of the first principle in the practical order, i.e., to judge with certitude about the primary precept of the natural law.[25] However, it is important to note that just as is the case with *intellectus*, so too with *synderesis*; it is not possible to attain this certain judgment until the human intellect has first understood the terms of the first principles. Thus, just as a child who is unable to comprehend the concept of being is unable to recognize a first principle in the speculative order (e.g., "it is not the same thing to affirm and to deny"), so also a child who is unable to grasp the concept of good and evil is unable to recognize the truth of the first principle in the moral order: that the good is what all desire. Obviously, then, there is no question of an innate knowledge of morality. Nor is it the case that the primary principles of the moral order are implanted in the mind. Rather, it is the case, according to Aquinas, that what is present in the very makeup of the human mind from birth is the presence of a habit, *synderesis*, by which one judges with certitude about the primary precept in the moral order. However, one is not *capable* of that judgment from infancy. The capacity or disposition is actualized only when the infant reaches the age at which she can distinguish good from evil.

3. Nature of Natural Law

It is instructive to observe Aquinas's method in showing how and in what order one recognizes the primary precepts of the natural law. He maintains that just as the concept of being is what first comes under the apprehension of the speculative intellect, the concept of the good is what first comes under the apprehension of the practical reason. "And so," says Aquinas, "the first principle in the practical reason is what is founded on the concept of good, namely, *the good is what all*

---

[25]*ST.*, I-II, 91, 3; 94, 2.

desire." Then, he proceeds to indicate that the primary precept of the law is, therefore, that the good is to be done and pursued and evil avoided. And he adds that

> all the other precepts of the natural law are founded upon this; so that all those things to be done or avoided pertain to the precepts of the natural law which practical reason naturally apprehends to be human goods.[26]

4. The First Precept of the Natural Law

It is important to concentrate for a moment on what Aquinas considers to be the first principle in the practical reason: *the good is what all desire.* This principle is his starting point as he engages the first question of the *Prima secundae.* There, he quotes Augustine to the effect that happiness is what all desire. It seems to me that this is a point worth pondering. Is it not true that all human acts are performed because of the desire of human beings for happiness? Certainly, what will make them happy is what is good. Someone may object that one who commits suicide does not desire happiness. But is it not precisely to escape one's present unbearable sadness or depression that one is driven to suicide? That is to say, does not the potential victim of suicide so act because of a desire for happiness? The problem occurs, then, not in affirming with certitude that happiness (the good) is what all desire but in determining in what that happiness (or good) consists. There is much disagreement among human beings about this point. For, as Aquinas himself notes, some think happiness consists in riches, some think it consists in pleasure, and others think it consists in something else. The point, however, is that although all may not agree as to what the good is, nevertheless, all people agree that the good is what all desire. When Aquinas formulates his ethical theory, he utilizes this fact as his starting point. When he discusses the nature of law and the natural law in particular, it serves also as the starting point. And so the first precept of law is that *good is to be done and pursued and evil avoided.* All the other precepts of the natural law are founded upon this first precept.[27]

---

[26] *ST.*, I-II, 94, 2.

[27] *ST.*, I-II, 1, 7 s.c. Cf. *ST.*, I-II, 1, 7. Someone may argue that a sadist does not desire the good. Still, the sadist desires what she or he perceives to be the good. Cf. Aquinas's statement (*ST.*, I-II, 8, 1) that it is only the good which attracts the will. Cf. *ST.*, I-II, 94, 2.

5. *Truths Self-evident* In Se *and* Quoad Nos

It has been customary among Thomists to say that the first precept as well as all other precepts of the natural law are self-evident to all. Thus, it is self-evident to everyone: a) that one ought to preserve one's own life; b) that there ought to be the conjugal union of male and female and the education of offspring; and c) that one ought to know the truth about God and live in society. St. Thomas himself says the common principles are known to all. Though known to all, reason can be impeded from applying the general principles to this particular situation or action. What Thomas says is that these precepts are self-evident in the same way as the first principles of the speculative intellect.[28] So it appears that the first precept and the others mentioned above are self-evident to us by the habit of *synderesis*. As to the secondary principles, they are not self-evident in the same way as the general principles. Why not? An important distinction made by Aquinas will, I think, clarify this matter. He argues that something can be self-evident in itself (*in se*) but not to us (*quoad nos*); or something can be self-evident both in itself and to us, such as the first principles in the speculative order, once their terms are understood. But there are other things which, though self-evident in themselves, are not self-evident to everyone. Aquinas gives the following example: "Man is a rational animal." To anyone who understands the meaning of the terms, "man," "rational," and "animal," this proposition is self-evident. But it is not self-evident to one who does not understand these terms.[29] Likewise, I would argue that it is consistent with Aquinas's thought to say that while the first, i.e., "the common", precepts are self-evident in themselves and to us (once the concept of the good is understood) because of the presence of the habit of *synderesis* in the human mind, the secondary precepts of the natural law, which are derived from the common precepts, are not self-evident to everyone, even though self-evident in themselves.[30] To take any other position makes

---

[28]These are the precepts of the natural law. Cf. *ST.*, I-II, 94, 2. Cf. Michael Cronin, *The Science of Ethics*, vol. 1, 4th ed. (Dublin: M. H. Gill and Son Ltd., 1939). He argues (pp. 510–512) that the primary precepts are self-evident. Fagothey and Murray (quoted above, n. 24) interpret the primary precepts as self-evident *quoad nos*. Cf. *ST.*, I-II, 94, 2; 4; 6.

[29]*ST.*, I-II, 94, 2. I think it is significant that Aquinas does not include here the precepts of the natural law as examples of propositions *per se* known commonly to all.

[30]Note that in both cases, that involving the primary precept and the other precepts founded upon it, they are not self-evident to us until the meaning of the terms is understood.

it very difficult to explain how there can be so much disagreement over issues that are directly based on the precepts of the natural law, such as suicide, artificial contraception, sterilization, abortion, private property, just wage, etc. If these things were self-evident *quoad nos*, there would not be so much disagreement about them among honorable people. Or to put the matter in another way, while everyone by the age of reason can recognize the term, "good," not everyone agrees upon that in which the good consists. And so they may not recognize that the secondary precepts of the natural law are the good that is to be done and pursued. In short, these precepts are self-evident in themselves (*in se*), but not self-evident to all (*quoad nos*). In today's world I wonder whether even all the general principles of the natural law are self-evident *quoad nos*. If, for example, procreation and education of children are precepts self-evident *in se* and *quoad nos*, why is there so much disagreement on these matters among honorable men and women? Perhaps it is because, although these precepts are known to all, reason may be impeded from applying the general principles to a particular action. If so, then perhaps it is preferable to argue that, indeed, only the primary precept of natural law is self-evident *in se* and *quoad nos*. For it is self-evident to all that the good is to be done and evil avoided, albeit not everyone agrees on that in which the good consists. After all, Aquinas himself argues that in a sense the natural law is one law, reducible to the primary precept, for all other principles flow from it.[31] In this way there is at least a starting point upon which all can agree. For if my opponent does not agree with the first principle of morality, is there any point in discussing the matter further?

6. The Role of the Virtues

Synderesis is the habit of mind by which one judges with certainty that good ought to be done and evil avoided. It is in this sense that Aquinas speaks of "the judgment of *synderesis*." By this judgment one recognizes that the common principles of the natural law are the good to be done. What perfects the human mind for matters which follow from the natural law is the presence in the human mind of the moral virtues. Whereas *synderesis* is a *natural* habit (or virtue) which

---

[31]*ST.*, I-II, 94, 6; *ST.*, I-II, 94, 2 ad 1.

perfects the human mind for a correct judgment about the primary precepts, the moral virtues can be either *acquired* or *infused*. The acquired moral virtues, e.g., prudence, fortitude, justice, and temperance, perfect the human mind for making sound judgments about a life of moral rectitude.[32] These virtues are acquired through practice and discipline. However, if the infused moral virtues are present, the judgment becomes connatural. What Aquinas means by this connatural judgment can be gathered by a brief look at the role of *caritas* (the virtue of charity or love). Just as *sapientia* is the root and guide of all the other intellectual virtues, likewise the theological virtue of *caritas* is the root and guide of all the moral virtues. As Aquinas says, "just as charity is the root and beginning of the virtues, so pride is the root and beginning of all vices."[33] This is why, when speaking of the moral order, Aquinas follows Saint Paul, 1 *Cor* 2:15, in saying that the spiritual man is the judge of all and is judged by no one. The spiritual man's judgment about what good ought to be done and what evil avoided in a specific instance has become connatural by the presence in him of the infused moral virtues and especially by the presence of *caritas*. This is not to say that one needs the infused moral virtues to be an ethician or an ethical person. Aristotle, to name an instance, lacked the infused moral virtues. He would never have said that it is good for human nature to die on a cross. But he surely possessed the natural and acquired moral virtues.[34]

Aquinas further comments on the distinction between the natural, acquired, and infused moral virtues. By the acquired moral virtues one judges according to human reason and, accordingly, directs one's good

---

[32] Aquinas treats the acquired moral virtues at *ST.*, I-II, 61, 2; 63, 2.

[33] *Super epistolas s. Pauli lectura*, cura Raphaelis Cai 3rd ed., vol. 1 (Marietti, 1953), II *Cor.* 12.7. Benoit Garceau, *Judicium: Vocabulaire, sources, doctrine de saint Thomas d'Aquin* (Montreal: Institut d'Etudes Medievales, 1968), especially pp. 226–234, has explained well the role of the moral virtues in guaranteeing a certain judgment. For a discussion of the acquired and infused moral virtues, see Odon Lottin, *Etudes de morale histoire et doctrine* (J. Duculot, editeur, Gembloux [Belgique], 1961), pp. 131–150.

[34] *ST.*, I-II, 58, 5. Also see *ST.*, II-II, 60, 1 ad 2; also *ST.*, II-II, 45, 2; also see n. 1 above. An example of a text in moral theology which takes into consideration the primacy of charity is Gerard Gilleman, S.J., *The Primacy of Charity in Moral Theology*, trans. William F. Ryan, S.J., and William F. Ryan, S.J. (Westminster, Maryland: The Newman Press, 1961). Some have suggested that Aristotle had the infused virtues. In that case I ask whether he acted for a supernatural end. Or were his good works directed to an end that did not surpass the natural power of man?

works to an end that does not surpass the natural power of man. On the other hand, by the infused moral virtues one judges according to divine reason, and because of the presence of the infused moral virtues, which cannot be present without *caritas*, the judgment becomes connatural to the one possessing the infused moral virtues.[35]

Thus, for Aquinas judgment with certitude in the moral order does not occur by proceeding deductively from a first principle which is known self-evidently. That one could take any position in the moral order and show its goodness or badness by tracing its derivation back to the primary precepts of the natural law is a position which, I fear, some Thomists have explicitly taught.[36] To speak from personal experience, my own ethics professor in college spoke of tertiary precepts of the natural law as if they were deductively derived from the primary precepts. Our inability to grasp this he explained by the fact that we were mere novices in the study of ethics; that we had not yet developed the necessary habits of mind. Of course, in one sense he was right; we indeed lacked the skill needed to reason ethically, but in another he was wrong; acquired moral virtues alone are not sufficient for reasoning ethically in all spheres of human conduct nor are they sufficient for obtaining apodeictic certitude about ethical matters.

7. Synderesis and the Precepts of the Natural Law

It is easy to make the mistake of thinking that *synderesis* contains the precepts of the natural law. As I mentioned above this is an issue that needs further discussion. Aquinas himself says in his *Commentary on the Sentences* that "In *synderesis* the universal precepts of the natural law are contained."[37] But how *synderesis* incorporates these precepts is explained and qualified later when Aquinas states that, although the natural law is not properly speaking a habit, still, in one way the natural law can be called a habit, insofar as the precepts of the natural law are held by a habit. In the same way the first principles in the speculative order are not identified with the habit of these principles, although they are the principles of which there is a

---

[35]*ST.*, I-II, 65, 2. Cf. *ST.*, I-II, 63, 1; 65, 2; 68, 1.

[36]See Thomas V. Upton, "Aristotle's Moral Epistemology: The Possibility of Ethical Demonstration," *The New Scholasticism*, vol. 46, n. 2 (1982), pp. 183. Cf. n. 24.

[37]II *Sent.* 2, 1, 2 ad 3: "In synderesi autem sunt universalia principia juris naturalis."

habit.[38] In short, the precepts are said to be in *synderesis* not properly but as held by the habit of *synderesis*.

8. Small Errors in the Beginning

Aquinas has remarked with regard to another topic that a small error in the beginning leads to a great error in the end.[39] This is why it is important not to make a mistake about his position regarding *synderesis*. Ethicians or natural law philosophers who misunderstand the relation of *synderesis* to the natural law and the moral virtues will be led to great errors in their moral philosophy.

Maritain and Synderesis

Maritain follows Thomas in saying that reason is the measure of human actions and that in order to measure human conduct reason itself must be measured by the natural law.[40] Moreover, natural law is natural both ontologically and gnoseologically. When Maritain says that natural law is natural ontologically his meaning is as follows: everything in nature is directed toward an end; some things achieve it as directed by nature (instinct); others (for example, human persons) achieve it with the intervention of free choice. But the proper end is present for both whether known by the agent or not. It is in this sense that the natural law is natural ontologically. That the natural law is natural gnoseologically refers to the natural law insofar as it is discovered and known by man. And man has a natural inclination to discover it. But the natural law is naturally known by man not conceptually or by way of reasoning. Rather, it is known connaturally. Maritain believes that this crucial point has been sorely neglected in moral philosophy.[41]

---

[38]*ST.*, I-II, 94, 1.

[39]*De ente et essentia*, c. 1: "Quia parvus error in principio magnus est in fine secundum Philosophum in primo Caeli et Mundii. . . ." Cf. Aristotle's *On the Heavens*, I, 5 (271 b 8–13).

[40]*Quelque remarques sur la loi naturelle*. In *Oeuvres Complètes*. Editions Saint-Paul, Paris, Vol. 9, 1990, p. 954.

[41]*Ibid.*, p. 956. Cf. *Man and the State* (Chicago: Chicago University Press, 1971), pp. 84–94, where Maritain distinguishes between the first element of the natural law (which is ontological) and the second (which is gnoseological). For Aquinas natural law *in se* is known connaturally only by those with the infused virtues.

In *Man and the State* he says that the natural law is "within the being of things as their very essence is, and . . . precedes all formulation, and is even known to human reason not in terms of conceptual and rational knowledge. . . ."[42]

Maritain is here criticizing the eighteenth-century view which wished to make the natural law a geometrical system. Already in the seventeenth-century "Pascal himself believed that justice among men should of itself have the same universal application as Euclid's propositions."[43]

Maritain comes close to the notion of *synderesis* in speaking of "pre-conscience", i.e., natural inclinations rooted in reason. These inclinations are not the same as animal instincts insofar as a thing is an animal; instead they are distinctly human inclinations, directed by nature toward an end with the intervention of free choice. These inclinations are grounded in the nonconceptual life of the intellect and become crystallized by reason as it reflects on the nature of human inclinations.[44]

For Maritain these inclinations presuppose a self-evident first principle. The other determinations of the natural law are discovered in the progress of the history of humankind.[45] This history makes gnoseological what is otherwise ontological, a distinction which is based on Aquinas's separation of the precepts as known *in se* and *quoad nos*.

Maritain's view that there is connatural knowledge of the natural law seems to be equivalent to Aquinas's position that natural law is known by *synderesis* and the infused virtues. However, at least in these texts, Maritain makes no reference to the need for the infused virtue of charity which, in my opinion, is the only sure guide in Aquinas's system for arriving at other principles related to the natural law. For Maritain these are discovered in the progression of human history.

The reason that Maritain does not consider the role of infused virtues, at least in the texts I have examined, is perhaps the same reason that keeps other moral philosophers from considering them. If one considers ethics as a strictly philosophical discipline, then one

---

[42]*Ibid.*, p. 91.
[43]*Ibid.*, p. 82.
[44]*Ibid.*, pp. 84–94.
[45]*Ibid.*, p. 90; also pp. 93–94.

should appeal to natural reason alone. Thus, one cannot consider the role of the infused virtues since that is the domain of theology. If one accepts this very rigid division, then philosophers like Maritain and others are justified in their exclusion of the role of infused virtues.[46] In that case, Maritain has certainly shown us how far one can proceed in developing an ethics without appeal to revelation. At least this is the case with the texts which I have examined.

Conclusion

My purpose in this paper has been to draw attention to a few points in Aquinas's moral theory, the neglect or misunderstanding of which, in my judgment, has lead to attacks on Aquinas' doctrine. Contrariwise, a correct understanding of these points not only makes Aquinas' doctrine more coherent but also furnishes an antidote for some current scepticism about ethics.

I close by calling to mind an important remark made by a philosopher who perhaps would be placed in a league with Aquinas and Maritain. Charles Pierce has remarked that no one philosopher will arrive at the whole truth. For that achievement the community of philosophers is required.[47] Taking to heart Pierce's remark, I do not claim to have said all there is to say about *synderesis*. Rather, I rely on the community of philosophers to further elucidate this issue in moral philosophy.

---

[46]See Maritain's Moral Philosophy: An Historical and Critical Survey of the Great Systems (London, 1964), p. x. Also consult his *Essay on Christian Philosophy* (New York: Philosophical Library, Inc., 1955), pp. 38–43; pp. 61–100; likewise review his *Science and Wisdom* (New York: Charles Scribner's Sons, 1940), pp. 107–127.

[47]Cf. Charles Peirce, "How to Make Our Ideas Real," in *Values in a Universe of Chance*, ed. P. Weiner (Stanford, California: Stanford University Press, 1958), p. 134.

A Fresh Look at the Principle of the Double Effect

W. L. Lacroix

While the Principle of the Double Effect has been receiving some attention in journals in recent years, ethicians still seem to be approaching it in ways similar to those earlier presentations that have made it unattractive and relatively useless: that is to say, as if it were some wondrous *a priori* formula theorized by ethicians with no basis in everyday human experience.[1] I would suggest that both attacks on and defenses of the Principle have concentrated on "how to apply it," rather than on "how the Principle originated" and on "how it is directive in application." Perhaps this concentration simply on application is not only historically unfortunate but also methodologically incorrect.

If our everyday experience were in a world in which conflicts of values or rights never arose, where existential (i.e., non-moral) evils were always avoidable by acting on reasonable judgments, then one's

---

[1]The following works represent recent efforts to discuss the Principle of Double Effect: Joseph T. Mangan, "An Historical Analysis of the Principle of the Double Effect," *Theological Studies* 10 (1949), pp. 41–61; Peter Knauer, "The Hermeneutic Function of the Principle of the Double Effect," *Natural Law Forum* 12 (1967), pp. 132–162; Philippa Foot, "The Problem of Abortion and the Doctrine of the Double Effect," reprinted in her book, *Virtues and Vices* (Oxford: Basil Blackwell, 1978), pp. 19–32; Joseph M. Boyle, Jr., "Toward Understanding the Principle of Double Effect," *Ethics* 90 (1980), pp. 527–538; Jonathan Bennett, *Morality and Consequences*, The Tanner Lectures on Human Values, III (Salt Lake City, Utah: University of Utah Press, 1981); G. E. M. Anscombe, "Action, Intention, and "Double Effect," *Proceedings of The American Catholic Philosophical Association* 56 (1982), pp. 12–25.

basic values, the ideals of virtues, and guides from specified and validated rights would give adequate direction for ethical decisions. However, humans quite often find themselves in situations that are not so simple. Sometimes the very actions done to support one value or right also have as their outcome the negation of another value or right. Sometimes no matter what alternative I choose, I am going to affect one human value positively and one negatively. Therefore, I am going to be *responsible for* (a broader expression, by the way, than "guilty of") the occurrence of an existential evil.

This ethical problem is radical: is it ever reasonable to cause or permit such a negation? It is here that the ethician must pay close attention to the explanations of ordinary people.

Some ethicians insist that certain values or rights are *a priori* sovereign. This is to say that after reflection the ethician identifies certain values as decisive *a priori* for any subsequent experience. Examples of this approach occur in diverse formulations of the Natural Law tradition and are sometimes evident in the handling of a) the natural biological processes of nutrition and generation; b) innocent human life; and c) the compensation for past injustices. Often in this tradition it is argued that the negation of such values can never be morally justified. Acts or policies that do so as means to some otherwise valid goal are always immoral.[2]

Of course, the obvious objection against this tradition is that it appears to neglect the process of induction moving from actual human decisions to the establishment of moral principle. The non-inductive approach would have a content-specific principle become universally decisive at some historical moment and would preclude taking into account later judgments by people trying to do the right thing in situations which involve the same value. It thereby would omit any historically emerging new subset of experiences which could challenge the *a priori* principles of a purely deductive morality. For example, consider the difficulty some natural lawyers have faced grappling with whether masturbation is wrong even if practiced for a medical reason, such as the need to acquire a semen sample so as to test it for sterility. Ignoring the peculiarities of such situations is clearly

---

[2]This position denies that there can be situational relativity in certain content-specific moral matters, albeit many values and rights are not of this sovereign quality and so disputes concerning these latter would be reasonable.

arbitrary and objectionable and betrays a failure to appreciate how ethical generalizations have been traditionally established in the first place: namely, out of reflection on the actual decisions of people in lived circumstances.[3]

In their effort to come to terms with decisions that grapple with concrete conflict, many past ethicians (some of an *a priori* disposition, others of a more inductive temperament) embraced a formal principle, which goes by the classic description: "The Principle of the Double Effect" (PDE). This Principle requires careful examination and commentary as it has not only suffered much (perhaps justifiably) at the hands of its detractors but has also been sometimes harmed by its advocates.

History seems to show that ethicians first uncovered the Principle by means of analyzing actual decisions of ordinary people in their effort to act well in situations involving conflict. The first use of this Principle seems to occur in Thucydides, specifically where the Athenians explain to the Boeotians why they seized a temple.[4] Aristotle later assumes the Principle in his discussion of actions mixing the voluntary and the involuntary.[5] Cicero appeals to it as he ranks differently the duties under justice in his analysis of how people can consider the existential evils of war to be justifiable. This ranking involves qualitative difference, not some utilitarian quantity.[6] Later, Athanasius, also in the context of war, affirms the PDE as he indicates that the physical action and its existentially evil results need not be morally decisive.[7] To name other instances, I will suggest later that the PDE is behind the difference between Abraham's response to Yahweh's request for the sacrifice of Isaac and Agamemnon's response to Artemis's request for the sacrifice of Iphigenia.

---

[3]See Aquinas, *Nicomachean Ethics Comm.* III, 10, 494. This is connected with the Aristotelian theme that *phronesis (prudentia)* is not scientific since it is concerned with the ultimate particular situation, "since the thing to be done is of this nature." It is not about types of particular situations because types of situations are universals (*Nicomachean Ethics.* 1142a 23–25). *Phronesis* is about the proportion of values as they appear in context (*Nicomachean Ethics.* 1106b 36–1107a 3). See Robert B. Louden, "Aristotle's Practical Particularism," in *Essays in Ancient Greek Philosophy IV: Aristotle's Ethics*, ed. John P. Anton and Anthony Preus (Albany, New York: SUNY Press, 1991, esp. pp. 164–166.

[4]Thucydides, *The History of The Peloponnesian War*, IV, 98.

[5]*Nicomachean Ethics.* III, 1110a 4–35.

[6]*De Officiis*, I, 160.

[7]Athanasius, *Epistola ad Amunem Monachum.*

It is important to stress that the PDE is not a principle that ethicians have made up. Ethicians have no special source of ethical knowledge, nor do they have a special authority to tell people how to make moral decisions. The only valid source for such a principle has been the articulations of good people as they have tried to explain why they acted as they did in the midst of ethical conflicts.[8] People who have tried to act rightly in situations involving conflict have been found to give rather consistent explanations for their conduct. Consider such statements as "I didn't want to, but I had no choice"; "I'm sorry about that but this was more important"; and "I didn't want to do more damage than I absolutely had to." Such remarks are frequently heard and, even more importantly, are considered proper. Over time a consensus has arisen to mandate these explanatory appeals as forms of ethical justification. Upon analyzing these appeals, ethicians discovered distinguishable elements in these explanatory articulations. The point of the analyses was to identify the intelligible structure within the ordinary good person's conflict resolution. So far, so good.

Unfortunately, proponents through the years ossified these "elements" into propositional phrases which they and others mistook as self-explanatory and absolute ethical guides. The following phrases typify how the elements have been put into propositional form:

1) the act must not be in itself evil;

2) the evil outcome must not be the means to the good outcome;

3) the evil outcome must be only permitted, not intended for itself; and

4) there must be proportionality, both in the sense of what intentionally is done for the sake of the intended outcome, and in the sense of the outcome intended in relation to the evil permitted.

When later medieval proponents tried to apply the PDE to new conflicts, they simply forgot the source of the Principle. They not only separated the phrases from the PDE as used in everyday moral decisions and from the articulated explanations (a perfectly acceptable

---

[8]Aquinas commented that in ethics it is a "serious defect" to spend time on "reason" and the "parts of the soul" rather than on the human actions themselves (*Nicomachean Ethics Comm.* I, 11, 136).

method, by the way, for formulating a principle in ethical analysis),[9] they also used the phrases as *a priori* boundaries for the application of the principle without seeing whether good people in these new conflicts agreed. (The recurrent "manual" case citing the removal of the bleeding uterus of the pregnant woman instead of direct abortion is a relevant example.)

When those who were not proponents of the PDE looked at the application of these phrases in new conflicts, they judged that the PDE forced one to take positions that were inadequate. Put in terms used above, the historical use by proponents of the PDE turned what was originally a formal principle gained by analysis into one that carried *a priori* sovereign content that set moral limits to actions, limits that good people would think irrational in real situations. A good test is whether in the application of the principle (where such *a priori* moral limits are absent), there might yet prevail a consensus of good people differing from what the principle interpreted as an *a priori* standard would imply.

With this history one might dismiss the PDE as a lost cause. I would be tempted to agree except that I continue to encounter obvious uses of the Principle in such areas as the "scrutiny" processes of Supreme Court decisions, in Due Process cases, and in debates on societal ethics. Consequently, I have asked whether the PDE might not be rescued from its epigones and made useful once again.

The PDE operates as a rational and thus as a non-relative principle. But it is a formal or procedural principle only. Recall that it emerged out of an analysis of the articulations of people who made hard, but what they thought were ethically defensible, decisions in conflicts as diverse as killing in war, breaking a promise, telling an untruth, and implementing affirmative action programs.

To effect this rescue, let us take the above four propositional phrases that attempt to express the PDE and see how such phrases have meaning drawn out of the actual moral experience of people.

1) The act must not be in itself evil. Because the use of the PDE only occurs when it is inevitable that a value will be negated (such a negation being equivalent to an existential evil), it is important to

---

[9]I thank my colleague, Rosemary Flanigan, CSJ, for advising me to add this clarification.

understand how the term "evil" is used in this requisite part. The action done, which for moral adequacy appeals to the PDE, acknowledges by that very appeal that an evil outcome is germane. This appeal to a principle to resolve an ethical conflict takes into account two important facts. First, there cannot be a question of a right or a value being lost prior to the action at hand. For example, if an "aggressor against my life or my property" did lose some basic right by such aggression, the principle would not apply. There would be no need for a principle to resolve a non-existent conflict.[10] Obviously, the first requisite for the PDE does not say that the action done cannot have any humanly evil outcome. By using the PDE an individual acknowledges that a humanly evil outcome will result no matter what one does. The question, of course, is whether such an outcome is morally tolerable.

Secondly, there cannot be reference here to "morally evil acts," i.e., acts that are asserted to be "intrinsically evil abstracted from any context." The whole point of the appeal to the PDE in a conflict is to use it to judge the morality of the possible action. One would be helpless to judge the action in a conflict situation *by means of* the PDE, if one of the elements requisite for use of the PDE *is the moral judgment itself* on the action. So the first requisite cannot require the moral judgment prior to the PDE's functioning in an actual situation. This would reduce the PDE to a simple tautology: "One cannot morally do a morally evil act." The whole point of the PDE, however, is to respond to the following question: "How can one morally do an action that effects an existential evil?" By using the PDE an individual affirms that the resultant negation of rights or values is not to be trivialized or ignored, but also that no right or value of itself is *a priori* decisive for the PDE resolution. To hold that a value or a right is *a priori* decisive (which would imply, of course, that any action negating it would be intrinsically wrong regardless of the situation) is, in fact, to decide a case of moral conflict by using some principle other than the PDE.

Nevertheless, some proponents envision the first requisite as a separate phase from the other parts of the PDE, a phase wherein one

---

[10]Minimally, those who advance this concept would have to consider the right to life to be a merit right only. Actually, the position of Locke and others, when they make a case for defending life and property against aggression, may be interpreted to appeal to a hierarchy of values or principles, which will be discussed later.

distinguishes humanly evil acts or outcomes in general from specifically identified acts or outcomes unexceptionally settled as morally evil prior to any actual conflict. Following this distinction, one tests whether the proposed resolution of the conflict would involve an *a priori* moral evil. Recently, for example, James F. Keenan has argued that the PDE "can only be not nonsense or not 'superfluous' when we have deontological, absolute prohibitions" on specific content values which cannot be intended as an end or chosen as a means.[11] Additionally, Bruno Schüller identified "the frustration of a natural faculty" or action without "required authorization" (e.g., killing in private self-defense) as specific deontologically unacceptable courses of action at issue for Catholic moralists.[12]

Obviously, this "where to apply" concentration is much too narrow to cover the many manifestations of the PDE by ordinary good people, who utter excuses like "I wouldn't have done it except that. . . ." What seems in the everyday application to be the intelligible content of this first requisite is this: one may not do the act if one foresees that the act will have only an existential evil as a result. In other words, the requisite demands that there be a "second effect" of the act, one which affirms a right or a value. To act only to bring about the first result—i.e., only the existential evil—would be irrational, and so would be to perform a morally evil act.[13]

2) The evil outcome must not be the means to the good intended. This requisite focuses on the relation of the two outcomes. It elaborates the articulated explanation of people wherein they claim that the resolution of the conflict is one in which they did not want to bring about the bad effect that they, in fact, produced; it is not as if the bad effect were unworthy of consideration except as a step on the way to an intended good. Ordinary people in those kinds of conflict-situations express their consensus in such terms as: "This (the good effect) was more important."

---

[11]James F. Keenan, "Taking Aim at the Principle of Double Effect: Reply to Khatchadourian," *International Philosophical Quarterly* 28 (June, 1988), p. 201.

[12]Bruno Schüller, "The Double Effect in Catholic Thought," in *Doing Evil to Achieve Good*, eds. R. McCormick and P. Ramsey (Chicago: Loyola University Press, 1978), p. 174.

[13]Aquinas said that "moral acts receive their species in virtue of what is intended." *ST.*, II-II, 64, 7. See also, I-II, 72, 1.

This source in experience is significant, for some proponents of the PDE often have interpreted this requisite as if it were saying "one may not do a morally evil act to achieve a good end." That such begs the question has been mentioned above.

Other advocates have interpreted the requisite to say that the evil effect, even as existentially evil, cannot be the means to the good effect. That this also cannot be correct seems clear from a common exemplary case: using physical force in self-defense. The agent's end is self-defense from the aggression. The act done involving physical force has two effects: a) of stopping the physical acts of the aggressor; and b) of physically injuring or killing the aggressor. I choose the act I do because I want to stop the physical acts of the aggressor. If I could talk her out of it, that would achieve the end of the act as means to my end as agent. But if I have to use physical force to stop her aggressive physical acts, then it is a feckless velleity to say the existential evil of physical injury is not a means. It is, indeed, the way that I stop the aggression and thereby achieve my end as agent.

So we must explore more carefully the relation of the evil outcome to the good outcome precisely in terms of "means" and "end." From the experience of people, the heart of the PDE is simply that, for the conflict resolution to be ethical, the agent must do that alternative action which will express the more qualitatively important right or value. The existential evil is caused/permitted in that context. What has this to do with "means" and "end"? Perhaps we could find help by asking why a negation of a value can be morally problematic. In its most severe expression the question asks: what morally is the problem with using a human being merely as a means? The consensus seems to be that using another human being as a means is morally acceptable as long as it does not debilitate, eliminate, or disdain the other's dignity. (For example, I may *pay* for "full service" at the gas station.) But to use another "merely as a means" is precisely to do something which debilitates, eliminates, or disdains the dignity of the one used. Now such a disdaining of the one who bears the burden of the conflict resolution would occur in the act if the value negated were the same as, equal to, or even higher than the value affirmed. For the act would say "such and such here is not one who has intrinsic importance."

This interpretation of the "merely as a means" principle ties in with the ordinary explanation from experience: that one acted for the more important value. The consensus explanation indicates that the correct resolution of the conflict is to act for the more important value. This does not mean that to act for the less important value is in itself unethical. The point rather is that, in a situation where conflicts come into play, to act for the less important value is to act in a way which expresses falsely that the negated value is less important.

This solution seems to require some ranking of values, a ranking somehow independent of the desires of the actor.[14] It is by this ranking that the actor can rationally settle which value to affirm and which to negate. The action is rational, if the value affirmed by the act is higher and belongs to all persons, including the persons who have another (lower) value negated by the act.[15]

The initial evidence for this hierarchy is that people are willing to sacrifice some values for the sake of others (e.g., to sacrifice personal comfort to help others; to risk life for a loved one; or to give misleading responses to keep secrets). With this evidence one can a) reflect on the hierarchy and find dependencies. One can see that "x" value loses its worth without "y" value. For example, property needs security, so one can b) see that some values include others in a descending scale: the right "to be recognized and treated as a person" is specified by the right "of all persons to a reasonable security within which to act as persons"; which is specified by the right "to security against unprovoked physical aggression"; which thus might be higher at times than the right to or the value of "physical life."

Our society has laws covering actions such as "justifiable homicide." In ordinary explanations of why it is morally correct to kill in self-defense, there are repeated references to the "aggressor" who "voluntarily attacked" the "defender" who "did not choose to be in the situation." All these references would be irrelevant if the value of physical life were the only value involved, or if the defense achieved were the only outcome of importance in the resolution of the conflict.

---

[14]Some such ranking of values is clearly implied in Aquinas's analysis of the morality of killing a malefactor for the good of the community (*ST.*, II-II, 40, a 1; 64, a 2, 3, and 7) and of doing physical harm for the sake of justice (*Quaestiones Quodlibetales*, 9, q. 7, a. 15; *ST.*, II, 188, 3 ad 1).

[15]Many presuppositions would be necessary for such a solution. Key elements of a solution are a) that there is, in fact, a hierarchy of values (acknowledging that not all values are of equal significance for persons); b) that the lower value must at times give way to the higher; c) that the negation of the lower value does not necessarily entail a limit on universal respect shown to all persons because there is still unlimited respect expressed in the higher; and d) that one should not *a priori* consider any value as absolute.

(Consider the explanation of the moral difference between killing in self-defense and killing in a duel.) Likewise, the claim by many, such as John Locke, that there is a loss of the right to life by the very commission of an unprovoked aggression must imply that such aggression violates a right more important than that of physical life. (With the acknowledgment of the hierarchy, of course, the claim that the aggressor loses the right to physical life is unnecessary.)

Interestingly, most trouble in resolving conflicts emerges because it is often impossible to settle which right or which value is more important (higher). This indicates that there is not one single hierarchy in human experience, but rather that there are many independent hierarchies. This would parallel the position that humans have many diverse goals in their pursuits, and that these goals cannot all be subordinated to one ultimate goal.[16] Of course, multiple and competing scales of values are a feature of ethics that makes the discipline untidy and troublesome. Perhaps one of the more troublesome clashes between hierarchies is that between the scale of values that pertains to an individual as an abstract person and the hierarchy of values that pertains to the individual as a member of a private or a public group.

3) The evil outcome must be only permitted, not intended for itself. Examples of explanatory phrases from experience relevant to this condition would be "I am sorry I had to do it, for I didn't want to"; "I wouldn't have done it had there been another way"; and "I had no choice." Such phrases bring out two aspects of this requisite: first, that the freely done act was judged somehow morally necessary (in self-defense, for example, the aggressor's act eliminated other ways for the defender to actualize the higher value); secondly, that the evil outcome was unwanted. Again, the act was necessary because it was judged only rational to affirm what was more important. Still, the act was unwanted because the agent continues to affirm the human value that the act negated. This point further supports the ordinary judgment that the negated right to the value is not lost.

---

[16]To use older terminology, not all "ends in themselves" are also "means" to one unifying "ultimate end," but may be constitutives in the aggregate that makes up the ultimate end. See Aquinas, *ST.*, I-II, 3, 2 ad 2; 1, 5 ad 1; 1, 6 ad 1 and 2.

Consciously one intends whatever is necessary to affirm the value supported. So one must intend the physical action that involves the existential evil (the negation of the value). But this requisite insists that one cannot ethically want the existential evil, and would avoid it if possible. Thereby, one still respects the value negated in the act. And yet the act is rational because it is necessary if one is to affirm the higher value belonging to all persons.

A satisfactory account of this third requisite perhaps can be crystallized in the following analysis: in consciousness one combines a) the intention to do whatever necessary to affirm the value supported;[17] and b) the sincere, conscientious effort to avoid complacency or indifference regarding the value negated. (Aeschylus makes Agamemnon's key character flaw—namely, his complacency in accepting the gods's decree to kill his daughter—the source of tragedy)[18] True, this negated value, as foreseen, may be psychologically intended. To deny this would be to indulge in mere "word-games."[19] When I strike at the physical aggressor in self-defense, I intend to stop her by an action which inflicts physical harm and may even risk her death. That action and its effects are precisely the means to stopping the aggression and to achieving self-defense. They are, therefore, as much intended as is the end. Harming or killing the aggressor is itself an existential evil, and yet must be, as means to the end, an intended effect of my action. The action taken involves intentionally brought about existential evil, even if I do not intentionally bring about the existential evil of her death. Thus, Aquinas's insistence that I cannot intend the death of the aggressor is morally a second question, since the first question is: "can I morally intend any existential evil?" In light of the above qualifications, the answer to this question derived from reflection on the explanations of good people is "Yes."[20]

---

[17]Aquinas, *De Veritate*, 22, 13c; I-II, 12, 1, esp. ad 4.

[18]Martha Nussbaum summarizes the flaw: "We notice the correctness of his [Agamemnon's] decision is taken by him to justify not only action but also passion: if it is right to obey the god, it is right to want to obey him [sic]." "Aeschylus and Practical Conflict," *Ethics* 95 (1985), p. 250.

[19]See Elizabeth Anscombe's medalist address at the American Catholic Philosophical Association, "Action, Intention, and 'Double Effect,'" *Proceedings of the American Catholic Philosophical Association* LVI (1982), pp. 12–25.

[20]*ST.*, II-II, 64, a. 7. Aquinas's analysis of "intention" played a major role in the manual articulation of the PDE. Problems arise if there is a move from "the act gets its moral specification

Of course, this requisite makes sense only if there is the reality of hierarchies of rights and values as taken when discussing the phrase or proposition in #2. The sign that the negation is unwanted will be the attentiveness to the fourth requisite of the PDE.

4) There must be proportionality, both in the sense of what intentionally is done for the sake of the intended outcome, and in the sense of the outcome intended in relation to the existential evil done. If one has a rational respect for persons, and if one acknowledges that these persons have rights and values that intelligibly coerce one's actions, then one will constantly take care so that encroachment upon rights and values by one's actions takes place only insofar as is necessary for the affirmation of higher conflicting rights and values. Expressions of this from common experience are that "I only did as much as I had to"; or that "more wasn't necessary"; or that "if there were a better way, I would have done that."

Three items are operative in such a proportionality judgment: a) how important is the value to be promoted? b) how important is the value to be negated? and c) how necessary are the means taken to promote the higher value? (Is there a feasible alternative? Is that alternative one that will do less existential harm?) The proportionality is always judged in the situation. It is never possible to set it *a priori*.

The evidence that proportionality is not an otiose guide comes from history. Those trying to act morally as heads of families, associations, or governments have made decisions, some of which, for a time at least, have achieved a consensus among others similarly positioned. Ordinarily, these consensus positions have been referred to by set phrases, such as "protecting the home"; "following sound business practice"; or "acting against unjustified aggression." These were shorthand for the message that, even though the actions taken were causing physical evils for some, reasonable people nevertheless considered them morally adequate ways to secure or advance important human values.

---

from what is intended" to "so if what is intended is an existential evil, intending it is a morally evil action." Good people would judge this to be true only if the intended existential evil were unnecessary for securing the higher value.

In conclusion, the PDE can be salvaged so long as the philosopher honors how ordinary reasonable people supply the starting point of ethical reflection and analysis. When this lesson is forgotten, a creeping *a priorism* corrupts moral philosophy. Aristotle and Aquinas were on guard against this sort of corruption. Their descendants, however, have too often lost sight of their example. As a result, the PDE has suffered at their disciples's hands, appearing muddled when it need not be.

"There Are No Sinners In Hell!": Moral Judgments and Love in the Philosophy of Jacques Maritain

John G. Trapani, Jr.

Introduction

Within the realm of ordinary discourse, we might understand a "sinner" to be one who commits a "sin," an action which violates God's law. Such disobedience, one might say, is rightly punishable. Since, in its ultimate expression, "Hell" is that eternal punishment which is a justified consequence of one's evil action, it is reasonable to conclude that there must be sinners in Hell. Moreover, it seems appropriate to proclaim this conclusion as the necessarily Christian position as well. Surely, our non-professional, non-philosophical, ordinary experience (and even some of our professional, philosophical ones) give ample testimony to the common, widespread acceptance of just such a position.

On this reckoning, then, the title of this essay may appear curious indeed. How is it possible, for an essay which concerns the philosophy of one of the twentieth-century's foremost Christian thinkers to have such a seemingly heretical and possibly scandalous title?

My response to that question, as a justification of the title's legitimacy, will consist of: a) an examination of the different types of moral judgments that function in moral experience; b) an exploration of Maritain's thinking about the role and influence that love plays in these various types of moral judgments and in our relationship with God; and c) a statement about the criteria that Maritain establishes for the determination of true moral culpability. My conclusion will show that, far from being a scandalous title and claim, the statement "There Are No Sinners In Hell," when understood correctly, is not only consistent with Maritain's ideas about morality, God, and the human person, it is actually a true and necessary conclusion as well.

Moral Judgments and Love

Moral judgments are essentially of two kinds: those in the *objective order*, which pertain to judgments about actions, and those in the *subjective order*, which concern judgments about the culpability or blameworthiness of persons. In either of these orders, we find that judgments may be either theoretical or concrete. Examples in the objective order might be theoretical: "Is stealing morally wrong?" and concrete: "Is it wrong for me to steal at this moment and in this situation?" To the theoretical belong abstract intellectual questions, while the concrete concerns the various unique circumstances attendant to the moral event, here and now. As philosophers we ask theoretical questions in both the objective and subjective orders; as ordinary human persons we often wrestle with the ambiguity and obscurity that comes from the necessity of making moral judgments of both kinds in concrete circumstances, when certainty and assurance may well be lacking. Although moral maturity and integrity may be understood as the integration of our professional, philosophical speculation with our concrete, personal choices and decisions, experience all-too-frequently provides us with sufficient testimony of the disparity between what we know we ought to do, on the one hand, and what we actually do, on the other. And while there are certainly many factors involved in both kinds of moral decision-making, love is principal among them. Thus, the question arises: in the philosophy of Jacques Maritain what part does love play in these two kinds of moral judgments, each considered both concretely and theoretically?

In his essay "Love in the Thought of Jacques Maritain,"[1] William Rossner, S.J., follows Maritain by first distinguishing between "natural" and "supernatural" loves and, secondly, by identifying two kinds

---

[1]William L. Rossner, S.J., "Love in the Thought of Jacques Maritain," in *Jacques Maritain: The Man and His Achievement*, ed. Joseph W. Evans (New York: Sheed and Ward, 1963), pp. 237–258.

of natural love. The first kind of natural love, "Love-of-Nature," concerns the love that all beings, both animate and inanimate, have for God. This metaphysical use of the word "love" is *not* what we commonly understand by this word; rather it refers to the amplitude of metaphysical being by which any natural existent, in its inner dynamism, is ordered toward "the good and the end to which it tends by the very necessity of its nature."[2] Maritain tells us that this type of love is true for "birds, moss, or inanimate molecules."[3] Although characteristic of all natural, created beings, it takes on special significance when predicated of human persons, endowed as we are with intellectual appetites. Even though Rossner actually discusses four different types or manifestations of this "love-of-nature," the central point for us *as persons* is that, just as the senses naturally love something that is pleasing to them, so the will naturally inclines toward any good whatsoever. This natural desire of the will ultimately seeks and delights only in God . . . even if the Divine is not explicitly known or understood as the object of this natural desire or love of our human nature.[4]

While this "love-of-nature," when specifically considered in relation to persons, concerns the metaphysical structure of the biologically affective as well as the intellectually affective dimension of human nature, it does not, of itself, establish the moral or genuinely human life of a person. For that we must consider the role and operation or willed-exercise of our intellectual appetite. This is what Rossner identifies, again following Maritain's terminology, as a "love-of-free-option." This now is love as it is more properly defined and understood: a freely chosen and willed-commitment to an intellectually apprehended good.

Although God is the Absolute Transcendent Good and the ultimate object of the will's desire, we do not see God's essence (which would *necessarily* determine the will's love if we did). In lived-experience we encounter many rival goods of many conflicting kinds, and as a result, we are left to contend with a conflict in our affections. When we look

---

[2]*Ibid.*, p. 247.

[3]Jacques Maritain, *Existence and the Existent* (New York: Pantheon Books, 1948), p. 42.

[4]William L. Rossner, S.J. "Love in the Thought of Jacques Maritain" in *Jacques Maritain: The Man and his Achievement*, ed. Joseph W. Evans (New York: Sheed and Ward, 1963), pp. 247–51.

to go beyond this experienced-confusion and choose to *orient* our lives to God as a desire on our part for the supreme good, we are casting ourselves "into the darkness of the Incomprehensible." Ultimately, at this foundational level, the will either gives itself to the good, to God, or it does not. This primal *character-orientation decision* cannot be avoided. And while it does not perfect us from error, wrong-doing, or sin, "the will, nevertheless, in choosing any moral good out of love for goodness, *de facto* extends its love to the True Good. . . ."[5] to God, even if God is not known as such.

This systematic delineation of the various types of love takes us into the heart of understanding the role of love in the various kinds of moral judgments. In his 1949 Princeton lectures, published as *An Introduction To the Basic Problems of Moral Philosophy*,[6] Maritain says that there are two sorts of inclination that operate in moral decision-making. The first of these concerns the laws of our more properly "animal" nature; these are the forces of instinct and heredity, and they are rooted profoundly in our biological nature. Distinguished from these lower influences, however, are those inclinations of our more properly "human" nature, that is, those which issue from our spiritual dimension: from the intellect and from the intellectual appetite (what Maritain also calls "connaturality"). These "higher" inclinations presuppose all the forces and complexities of our lower nature but, as is so characteristic of Maritain's thinking in regard to the many forms of practical knowledge, they are "passed through the lake of Intellect (functioning unconsciously)."[7] All of these influences and forces occur at a pre-philosophical or pre-conscious level, though they are purified and informed by the individual person's love-of-nature which *orients his or her basic character*.[8]

Maritain also points out that in the concrete order, where confusion and difficulty abound, each of these types of inclination can be perverted. Moreover, these two types of inclination, operating as they do below the level of conscious self-reflection and self-understanding, are frequently in conflict, or they are so intermingled with each other

---

[5]*Ibid.*, p. 253.

[6]Jacques Maritain, *An Introduction To The Basic Problems of Moral Philosophy* (Albany, New York: Magi Books, 1990).

[7]*Ibid.*, p. 54.

[8]*Ibid.*, pp. 50–59.

that it is not uncommon that "the natural tendencies and inclinations born of reason may be overcome or warped by the other instincts."[9]

Thus, in all the darkness that may come from the absence of objective certitude in concrete moral decisions, or from the confusion or conflict that we often introspectively experience, in the final analysis we are called to consult and act upon, in truth of conscience, that orientation of our being toward the Universal Good or God. This is what Rossner identified as the human version of love-of-nature, which underlies any and all of our acts of free-option or free choice. For as Maritain himself says, all the rules and objective norms of morality can neither be applied nor applied well "unless they are embodied in the ends which actually attract my desire and . . . will."[10] As a person is, so will the ends appear. For if we do not recognize the relationship between those moral laws or values which rule our lives and the ends upon which we make our life depend, we may not succeed in choosing what our inmost being desires, the Good.[11]

These insights introduce us to a consideration of the tension between the moral value of external acts and the moral value of "intention" or the internal acts of the will. In this way Maritain establishes the criteria for true moral culpability.

True Moral Culpability

After acknowledging that culpability (or "fault" as he calls it) is not easy to explain, Maritain identifies four factors that are involved in the determination of moral blameworthiness.[12] The first element refers to the act or action itself; it is the external act which may be determined as evil if it fails to conform with the principles of right reason. "Here," Maritain tells us, "the object alone is considered, in itself, not taking into account the intentions or the will of the subject."[13] While this objective immoral act is important, the commission of it is alone not sufficient for a conclusion of moral culpability.

The second element which Maritain explores is the role and activity of the will in the evil or immoral act. The realization of the absolutely

---

[9]*Ibid.*, p. 62.
[10]Jacques Maritain, *Existence and the Existent*, p. 52.
[11]*Ibid.*, p. 53.
[12]Jacques Maritain, *Moral Philosophy*, pp. 188–97.
[13]*Ibid.*, p. 188.

essential part played by the will has been slow to develop over the course of the history of moral consciousness he tells us, and, we might add, is also slow to appear in those whose own understanding of morality is likewise limited and immature. As we consider the act of the will, we also need to consider both the intentions and the circumstances that are involved, concretely, in each individual case, bearing in mind that no two cases are ever the same.[14]

Maritain points out that it is possible for an innocent person to commit an evil action in the objective order with no evil or malice intent; confoundingly, he also points out that it is equally possible to have malicious intent which commits an innocent act. In the former case, the action may occur out of ignorance or through what Maritain calls an "invincibly erroneous conscience." In neither of those cases of interior innocence is moral fault to be attributed. For example, Maritain writes that "for many poor urchins in certain big cities, stealing is not a sin, it's a sport. They are so invincibly convinced of this that there is no moral fault in their thefts."[15]

Those of evil intention, even if their actions be innocent or morally appropriate or acceptable in their own right, are not dealt with in so kindly a fashion. For in their "malicious innocence there is no innocence at all, but rather diabolical malice."[16]

"Invincible error" is not always sufficient to mitigate or exonerate moral responsibility, however; in some cases, the moral agent must bear responsibility for an insufficiently informed conscience. There are many factors which Maritain identifies in this context, and they serve to increase or decrease the degree of personal responsibility. These factors include violence of the passions; "tricks of the Unconscious"; mental imbalance; obsessions; compulsions, addictions, hereditary predispositions; hormonal imbalance; and other psychological dynamics which may be involved in the determination of fault. The entire range of these subjective internal psychic energies constitute what Maritain identifies as the third element in the determination of fault.

In her article "Aquinas's Assent/Consent Distinction and the Problem of 'Akrasia,'" Judith Barad provides an additional consideration to this discussion of moral fault.

---

[14]Jacques Maritain, *Existence and the Existent*, p. 51.
[15]Jacques Maritain, *Moral Philosophy*, p. 192.
[16]*Ibid.*, p. 192.

The problem of *akrasia* [moral weakness] is that we are aware that we judge certain actions (primarily those involving the bodily enjoyments) to be morally bad and not to be done, and yet go against that judgment by performing the actions."[17]

A Socratic interpretation would place the emphasis on a failure of insight or a lack of knowledge and truth. By contrast, Barad argues that the intellect may terminate in an assent to a proposition involving a commitment to a universal good or principle without the will's consequent choice (in a particular case) to act upon that knowledge. We may know that something is truly wrong and yet do it anyway. Barad points to Aquinas in recognizing that two acts of will are therefore necessary in order to execute a genuinely moral action involving personal responsibility. First, we must understand the good and will it in a general way. This is *assent*. Secondly, however, "a more intense act of will is required to make this principle the one we will act on in a given situation. If this will-act does not occur [*consent*], a likely result will be 'weakness of will,' for propositional assent is not sufficient to guarantee action."[18]

This moral weakness may constitute the vast majority of what ordinary folks may understand by the term "sin," which in turn helps us to understand how we may genuinely love the good and yet may occasionally fail to do it. This is, I think, precisely what Maritain had in mind when he wrote:

> Yet, in order that a man follow [the objective norms of morality], at the moment of temptation they must not merely resound in his head as mere universal rules which suffice to condemn him though not to set him in motion. [Otherwise] . . . he will not do the good he loves . . . , but he will do the evil he does not wish to do.[19]

Sin on this account issues from weakness, not from any malice or willed-intention of evil; instead it is the sin of those who yet love the Universal Good or God but who, at this juncture in their life's journey, may lack the sufficient strength or virtue they ultimately need in order to eventually succeed at doing the good which they also love.

---

[17]Judith Barad, "Aquinas's Assent/Consent Distinction and the Problem of *Akrasia*," *The New Scholasticism*, LXII, Winter 1988, p. 98.

[18]*Ibid.*, p. 110.

[19]Jacques Maritain, *Existence and the Existent*, p. 53.

To return now to Maritain's account of the elements of moral fault, I will discuss the fourth factor, which brings us to our conclusion. After observing that sin is always *against* something, Maritain identifies the three categories against which sin may be directed:

a) sin against the universe of society;

b) sin against the universe of being or creation; and

c) sin against the transcendent Whole or God.[20]

Different "sins" may vary in their degree of seriousness when considered from the perspective of these different categories; some may be severe in one category but of little significance in another. Maritain observes that for us in the Judeo-Christian tradition, seriousness of fault or sin lies chiefly in its being an offense against God, the Alpha and Omega of all goodness. But if God is pure act, self-subsisting Goodness, and absolutely immutable, what sense does it make to refer to sin as an "offense against God?"

Maritain's response is simple. "Sin is something which God *does not desire* and desires not to be."[21] When I sin my good and the good of all creation which God desires and loves will now be prevented from coming into being. Maritain concludes by saying that:

Moral fault affects the Uncreated, in no way in Himself, since He is absolutel invulnerable, but in the things and the effects He desires and loves. Here, one can say that God is the most vulnerable of beings. No need for poisoned arrows, cannons and machine guns—an invisible movement *in the heart of a free agent* is all that is needed to wound Him, to deprive His antecedent will of something here below which it desired and loved from all eternity, and which shall never be.[22] (underscore mine)

Conclusion

When we reflect back over the various types of moral judgments which we distinguished at the outset, we can now appreciate Maritain's insights of concerning the part that love plays in each of them. Several conclusions stand out.

---

[20]Jacques Maritain, *Moral Philosophy*, p. 194.

[21]*Ibid.*, pp. 196–97.

[22]*Ibid.*, p. 197.

I. *In the objective order of judgments about actions:*

A. *Conclusion #1 (as applied to theoretical judgments).* Philosophical analysis can successfully enable us to establish moral rules that are in keeping with the loving nature of God, of the created universe, of the human person, and of the precepts of right reason. In this category love plays an admittedly minor and less active role.
B. *Conclusion #2 (as applied to concrete judgments).* Moral judgments about actions which occur in concrete situations proceed from the mysterious inwardness of an individual's Self, the fabric of which involves and may include the secret depths of one's being, the spiritual orientation of one's loves, and the whole complex interrelation of biology, psychology, intellect, will, and Divine Grace. When making these concrete decisions we ought to be a) guided by an intellectual commitment to ethical principles; b) strengthened by moral virtues (which are always in need of additional improvement); c) animated by a love for the Good in all things, all the while that we are d) conscious of the epistemological limitation and darkness in which we often must proceed; and e) mindful of, and humbled by, our intellectual and moral weaknesses and vices.

II. *In the subjective order of judgments about persons:*

A. *Conclusion #3 (as applied to theoretical judgments).* Understanding the complexity of human nature, we can also understand, in a universe created by a loving God whom all of that creation loves in return, that the determination of fault or moral culpability involves many complex factors. In the final analysis, love (God's and our own) is salvific; wickedness and malice are those serious obstacles to an interior life of love which wills the good. Thus, while moral damnation is certainly possible, *it is not reducible to the commission of an external action alone.*

B. *Conclusion #4 (as applied to concrete judgments)* Humanly-made moral judgments which attempt to assign interior moral fault or culpability, whether to others or ourselves, are ultimately an impossibility. We may judge the sin but never the sinner; we may judge material or legal liability or responsibility but not *moral* guilt. For judgments of the latter are made by God alone, Who understands the deepest recesses of the heart. Maritain says: "It is said of the church that 'she does not judge of interior dispositions;' this applies all the more to human society. It cannot undertake to mimic God's justice."[23] Nor can we mimic God's justice individually. We can understand how complex it is to determine moral fault, and we can speculate on and hope for Divine mercy; but we simply do not know what God's justice, mercy, and love are in themselves; nor do we understand how they might work.

Thus, love brings us into being; it permeates our nature, and it calls us to grow in our own capacity as loving persons and stewards of God's creation. We can understand that love of universal goodness makes us better, makes our world better, and makes our choices and moral judgments better: objectively, to proceed toward the Truth, and subjectively, to proceed with compassion in our vast network of relationships. Moral weakness has no ultimate strangle-hold upon us. We are comforted by the words of St. John of the Cross: "In the hour of our lives, we will be judged on how we have loved."

In this way too we can understand Maritain's entry in his *Notebooks* on the 29th of March, 1910 (Easter Tuesday), when he wrote: "Leon Bloy comes to see us. 'There are no sinners in Hell,' he tells us, 'for sinners were the friends of Jesus. There are only the *wicked*.' "[24]

---

[23]*Ibid.*, pp. 193–94.

[24]Jacques Maritain, *Notebooks*, (Albany, New York: Magi Books, 1984), p. 62.

The Existential Ethics of Maritain and Rahner

Joseph L. Pappin, III

Introduction

The paradoxical Sartrean proclamation that "man is condemned to be free" rolls down the corridors of the twentieth-century. Although this proclamation strikes us as bizarre in its formulation, both Rahner and Maritain agree in holding that freedom is inescapable. We cannot escape the exercise of freedom, a freedom which is not simply a series of unrelated actions, of neutral import, easily withdrawn, without consequence, but a freedom which in its finality aims at nothing less than the total enactment of the person.

Sartre makes several incredible claims toward the end of *Being and Nothingness*. The great atheistic existentialist argues that "to be man means to reach toward being God." Thus, continues Sartre, "man is the being whose project is to be God."[1] How is this to be accomplished? It is the goal of human freedom, and yet it is impossible. For to achieve it man would have to be a "freedom thing," a "being-for-itself and in-itself," the fusion of consciousness and being. But, as freedom implies lack, man's project is doomed, but he cannot escape the attempt.

Furthermore, the condition of human freedom is an essenceless, and yet human, reality. There is no law of nature, or human nature, to realize. Essence annuls freedom. Freedom and law are incompatible.

---

[1]Jean-Paul Sartre, *Being and Nothingness*, trans. Hazel Barnes (New York: Washington Square Press, 1966), p. 724.

Freedom posits its own values and the source is passion. The ground of an existential ethics is the lack of being and the striving toward a contradictory ideal. For Sartre freedom and the responsibility to universalize freedom for all humankind is the ultimate value.

The Sartrean backdrop helps us to locate the existential nature of Rahner and Maritain's existential ethics. It is the aim of this comparative paper to explore the themes of human freedom; the tension between person and nature; God and the existential condition. Such a discussion must culminate in the crucial theme of freedom and the moral law and the pivotal role of conscience, noting here the difference between the existential ethics of Rahner and Maritain and that of Sartre.

Human Freedom

As with all of Rahner's thought, human freedom emerges within the infinite horizon of being, disclosed through transcendental experience. Spirit, in effect, means the transcendence of the person beyond any categorial object toward the unthematic "grasp of absolute being and absolute good."[2] Or, as Rahner boldly declares in *Hearers of the Word*, "man is the absolute transcendence toward the absolute value which is God's pure being."[3] Spirit as transcendence displays an *a priori* and essential openness to being. The human subject is "pure openness for absolutely everything, for being as such."[4] This *a priori* structure is revealed to spirit in every act of everyday knowing and willing, because, as knowing discloses categorial, and hence discloses limited objects, the realization of limits is at the same time a surpassing of all limit. So, Rahner's famous pre-apprehension of being is antecedent to all knowing, permitting, in fact, the actualization of the potency for knowledge. Accordingly, "in knowledge not only is something known, but the subject knowing is always co-known."[5] We achieve self-awareness in and through the act of knowing; spirit is being-present-to-itself. Likewise, it must be emphasized that spirit is luminous to itself

---

[2] Karl Rahner, *Theological Investigations*, Vol. XVI, trans. David Morland O.S.B., (New York: The Seabury Press, 1979), p. 25.

[3] Karl Rahner, "Hearers of the Word," trans. Joseph Donceel, in *A Rahner Reader*, ed. Gerald A. McCool (New York: The Seabury Press, 1975), p. 42.

[4] Karl Rahner, *Foundations of Christian Faith*, trans. William V. Dych (New York: The Seabury Press, 1978), p. 20.

[5] *Ibid.*, p. 18.

by way of its free acts. Our free acts do not simply posit something external to ourselves. Rather, as we move toward self-enactment, we must take possession of ourselves and of our creative powers. This is only accomplished through the return of the subject to itself, which is only possible for spirit as incarnate. Spirit's incarnational existence is, moreover, necessary for freedom. Rahner concludes, therefore, that "free action is luminous in itself" while "dark for others."[6]

As present-to-oneself in the presence of the other and as experiencing the transcendence of spirit beyond all limited objects, the human person transcends himself in a way that orients him toward God. Rahner concludes that the essential nature of freedom is only conceivable in and through the transcendent reference of the human spirit in knowledge and freedom to that being, or rather person, whom we call God."[7]

Thus, freedom moves toward or away from God with the final disposition of the human subject held in the balance. True, it is that freedom is primarily directed toward the objects of experience, and through our actions we become what we are, nonetheless—and here Rahner is emphatic—freedom "is primarily and unavoidably concerned with God himself."[8] How does freedom stand with Maritain?

To recapitulate in detail Maritain's philosophy of freedom would be out of place. Instead, let us briefly re-state some of the essentials of Maritain's doctrine in order to formulate, in comparison with Rahner, his existential ethics.

The person is possessed of appetites which in themselves are blind. Yet the appetites are powers tending toward either the good of the senses or the good as apprehended by the intellect. The appetite as informed by the intelligible good is the will. The will requires a judgment to produce its proper object. The primordial act of the will is to love, and thus the goal or ultimate end of the will lies in the surrender of itself to the desired end.

Furthermore, prior to the judgments of the intellect concerning the good, "there are in the will," writes Maritain in his work on Bergson, "upon the simple apprehension of a good, undeliberate movements for

[6]Karl Rahner, "Hearers of the Word," p. 39.

[7]Karl Rahner, *Theological Investigations*, Vol. XVI, p. 66.

[8]Karl Rahner, *Theological Investigations*, Vol. VI, trans. Karl-H. and Boniface Kruger (London: Darton, Longman and Todd, 1969), p. 182.

which we are not responsible."[9] Yet the full act of the will follows on the act of the intellect. The will cannot will the evil, for to will the good "is the very urge and expression of its being." Contrast this with Sartre who declares that "human reality through its very upsurge decides to define its own being by its ends."[10] These ends reflect one's project, freely chosen, without reason, and, hence, unintelligible.

Maritain claims that necessity lies at the foundation of the will, because the will necessarily wills the "absolute and universal good."[11] What is not "absolute and universal" cannot determine the will with necessity. Moreover, "in any particular good which it knows," Maritain continues, "the intellect sees that this good is not universal."

Rahner likewise holds that the spirit recognizes the limited nature of finite goods within the horizon provided by the transcendental experience of infinite reality. In fact, the absolute good is mediated in its immediacy through the limited good grasped categorially. For Maritain that there is indetermination in the will is due to the fact that all goods simply fall short of *the* good. So this is why "every will, even the most perverse, desires God without knowing it."[12]

For all the freedom that marks our being, necessity imposes itself upon us through the tension revealed between person and nature.

The Great Divide: Person and Nature

For Rahner the human subject is "on the way," but it suffers the internal divide between spirit and matter, person and nature. As finite, spirit requires the otherness of its own materiality and discovers the barrier to its own complete self-realization, dispersed as it is in space and time. Yet matter is required for the enactment achieved through knowing and willing and is required for the self-presence which is mediated through sensibility. Thus, the ambivalence of finite spirit lies in both the necessity of materiality for self-transcendence and the inherent limits due to matter. On the one hand, the experience of transcendence as unlimited and as the goal of one's striving offers the

---

[9]Jacques Maritain, *Bergsonian Philosophy and Thomism*, trans. Mabelle L. Andison (New York: Philosophical Library, 1955), p. 266.

[10]Jean-Paul Sartre, *Being and Nothingness*, p. 572.

[11]Jacques Maritain, *Bergsonian Philosophy and Thomism*, p. 268.

[12]*Ibid.*

awareness that as striving one has not yet achieved the full enactment of one's essence. On the other hand, in the desire for the completion of oneself through transcendence, one discovers the inertia and weight of one's own nature. Rahner makes it clear in his essay on "The Theological Concept of Concupiscentia" that this resistance inherent in the "dualism of person and nature . . . arises from the materiality of the human being, from the real differentiation of matter and form which prevents the form from bringing itself fully to manifestation in the 'other' of matter."[13] The duality of form and matter in the subject reflects the duality of spirit and sensibility. Yet the ambiguity and ambivalence lies in the necessity of matter for spirit's enactment through the otherness of matter, positing as it does the person as "spirit in the world."

But as spirit is transcendence and as spirit necessarily enacts itself through sensibility, it intends the eternal as the incomprehensible orientation of its striving. Rahner holds, then, that "Freedom is self-achievement of the person, using a finite material, before the infinite God."[14] But more than this, spirit-in-the-world requires the community of other finite spirits as the end of spirit is achieved through the love of the incomprehensible One. Thus, Rahner states that "Freedom . . . is the *manner* of the appropriation and realization of the person and of his absolute dignity before God and in the community of other persons, using finite decided materials."[15]

Just as Rahner posits the dualism of spirit and matter, of person and nature, so does Maritain. The person is "one substance," Maritain writes, "which is both carnal and spiritual."[16] Distinguishing between individuality and personality, he notes that individuality tends to dispersal, expressing an avidity to matter, while "personality is the subsistence of the spiritual soul communicated to the human composite."[17] Personality signifies both a "generosity and expansiveness of being,"

---

[13]Karl Rahner, *Theological Investigations*, Vol. I, trans. Cornelius Ernst (Baltimore: Helicon Press, 1961), p. 364.

[14]Karl Rahner, *Theological Investigations*, Vol. II, trans. Karl-H. Kruger (London: Darton, Longman and Todd, 1963), p. 246.

[15]*Ibid.*, 247.

[16]Jacques Maritain, "The Individual and the Person," in *The Social and Political Philosophy of Jacques Maritain*, ed. Joseph W. Evans and Leo R. Ward (Garden City, New York: Image Books, 1965), p. 19.

[17]*Ibid.*, p. 21.

tending in a dynamic way to the perfection of itself in communication with others in knowing and loving. This communication in dialogue is not appended to personality; rather it is at the core of its essence as incarnate spirit.

While for Rahner spirit is transcendence, the openness of being for the absolute infinity of being, Maritain in "The Conquest of Freedom" likewise holds that "Spirit . . . implies a sort of infinity; its faculty of desire goes out of itself to a good which completely satisfies it, and therefore to a good without limits, and we cannot will anything except in the willing of happiness."[18] At the root of personality, thus, is spirit. Moreover, personality, tending as it does to the Subsistent Good, remains a mystery. This mysteriousness is a result of personality and freedom being "too purely intelligible relative to our intelligence. They exist in us," Maritain exclaims in *Moral Philosophy*, "as something obscure *for us*. . . . Our intelligence grasps them without comprehending them. Even more than the universe itself, individuality, personality and freedom are known by us and intelligible to us as mysteries, and in the mystery of existence."[19]

God, Freedom, and the Existential Condition

The existential condition in which the human being finds itself is that of a personal subject, never as a purely neutral stuff to be crafted at will, nor to be re-made at a whim. Rahner speaks of the "freedom of being" as being the "transcendental mark of human existence itself."[20] The person is "never just 'something there' but always already 'for himself', 'existing'."[21] Bearing this "transcendental mark," the human being discovers in its freedom the capacity for the eternal, the capacity not simply for an endless series of possible revisions of destinies, but the capacity "to do something uniquely final, something which is finally valid precisely because it is done in freedom."[22] This capacity for the eternal and the need to "do something uniquely final" requires freedom to will death. It is inconceivable that we should endure the

---

[18]*Ibid.*, p. 26.

[19]Jacques Maritain, *Moral Philosophy* (New York: Charles Scribner's Sons, 1964), pp. 143–144.

[20]Karl Rahner, *Theological Investigations*, Vol. VI, p. 184.

[21]*Ibid.*, p. 185.

[22]*Ibid.*, p. 186.

infinite extension in time and the transitory character of temporal existence. Here, nothing is final. Indeed, Rahner declares in his essay "On Christian Dying" that such a condition is "tantamount to being damned."[23] Rahner discovers in the depths of our existence a craving "for that which is imperfect in use to be brought to an end in order that it may be finally perfected."[24] Yet what is it that is finalized through freedom? Ultimately it is the final disposition of the person as a self before the Eternal, which is God. In this respect, freedom has to do with God. "Freedom is the freedom to say 'yes' or 'no' to God," Rahner claims, "and therein and thereby is it freedom in relation to oneself."[25] Our lives become a response and answer "to the question in which God offers himself to us as the source of transcendence."[26] Consequently, "The ultimate act of freedom," Rahner concludes, is one "in which [the person] decides his own fate totally and irrevocably," being "the act in which he either *willingly accepts or definitely rebels against* his own utter impotence, in which he is utterly subject to the control of a mystery which cannot be expressed—that mystery which we call God."[27] What depiction of the existential condition is provided by Maritain?

In an essay on "The Immanent dialectic of the First Act of Freedom," Maritain indicates how the original act of freedom emerges. The child, confronted with its first potentially moral decision, rises above the deterministic encumberments of its young existence to discover an inclination to the moral good as the good, combined with a deliberation upon the self in an act of self-possession. The child is able to turn away from the clamoring within itself for gratifications, the good that ought to be done, and away from the evil to be avoided. Maritain identifies this as the "primary implication of the first act of freedom when it is good."[28] The second implication of this act of freedom is the realization that there is a moral law transcending all empirical realities, and governing our human actions, a moral law which entails the notion of the morally good act which ought to be done. This leads

---

[23]Karl Rahner, *Theological Investigations*, Vol. VII, trans. David Bourke (London: Darton, Longman and Todd, 1971), p. 290.

[24]*Ibid.*, p. 291.

[25]Karl Rahner, *Foundations of Christian Faith*, p. 100.

[26]*Ibid.*, p. 101.

[27]Karl Rahner, *Theological Investigations*, Vol. VII, p. 291.

[28]Jacques Maritain, *The Range of Reason* (New York: Charles Scribner's Sons, 1958), p. 168.

to the first precept of the moral law demanding that my actions in fact be good. This law points to a separate good toward which I strive "because it is both *the* Good and *my* Good."

While the child does not think explicitly of God, he does will the good as the good and as the purpose and meaning of his life. Maritain concludes that "God is thus naturally known, without any conscious judgment, in and by the impulse of the will striving toward the Separate Good, whose existence is implicitly involved in the practical value acknowledged to the moral good." Maritain underscores the claim that this is a "purely practical cognition of God" so that we strive toward God as our ultimate end, knowing "God (unconsciously) without knowing Him (consciously)."[29]

The real test of a Thomistic existential ethics as a response to Sartre's ethics lies in the treatment of freedom and the moral law.

Freedom and the Moral Law

These questions must be finally posed to Rahner: Can one seriously hold to the reality of a "human nature" and to the existence of God, and yet put forward an "existential ethics"? Can there be an existential ethics without succumbing to a massive nominalism, mired in the multiplicity of possibilities entailed by one's situation, a situation, moreover, which moment by moment transfigures itself? Can we honestly hold to an ethic of radical freedom when one's choices take place within the necessity imposed upon the person who must say "yes" or "no" before God, even if the person denies God altogether? Clearly, Sartre would hold that Rahner's philosophy of freedom is totally nonexistential. In *Being and Nothingness* Sartre proclaims that "Human reality can not receive its ends, as we have seen either from outside or from a so-called inner nature. It chooses them and by this very choice confers upon them a transcendent existence as the external limit of its projects. . . . Thus since freedom is identical with my existence, it is the foundation of ends which I shall attempt to attain either by the will or by passionate efforts."[30] The positing of my ends is accomplished, Sartre argues, by a "sudden thrust of the freedom which is mine."[31]

---

[29]*Ibid.*, p. 70.
[30]Jean-Paul Sartre, *Being and Nothingness*, p. 572.
[31]*Ibid.*

Rahner is not uninstructed by the arguments of the existentialists. He sets out to avoid a deductive, essentialistic ethics that would somehow treat the moral ought as a mere intersection of the universal norm and the concrete case. Yet there is a moral law; there is a formal structure given to our existential reality. However, this structure does not override the existential uniqueness of each person as he stands personally before the abyss of the "infinity of reality,"[32] and experiences the singularity of the call of the Holy Mystery to self-transcendence. There is a moral law, and this law does not liquidate freedom; rather it is necessary to its realization. In his essay on "The Dignity and Freedom of Man," Rahner claims that "The moral law as such (in contrast to the forced compliance with it) is not a limitation of freedom, since it does after all presuppose freedom of its very nature and turns to it (since it is fulfilled only when it is obeyed freely), and since it orientates freedom to its own essential goal, namely, the true achievements of the person."[33]

Now the question emerges whether there is a "concrete imperative" which clearly indicates how the moral law is to be realized in the concrete particular? A problem emerges, namely, the universality of the law and the array of possibilities that floods every concrete case. Even more, for Rahner, the central issue revolves around the call of the individual subject, who is *individuum ineffable*, who is not merely an instance of a universal norm. God has called the person to loving surrender in the Holy Mystery. Moving to the complexity of the issue, Rahner maintains that an "existential ethics . . . relates . . . to the *substantial nature* of man . . . as principle of the origin and actualizing of the historic-personal activity," which "must achieve itself constitutively in the positivity of each single, uniquely one con-cretion of the individual decision."[34] The recognition of such a nature does not entail the entrenchment of an essentialistic ethics positing in deductive fashion ethical norms. For Rahner "there is an individual ethical reality of a positive kind which is untranslatable into a material universal ethics; there is a binding ethical uniqueness. . . ."[35] Furthermore, to know Rahner is to know of his claim of a "supernatural existential," which

---

[32]Karl Rahner, *Foundations of Christian Faith*, p. 33.
[33]Karl Rahner, *Theological Investigations*, Vol. II, p. 249.
[34]*Ibid.*, p. 228.
[35]*Ibid.*, p. 229.

states that "man is the event of God's absolute self-communication."
This is a "free and unmerited grace, of a miracle of God's free love
for spiritual creatures." For Rahner the supernatural existential "is
given to everyone who is a being of unlimited transcendentality as a
fulfillment essentially transcending the natural."[36]

Now all of this may seem to signal not only the impossibility
of an essentialistic ethics but also the suspension of all moral law
in lieu of the radical singularity of the supernatural existential as a
call and communication to each individual. In the *Theological Investigations* Rahner effectively refutes such a claim: "There can be
nothing which actually ought to be done," Rahner states, "or is allowed
in a concrete or individual situation, which could lie outside these
universal norms."[37] This brings us back to the question which asks
if that which we ought to do is only the "intersection of the law and
the given situation."[38] For Rahner we must recall the uniqueness of
our moral acts and the eternal destiny of the human person. Each
moral act is not simply one bound by space and time. Instead, the
person's "acts have a meaning for eternity, not only morally but also
ontologically."[39] Thus, Rahner concludes that while there cannot be
a moral science of the individual as individual, there is a "universal
formal ontology of individual reality, so . . . there can and must be a
formal doctrine of existential concretion, a formal existential ethics."[40]
Conscience performs the existential role of recognizing the moral law
and the possibilities emerging out of the unique situation in order
to determine what is to be done. Such a role of conscience requires
the self-knowledge which emerges from transcendental experience,
placing the spirit in openness before the unthematic presence of infinity, allowing the spirit to be present-to-itself as one dynamically
tending in knowledge and love to absolute being. The infinite reality of absolute being, while transcendent, is nonetheless intimately
present to us as the absolute good providing the horizon for the
finite goods and values to take their proportional place in the ethical
range of possibilities. It is, as always, the transcendence of spirit

---

[36]Karl Rahner, *Foundations of Christian Faith*, pp. 126–127.
[37]Karl Rahner, *Theological Investigations*, Vol. II, p. 222.
[38]*Ibid.*
[39]*Ibid.*, p. 225.
[40]*Ibid.*, p. 229.

toward the unlimited good of absolute being which allows for the non-reflective self-presence of the spirit to emerge in all its positive uniqueness.

Maritain criticizes the existential ethics of Sartre, noting that the formal element of such an ethics consists "in pure liberty alone." To the perplexed youth seeking moral counsel, a Sartrean ethics advises that "his liberty itself will tell him how to make use of liberty."[41] Instead, Maritain holds that the root of liberty lies in reason. Maritain claims that there are objective moral norms, that they are known both by reason and natural inclination, but that they are not applied in deductive, case-book fashion. Maritain opposes a Kantian ethics which replaces the Good by the Norm, where Pure Reason attempts to displace God.[42] While there is indeed the knowledge of natures providing formal norms of conduct, these norms are not mere universals, imposing duties and obligations, condemning me to guilt. Rather, objective norms of morality, Maritain reasons, must be "embodied in the ends which actually attract my desire and in the actual movement of my will." The human person "must recognize in them . . . an urgent demand of his most highly individualized, most personal desire, for the ends upon which he has made his life depend."[43] What is at stake here in the obedience to the law is not the negation of freedom, but, through love, the realization of one's own deepest desire, harmonizing "his will with the law (since it remains a will to the good) and makes him identify his *self*," according to Maritain in *Existence and the Existent*, "with the *everyman* who is subject to the universal precept."[44] Expressed negatively, to suppress universality and the law is to suppress freedom which is rooted in reason.

Now, just as for Rahner, what Maritain terms the "existentiality of the moral judgement" is realized through the "judgement of the moral conscience."[45] It comes down in the practical sphere of freedom to the virtue of prudence which alone can determine what ought to be done in the context of the moral situation and particular circumstances

---

[41]Jacques Maritain, *Existence and the Existent*, trans. Lewis Galantiere and Gerald B. Phelan (New York: Vintage Books, 1966), p. 60.

[42]Jacques Maritain, *Moral Philosophy*, p. 113.

[43]Jacques Maritain, *Existence and the Existent*, pp. 52–53.

[44]*Ibid.*, p. 58.

[45]*Ibid.*, p. 50.

which are unrepeatable and unique to the moment. As Maritain enjoins, "No knowledge of moral essences . . . no casuistry, no chain
of pure deduction, no science, can exempt me from my judgement
of conscience." Maritain forcefully concludes that while the universal
precept is enunciated in the major premise of the practical syllogism,
both the minor and conclusion operate on a different level, for "they
are put forward by the whole subject, whose intellect is swept along
the existential ends by which (in virtue of his liberty) his appetitive
powers are in fact subjugated."[46] Just as the first teaching of Thomistic
existentialism is "the perfection of human life," Maritain asserts that
this is achieved only in charity: "All morality thus hangs upon that
which is most existential in the world. For love . . . does not deal with
possible or pure essences, it deals with existents."[47]

Conclusion

Separating the existential ethics of Rahner and Maritain from that
of Sartre is the reality and necessity of the moral law, reflecting
human nature. Whereas for Sartre God is an impossible ideal to which
everyone aspires, for Rahner and Maritain it is the eternal destiny
that belongs to every human person, a destiny that signals both the
existential uniqueness of the person and the ground of the moral law.
Also, for both Maritain and Rahner, antecedent to the exercise of
freedom is a pre-conceptual knowledge of God. For each this entails a
striving for the perfection of one's being through the love of God and
one's fellow human beings with the shaping of the self the result of
the exercise of one's freedom. Rather than a condemnation to freedom
within an absurd universe, this is the person's authentic and existential
liberation.

---

[46]*Ibid.*, p. 52.
[47]*Ibid.*, p. 49.

Three Rival Versions of Nonmoral Goodness

Thomas Loughran

Moral theory requires for its development an account of human well-being, of what it is for a thing to be good for a person—a theory, that is, of nonmoral goodness. Contemporary moral theorists—notably the so-called "new natural law theorists" and consequentialists alike—have come under fire for their failure to provide defensible accounts of nonmoral goodness.[1] This essay will present in outline three important rival approaches to the question of nonmoral goodness—natural law, communitarian, and informed-desire approaches—and will identify some significant strengths and weaknesses within and some principle differences among these rival versions. One of these approaches, the full-information informed-desire approach of recent popularity, will be developed to overcome its shortcomings by incorporating natural law and communitarian resources. Finally, the resulting view will be presented as maintaining the strengths and avoiding the weaknesses of each of the three rival approaches discussed, and thus as showing more promise than they for serving as the foundation of moral theory.

---

[1]See Russell Hittinger's *Critique of the New Natural Law Theory* (Notre Dame, Indiana: University of Notre Dame Press, 1987). His critique is more precisely that the natural law theories of Grisez and Finnis fail to provide the philosophy of nature on which an adequate account of the basic human goods must rest. See David Sobel's "Full Information Accounts of Commensurating Well Being," *Ethics*, Vol. 104, No. 4 (July, 1994), pp. 784–810, where he brings criticism of full-information accounts of well being to bear on what he calls the "standard consequentialist position."

I

Human action can be considered in terms of three logical components: apprehension, appetite, and the causes operating on these. The
first component can be loosely called reason; the second, desire; and
the third, the external causal influences on human action, including
those in the observable and immediate environment of the agent, an
environment which is prominently social in nature. The precise nature
and causal relationships among these features of human action matter
much for moral theory, but can be set aside for present purposes.[2]
They are distinguished here only to suggest that attending to these
components severally without adequate consideration of the three together leads to rival approaches to nonmoral good.

A Natural Law Approach

If we begin thinking about nonmoral goodness by attending introspectively to the process of reasoning about action (to delibertion),
we notice chains of motivation in ourselves which converge into a
reasonably limited number. In the attempt to categorize the wellsprings
of human action, we in effect survey human nature, noticing its various
aspects, functions, and ends. We have purposes related to our animal
nature: there are goods of food, physical comfort and pleasure, and
the like. Insofar as we are rational, there are goods of knowledge
and education. We are social in nature; there are goods of friendship,
community. We are sexual in nature; there are goods of procreation
and family. We are consciously contingent beings, suggesting goods
in the area of religion.

Lists such as these of the basic human goods, made with greater
care but usually mentioning goods of less than a dozen or so kinds,
have become associated with natural law theory.[3] The evident virtue
of generating an account of nonmoral good by reflecting on human
deliberation and human nature is that the list produced is likely to

---

[2]For a sketch of the nature and causal relationships of these faculties which motivates and
supports the view of nonmoral goodness presented here, see my "Freedom and Good in the
Thomistic Tradition," *Faith and Philosophy*, Vol. 11, No. 3 (July, 1994).

[3]See Mortimer J. Adler, "A Dialectic of Morals," *The Review of Politics*, 1941, p. 42; John
Finnis, *Natural Law and Natural Rights* (Oxford: Clarendon Press, 1980), pp. 86–90; Germain
Grisez, *The Way of the Lord Jesus*, Vol. 1, *Christian Moral Principles* (Chicago: Franciscan
Herald Press, 1983), p. 124.

be applicable to and assessable by most, if not all, rational human beings. The substantial agreement among human beings about basic human goods is easily explained on this approach: human beings are generally alike, with similar capacities for activity and similar states constituting the actualization or fulfillment of those capacities.

But any such analysis of human nature and human ends is likely to be as thin as it is general, and their lack of specificity is perhaps the principle weakness of such approaches. The most important questions human beings have concerning how to weave successful individual human lives and successful communities from the fabric of human nature seem unaddressed on this thin natural law approach. It is far from clear how introspection into human nature helps to adjudicate the controversy between rival ways to prioritize and achieve goods drawn from the many areas of human activity which when considered abstractly are relatively uncontroversial. So, the appealing universality of natural law accounts of nonmoral goodness seems inescapably linked to an unappealing vacuousness.

A Communitarian Approach

The relative lack of content in accounts of nonmoral goodness resulting from natural law approaches might prompt attention to those elements in the whole context of human action from which the details of successful decisions are drawn: to the particular environment, the concrete social context, within which decisions are made. Only in the concrete situation in which the individual human agent actually deliberates can be found the data which give substance and intelligible form to human action. In fact, merely general accounts of human ends seem unable by themselves to supply any direction for human action at all. For the question as to whether the fulfillment of some human function is good for a person seems to depend on what actual human agents would do under fully specified circumstances. These would be circumstances, of course, in which the available options might not permit the actualization of a given human function at a cost which any human being would judge to be worth paying. What is good for human beings, then, would seem to be a function of the concrete circumstances in which human beings find themselves. Human beings do not find themselves within such circumstances alone; they belong to communities. Within such communities wisdom is gathered about how to transform one concrete set of physical and social circumstances into some alternative concrete set of circumstances toward which its members are more inclined. What is good for human beings, it might thus seem, is inescapably tied to concrete human communities rather than to abstract human nature.

In focusing on the specific causes giving substance to the deliberations of existing human beings, communitarian approaches of this sort promise the kind of detailed answers to the actual questions human beings have about their good, details which natural law approaches seem unable to provide. Such details can be accumulated, moreover, bringing about in time a practical wisdom about how human beings in such and such kinds of community can respond to such and such kinds of challenges and opportunities. So, perhaps the principal strength of communitarian approaches to nonmoral good is their ability to provide detailed accounts of what is actually good for human beings.

But such detailed accounts will vary from one community to the next. Different stores of practical wisdom suitable fo solving different sets of problems emerging from different particular sets of concrete physical and social circumstances will characterize different communities; what is good for a human being would seem to be relativized to the mode of community life in which he or she participates. Whose values, which store of practical wisdom to use in choosing from among rival modes of community life would seem to be questions which admit only question-begging answers, given only the resources afforded by a communitarian approach. Moreover, insofar as this feature of communitarian rational justification is noticed by members of a given community, the lack of theoretical support for the actual practice of community life may erode the motivational link between community values and individual action. Once it is noticed that membership in this particular community is not the only option available to its members, and that in the end only question-begging justification can be given for supposing that remaining within this community is good for its members, the inclination of those members to think and act in ways characteristic of mature members of that community may diminish. But one characteristic of nonmoral good which must be included in any account of it is the connection between the good and human inclination. A state of affairs which when adequately understood fails to motivate a given individual is, at least on the face of it, improperly called her "good." These three features—relativism, resourcelessness for guiding choice among rival modes of community life, and the resulting motivational skepticism—seem the biggest weaknesses of communitarian approaches to nonmoral good.

An Informed-Desire Approach

The importance of the link between nonmoral good and human motivation has led many to build their accounts directly from the phenomenon of human inclination, or desire. While surely not everything that is desired is good *simpliciter*, it has often been maintained that the good is what would be desired under some circumstance or other. Attempts to specify those circumstances have focused on the elimination of cognitive defects—ignorance and error—and have resulted in what are known as informed-desire accounts of well-being or of nonmoral good.[4] Recent informed-desire approaches have pointed toward the ideal state where ignorance and error are removed from practical judgments, so that an agent would be fully and vividly aware of all of his or her options; such attempts have been called full-information accounts. Surely, no existing human being is ever in circumstances such as these, and so the good for any individual has accordingly been defined roughly as what her idealized fully-informed self would advise her actual self to do. This turn in informed-desire theory has been toward what have been called "Ideal Advisor" accounts of nonmoral good.[5]

The virtues of informed-desire approaches have been characterized as their ability to capture a pair of intuitions about nonmoral good, the epistemic and internalist intuitions.[6] These intuitions correspond roughly to the "informed" and "desire" components of such accounts. The epistemic intuition is the recognition that information generally improves desire or inclination, and that choices are rightly criticized by pointing out relevant information not adequately considered by the agent.[7] The internalist intuition is roughly that whatever is meant by something being good for a person, it must include some connection

---

[4]Recent statements of informed-desire approaches include those of Richard Brandt, *A Theory of the Good and the Right* (Oxford: The Clarendon Press, 1979); Peter Ralton's "Facts and Values," *Philosophical Topics* 14, Fall, 1986, and "Moral Realism," *Philosophical Review*, 95, April, 1986; and James Griffin's *Wellbeing* (Oxford University Press, 1988).

[5]The "Ideal Advisor" handle is taken from Connie Rosati's "Persons, Perspectives, and Full Information Accounts of the Good," forthcoming in *Ethics*, Vol. 105 (January, 1995).

[6]Don Loeb's unpublished paper, "Full-Information Accounts of Rational Desire and Individual Good," is helpful concerning the nature of and the interplay between these two intuitions.

[7]The epistemic intuition is reminiscent of Aquinas's claim that some error of judgment is necessarily involved in any instance of sin: *ST.*, I, 63, 1 ad 4m; *ST.*, I-II, 58, 2 and 77, 2; *ST.*, II-II, 53, 2.

to desire, or more properly to some motivational disposition internal to that person; this is just the intuition about the link between motivation and nonmoral good against which the communitarian approach, as outlined above, seems to fall short.

In spite of the initial appeal and popularity of full-information accounts, they have been subject to considerable recent criticism.[8] As do the virtues, so the vices of full-information informed-desire accounts correspond roughly to "informed" and "desire" aspects. First, the notion of an ideally-informed human being seems incoherent, on account of both the amount of information relevant to human choices, and of the impossiblity of being at once fully and vividly aware of certain kinds of information. As to the amount of information, it seems any being who was simultaneously fully and vividly aware of all of her possible options would not *be* a human being, and thus would not be the identical fully-informed "self" for any human being. Nor is it clear that any being could have a complete and simultaneous grasp of certain kinds of experiences. No one who knows what it is like to have deep compassion for other human beings could be also fully and vividly aware of what it is like to take delight in the sufferings of others, one might think. So, it seems that no human being could fully grasp the amount and kinds of information relevant to human choices.

Secondly, it seems that any person who could experience delight at the sufferings of others would not be the kind of person whose advice we would want to take. In general, persons reared differently will have different perspectives and different reactions (like sorrow or delight) in otherwise similar circumstances (like witnessing the suffering of others). The hope of ideal advisor theories is to characterize some fully-informed state which will neutralize the effects of those differences. But the nature of past experiences seems, at least generally, to affect the way one reacts to any future set of experiences, including (were it possible) all experiences considered nearly at once. So the desires emerging from exposure to full information would be different for a person were she to have undergone one formation rather than another. Such desires would retain the incommensurability which appeal to the notion of full information was intended to eliminate.

---

[8]See the papers by Sobel, Rosati, and Loeb.

Ideal advisor versions of full-information theory attempt to specify some single neutral and authoritative set of information conditions such that the desires of persons in those conditions for their real-world counterparts would constitute the good for their less knowledgeable selves. These attempts have been judged by reluctant critics of full-information theory to have run into a blind alley.

Differences Among These Three Approaches

Three different approaches to understanding nonmoral good have thus far been sketched, each one corresponding to an initial emphasis on a different component of human action: natural law approaches to an initial emphasis on the role of reason, informed-desire to inclination, and communitarian to the proximate causes of these two components. Nothing said here shows that these approaches are ultimately incompatible with one another. Yet each approach can be developed in ways whch focus on the role of one component to such an extent that inadequate attention is given to one or both of the remaining components. Rival accounts of nonmoral good will emerge from such unbalanced emphases. Three approaches have been sketched in just such an unbalanced manner for the purposes of illustration, and the resulting conflicts among them can be seen in three areas: regarding the source of knowledge of nonmoral good, the scope of judgments about it, and the motivational force of those judgments.

On the natural law approach sketched above, human nature determines the character of human good, and all rational human beings have cognitive access to that character through the introspection which reason affords. Community life may be needed to attain a full measure of rationality and is surely needed to achieve the goods revealed to rational persons through introspection. On the communitarian approach, however, community life plays a deeper role. For that approach insists that it is not human nature but rather concrete social life which determines the character of the good for members of a community. Members depend on life in community not only in the ways the natural law approach would admit but also for the kind of specific education which enables maturity in that community and adequate knowledge of the good for mature members of that community. The ideal advisor approach differs from each of the previous two in insisting that the good for any given human being is determined not by human nature nor by the character of social life but instead by each human being's own dispositional properties to incline in certain ways were each fully rational and in fully-informed circumstances. Community life is necessary for the actualization of those circumstances—for scientific progress and education, at least—but it does not determine the character of the good for human beings other than by providing or restricting the range of options for individual choice. So, for knowledge of the good, the natural law approach seems to suggest introspection; the communitarian approach, formation to maturity in one's own mode of community life; and the ideal advisor approach, an education toward that fully-informed and impartial perspective which is taken as the ideal of all rational inquiry.

The judgments about nonmoral good which result from these diverse kinds of procedures for acquiring knowledge of it are likely to differ from one another with respect to the scope of their applicability. Judgments about the requirements of human nature arrived at through introspection will be universal in scope: if knowledge, friendship, and the like are goods for any human being, they are goods for all human beings, insofar as they are a function of the human nature which all human beings share. On a communitarian approach, however, the judgments about the good made by mature members of a given community will apply (at best) only to members of that community, since those judgments represent the best advice which the most experienced members of that community have for succeeding in their particular mode of life. (Mature members of a given community may recognize some range of diverse roads to maturity suitable for persons of different temperament, and so the scope of at least some of their judgments about nonmoral good may be narrower than community-wide.)

For the ideal advisor theorist, judgments about nonmoral good are at their foundation restricted in scope to the individual agent's own good, since the desires of each fully-informed and rational individual are taken as normative. It may be possible, on this view, to arrive at tentative conclusions about what is good for any member of a given community or for all human beings. But all judgments about nonmoral good which apply to more than single individuals would have a derivative character, resting upon empirical observation of what a range of individual human beings actually desire in conditions maximally approximating ideal conditions. Thus, while natural law approaches yield judgments about nonmoral good which are immediately universal in scope, communitarian approaches yield judgments whose scope is communitarian, and ideal advisor approaches yield judgments which apply primarily only to single individuals.

The ideal advisor approach is intended to establish a clear motivational link between nonmoral goods and the individual human beings whose goods they are. The motivational link between an individual and his or her nonmoral good considered along ideal advisor lines can be expressed this way: "This is exactly what you yourself would choose, were you fully aware of exactly that information which you yourself would deem relevant to this choice." The parallel expression of motivation for communitarian approaches is this: "This is exactly what you yourself would want, were you to be formed to maturity in the mode of community life in which you actually live." There is an important difference between ideal advisor and communitarian expressions of the motivational link. Human beings naturally incline toward information about their options, but they do not (so obviously, at least) naturally incline toward participation in whichever mode of community life they find themselves. The question "why should I seek information about my options?" falls flat, whereas the question "why should I be formed to maturity in the community in which I live?" may capture a genuine concern for some human beings. Persons content to continue in their current mode of community life would perhaps be motivated by knowledge about how they would choose as mature members of that community, but persons not so content would perhaps not.

The expression capturing the same motivational connection for natural law approaches—"this is exactly what you yourself would want," etc.—is more difficult to isolate: "were I to fulfill my human nature," perhaps. Once it is noticed that the dimensions of human fulfillment can come into conflict, no description of some general area of activity will seem to have motivational force for human beings other than in an "other things being equal" sense: "I will pursue the good of knowledge, unless I have to let my family starve to do it." So, the ideal advisor approach seems to offer the clearest connection between judgments about nonmoral good and human motivation; the communitarian approach seems to offer a firm connection for some kinds of persons; the natural law approach suggests only a *prima facie* connection.

Three approaches to nonmoral good have thus far been sketched, each introduced as arising from initial consideration of a different feature of human action. The approaches suggested by each of these three different initial considerations point as they mature to accounts of nonmoral good which conflict with respect to knowledge of the good, the scope of judgments about the good, and the motivational force of such judgments. Yet it is far from clear that merely beginning from reflections on different features of human action must drive the accounts built on those reflections to lasting conflict. In the following section, the approach building upon reflection on human inclination and leading to full-information informed-desire accounts will be developed in a way incorporating key features of natural law and communitarian approaches. In developing the informed-desire approach in this way, its turn toward ideal advisor theory will seem a mistake, and the resulting view will be no less a natural law and a communitarian position than a full-information informed-desire account.

II

The chief difficulties for ideal advisor theory have been presented as twofold: given the amount and kinds of information relevant to human choices, the notion of a fully-informed human being seems incoherent; given the effects of past experiences on a person's perspective, the desires which would emerge from exposure to full information would be in any case incommensurable. It is in the development of solutions for these difficulties that the informed-desire, communitarian, and natural law approaches to nonmoral good can be reconciled.

The problem presented by the vast amount of experiential information relevant to our practical judgments can be mitigated in part by analysis. The good can be analyzed as roughly that which would be chosen over any—rather than over all—of its competing options were each pair fully known. This strategy of pairing options for comparison eliminates the need for reference to some impossible single instance of immediate cognitive awareness of all relevant information about all options. Yet it is not clear that postulating an enormously long series of consecutive cognitive comparisons between pairs of options by a single agent is more within reach of human cognitive capacity than is instantaneous practical omniscience. Ideal advisor theory has sought to link the choices of each human agent to all relevant information solely through idealized cognitive contact between the individual agent and that information; this is a first area in which a successful full-information account must depart from an ideal advisor approach.

It is possible that other people who are themselves in cognitive contact with information about an agent's options can shape that agent's choices through intentional arrangement of the circumstances within which that agent's choices are made. Parents, for example, instill a habit of truth-telling in their children through the placement of a system of rewards and disincentives which intentionally mirror the positive and negative consequences which children will later learn truth-regarding speech to have. Many parents believe that the habit of truth-telling is what their children would prefer to have acquired, were they to come to experience what these parents already have experienced about truth-regarding speech.

To reasonably intend benefit to their children by cultivating in them the habit of honesty, parents require as resources not only the craft of shaping children's perceptions so as to guide their children's choices—the craft of child-rearing—but also at least rough varieties of historical awareness and of a philosophy of nature. Parents require some access to knowledge of how a range of other human beings have reacted to a spectrum of experiences related to truth-telling; this is a kind of historical awareness. They must have grounds, moreover, for assuming that their own children are relevantly similar to the human beings included in that knowledge base, that the circumstances their children will encounter are known in relevant respects, and that those circumstances are similar, again in relevant respects, to the circumstances in which parents have observed the behavior of other human beings regarding truth-telling. These grounds are part of a working philosophy of nature: a theory of human nature and of human circumstances.

Relying on these resources, parents attempt to link their children's choices and resulting characters to more information about their children's options than that with which their children are in cognitive contact. But as much as they might like to be, no parents are themselves aware of all the information relevant to their children's choices; to suppose that they were would be to try to solve the information problem merely by pushing it back a generation. Yet a child raised by an intelligent and concerned parent may have her choices intentionally linked, if not to all relevant information, at least to more information than the child could have acquired on her own. Of course, some of that benefit is transmitted through cognitive channels: through story-telling, example, advice, etc. But some benefits come not through what a child experiences, but rather through what she does not experience.

Step-saving omission of options can be prompted by a wealth of experience and yet produce benefits which take none of the child's time to accrue. An analogy with technology is apt. The contemporary consumer, faced with the problem of reproducing high-quality sound, can by visiting an audio showroom encounter a range of options all of which are far beyond what a person in a technologically less advanced society could ever hope to produce by way of solutions to that problem. The hours of investigation of the properties of materials, theories of electricity and of sound which went into the production of the applications of technology presented to the consumer as options are together beyond the capacity of a single human being. Yet the length of time required for the consumer to make a successful choice is simply independent of the time spent developing the technology. In a similar way a child brought up in a given political order, taught a given language, initiated into a given form of liturgy, exposed to a given curriculum, and in general introduced to a given variety of activities in a certain order may choose from among the options presented in these contexts in ways which are causally linked to an indefinitely large pool of human experiences. Yet she may do so without herself being aware of those experiences. This possibility of noncognitive contact between agents and information about their options suggests, as an alternative to ideal advisor theory, an Ideal Tradition approach. How, or what could an "ideal tradition" be?

To perform a function analogous to that for which the notion of ideal advisor was created—to provide a theoretical link between the desires an agent has and full-information about his or her options— an ideal tradition would at the very least have to ground the kind of assumptions which ordinary parents were described as making in the rearing of their children. An ideal tradition must provide its members with reasons for supposing that it is a source of knowledge about how any and all of its members would choose in a variety of adequately-informed circumstances. The mature members of an ideal tradition would have knowledge of what those actual experiences have been, a kind of historical awareness. From their knowledge of these experiences, the mature members of an ideal tradition would have formulated an account of the nature of human beings and human circumstances—a philosophy of nature—grounding both a measure of successful prediction of the behavior of all of their members in future circumstances, as well as reasoned accounts of how their members would behave in other counterfactual circumstances. This philosophy of nature can be tested, refined, and confirmed or falsified in the track record of the tradition's success in forming its members to maturity and in maintaining their allegiance to the tradition as they encounter other ways to live, thereby adding to the tradition's store of practical wisdom.

This engagement of the mature members of an ideal tradition with a variety of other ways to live, the source of tradition-enriching experience, is also a source of tradition-sharpening challenge. For among these other and different ways to live are memberships in other communities, different traditions with different histories and rival accounts of human beings and their world. This diversity of rival perspectives raises at the level of community the same relativism-of-perspectives problem which ideal advisor theorists encounter at the level of the individual. Even given the success of a tradition in forming and predicting the behavior of its own members—and it might well fail at this—it remains possible that those same members might have behaved differently in otherwise similar circumstances had they received a different formation. Any formation they have received connects the members of a tradition with a particular set of circumstances as experienced by a particular and finite set of human beings who have themselves been formed in some particular way. But there are other sets of circumstances which other sets of persons, nurtured by different formations, have, might have, or might yet have experienced. All perspectives, all communities, regardless of the richness of their store of practical wisdom, are particular; each has a particular and different effect on the ways their members experience the world and react to it. Whose account of maturity—that is to say, which mode of community life—is normative for defining the good for any or all human beings?

The full-information informed-desire approach to nonmoral good suggests a fully-informed comparison of rival traditions as a way to approach the relativism-of-perspectives problem, where the good for any individual is to be defined by her own inclinations as she emerges from such a comparison. That tradition which would be chosen over any of its rivals in fully-informed choice scenarios would have claim to being the best tradition for the human being who chose it. Yet the relativism-of-perspective problem is easily reformulated for fully-informed choice between pairs of rival traditions. For any two traditions, there are always at least two pathways to full information. A person can be formed to maturity, first, in one tradition, and then to the kind of imaginative maturity which MacIntyre calls "second first-language competency" in the second, or vice-versa. There are, in effect, at least two incompatible sets of full information for every pair of rival traditions, since there are at least two different sets of experience, two different formations, which lead to that fully-informed state.

It is possible that a given individual might choose the same tradition of a pair regardless of which tradition first formed him or her to maturity. Narrative history of full-information encounters between rival traditions—history recounting the deliberations and choices of persons formed to maturity in one tradition and to imaginative maturity in a second—is the locus of evidence bearing on which tradition or traditions human beings would choose if fully informed. Yet such a tradition may indicate that persons in a fully-informed comparison of a pair of traditions would judge differently, depending on which tradition first formed them to maturity; traditions may be incommensurable in this sense. This latter possiblity suggests something about the aim of rational inquiry in any tradition claiming to be ideal, as well as about the nature of the practical wisdom which would have to be stored in such a tradition.

To help its members rationally adjudicate between rival traditions they may encounter, as well as to preserve itself as a tradition while enlarging the pool of experience upon which it draws, an ideal tradition will aim to establish asymmetry between itself and its rivals, asymmetry which can be importantly threefold. A successful tradition will develop resources to characterize the life and thought of rival traditions not only in its rival's own terms—enabling its members to achieve second first-language competency in rival traditions—but also in terms of its own categories. The successful tradition will, moreover, generate an explanation in its own terms of problems internal to its rival traditions, both those which are recognized as such by the mature members of those rival traditions, as well as those which are not. Thirdly, the successful tradition will marshal these resources of characterization and explanation to develop strategies for persuading the mature members of rival traditions of its superiority over those rivals. This persuasion will involve translating the power of the superior tradition's own understanding of those problems recognized by the mature members of rival traditions as internal to those traditions into terms which retain a measure of persuasive force for persons formed to maturity in those rival traditions.

It is possible that one tradition might succeed in establishing asymmetry between itself and any rival tradition at the first, the second, or even only at the third of these levels of characterization, explanation, and persuasion. In so doing, a tradition will be gathering resources for demonstrating its rational superiority over its rivals both to its own members on one set of criteria, and to members formed to maturity in rival traditions on a different set of criteria. A tradition which accumulates in its store of practical wisdom the resources for converting to it a range of mature members from a range of rival traditions in fully-informed choice scenarios, as well as for maintaining the allegiance of a range of its own mature members in similar fully-informed circumstances, would have claim to being objectively preferred by fully-informed human beings—to being better for human beings—than the rival traditions with which it has undergone such comparison. Rational agreement would have been achieved without neutrality of standards.[9] This strategy of achieving rational decidability without eliminating incommensurability is a second major departure from ideal advisor theory on the road to a successful full-information informed-desire account of nonmoral good.

The major difficulties facing full-information informed-desire theory in its ideal advisor incarnation were presented as twofold: first, the notion of full information seemed incoherent, due to the amount and kinds of information relevant to human choices; secondly, the desires elicited from exposure to full information would in any case be incommensurable, due to the effect which rival formations have on human perspectives. This second difficulty may yield to the possibility of non-neutral rational agreement between mature members of nonetheless incommensurable traditions. The first difficulty, insofar as it is grounded in the amount of information relevant to rational choice, may yield to the possiblity of the kind of noncognitive formation afforded by certain kinds of community. What remains is the alleged

---

[9]"And it is of course this very same conception of reason that the genealogist rejects, so that genealogist and encyclopedist agree in framing what they take to be both exclusive and exhaustive alternatives: *Either* reason is thus impersonal, universal, and disinterested *or* it is the unwitting represenation of particular interests, masking their drive to power by its false pretensions to neutrality and disinterestedness. What this alternative conceals from view is a third possibility, the possibility that reason can only move toward being genuinely universal and impersonal insofar as it is neither neutral nor disinterested, that membership in a particular type of moral community, one from which fundamental dissent has to be excluded in a particular type of moral community, one from which fundamental dissent has to be excluded, is a condition for genuinely rational inquiry. . . ." Alasdair MacIntyre, *Three Rival Versions of Moral Enquiry* (Notre Dame, Indiana: University of Notre Dame Press, 1990), pp. 59–60.

incoherence of the notion of full information grounded in the difficulty of combining certain kinds of information.

Imagine a tradition which developed a highly refined mode of life centering around a ritual which was held in secret and which required participation in, say, human sacrifice for admission. Could a mature member of a Christian tradition achieve second first-language competency in such a tradition? Probably not. The impossibility of a single individual having simultaneously full and vivid appreciation of such rival modes of human life may well count against the coherence of the kind of practical omniscience described by ideal advisor theorists, perhaps a redundant mortal wound. For the full knowledge in terms of which a person's good is defined is for ideal advisor theorists cast in terms of how a person would choose in light of a complete and fully vivid grasp of simultaneously all relevant information, and it is likely that no such complete grasp is possible for some pairs of options.

In a parallel fashion ideal tradition theory must admit that second first-language competency in certain kinds of traditions may be incompatible with mature membership in certain other kinds of traditions. But the impact of that admission is different for ideal tradition theory that it would be for ideal advisor theory. Full knowledge on an ideal tradition approach must be understood not in terms of any idealized experience by a single person, but rather in terms of the successive experiences of a number of persons whose reactions in given circumstances are thought to be similar within a range indicated by a theory of human nature and human circumstances. Such a theory of human nature can in principle enable prediction of how a given human being would choose in each of a pair of circumstances which could not both obtain in the life of a single person, just as such a theory can and does enable prediction of how a given human being's body would undergo physical changes in each of a pair of circumstances which could not both obtain in the life of a single person. A person's being burned to death is incompatible with the same person's being frozen to death, and yet we affirm the untestable hypothesis that the same human being could die either way. We affirm this because we have a theory of kinds from which we infer that one human being's being frozen to death is indicative of what would have been the burn victim's fate in relevantly similar circumstances. Just so, a theory of human nature could in principle enable the prediction that just as one human being was persuaded away from a given tradition with a given set of considerations, so would another person have been similarly persuaded, even though that person's membership in a given tradition precludes the direct testing of that prediction. These kinds of problems deserve more precise formulation and more careful response. But enough has been said to make it plausible that an ideal tradition approach to these problems is considerably different and more promising than that of ideal advisor theory.

It seems, then, that full-information informed-desire theory can overcome its major weaknesses by abandoning some of its traditional assumptions and employing resources drawn from natural law and communitarian approaches. The difficulties concerning the coherency of the notion of full information and the incommensurability of perspectives can be resolved by abandoning reference to the ideal of a neutral and practically-omniscient perspective and substituting for it the ideal of non-neutral and practically-achievable maturity in an ideal tradition. A tradition is an ideal tradition insofar as it is equipped with a narrative history, a philosophy of nature, and the resources necessary to defend them successfully in dialectical engagement with conflicting accounts offered by any rival tradition. Maturity in such a tradition is the closest to ideal advisor status that human beings can hope to obtain.

III

The view which emerges from the importing of natural law and communitarian resources for the resolution of the central problems facing full-information theory is as much a natural law and communitarian theory as it is an informed-desire approach. The ideal tradition theory is a natural law approach insofar as its aim is to articulate a theory of human nature which correctly identifies universal human tendencies toward a range of ends. Mature inhabitants of any ideal tradition would be able to explain whatever measure there is of universal human agreement about human goods as a manifestation of these universal human tendencies, and can offer some account of *synderesis* as the ground of the universal human recognition of these ends as ends. But the ideal tradition approach avoids the thinness of some natural law accounts of the human good by insisting both that the ends which *synderesis* reveals require clarification and prioritization by prudence, and that the demands of prudence are not universally accessible but rather are more or less so in various forms of social life. Ideal tradition is thus communitarian in its insistence on the importance of certain kinds of community life for gathering, storing, and transmitting practical wisdom. Yet its natural law resources have been shown to arm ideal tradition theory to confront relativism and resourcelessness in the face of intra-community assessment.[10] Finally, because the theory of human nature to which the ideal tradition would appeal would be falsified insofar as it ultimately failed to account for the behavior of even a single human being, the goods specified by that theory are good only insofar as they would have motivational force for any human being with any prior formation were those persons to undergo a full-information comparison of the ideal tradition with any other, and subsequently be formed to maturity in the ideal tradition they would have chosen. Thus, ideal tradition theory is a full-information informed-desire theory, one which preserves the epistemic and internalist virtues of such approaches without succumbing to the incoherence and relativism with which ideal advisor theories stand accused.

So the ideal tradition approach is at the same time a natural law, communitarian, and full-information informed-desire approach, one which shows promise for preserving the resources and avoiding the difficulties of each of the three approaches; these approaches to nonmoral goodness turn out not to be rivals after all. As each approach was seen to emerge from consideration of apprehension, appetite, and their proximate causal influences respectively, they seemed to suggest conflicting implications regarding knowledge of the good, the scope of judgments about it, and the motivational force of those judgments. Yet the ideal tradition approach has the resources to resolve these apparent conflicts by distinguishing their elements and uniting them in a coherent account.

Ideal tradition theory affirms that knowlege of basic human goods can be achieved through introspection. But knowledge of *the* human good—a unified life within which the basic goods are organized and prioritized in a way toward which any human being from any background would incline were she formed to maturity in the ideal tradition—requires participation in a certain form of community life, a life characterized by a shared philosophy of nature and a common

---

[10]Whether relatvism can be overcome is an empirical question on this view; for all we know it is possible that some tradition can demonstrate the kind of asymmetrical resourcefulness described herein, but only in history can evidence be gathered that any such tradition remains a candidate to be actually such.

awareness of the history of their tradition. Education in such a community does not aim at a neutral outcome. But it does aim at forming human beings whose perspective is objectively and demonstrably superior to any other human perspective for any other human beings, even while there is no universally persuasive way of accomplishing that demonstration.

The judgments about the good made by human beings formed to maturity in that tradition will be universal in scope insofar as the theory of human nature and of human circumstances internal to that tradition identifies a range of common human dispositions to choose in various ways under various fully-informed circumstances. Among these common dispositions will be those toward mature membership in this ideal tradition. But circumstances consisting in different upbringings and relevant genetic differences will impact both the way any human being would be persuaded to inhabit the ideal tradition, as well as the way he or she would live out mature membership in it. So, some judgments about the good will be universal in scope, some will be kind-of-person- or kind-of-circumstance-specific, and some will be applicable only to particular individuals or sets of circumstances.

There will, of course, be judgments about the good which are general and have at best *prima facie* motivational force for anyone. But all-things-considered judgments about a given person's good will have actual and all-things-considered motivational force for her if she is formed to maturity within the ideal tradition. Moreover, insofar as that tradition has proven it can live up to its promise to be able to overcome all rival traditions in dialectical engagement, it contains in its store of practical wisdom the various resources needed to persuade any person from any perspective who enters into a full-information comparison of the ideal tradition with any other perspective. Thus, the ideal tradition's claims about what is universally good for human beings will have dispositional motivational force for all human beings.

This ideal tradition account of how the good is known and of the scope and motivational force of various judgments about it is just a promissory sketch. Yet enough has been presented to render plausible the claim that the ideal tradition approach to nonmoral good is a promising candidate in a field which has been noteworthy for its lack of a front-runner. The ideal tradition approach is, of course, very much like the view of the good which Alasdair MacIntyre ascribes to St. Thomas. How much so is a question which must remain for another occasion.

Tradition as "Bearer of Reason" in Alasdair MacIntyre's Moral Inquiry

Alice Ramos

Introduction

Alasdair MacIntyre rightly notes that the conception of rationality and truth as embodied in tradition-constituted inquiry is at odds with the Cartesian account of rationality. Descartes's description of his epistemological crisis is such that its starting point—a radical doubt—lacks all reference to a background of well-founded beliefs; Descartes thus starts from the assumption that he knows nothing until the moment in which he can discover a first principle, with no presuppositions, on which everything else can be founded.[1] Descartes's doubt is to be, in MacIntyre's own terms, a "contextless doubt."[2] As MacIntyre describes Descartes's enterprise, it is evident, however, that it is doomed to failure, for a radical doubt would dissociate Descartes from language and from a tradition from which he had inherited his epistemological ideals. According to MacIntyre,

> To say to oneself or to someone else "Doubt all your beliefs here and now" without reference to historical or autobiographical context is not

---

[1]Alasdair MacIntyre, "Epistemological Crises, Dramatic Narrative, and the Philosophy of Science," in Gary Gutting, *Paradigms and Revolutions* (Notre Dame, Indiana: University of Notre Dame Press, 1980), p. 59.

[2]*Ibid.*

meaningless; but it is an invitation not to philosophy, but to mental breakdown, or rather to philosophy as a means of mental breakdown. Descartes concealed from himself . . . an unacknowledged background of beliefs which rendered what he was doing intelligible to himself and to others.[3]

It is this reference to a historical context or tradition which accounts for the intelligibility of one's story, of one's narrative, in the search for truth. To put one's whole background of beliefs also into question is to render one's story totally unintelligible to oneself and to others. An example of this is Hume's radical skepticism, which as MacIntyre describes it, may be termed a first-person epistemological project.[4] If tradition then is precisely the context which renders argumentation intelligible, then a separation from tradition will constitute an impoverishment of rational inquiry. The displacement of tradition will not therefore lead, as was once thought, to greater enlightenment, but rather to the darkness of irrationalism. This has been proven not only in the epistemological realm, but also in the area of ethics which concerns us here. The Enlightenment project of morality has exalted the ideal of universality and autonomy, and displaced authority and tradition. The Kantian solution to morality, like the Cartesian solution to epistemology, has failed, and with these failures, we have witnessed the degeneration of our moral and intellectual traditions. In order to transcend the Enlightenment project of morality, MacIntyre draws upon the resources of the Aristotelian-Thomistic moral tradition.

My purpose in this paper is to focus first briefly on MacIntyre's return to the Thomistic tradition, which he does in an innovative way, for according to MacIntyre himself, the recovery of a tradition can sometimes only be made possible through "a revolutionary reconstitution."[5] The latter is realized by MacIntyre through an approach or methodology which he terms "unThomistic." I will then turn to the theistic version of classical morality, which in the Thomistic tradition is seen as complementing and enriching the Aristotelian

---

[3]*Ibid.*, p. 63.

[4]Alasdair MacIntyre, *First Principles, Final Ends and Contemporary Philosophical Issues*, The Aquinas Lecture (Milwaukee, Wisconsin: Marquette University Press, 1990), p. 12.

[5]"Alasdair MacIntyre, "Epistemological Crises, Dramatic Narrative, and Philosophy of Science," in Gary Gutting, *Paradigms and Revolutions* (Notre Dame, Indiana: University of Notre Dame Press, 1980), p. 63.

framework. What I wish to emphasize is that Kant's ethical construction has its roots in deviations from the Thomistic moral tradition, and that new theologians themselves, in debt to Kant's secularized rational moral theology, are in effect in a traditionless state. MacIntyre's return to Thomism shows that when moral rules and laws are placed within their proper context, they are retrieved from irrationalism and thus acquire once again their eminently reasonable character.

A Return to Thomism:
A Theistic Version of Classical Morality

If it is true that some of MacIntyre's critics find him unThomistic, although they do recognize his attempt to defend Thomism, it is also true that MacIntyre himself does not wish to present his arguments in a Thomistic way. Too much has happened in the history of philosophy to think that a revival of Thomism can occur in a traditionally systematic Thomistic fashion. In speaking about the contemporary rejection of the concept of a first principle, MacIntyre notes that this question cannot be addressed solely with the resources provided by Aquinas and his predecessors:

> It seems that, if this central Aristotelian and Thomistic concept is to be effectively defended, in key part it will have to be by drawing upon philosophical resources which are themselves—at least at first sight—as alien to, or almost as alien to, Thomism as are the theses and arguments which have been deployed against it. We inhabit a time in the history of philosophy in which Thomism can only develop adequate responses to the rejections of its central positions in what must seem initially at least to be unthomistic ways.[6]

Now, these unthomistic means to which MacIntyre resorts are similar to what Nietzsche called a genealogy. The genealogical narrative has as its purpose that of disclosing something about the activities, beliefs, and presuppositions of some class of persons. It normally explains how they have come to be in a type of predicament which they cannot explain out of their own conceptual resources. Genealogy provides, according to MacIntyre, "a subversive history."[7] As is known, Nietzsche

---

[6]Alasdair MacIntyre, *First Principles, Final Ends and Contemporary Philosophical Issues*, The Aquinas Lecture (Milwaukee, Wisconsin: Marquette University Press, 1990), p. 2.

[7]*Ibid.*, p. 57.

"used genealogy as an assault upon theological beliefs which Thomists share with other Christians and upon philosophical positions which Aristotelians share with other philosophers."[8] To thus adopt the methods of genealogical narrative is certainly to have recourse to un-Thomistic means. But as MacIntyre sees it, these are to be put to the service of Thomistic ends, for what his own genealogical construction reveals is that "the predicaments of contemporary philosophy, whether analytic or deconstructive, are best understood as a long-term consequence of the rejection of Aristotelian and Thomistic teleology at the threshold of the modern world."[9] So, whether in the epistemological or moral realms, what MacIntyre sees as missing within contemporary inquiry is the teleological scheme.

For those who have read *After Virtue*, this comes as no surprise. MacIntyre's chapter on why the Enlightenment project of justifying morality had to fail pinpoints the rejection of the teleological view of human nature as the reason why the whole project of morality in the modern age becomes unintelligible. He cites the Aristotelian teleological scheme, with its contrast between man-as-he-happens-to-be and man-as-he-could-be-if-he-realized-his-essential-nature, and the precepts of rational ethics, which permit the passage from potentiality to act and therefore the realization of man's nature and the attainment of his true end. But MacIntyre also notes that to this scheme was added, without any essential alteration, a framework of theistic beliefs, as the Christian one which is elaborated by Aquinas.[10] So, as MacIntyre presents it, the Christian framework does not alter the Aristotelian scheme but rather complements it and adds to it another dimension, thus enriching it. The theistic version of classical morality presents reason as instructing man with respect to what his true end is and how to reach it. Moreover, while it insists that the precepts of ethics are, as in Aristotelianism, teleological injunctions, it transcends Aristotelianism by affirming that its precepts are also expressions of divine law. In a well-ordered Christian tradition such as that of Thomism, there is no conflict between the obligation imposed by practical reasoning and the obligation imposed on man by divine law. This absence of conflict is implicit in the following:

---

[8]*Ibid.*, p. 58.

[9]*Ibid.*

[10]Alasdair MacIntyre, *After Virtue* (Notre Dame, Indiana: University of Notre Dame Press, 1984, second edition), p. 53.

To say what someone ought to do is at one and the same time to say what course of action will in these circumstances as a matter of fact lead toward a man's true end and to say what the law, ordained by God and comprehended by reason, enjoins. Moral sentences are thus used within this framework to make claims which are true or false. Most medieval proponents of this scheme did of course believe that it was itself part of God's revelation, but also a discovery of reason and rationally defensible.[11]

This area of agreement does not survive. Its extinction, as MacIntyre himself recognizes, was not merely due to the new conception of reason embodied in seventeenth-century philosophy and science, which led to the Enlightenment; but additionally, and perhaps surprisingly, it was due to Protestantism, Jansenist Catholicism, and a Scholasticism that was not Thomistic. Thus, we might say that it was due in part to a Christian tradition that was not well-ordered. What I wish to emphasize here is that the dissociation between theism and morality was not exclusively an Enlightenment or Kantian discovery, but rather that it had its roots in a deviated theistic version of human nature and morality.

If Hume is indeed important for the Enlightenment project of morality, this is so because he comes upon an ethics which has been evacuated of its theistic content and rendered in effect contextless and thus unintelligible. In her essay "Modern Moral Philosophy," which has influenced MacIntyre's own thought, Elizabeth Anscombe says:

Hume discovered the situation in which the notion 'obligation' survived, and the word 'ought' was invested with that peculiar force having which it is said to be used in a 'moral' sense, but in which the belief in divine law had long since been abandoned: for it was substantially given up among Protestants at the end of the Reformation. The situation . . . was the interesting one of the survival of a concept outside the framework of thought that made it a really intelligible one.[12]

Anscombe continues:

They did not deny the existence of divine law; but their most characteristic doctrine was that it was given, not to be obeyed, but to show man's incapacity to obey it, even by grace; and this applied not merely to the

---

[11]*Ibid.*
[12]G. E. M. Anscombe, "Modern Moral Philosophy," *Philosophy*, 33, 1958.

ramified prescriptions of the Torah, but to the requirements of 'natural divine law.'[13]

Anscombe's essay ties morality to religion, and although in *After Virtue* MacIntyre follows to a great extent the Aristotelian tradition of virtue ethics, it is my contention that MacIntyre has an acute interest in the relationship between theism and morality. I will try to show this by reference to some of MacIntyre's earlier writings, as well as to some of his work in the last few years.

A Non-Thomistic Christian Moral Tradition as Precursor of Kant's Ethical Construction

It is well to note first of all that Anscombe's essay dates from 1958, and that in 1967 MacIntyre contributed two essays to the lecture topic, *The Religious Significance of Atheism*, presented at Columbia University, along with Paul Ricoeur. In the first of these two essays, "The Fate of Theism," MacIntyre notes that in an effort to render theism intelligible or perhaps palatable to the secular-minded man, theologians have evacuated theism of its content, and in so doing they have failed in their attempt to have theism accepted by a secular audience.[14] Nineteenth-century theists argued that the loss of theistic belief results in moral collapse; one has only to think of Dostoyevsky's famous phrase: "If God does not exist, then everything is permitted." However, in his second essay "Atheism and Morals," MacIntyre questions the Dostoyevskian contention: "What I am principally concerned with here are the logical connections between belief in God and morality; my contention is that theism itself requires and presupposes both a moral vocabulary which can be understood independently of theistic beliefs, and moral practices which can be justified independently of theistic beliefs."[15] The problem which arises here, according to MacIntyre, is that "we ought to do what God commands, if we are theists, because it is right in some independent sense of 'right,' rather than hold that what God commands is right

---

[13]*Ibid.*

[14]Alasdair MacIntyre, "The Fate of Theism," in *The Religious Significance of Atheism* (New York: Columbia University Press, 1967), pp. 26–29.

[15]Alasdair MacIntyre, "Atheism and Morals," *ibid.*, p. 32.

just because God commands it, a view which depends upon 'right' being defined as 'being in accordance with what God commands'."[16] What MacIntyre wishes to emphasize, and rightfully so, is that man should have *reasons* for doing what is good or right, rather than simply appeal to divine *power* when he obeys divine commandments. "If God's commands are not to be mere fiats backed by arbitrary power then they must, [according to MacIntyre], command actions which can be seen to have [reasonable] point and purpose independent of, and antecedent to, the divine utterance of divine law."[17] The practice of making moral judgments pre-existed the utterance of theistic moral injunctions. These points were especially well understood by many medieval theologians, the most important of which was Aquinas.

For MacIntyre theism requires an independently understood moral vocabulary and independent moral practices, which must be of a certain kind. What theism presupposes and requires morality to be is in effect what morality has been *traditionally* considered to be, and no longer is.

> What morality is required to be by theism and what it usually has been considered to be is a set of rules which are taken as given and are seen as having validity and authority independent of any external values or judgments. It is essential to morality so conceived that we accept the rules wholly and without question. We must not seek rational grounds for accepting them, nor can we decide, on rational grounds, to revise them. . . . When morality is considered in this light, theories about morality are accounts of why the code of moral rules includes the items that it does and no others. Platonic and Aristotelian morality offer theories of this kind. Aristotelianism grounds its explanation in the view that human nature has certain inherent goals, needs, and wants. The cogency of this theoretical explanation depends on the fact that the society which upholds the given moral rules agrees upon a way of life defined in terms of just those goals, wants, and needs.[18]

When morality is thus understood, the theistic framework completes that of a natural morality, in such a way that there is no arbitrariness but rather reinforcement.

---

[16]*Ibid.*, p. 33.
[17]*Ibid.*, p. 35–36.
[18]*Ibid.*, pp. 36–37.

Theism furnishes an explanation for the authority and the fixed character of the rules, both by according them divine status and by providing grounds for the underlying belief in a single determinate human nature. God created men with just those goals, wants, and needs which a way of life embodying the given rules will enable them to achieve. To the natural morality of men theism adds rules concerned with man's supernatural end, and a set of beliefs and practices concerning guilt, repentance, and forgiveness to provide for moral, as well as religious failure. Theism and morality of this kind naturally and easily reinforce one another.[19]

According to MacIntyre, the traditional attitude to moral rules which theism required has decayed, and this decay has been to a great extent prior to the loss of theistic belief, for which reason he holds that a change in the character of morality is in part responsible for the modern man's inability to accept theistic beliefs. The Dostoyevskian contention about the relation between theism and morals is thus inverted. One of the causes that MacIntyre cites for the decay of the traditional attitude to moral rules is the impact of certain versions of Christianity. There is no doubt that MacIntyre sees this deviated Christian tradition as having exercised enormous influence; he refers to it not only in his essay "Atheism and Morals," but also in *Against the Self-Images of the Age*, in *After Virtue*, and in *Three Rival Versions of Moral Enquiry*. The most important culprits here are Protestantism and Jansenist Catholicism. Both these versions of Christianity present a human nature which has been corrupted by original sin; man's will and reason are so depraved that they cannot possibly adhere to the moral law except by the aid of grace. It is not surprising then that justification should become a matter of faith alone. "The consequence of [the Protestant and Jansenist Catholic] view is that from any human standpoint the divine commandments do become arbitrary fiats imposed on us externally; our nature does not summon us to obey them, because we cannot recognize them as being for our good. The motives of hope of eternal reward and fear of eternal punishment then must completely replace temporal motives for morality."[20] Such a theistic framework leaves man morality-less; he no longer recognizes in his nature an internal finality which is not at odds with an external

---

[19]*Ibid.*, p. 38.
[20]*Ibid.*, p. 39.

finality (the good for man is God and the way toward this good is adherence to the natural moral law; in other words, actions in conformity with his nature, which in a theistic framework are seen as God-given). Theism and morality thus become dissociated; theism no longer grounds morality; the two no longer reinforce one another. As a result, secularization ensues. Certain realms of human life become autonomous in their norms because they are not considered to belong to the realm of salvation and damnation, and yet paradoxically success, for example, in the economic realm, is seen as a sign of redemption. The theistic framework then seems to provide for no more than divine arbitrariness. If man considers himself to be one of the elect, then the only restraint put on his actions is external—namely, the threat of punishment.

It was precisely this type of Protestant ethic which was inherited by Kant; it is no wonder then that there should be in Kant a distinction made between phenomenal man, as a creature of nature, led by the desires and goals inherent in his nature, and noumenal man, as the self-determining personality or individual, who is an autonomous moral agent, imposing laws on himself, with no other authority than the self as a rational agent. MacIntyre sees Kant as a coherent analyst of the change which had in part already occurred in the character of morality and of the split between theism and morality. Kant had inherited the Protestant denial of the essential integrity of fallen human nature; in declaring man's autonomy from his nature, moral injunctions have only the authority of each individual's will. Such an ethic is inconsistent with the morality that theism really requires. The only reason why Kant invokes theism is to insure that man will be rewarded for his virtuous living. The effect of "radical evil," as Kant puts it, on man's nature is such that morality cannot possibly be derived from theism, if God is to be considered good.

> [F]or Kant the heterogeneity, the variety, the incompatibility, which mark man's natural goals, needs and wants entail that these can provide us with no stable criteria. He cannot find, as the medieval Aristotelian would, any point or proof for morality in terms of the satisfaction of the needs and wants of a human nature created by God to be of a certain determinate kind.[21]

---

[21]*Ibid.*, p. 42.

Theism is thus relegated to a tenuous position, for, as was suggested above, God is needed only to apportion happiness for man's goodness, in another life.

If there is then no stable criteria to which man can appeal to determine the morality of his actions, since recourse to a single determinate human nature has been abandoned for moral prescriptions which have no authority other than that derived from the autonomous moral agent, it is then not surprising that moral disputes should seem insoluble. As MacIntyre notes: "Theism has lost the morality which it logically presupposed; and the lack of social contact between theism and contemporary morality is at least partly to be explained by the lack of logical connection between theistic beliefs and modern moral belief."[22] If Kant was the coherent and consistent interpreter of a deviated Christian tradition, it would seem that the new theology which has emerged from the radicalization of Kant's own theological construction cannot provide any justification for these rules and thus their adherence to the rules seems "arbitrary and irrational."[23] Traditional Christianity then appears as false and as having been secularized not from without, but rather from within. "The new theism turns out to be in morals as in theology the project of retaining a religious vocabulary emptied of belief-content."[24] If this new theism is in effect a product of the Enlightenment, caused by the rationalism of such thinkers as Kant but also due to the impact, as we have shown, of Protestantism and Jansenist Catholicism, then the Enlightenment's attempt to replace the irrational, traditional world view with a rational, progressive one has indeed been thwarted. What is now apparent is that the rational, progressive world view with its attempt to cut itself off from tradition and all beliefs is in effect an invitation to irrationalism.[25]

Rehabilitation of Tradition: the Thomistic Tradition

It is perhaps this irrationalism which best characterizes the postmodern age and which MacIntyre, along with other philosophers,

---

[22]*Ibid.*, p. 44.

[23]*Ibid.*, p. 46.

[24]*Ibid.*, p. 53.

[25]See Alasdair MacIntyre's discussion of Descartes's rejection of tradition in "Epistemological Crises, Dramatic Narrative, and the Philosophy of Science" in Gary Gutting, *Paradigms and Revolutions* (Notre Dame, Indiana: University of Notre Dame Press, 1980), pp. 59–64.

is trying to supersede, through a rehabilitation of that which has been rejected, namely, tradition. If the Enlightenment pitted tradition against the progress of reason, MacIntyre considers tradition a bearer of reason, for we cannot really understand our actions and our very selves unless the narrative of our life is ultimately embedded within a tradition. The story of our life is accordingly only made intelligible through reference to a tradition.

> A living tradition then is an historically extended, socially embodied argument, and an argument precisely in part about the goods which constitute that tradition. Within a tradition, the pursuit of goods extends through generations, sometimes through many generations. Hence the individual's search for his or her good is generally and characteristically conducted within a context defined by those traditions of which the individual's life is a part, and this is true both of those goods which are internal to practices and of the goods of a single life.[26]

MacIntyre's appeal to tradition in *After Virtue* is thus made in order to provide a context which will render man's actions intelligible. When man seeks for the good or exercises the virtues, he does so not *qua* individual, but rather as the bearer of a particular social identity. To this effect,"What I am, therefore, is in key part what I inherit, a specific past that is present to some degree in my present. I find myself part of a history and that is generally to say, whether I like it or not, whether I recognize it or not, one of the bearers of a tradition."[27]

MacIntyre further elaborates his thoughts on tradition in *Whose Justice? Which Rationality?* Education in the virtues is for MacIntyre what permits one to justify one's actions, and in order to become virtuous, one has to enter into a craft-like tradition, in which one accepts the authority of others, the standards, the rules. In a craft the apprentice learns from the instructor how to apply relatively simple rules: he acquires the disposition to do what the rule prescribes. In a similar manner, in moral education one learns certain rules or truths and one applies them in particular situations; where it is difficult to see if the rule applies to the case, then one has to apply right judgment. The virtuous person does not abide by rules, but rather is the one

---

[26]Alasdair MacIntyre, *After Virtue* (Notre Dame, Indiana: University of Notre Dame Press, 1984), p. 222.

[27]*Ibid.*, p. 221.

who knows how to exercise judgment in particular cases. Because the virtuous man has not only knowledge of the good, but is good himself, he will know what the appropriate course of action should be in a given situation. His practice of virtue informs his desires by reason. But, as MacIntyre insists, one becomes virtuous, rational, by participating in a rational practice based community, and not simply as an autonomous individual. It is thus necessary to establish relationships with persons so as to learn what one's good is; one needs therefore the support and advice of others.

The comparison of moral inquiry or moral education to the craft-like tradition is continued in *Three Rival Versions of Moral Enquiry*, according to which progress in inquiry and in the moral life will be predetermined by the nature of a prior commitment, that is, commitment to a tradition. As in a craft, the apprentice relies on the rational teaching authority of the master, so also in the practice of the "craft" of moral inquiry, a teacher is needed. MacIntyre recognizes that this conception is at odds with that of the encyclopedist and the genealogist: for the former, authority comes from within, whereas for the latter, authority represents the will to power and therefore should be resisted. MacIntyre is presenting the Thomistic tradition as the rational alternative to the encyclopedist and to the genealogist. In Thomism initiation into the moral life is initiation into a tradition, by way of a teacher; both virtue and practical reasoning are acquired within a community, through acceptance of an authority within that community. Since MacIntyre sees Thomism as a synthesis, as it were, of Aristotelianism and of Augustinianism, it is interesting to note MacIntyre's Augustinian-Thomistic side, for when he speaks of acceptance of tradition, of authority, as the way to advance toward the truth and toward perfection or goodness, he observes in an Augustinian way that faith in authority, or faith in tradition, precedes rational understanding. This is certainly reminiscent of Augustine's faith seeking understanding, and it is, in my opinion, in consonance with MacIntyre's own self-description as an Augustinian-Christian.[28] What I believe MacIntyre wishes to emphasize here is that faith in tradition, in authority, is not a blind surrender to the irrational, but

---

[28] Alasdair MacIntyre, *Whose Justice? Which Rationality?* (Notre Dame, Indiana: Notre Dame University Press, 1988), p. 10.

rather a movement toward meaning and truth itself. We can create meaning, advance in the truth, only because meaning and truth are already present. And the acceptance of that meaning and truth is faith. We have to stand in the truth, that is, accept the authority of another, be committed to the truth, in order to understand. Faith thus conceived makes understanding possible; in the last analysis, we could say that faith is a deciding for the truth; this conception of the faith is certainly very different from the Enlightenment stance, in which as we noted above, faith is pitted against reason. Faith here is seen as reasonable, because authority and tradition are bearers of reason, and faith in authority and tradition permits advancement in reasoning or the true progress of reason, that is, man's ever better understanding of the truth, which also advances his own perfection and goodness by the correction of his will.

It seems to me that MacIntyre's work is to a great extent an effort to reconcile in a sense faith and reason, tradition and progress, the particular and the universal. It is for this reason, I believe, that MacIntyre's reference to *Aeterni Patris* in *Three Rival Versions of Moral Enquiry* is particularly fortunate, since this encyclical calls for a return to the scholastic thought of St. Thomas (it is well to note that not all scholastic thinkers are Thomists and that the influence of these non-Thomistic scholastic minds, such as Duns Scotus and William of Ockham, has led to deviations in traditional Christianity and in the Thomistic tradition), in which faith and reason are not antagonistic toward each other. Rather each helps the other so that there is no contradiction: reason is illumined by faith and faith is better understood through reason. It is this effort of reconciliation, of harmonizing, without accomodationisms, which we see in MacIntyre's work. The theistic framework is not something superfluous or extrinsic to the moral framework, as we saw, for example, in Kant. The moral life is not simply for self-perfection, but is rather for the ordering now of man's life to God. God is thus not extrinsic to morality. This was MacIntyre's point when he reversed the Dostoyevskian contention: "If everything is permitted, then God does not exist." In line with this, MacIntyre makes the following observations:

> Modern Catholic protagonists of theories of natural law have sometimes claimed that we can fully understand and obey the natural law without any knowledge of God. But according to Aquinas all the moral precepts of the Old Law, the Mosaic Law summed up in the Ten Commandments, belong

to the natural law, including those which command us as to how we are to regard God and comport ourselves in relation to Him. A knowledge of God is, on Aquinas' view, available to us from the outset of our moral enquiry and plays a crucial part in our progress in that enquiry. And it would be very surprising if this were not so: the unifying framework within which our understanding of ourselves, of each other, and of our shared environment progresses is one in which that understanding, by tracing the sequences of final, formal, efficient, and material causality, always refers us back to a unified first cause from which flows all that is good and all that is true in what we encounter. So in articulating the natural law itself we understand the peculiar character of our own directedness and in understanding the natural law better we move initially from what is evident to any plain person's unclouded moral apprehension to what is evident only or at least much more clearly to the *sapientes*, those whom Aquinas saw as masters of the master-craft (I-IIae 100, I), and to what supernatural revelation discloses. But in so doing we progress or fail to progress, both as members of a community with a particular sacred history, the history of Israel and the church, and as members of communities with secular political histories.[29]

Man does not therefore have, as it were, two finalities, one natural and one supernatural, one known through reason and another known only through faith; man is simply ordered to God, and in our understanding of the natural law, we understand, as MacIntyre puts it, "the peculiar character of our own directedness."

Elsewhere MacIntyre points out that obedience to the natural law is in effect obedience to God; the "ought" of moral obligation, of obedience to God because He commands what is right, is not extrinsic to the "ought" of practical reasoning; in other words, moral obligation is not to be identified as an obligation simply in virtue of the command of another, but rather because of what it enjoins in the doing or achieving of something good.

[T]o know that God commands those precepts of the natural law, in obedience to which one's good is to be realized, gives one no further, additional reason for obedience to those precepts, except insofar as our knowledge of God's unqualified goodness and omniscience gives us reasons for holding

---

[29]Alasdair MacIntyre, *Three Rival Versions of Moral Enquiry* (Notre Dame, Indiana: Notre Dame University Press, 1990), pp. 141–142.

his judgments of our good, as promulgated in the Old and New laws, to be superior to our own. The "ought" of "One ought to obey God" is the same "ought" as the "ought" of "To do so and so is the good of such a one; so such a one ought to do so and so"—the same "ought," that is, as the "ought" of practical reasoning.[30]

MacIntyre's return to the Thomistic tradition shows then the interpenetration of theism and morality. His return to Thomism also emphasizes how the individual moral life is set within a tradition, in which the rational teaching authority of another is accepted so as to progress in truth and in virtue.[31]

---

[30]*Ibid.*, p. 154.

[31]This paper is the result of research initiated during an NEH Summer Seminar for College Teachers at Boston University on the Enlightenment and its twentieth-century critiques.

Ethics and the Turn
to Narrative

Thomas Hibbs

In recent years dissatisfaction with the barren formalism of ethics has led moral philosophers to revitalize their discipline. In the wake of the critique of academic moral philosophy, terms such as "experience" and "narrative" have become pervasive. The emphasis has shifted from analysis to stories, the stories of individuals and communities, even stories of the history of moral philosophy.[1] The impetus behind the turn to narrative has had much to do with a reaction against Kantian ethics. In place of formalism, universality, necessity, and deductive clarity, narratives highlight contingency, particularity, and moral conflict. Often the turn to narrative has coincided with a return to pre-modern moral philosophy and to the literary genre of tragedy. But just how compatible is the turn to narrative with pre-modern ethics, especially Thomistic ethics? There are, I think, many features of narrative ethics that a Thomist can find congenial. The emphasis upon insoluble contract and upon tragedy as the dominant narrative of human life is problematic, however. In what follows I want to sketch the virtues and vices of narrative ethics. As a corrective to certain tendentious features in narrative ethics, I will provide a reading of the narrative structure of Thomas's own writing.

---

[1] Three of the most popular recent books in ethics—Alasdair MacIntyre's *After Virtue*, Martha Nussbaum's *The Fragility of Goodness*, and Charles Taylor's *Sources of the Self*—are works of retrieval and works that focus upon the importance of narrative.

As I noted above, the resurgence of interest in narrative parallels and intersects with a return to experience in ethics.[2] Like "experience," "narrative" is invoked in such a variety of contexts and is used in so loose a manner as to render it devoid of meaning. Given the connection between these terms, Thomas's discussion of experience may prove helpful. The Latin nouns *experientia* and *experimentum* are allied to the deponent verb *experior*, which is passive in form but active in meaning. The verb means "to try, prove, test, or ensure." *Expertus*, the past participle of *experior*, means "tried, proven, or known by experience." That the verb as a deponent is instructive, since the Latin deponent is akin to the Greek middle voice, in which the subject both effects the action and is affected by it. The role of "experience" in the Aristotelian-Thomistic account of human knowing preserves two important features of the etymology of *experior*: first, the characterization of knowing as an undergoing or suffering, as involving both passivity and activity, and, secondly, the claim that knowledge arises from experience as from a dialectical testing or trial of sensible particulars. A return to the Thomistic understanding of *experientia* would help to combat what Charles Taylor has identified as two dominant features of the modern conception of the person: disengaged reason and the punctual self.[3]

Following Aristotle Thomas holds that experience is a necessary but not a sufficient condition of knowledge. Experience results from memory which in turn arises from the perception of sensible particulars. Experience notes similarities and regularities among a related set of singulars; it collates particulars and thus makes them amenable to intellectual insight. Experience remains at the level of particulars; only reason, which grasps the "why," can supply insight into a related set of particulars, an insight that issues in a universal. The route from *senus* through *memoria* and *experimentum* to *ratio* involves what Thomas calls the abstraction of the universal from sensible particulars. It is important to note, however, that the intellect primarily grasps not an abstract universal but the nature of sensible

---

[2] A Previous draft of the section on experience was presented at a session of the Catholic Theological Society of America, June 1992 in Pittsburg.

[3] *Sources of the Self: The Making of the Modern Identity* (Cambridge, Massachusetts: Harvard University Press, 1989), pp. 143–76.

particulars.[4] More generally, Thomas argues that the intellect is a potency made actual through interaction with the sensible world.

Since the embodiment of the soul is natural and perfective, the intellect of rational animals is inoperable apart from sense experience and imagination. Moral knowledge does not, of course, rest in the universal. Its term is a particular; thus it is involved more intimately with experience, as is evident from Aristotle's exclusion of inexperienced youth from the study of moral philosophy.

Experience, then, is the ineliminable starting point of human thinking, and yet Aristotle and Aquinas underscore its limits as well. The insufficiency of experience as a guide in ethics seems to become more pronounced in the move from Aristotle's theory of the virtues to Aquinas's theory of natural law. Does not the universality and necessity of the natural law lie beyond the purview of narrative? This is precisely the objection some Thomists have leveled against MacIntyre's narrative rendering of Aquinas.[5] Concerning the first principles of the natural law, Thomas holds that the most common precepts are grasped by all. But commentators have noticed a gap in Aquinas's account of the natural law, namely, the lack of a discussion of the precepts that would mediate between the most common principles and particular circumstances. There is certainly room for development of the intermediate precepts. Still, the variability and contingency of particular circumstances make application of both primary and intermediate principles difficult. The "more there is descent to proper or particular matters, the more defect is found."[6] Even if the gap in the account of moral precepts can be partly filled by further casuistry, such reasoning must ultimately be put at the service of prudence, which is said to command (*praecipere*) particular actions. By enriching and refining our appreciation of the human condition, narratives can provide

---

[4]*ST.*, I. 84, 7, where Thomas argues that every act of knowing requires conversion to a phantasm. This is necessary not only because of the poverty of the intellect, which needs the assistance of images, but also because the intelligible species is not "truly and completely known unless it is known as existing in the particular" (*cognosci non potest complete et vere, nisi secundum quod cognoscitur ut in particulari existens*). Thomas proceeds to argue that the intelligible species is not the *quid* but the *quo* of knowledge. The intellect primarily and directly knows the nature of the thing (*ST.*, I, 85, 1).

[5]See Robert P. George, "Moral Particularism, Thomism and Tradition," *The Review of Metaphysics* 42 (1989), pp. 593–605.

[6]"Quanto magis ad propria descenditur, tanto magis invenitur defectus," *ST.*, I-II, 94, 4.

a vicarious education in prudence, which is "perfected through memory and through experience to a prompt judgement of particulars."[7]

The connection between reason, experience, and sensible particulars can be assisted or obstructed and is always mediated by passions, habits, customs, and so forth. While Thomas argues that the basic precepts of the natural law are *per se nota* or self-evident, he adds that their evidence presupposes an apprehension of the meaning of the terms. The latter can be grasped only through experience (*ST.* I-II, 94, 2). The ground of the natural law, moreover, is not an abstract set of propositions, but the order of natural inclinations.[8]

The importance of experience and rightly ordered inclination in the account of the natural law points the way to a role for narrative in moral education. Because narratives engage us concretely as whole human beings, not just as intellects, they operate at the level of "sympathy or connaturality," the importance of which needs no defense among those familiar with Maritain. By informing the imagination and addressing the passions, they can help to provide the sort of education that Aristotle describes as the necessary starting point of the good life. "Moral virtue has to do with pleasure and pain. For through pleasure we do base things and through pain we flee noble deeds. Thus it is necessary to have been well brought up from youth . . . so as to delight in and be grieved at the things we ought. For this is the right education."[9] Aristotle returns to this topic in the final book of the *Politics*, where he discusses education in the *polis* and argues that music and poetry have the "power to form character."[10]

The distinction between the *ordo inveniendi*, the order of discovery, and the *ordo demonstrandi*, the order of proof, is germane. Since narratives operate at the level of experience and appeal to our passions, they may well serve to aid us in discovering the precepts as natural inclinations; they may initiate a process of recognizing, recollecting, and reordering our natural inclinations. In Aristotle and Aquinas the appeal to experience is often dialectical in character; it

---

[7]"Perficitur per memoriam, et per experimentum ad prompte iudicandum de particularibus expertis," *ST.*, II-II, 47, 3, ad 3.

[8]Even fundamental precepts, for instance, the one against theft, can be abolished from the human heart "on account of depraved customs and corrupt habits" (*propter pravas consuetudines et habitus corruptos*), *ST.*, I-II, 94, 6.

[9]*Nicomachean Ethics*, 1104b11–13.

[10]*Ibid.*, 1340b13.

seeks to return us to certain features of the phenonema that have been overlooked or remain in need of explanation. Stories may not provide demonstrations, but they can be of assistance as dialectical starting points for moral reflection. If narratives are to be tools of criticism and appraisal, they must be open to dialectical engagement. The most illuminating narratives provoke inquiry.

While the turn to narrative has often been motivated by a repudiation of rational discourse, it has also been motivated by the desire to find more adequate philosophic means of understanding moral knowledge and action. In their introduction to an anthology entitled *Why Narrative?*, Stanley Hauerwas and L. Gregory Jones trace the turn to narrative to a "recognition that rationality, methods of argument, and historical explanation have, at least to some extent, a fundamentally narrative form."[11] From a Thomistic perspective the turn offers a welcome corrective to certain tendencies in modern ethics. Narrative accounts of human action underscore the complexity of human action and link the intelligibility of particular actions not just to intentions or consequences, but also to the habits, characters, and histories of individuals and communities. As Martha Nussbaum puts it,

> A whole tragic drama, unlike a schematic philosophical example . . . , is capable of tracing the history of a complex pattern of deliberation, showing its roots in a way of life and looking forward to its consequences in that life. As it does all of this, it lays open to view the complexity, the indeterminacy, the sheer difficulty of actual human deliberation.[12]

There is yet another reason to think that the turn to narrative might be auspicious for Aquinas's ethics. It is well known that modern moral and political thought involves a decisive rejection of classical philosophy; what is less appreciated is the simultaneous subordination of poetry to so-called historical fact. Machiavelli accentuates the gap between "how one lives and how one ought to live" and repudiates "imagined republics" in favor of the "effectual truth" of history.[13] Hobbes ties political philosophy to history, which he calls "knowledge

---

[11]*Why Narrative? Readings in Narrative Theology* (Grand Rapids, Michigan: Eerdmans, 1989), p. 4.

[12]Martha Nussbaum, *Fragility*, p. 14.

[13]*The Prince*, trans. De Alvarez (Irving, Texas: University of Dallas Press, 1980), p. 93.

of fact."[14] But what is the significance of the preference for history? An initial answer can be had from Aristotle's remark in the *Poetics* that, while the historian describes what "has come to be," the poet describes "the sort of thing that might come to be." He continues, "Thus poetry is more philosophic and of graver import than history." For its statements are "more of the nature of universals," while those of history are "according to particulars." The tradition of viewing poetry in this way stretches from Aristotle to Philip Sidney's *Defense of Poesy*. In the latter work, poetry is said to have as its goal "to lead us to as high a perfection as our degenerate souls can be capable of." The poet does this by describing nature not just as it is but as it might be if it were to achieve the excellences of which it is capable. Poetry has the ability to mediate between the universal and the particular; as Sidney puts it, the poet "couples the general notion with the particular example."[15]

Two characteristics of poetry—as having to with universals and as serving the attainment of human perfection—run counter to the dominant early modern views of knowledge and of human nature. Poetry is open to the dimension of depth in the human person, to the often unrealized but latent capacities for moral excellence.[16] Thus, a return to narrative, as understood in Aristotle and Sidney, is an implicit return to a teleological understanding of human nature.[17] As Alasdair MacIntyre puts it: "In what does the unity of an individual life consist? The answer is that its unity is the unity of a narrative embodied in a single life. To ask 'What is the good for me?' is to ask how best I might live out that unity and bring it to completion. To ask 'What is the good for man?' is to ask what all answers to the former question must have in common."[18]

---

[14]*Leviathan*, ed. Michael Oakeshott (New York: MacMillan Press, 1962), p. 69.

[15]*Sir Phillip Sidney: Selected Prose and Poetry*, ed. R. Kimbrough (Madison, Wisconsin: University of Wisconsin Press, 1983).

[16]The problem of whether "ought" can be derived from "is" pre-dates Hume; it can be traced to the early modern preference for historical fact. Admittedly, the turn to narrative will not resolve all the questions concerning the debate. But it does return us to an often forgotten fact, namely, that the descriptive and evaluative are inextricably bound in our ordinary language.

[17]I am grateful to Deal Hudson for pointing out this connection to me.

[18]Alasdair MacIntyre, *After Virtue*, p. 203. In *After Virtue*, MacIntyre develops an account of social teleology as a substitute for what he oddly calls the "metaphysical biology" of Aristotle. In this work MacIntyre does not see that his persistent use of teleological language and of the language of potency and act needs some sort of natural teleology. In *Three Rival Versions of*

Is it mere coincidence that the quest for human excellence survives in literature long after it has been ostracized by the philosophers? Sidney describes poetry as "a speaking picture, with this end,—to teach and delight." But one might object that this view of the poet's goal is misleading, that it reduces the poet to the moralist. As Maritain rightly insisted, *poesis* and *praxis* should not be conflated. "Art operates for the good of work done, ad bonum operis."[19] Art is not *recta ratio agibilium*, but *recta ratio factibilium*. The danger of Sidney's description, however, is not that it would collapse ethics and poetry, but poetry and rhetoric. Some clarification can be found in C.S. Lewis's contrast between rhetoric and poetry, a contrast that brings out the indirect way in which poetry promotes the good.

> The differentia of rhetoric is that it wishes to produce in our minds some practical resolve . . . and it does this by calling passions to the aid of reason. Poetry aims at producing something more like vision than it is like action. But vision, in this sense, includes passions. Certain things, if not seen as lovely or detestable, are not being accurately seen at all. . . . In rhetoric imagination is present for the sake of passion, while in poetry passion is present for the sake of imagination, and, therefore, in the long run, for the sake of wisdom or spiritual health—the rightness and richness of a man's total response to the world.[20]

Lewis goes on to note that the rectitude inspired by poetry contributes "indirectly to right action." Thomas himself states that poetry leads to "virtue by a pleasing image."[21]

The most troublesome features of the turn to narrative lie not in the risk of confusing poetry and rhetoric, but elsewhere. One of the welcome motives behind the turn to narrative is the attempt to counter reductionistic notions of autonomy and atomism; yet narrative ethics often embodies a reductionism of a different sort. It risks abandoning

---

Moral Enquiry (Notre Dame, Indiana: University of Notre Dame Press, 1989), however, he seems less reticent to adopt traditional accounts of teleology. He writes, "Evaluative judgements are a species of factual judgement concerning the final and formal causes of activity of members of a particular species" (p. 134). He also insists that the practical portion of the *ST.* can be understood only by reference to the preceding theoretical sections (p. 135).

[19]Jacques Maritain, *Art and Scholasticism*, trans. J. F. Scanlon (New York: Charles Scribner's Sons, 1947), p. 12.

[20]*A Preface to Paradise Lost* (New York: Oxford University Press, 1961), pp. 53–54.

[21]Prologue to the commentary on Aristotle's *Posterior Analytics*.

moral inquiry to a set of utterly incommensurable stories.[22] Although Aristotle understands ethics as a science only in a diminished and analogous sense, he nonetheless resists the temptation to conflate ethics and literature. When it jettisons altogether the dialectical or scientific character of ethics, narrative ethics replaces the autonomy of the Kantian agent with the autonomy of the story. Understood thus, narrative ethics would mark not so much a return or an advance, as a capitulation to the modern way of framing the moral question. Either there is Kantian autonomy and universality or there is the relativity of stories.

The autonomy of stories and their inevitable and irreconcilable conflicts are prominent in even the most philosophically trained advocates of narrative. For example, Hauerwas, Nussbaum, and MacIntyre accentuate the role of moral dilemmas in the moral life and fittingly see the genre of tragedy as best capturing the narrative structure of human life.[23] Hauerwas sees a truthful narrative as one that "gives us the means to accept the tragic without succumbing to self-deceiving explanations." The Christian narrative gives us the "skills to live joyously in the face of the tragic."[24] In *After Virtue*, a seminal text in the turn to narrative, MacIntyre advocates a combination of Aristotle's ethics with the Sophoclean insight concerning tragic conflict. Unlike Nussbaum, MacIntyre at least admits that he is imparting the Sophoclean emphasis into his reading of Aristotle. For Nussbaum tragedies capture the vulnerability and fragility of the human condition, features of our condition that Platonic, Kantian, and Christian moral thought overlook. She writes, "They offer no solution in bewildering tragic situations—except the solution that consists in being faithful to or harmonious with one's sense of worth by acknowledging the tension and disharmany."[25]

---

[22]The emphasis upon incommensurability follows upon the purported centrality of moral dilemmas. See Bernard Williams, *Moral Luck: Philosophical Papers, 1973–1980* (Cambridge: 1980).

[23]Stanley Hauerwas, *Truthfulness and Tragedy* (Notre Dame, Indiana: University of Notre Dame Press, 1981), Martha Nussbaum, *The Fragility of Goodness* (Cambridge: Cambridge University Press, 1986). These views should not be collapsed. Hauerwas speaks of the Gospel as urging truthfulness and charity in the face of tragic situations, while MacIntyre speaks of the tragic confrontation of "good with good." Nussbaum's position is, I think, the most contrary to that of Aquinas.

[24]Martha Nussbaum, *Truthfulness and Tragedy*, p. 12.

[25]Martha Nussbaum, *Fragility*, p. 81.

As MacIntyre would later note, there is no place in Aquinas's ethics for tragic dilemmas *simpliciter*, that is, for dilemmas that are not rooted in some prior sin or error.[26] Indeed, the closest analogue in Thomas to the moral dilemma is what he calls *perplexus*, the state of moral conflict resulting from an antecedent sin.[27] Thomas's account of the origin of moral perplexity indicates that more is at stake in the debate over moral dilemmas than the opposition of a calculative and abstract conception of moral reasoning to a personalist narrative embracing the concrete and contingent. Indeed, Thomas's simultaneous emphasis upon the centrality of prudence and his repudiation of moral dilemmas reveals this opposition to be a false one. Instead, the fundamental opposition is a metaphysical one. On the one hand, there is the position, intimated in Plato and Aristotle, made explicit in the Christian tradition, that grounds all things in a transcendent source and paradigm of the Good, and that sees evil as dependent and parasitic upon the good, as impotent non-being. On the other hand, there is some version of the Manichean view of the inseparability of good and evil. John Milbank argues that tragic narrative affirms an "ontological violence" at the roots of the natural and moral cosmos.[28] The Platonic critique of tragic poetry can be understood in this light. Socrates castigates the poets for presenting divine beings in states of conflict and for presenting noble souls as ending in destruction. Both René Girard and Paul Ricoeur see tragedy as an expression of "primordial incoherence."[29] Such an ontology partly explains the preference for

---

[26]Alasdair MacIntyre, *Whose Justice? Which Rationality?* (Notre Dame, Indiana: University of Notre Dame Press, 1988), pp. 183–188.

[27]*ST.*, I-II, 6, ad 3.

[28]Nussbaum's position, which speaks of the harmony of conflicting values and forces, is not far from the Nietzschean affirmation of difference. The aesthetic distance requisite for such an affirmation involves either ignorance or celebration of the real violence ensuing from the conflicts. See Milbank, *Theology and Social Theory: Beyond Secular Reason* (Oxford: Blackwell, 1991).

[29]Paul Ricoeur, *The Symbolism of Evil* (New York: Harper, 1967), p. 219. René Girard, *Violence and the Sacred* (Baltimore, Maryland: Johns Hopkins University Press, 1977). Girard sees Aristotle's account of tragedy as continuous with the origins of tragedy in religious rituals. He writes, "Katharsis refers primarily to the mysterious benefits that accrue to the community upon the death of a human katharma or pharmakos. The process is generally seen as a religious purification and takes the form of cleansing or draining away of impurities" (p. 287). More pointedly, "On closer inspection, Aristotle's text is something of a manual of sacrificial practices, for the qualities that make a good 'tragic' hero are precisely those required of the sacrificial victim" (p. 291). A more traditional reading of Aristotle's *Poetics* can be had

tragedy in postmodern thought from Nietzsche to Heidegger and into certain strains of deconstruction.

Another danger in the turn to poetry has to do with the temptations of *technē*, the temptation to construct a whole which claims reality but in fact is merely a substitute for it. The philosophic objections to these poetic tendencies can be found in Plato's *Ion* and *Republic*. According to the divided line, the first step in the ascent to the Good involves grasping an image as an image. In the Allegory of the Cave, the citizens see images as things, images that are presented by the poets. Thus, the poets inhibit the ascent to the Good by presenting images as realities. That Thomas shares this concern is evident from his attempt to rebut the objection that the use of images in scripture obscures the truth. He counters that scripture does not allow its audience "to rest in likenesses but raises them to the knowledge of intelligible things." Moreover, "those things taught metaphorically in one part of scripture are taught more openly in other parts. The very hiding of truth in figures is useful for the exercise of thoughtful minds."[30]

Maritain was acutely aware of this danger. He writes, "Poetry (like metaphysics) is spiritual nourishment, but the savour of it is created and insufficient."[31] Indeed, part of the project of *Creative Intuition in Art and Poetry* is to salvage modern notions of creativity by returning and subordinating them to God's creativity. The artist, Maritain writes,

---

in Amelie Rorty's "The Psychology of Aristotelian Tragedy," in *Essays on Aristotle's Poetics*, ed. Richard Rorty (Princeton, New Jersey: Princeton University Press, 1992), pp. 1–22. Rorty argues that Aristotle's understanding of tragedy involves thoroughgoing transformation of the received view, which had been vitiated by the Platonic critique. Thus, Aristotle underscores the "representational truthfulness" of tragedy, and does not see it as a vehicle for reconciling the audience to unintelligible forces, forces which engender religious ecstasy and which inspire horror rather than pity and fear (p. 4). Rorty rightly insists upon Aristotle's variance from the tradition, yet her own emphasis upon the way in which fundamentally virtuous persons can unintentionally engender their own destruction brings to the fore the inseparability of order and disorder. She writes, "The plot unfolds from the protagonist's *hamartia*, a waywardness whose consequences reverses the eudaimonia that normally attends virtue" (p. 10). The protagonist's reversal (*peripeteia*), furthermore, "coincides with insightful recognition (*anagnorisis*)" and "fulfills the ancient command to know oneself" (p. 12). The fulfillment of the imperative of Greek ethics is precisely what leads to the destruction of the protagonist.

[30]*ST.*, I, 1, 9, ad 2. "Non permittat in similitudinibus permanere, sed elevet eas ad cognitionem intelligibilium. . . . ea quae in uno loco scripturae traduntur sub metaphoris, in aliis locis expressius exponuntur. Et ipsa etiam occultatio figurarum utilis est ad exercitum studiosorum et contra irrisiones infidelium."

[31]Jacques Maritain, *Art and Scholasticism*, p. 78.

is "an associate of God in the making of works of beauty; by developing the faculties with which the Creator has endowed him . . . and by making use at created matter, he creates in the second degree."[32] Maritain finds the basis for this understanding of the artist in Thomas's statement that the "operation of art is founded upon the operation of nature, and this upon creation."[33]

An acceptable alliance between narrative and Thomistic ethics requires that narratives meet certain criteria: they would have to avoid presenting violence or strife as primordial; they would have to undermine the autonomous creativity of the poet; they would have to provoke inquiry; and they would have to eclipse the tragic view of human life. Such strategies, I would argue, are operative in Aquinas's own texts and in the tradition of Christian poetry. The Christian tradition, of course, has not ignored the importance of tragedy for understanding the human condition. But it has never seen tragedy as the whole story or even as the fundamental story. The greatest Christian poems, those of Chaucer and Dante, for example, are comedies.[34]

But what does comedy have to do with Aquinas? It seems clear enough that Aquinas would object to making tragic conflict or moral dilemmas the focus of ethics. It also seems indisputable that Thomas's *Summa Theologiae* exercised some influence on Dante's *Divine Comedy*. But does Thomas himself countenance a narrative conception of the good life? A critic might argue that Thomas did not write narratives and that, as an ethicist, he does not look to stories for assistance, but to moral philosophy and the edicts of scripture. Clearly, Thomas's writings cannot be reduced to narratives. There are, however, in his texts a number of the themes characteristic of narrative ethics. First, Thomas's account of the virtues lends itself to narrative description. Secondly, Thomas links the intelligibility and force of law to the common good; thus the natural law presupposes participation in social practices. Thirdly, Thomas sees philosophy not as a set of abstract propositions, but as a way of life, having its own *telos*, an end that is enacted in the speculative virtues of human beings. Finally, Thomas regularly adverts to scripture, not just to specific propositions

---

[32]*Ibid.*, p. 49.

[33]"Operatio artis fundatur super operationem naturae, et haec super creationem" (*ST.*, I, 45, 8).

[34]MacIntyre appears to be moving in this direction; in *Three Rival Versions*, he focuses on the parallels between Aquinas's ethics and Dante's Divine Comedy (p. 142–48).

or doctrines, but also to its narrative structure and peculiar mode of teaching. In what follows I will focus on the last two.

Before turning to the role of narrative in Aquinas, it is important to note that the claim concerning the narrative structure of the philosophic life in no way entails the reduction of philosophy to literature. Thomas does not rebut the claim that poetry is the "weakest teaching" (*infima doctrina*).[35] He sees the philosophy of Plato and Aristotle as superseding the materialist assumptions of the earliest philosophers, who supposed that all things were material, including the human mind.[36] Indeed, the philosophers attempt to supplant the tragic vision of the poets with the speculative pursuit of truth about nature, man, and the divine. Nonetheless, the origin, structure, and culmination of *theoria* can be described in narrative terms.

Thomas describes the narrative structure of the philosophic life in the opening chapters of the *Summa Contra Gentiles*, in the famous discussion of the twofold mode of truth. Thomas distinguishes between the portion of truth that "exceeds every capacity of human reason," and the portion "to which even natural reason is able to attain."[37] In ascending from sensible things to the divine, philosophers have attained some knowledge of God. What the philosophers have demonstrated about God overlaps with a segment of what scripture reveals; in this Thomas finds an initial confirmation of the compatibility of reason and faith. The goal of the natural aspiration to know is an understanding of the highest things, which is a cause of vehement joy (*vehemens . . . gaudium*). While Thomas is impressed by the achievements of philosophy, he notes that its success has been rare and imperfect. The philosopher grasps only that God is, not what He is. The desire to know, then, remains unsated, and philosophy, inconclusive. Apart from revelation, the human race would remain "in the blackest shadows of ignorance."[38]

In spite of the philosopher's success in overcoming the tragic vision of the poets, tragedy itself is not fully eradicated. Maritain grasps

---

[35]*ST.*, I, 9, obj. 1 and ad 1.

[36]*ST.*, I, 84, 1.

[37]*SCG.*, I, 3. "Quae omnem facultatem humanae rationis excedunt . . . ad quae etiam ration naturalis pertingere potest."

[38]*SCG.*, I, 5. "Remaneret igitur humanum genus, si sola rationis via ad Deum cognoscendum pateret, in maximis ignorantiae tenebris."

the tragic character of the life of the philosopher. In the opening chapter of *The Degrees of Knowledge*, entitled "Majesty and Poverty of Metaphysics," the author eloquently captures the glory and fragility of the philosophic life: "Its majesty; that it is wisdom. Its poverty: that it is human science." He expatiates, "That, then is the poverty of metaphysics (and yet its majesty, too). It awakens a desire for supreme union, for spiritual possession completed in the order of reality itself and not only in the concept. It cannot satisfy that desire."[39] The potential sources of tragedy in Aristotle's philosophy are numerous: a) the philosopher aspires to a vision of that which escapes his natural capacity, b) the natural end is understood in terms of what happens always or for the most part, yet only the few attain contemplation, and even the active virtues are beset by the afflictions of fortune, c) the philosopher's grasp of the good places him in tragic isolation from the rest of mankind,[40] and d) since the intellect has a *per se* operation it is subsistent and separable from the body, yet, given the need for phantasms, the vexed question remains of how such a separated intellect could operate and how it could survive separate from the whole of which it is naturally a part.

The depiction of the philosophic life in terms of a tragic narrative is instructive. In her preference for tragic narrative over speculative philosophy, Martha Nussbaum overlooks Maritain's insight concerning the tragic character of speculative philosophy. Two features of Nussbaum's account are objectionable. First, she underestimates Aristotle's emphasis upon self-sufficiency and immunity to conflict in the account of the good life. Secondly, Nussbaum's description of the theoretical life as an attempt to escape from the limitations and fragility of human existence misses the mark.[41] For both Plato and Aristotle the life of contemplation is more fragile and more vulnerable than is the active life. Its grandeur and pedagogical utility consist in its pointing to and partially realizing the *summum bonum*. Its inability to achieve the highest good is, as Maritain notes, the source of its

---

[39]Jacques Maritain, *The Degrees of Knowledge*, trans. Gerald B. Phelan (New York: Charles Scribner's Son, 1959), p. 7.

[40]One pre-eminent in "virtue and political capacity" may "truly be deemed a God among men." *Politics*, III, 13 (1284a10–15). Compare the better known statement, "He who is unable to live in society . . . must be either a beast or a god." I, 2 (1253a28–30).

[41]For a more sustained response to Nussbaum, see my "Transcending Humanity in Aquinas," forthcoming in the *American Catholic Philosophical Quarterly*.

poverty or misery. Yet this is not the pre-philosophic and apparently necessary misery of the tragic hero; nor is it the misery of modern nihilism. What distinguishes the philosophy of Plato and Aristotle is its incompleteness, which is occasionally expressed as hopefulness. The persistent possibility of (in Socrates's case, faith in?) immortality is thus crucial to philosophy's circumvention of an all-encompassing tragic vision.

For Thomas philosophy is one of two means of access to the highest things. Thomas discusses the other way in the final book of the *Summa Contra Gentiles* where he distinguishes the way of ascent from the way of descent. The only efficacious means to the end sought in the way of ascent is the way of descent, the way of incarnation, which bridges the "unmeasured distance between the natures" of God and man. Given the limits to human reason, the adverse consequences of sin, and the natural desire to know the highest things, God's act of revelation (*revelare*) is an act of mercy (*clementia*). As Maritain puts it: "Exceeding human effort, gift of a deifying grace and the free largesse of uncreated Wisdom, there is at its source that Wisdom's foolish love. . . . Only Jesus crucified, the Mediator lifted up between heaven and earth, gives access to it."[42]

In Thomas's discussion of the Incarnation, dialectical arguments precede the arguments from fittingness. Thus, reason prepares the way for, and removes impediments to, the reception of the Christian narrative. On behalf of the fittingness of Christ's assuming human nature, Thomas returns to the dominant image of the *Summa Contra Gentiles*, the notion of man as a microcosm, existing on the horizon of the worlds of spirit and matter: "Man, since he is the term of creatures, presupposing all other creatures in the order of generation, is suitably united to the first principle of things to finish a kind of cycle in the perfection of things."[43]

The reference to the "completion of the cycle" indicates that creation has a beginning, middle, and end, that the narrative of scripture manifests rather than obscures the order of nature. Later on in the fourth book Thomas argues that the supposition of an infinity of souls

---

[42]Jacques Maritain, *The Degrees of Knowledge*, p. 7.

[43]*SCG.*, IV, 55. "Homo etiam, quum sit creaturarum terminus, quasi omnes alias creaturas naturali generationis ordine praesupponens, convenienter primo rerum principio unitur, etiam ut quadam circulatione perfectio rerum concludatur."

is contrary to the notion of an end. When coupled with the dialectical arguments against the eternity of the world, the argument against an infinity of souls underscores the limits to philosophy and paves the way for the Christian narrative. Thomas also argues that the best, probable argument against the eternity of the world can be taken from "the end of the divine will," which is to "manifest His goodness in His effects." That God is the absolute source of all goodness and power is most evident from the temporal beginning of the world.[44] Thus, the doctrine of creation *ex nihilo* precludes the possibility that in the roots of things there is conflict and violence. Instead, infinite goodness is the source of all things.[45] He concludes: "The preceding considerations enable us to avoid various errors made by pagan philosophers: the assertion of the world"s eternity; the assertion of the eternity of the world's matter, out of which as a certain time the world began to be formed, either by chance, or by some intellect, or even by love or strife."[46]

In the discussion of creation, Thomas compares God to an artist whose wisdom and goodness are manifest in creation. He begins by reworking the language of physical *productio* or *poesis*, which involves the inducing of form within pre-existing matter. God's artistry presupposes nothing and is not limited to a particular species or genus. God acts, moreover, not through some power inherent in him, but through his whole being. In creation there is neither motion nor change. Instead, creation is understood as a unilateral relation of dependency of the creature upon God (*ipsa dependentia esse creati ad principium*).[47] According to Thomas, the productive *technē* of

---

[44]*SCG.*, II, 38. "Finis enim divinae voluntatis in rerum productione est eius bonitas, in quantum per causata manifestatur: potissime autem manifestatur divina virtus et bonitas per hoc quod res aliae praeter ipsum ab ipso esse habent, quia non semper fuerunt. Ostenditur etiam quod non agit per necessitatem naturae, et quod virtus sua est infinita in agendo. Hoc enim convenientissimum fuit divinae bonitati, ut rebus creatis principium durationis daret."

[45]As Ricoeur notes, pagan myths envision creation as the introduction of order into a pre-existing state of chaos (p. 172). The image persists in Plato's *Timaeus*. In Aristotle, the topic is not directly addressed, yet, as Aquinas implies, the supposition of the eternity of the world obscures the absolute dependence of all things upon God.

[46]*SCG.*, II, 38. "Ex his autem quae praedicta sunt, vitare possumus diversos errores gentilium philosophorum quorum quidam posuerunt numdum aeternum, quidam materiam mundi aeternam, ex qua ex aliquo tempore mundus coepit generari, vel a casu, vel ab aliquo intellectu, aut etiam amore, atu lite."

[47]*SCG.*, II, 18.

any creature is but a diminished participation in divine creativity. As Maritain puts it, "only on the high summits of divinity, does the idea as artisan-form obtain the complete fullness required of it by its notion."[48]

Thomas underscores the pedagogical role of creatures in manifesting God to man. But creation is only one made of divine self-manifestation. As Thomas puts it, "All creatures are related to God as art products to an artist. . . . Consequently, the whole of nature is like an artifact of the divine artistic mind. But it is not contrary to the essential character of an artist if he should work in a different way on his product even after he has given it its first form."[49]

In the Christian narrative the first manifestation of God in creation is ordered to the revelation of God in scripture and in the person of the Son. The theological account of the human condition has the intelligibility and unity of a dramatic narrative. It locates man within the context of salvation history and its narrative moments, before the law, under the law, and under grace. While Thomas holds that revealed truths are doctrines, amenable to articulation in propositions, the intelligibility and practical import of the propositions supposes a larger context and requires a precedent grasp of a particular narrative account of human life. The incarnation, for example, fittingly occurs after the human person has been left alone "to discover that he was not equal to his own salvation: not equal by natural knowledge for before the time of the written law man transgressed the law of nature; nor equal by his own virtue, for, when he was given knowledge of sin through the law, he still sinned out of weakness."[50]

The emphases upon human sin as the origin of evil and upon the teleologically ordered nature of time are crucial elements in comic

---

[48]Jacques Maritain, *Art and Scholasticism*, p. 70.

[49]*SCG.*, III, 100. "Omnes creaturae comparantur ad Deum sicut artificiata ad artificem . . . unde tota natura est sicut quoddam artificiatum divinae artis. Non est autem contra rationem artificii, si artifex aliter aliquid operetur in suo artificio, etiam postquam ei primam formam dedit. Neque ergo est contra naturam, si Deus in rebus naturalibus aliquid operetur aliter quam consuetus cursus naturae habet."

[50]*SCG.*, IV, 55. "Relinquendus igitur aliquando fuit sibi, ut experiretur quod ipse sibi non sufficeret ad salutem, neque per scientiam naturalem, quia ante tempus legis scriptae homo legem naturae transgressus est, neque per virtutem propriam, quia, data sibi cognitione peccati per legem, adhuc ex infirmitate peccavit."

narratives. As Ricoeur notes, the shift from tragic to comic necessitates that "guilt must . . . be distinguished from finiteness."[51] Concerning time Frye states, "In comedy time plays a redeeming role: it uncovers and brings to light what is essential to the happy ending."[52]

It is important to see that the recovery of the comic provides us with a viable alternative to Kantian ethics, that is, that the comic does not involve Stoic indifference to contingency and suffering. The Christian narrative overcomes tragedy, not by ignoring or escaping from the tragic character of human life, but by embracing it. As Hauerwas puts it, "We believe, on the basis of the cross, that our lives are sustained by a God who has taken the tragic into his own life . . . we are freed from the obsession of securing our significance against death. We are thus given the time and space that provides the condition for faithfulness."[53]

Thomas underscores the role of redemptive suffering in the life of Christ, who for the love of men bore "not just any sort of death, but a death abject in the extreme." By "bearing in themselves the marks of the passion of Christ," believers expose themselves to dangers.[54]

With its doctrines of creation *ex nihilo*, original sin, and redemptive suffering, the comic vision of Christianity eclipses the tragic narrative of pagan philosophy. Comic reversal is evident in the themes of communion, restoration, and elevation. What might appear to be a primal loss is but one act within a larger story. The divine artist inscribes tragedy within comedy, as the narrative of revelation eclipses the narrative of pagan philosophy.[55]

Much more could and should be said on behalf of comic narrative. Without its recovery we are left with the alternative of Kantian systematics or tragic narrative. As we have seen, this way of framing the issue obscures important features of both ancient and Christian moral thought. Appraising the ethics of narrative, especially of tragic narrative, from a Thomistic vantage point helps to clarify what is at stake in the contemporary turn to narrative. It should also help to open

---

[51]Paul Ricoeur, *The Symbolism of Evil*, p. 222.

[52]Northrop Frye, *Anatomy of Criticism* (Princeton, New Jersey: Princeton University Press, 1957), p. 213.

[53]Stanley Hauerwas, *Truthfulness and Tragedy*, p. 12.

[54]*SCG.*, III, 55.

[55]Again, Maritain, "to establish fully the dignity and nobility of art, we have found it necessary to go back as far as the mystery of the Trinity." *Art and Scholasticism*, p. 97.

new avenues of exploration concerning the link between the moral life and narrative. Finally, the inquiry brings to the fore a neglected feature of Thomas's own writings, namely, their literary character. While Thomas's thought cannot be reduced to narrative, the intimate connection in his texts between form and content buttresses the claim that for Thomas the dominant narrative conception of human life is comic, not tragic.[56]

---

[56]I am indebted to Patrick Downey for his suggestions about comic narrative and for pointing me to Frye, Girard, and Ricoeur.

Maritain's Unnatural Acts

Roger Duncan

To call any act "unnatural" these days seems quaint to many, as does talk about "natural law." But even among philosophers who accept some version of natural law, critiques of the notion of "unnatural" have made many wary of appeal to it as a basis for moral evaluation. Whle every wrong or sinful act goes counter to natural law, what makes such acts wrong might never involve some narrower, more dubious sense of "unnatural" as, for instance, that the term has been used in relation to sexual perversion.

The question of the morality of contraception has focused these issues for Catholics; the simplest thing to say about contraception is that it is an unnatural act. The question is whether it makes any sense to say this, and what that sense might be. This paper attempts a "Maritainian" contribution to the discussion, though Maritain himself, to my knowledge, did not say anthing about contraception or, except indirectly, about "unnaturalness" as applied to human acts.

There are philosophers who want to oppose contraception but wish at the same time to avoid the term "unnatural" for reasons which would clearly be opposed by Maritain. Germain Grisez, for instance, rejects the "traditional" argument, which he represents as follows:

Major: To prevent any act from attaining its natural end is intrinsically immoral.

Minor: Contraception prevents sexual intercourse from attaining its natural end.

Conclusion: Contraception is immoral.[1]

---

[1]Germain Grisez, *Contraception and the Natural Law* (Milwaukee, Wisconsin: The Bruce Publishing Company, 1964), p. 20.

Grisez's chief objection to this argument is that, basing its prohibition solely upon a consideration of "natural" teleology, it requires an illegitimate move from an "is" to an "ought."[2]

But *this* objection, exploiting a rigid fact-value dichotomy, is surely a Humean red-herring, accepted by certain Catholic philosophers, who for presumably Humean reasons reject the metaphysically rich Thomism of Maritain and of Thomas himself. In reply to them we would say with Maritain, who insisted on the grounding of ethics in metaphysics, that, while there are certainly facts from which the derivation of an "ought" would be impossible, there are other facts—facts of a metaphysical nature (though available to the non-metaphysician)—which contain prescriptions and proscriptions implicitly.[3]

Roughly, Good is a transcendental of being. Insofar as I cognize the being of something, I recognize what is "due" it. For example, I know that the blind cow is missing something it ought to have. Insofar as the presence or absence of such natural evil in my own act depends on my free will, the ought takes on the force of moral prescription.[4] The rejection of Humean "being-blindness" takes us only part way. Our question is whether we can discover a "narrow" sense of "unnatural" which will authorize syllogisms similar to the one Grisez rejects.

It might help at this point to list several meanings of "unnatural" relevant to moral discourse.

1) The general sense, mentioned above, according to which "every sin is unnatural."

2) "Contrary to basic human inclination"; e.g., living in isolation, or not feeding the baby.[5]

3) A *privation* within an act, so that an essential ingredient of the act is missing, and consequently it looks like trying to bake a cake without an oven. St. Thomas uses this sort of criterion in talking about

---

[2]*Ibid.*, p. 22, 50.

[3]Jacques Maritain, *An Introduction to the Basic Problems of Moral Philosophy* (Albany, New York: Magi Books, 1990), p. 49. Cf. Henry B. Veatch, Natural Law and the Is-Ought Question," in *Swimming Against the Current in Contemporary Philosophy* (Washington, D.C.: The Catholic University of America Press, 1990), pp. 293–311. See also Ralph McInerny, *Ethica Thomistica* (Washington, D.C.: The Catholic University of America Press, 1982), pp. 50–62.

[4]Jacques Maritain, *An Introduction to the Basic Problems of Moral Philosophy*, pp. 47–53.

[5]St. Thomas derives the natural law from human inclinations: *ST.*, I-II, 94, 2.

homosexual acts, where he argues that the plumbing, so to speak, is all wrong.[6]

4) "Against nature" in the sense that you cannot commit an act in question without dire consequences, as when we say, "if you don't exercise, nature will get you back"; such is the sense when we give warnings about polluting the environment.

5) "Artificial" as, for instance, in the claim that bottle feeding is unnatural.[7]

6) Another meaning might be "the frustration of a natural tele-ology." Grisez thinks this is the issue in the "traditional" syllogism as presented above, and remarks that it would rule out the use of earplugs.[8]

I do not pretend this to be an exhaustive list. But it may help bring into relief the project of suggesting a meaning of "unnatural" distinct from all of the above, and crucial to the question of the morality of contraception.

We may get closer to this notion by listening to Grisez again. Of course, he wants to recast the whole argument against contraception in terms of the Grisez-Finnis machinery of basic "human goods." It is not my purpose here to give a detailed criticism of that system, a job which has been done ably by Russell Hittinger and others.[9] But on the way to his own formulation Grisez makes the following helpful remark:

> Normally one has no obligation to engage in sexual relations . . . but if intercourse is carried on to the point where procreation might follow unless we act to prevent it, then the full force of obligation falls upon us. We need not act, but if we do act, we may do nothing to prevent the procreative good from being realized. Positively to do any such thing by direct volition will set us absolutely at odds with the essential human good which our very action has made proximately possible of attainment.[10]

---

[6]*ST.*, II-II. 154, 11.

[7]This seems to be a particularly culture-relative criterion, e.g., the Amish refuse zippers and automobiles on this basis. But this notion of "unnatural" gains some force when combined with the consequential considerations of #4. For example, bottle feeding may subtract important nurturing ingredients.

[8]Germain Grisez, *Contraception and the Natural Law*, p. 90.

[9]Russell Hittinger, *A Critique of the New Natural Law Theory* (Notre Dame, Indiana: University of Notre Dame Press, 1987).

[10]Germain Grisez, *Contraception and the Natural Law*, p. 90.

What is helpful about this statement is that it recognizes that the problem is that there is some sort of contradiction within the contraceptive act. Having initiated this act of intercourse, it says, one may not then undertake a second act cutting across the first.

Consider the issue of lying as Thomas deals with it in the *Summa Theologiae*. In answer to the question as to whether it is always wrong (sinful) to lie, St. Thomas says "yes," because lying is *unnatural*.[11] Speech is ordered to truth.[12] I do not have to speak, but once I choose to do so I may not then by a lie act contrary to the purpose of speaking, which is the truth.

The discussion may be advanced by noting the difference between Thomas's account and Grisez's statement about contraception. 1) Thomas unabashedly specifies that the lie is "unnatural." 2) While for Thomas a "good" is involved (the virtue of "truthfulness"), he gives the point a different spin. It is not that, having once launched ourselves into the pursuit of some basic human good we may not *then* turn back,[13] but rather that, having chosen to speak, we may not *concomitantly* deform our act. To do so would be to make inner gears grind against each other, so to speak. A speech act is by its very nature an act "toward" truth. Hence, to act against truth, while at the same time acting toward it, does inner violence to the agent. As Josef Pieper once observed, lying "splits the soul."

Grisez presumably avoids a parallel account in the case of contraception for reasons connected with two examples: the vomitorium and earplugs. First, the vomitorium.[14] If in our characterization of acts as unnatural we were to leave out reference to serious or basic "human goods," we would, Grisez fears, in the end be making trivial prohibitions, like telling the gluttonous ancient Romans that they must keep down their food even when, by use of the vomitorium, they could continue the banquet. But is this issue really so trivial? Is not there a perversion here? Even if a Roman says "I am not eating just for pleasure but for the good fellowship of the feast," would not we want

---

[11]*ST.*, II-II, 110, 3.

[12]*ST.*, II-II, 110, 1.

[13]Grisez's analysis necessarily underscores this temporal aspect of choice: "Having gone this far we may not turn back." The example he adduces—the unjustifiability of undoing a life-prolonging measure we have decided to try—is unconvincing. Germain Grisez, *Contraception and the Natural Law*, pp. 88–89.

[14]*Ibid.*, p. 30.

to counsel him seriously against the separation, say, of the nutritive from the convivial good?

As for the earplugs, the disanalogy supports our point. For there is no *act* involved in hearing, as contrasted with a choice to listen to something in particular. One just hears, automaticaly, whether one likes it or not, and sometimes it makes perfect sense to cut off or plug up the hearing. We are not concerned with the question of interrupting the teleology of a power—the notorious "perverted faculty" argument. We are concerned with the moral impropriety of the destructive interior attempt to perform *two acts at once*, one cutting across or cancelling out the other.

I propose, then, that we develop a concept of "unnatural in the strict sense" to apply these cases of double-edged, self-contradictory acts. Lying will be unnatural in this sense, as an inner violence blunting the agent's capacity to relate to reality. Contraception will be deficient in the same sense except with the interesting twist that it is related to the complexity of the soul-body constitution of the human being. Contraceptive acts split soul and body by treating the procreative aspect as if it were "purely biological" and deforming the physical act to conform to a supposedly "spiritual" unitive aspect. The contraceptor thinks he is a "ghost in a machine."

In case it should be asked why or how human beings can suffer this inner act of collision in the first place, Maritain's analysis can help. "Inclinations of our animal nature," he tells us, "are grasped and transferred into the dynamism of the intellect's field of apprehension" so that "properly human inclinations" contain a complexity.[15] We might say that a properly human act is layered, or that there is an inner articulation of levels within the unity of the one act, giving the agent the possibility of initiating the act and yet simultaneously trying to stifle one of its aspects. In our vomitorium example the nutritive aspect of animal activity is altogether disregarded for the sake of the convivial expression of human feasting. It is all too easy, once it occurs to somebody, to try to split the act by a direct act against one of its aspects.

The analogy which treats contraception as a kind of "lie with one's body" may be helpful in answering some of the objections frequently

---

[15]Jacques Maritain, *An Introduction to the Basic Problems of Moral Philosophy* (Albany, New York: Magi Books, 1990), p. 54.

brought against *Humanae Vitae*. One of these objections is to the effect that the general principle of the unity of the unitive and procreative meanings of human sexuality is preserved by a life-style of generous intent to have children, without interpreting the principle to entail that "each and every marital act" must be "open to procreation." But with our analogy we can see what is wrong with this; we can see why we would not want to say: "Telling the truth in general is what counts; a lie now and then is all right." To be sure, a single swallow does not make a summer, and a virtue is not made or broken by a single act. But a single act may damage the power, an insight with which Christian moral seriousness has always complemented Aristotelian virtue ethics.

One frequently hears the accusation that *Humanae Vitae* inconsistently allows, under certain conditions, natural spacing of births by recourse to periodic abstinence. The idea is that intercourse intentionally taking advantage of infertile periods is, after all, subtly contraceptive. But from the standpoint taken here, the question would be: Exactly where is the contraceptive *act* in these cases?

The history of moral theology around the question of lying points the way here. The problem with lying is not deception as such, which in many cases may be justified. In any case, despite the *prima facie* goodness of truth, there are many cases where I ought to choose not to speak. What I may not do is perform an act "unnatural in the strict sense."

To call contraception "unnatural" is not to say all there is to say about the evil of contraception. Philosophy, after all, can only say so much about such an issue; even moral philosophy which is "subalternated" to moral theology, as Maritain puts it, suffers this constraint. True, we can derive an "ought" from an "is." But for positive guidance toward the good life, philosophy must, like Dante's Virgil, point us to a higher horizon. This higher source, in the form of the continually renewed teaching of the Church's Magisterium, has lately been pointing us toward that irreducibly sexual (though analogically so) communion of persons celebrated by Pope John Paul II in his "theology of the body" in terms of the "original unity of man and woman."[16] Within this theological context contraception will be viewed as a block within the process by which we move toward the fulfillment of participation

---

[16]Pope John Paul II, *The Original Unity of Man and Woman* (Boston: Daughters of St. Paul, 1981).

in the very life of the Trinity. Contraception blocks fullness of com-munion: it avoids both the fruitfulness and the abstinence by which the personalizing process is advanced.

In this article I have tried to speak in the spirit of Jacques Maritain who, no matter how sophisticated or creative his own expression of his master's thought, he always preferred a kind of "paleo-" Thomism to any form of "neo-Thomism." But just as Maritain was able to advance Thomistic thought through a sensitivity to problems raised by the neo-Thomists, he was not blind to problems surrounding the "is-ought" issue. Accordingly, he developed a nuanced position which deserves study. "I do not think that the passage from metaphysical or transcendental good to moral good takes place by a simple logical particularization; it supposes the appearance of a new datum: moral experience. But it remains ontological by nature, a particularized on-tological good."[17]

In order to see what is involved here, consider what an objector might say to our thesis at this point: "In developing the notion of 'unnatural in the strict sense' haven't you merely displaced the sticking point? How can you explain why I ought not to act 'self-destructively' without appealing to some sort of 'categorical imperative' of the sort that interests Grisez and Finnis, something like 'Do not act directly against a basic good," in this case, human life?"

The objection is in a sense well-taken. An ethics of self-fulfillment will have a difficult time grounding prohibitions against self-destruc-tion on the *telos* toward happiness without sooner or later adverting to wht Maritain always insisted was the key to a properly Christian, but not yet theological, ethics: *recognition of the objective good of being*. If I am truly to act toward my happiness (the order of exercise), then I must transcend myself sufficiently to honor goods that are simply good in themselves—the *bonum honestum* (the order of specification). The good here is, however, not limited to "human goods"; it ranges analogically as widely as being itself. Of course, honoring *this* good will have implications for my own being in a primary way because my own being is the only being I am always successful at damaging if I act against it. Within this perspective unnatural acts in the strict sense will be *ipso facto* prohibited.

---

[17]Jacques Maritain, *An Introduction to the Basic Problems of Moral Philosophy* (Albany, New York: Magi Books, 1990), p. 68.

In sum, for a reconstructed Maritainian position there is nothing wrong with traditional "biologistic" objections to contraception provided we recognize that we are talking not about preserving faculties from frustration but about protecting the integrity of *acts*, and that what renders an act unnatural in the strict sense is a "short-circuiting," an interference, which works against the inner unity, and thus the being, of the agent.

Maritain and the Pursuit of Happiness in the Light of Claudel, Péguy, and Bernanos

William Bush

During the summer of 1942, Maritain tells us, he wrote *Christianity and Democracy*.[1] As was to become his wont, he there vaunts American democracy, contrasting it with what he had known in Europe.

> There is one thing that Europe knows well, that she knows even too well; that is the tragic meaning of life. After a thousand years of suffering she has learned to know what man is and at what cost the slightest progress is accomplished. . . . There is one thing that America knows well. . . . She knows that the man of common humanity has a right to the "pursuit of happiness"[2] . . . .

Seven years later Maritain was invited to give six lectures under the auspicies of the Charles R. Walgreen Foundation. These 1949 lectures became the volume entitled *Man and the State*.[3] Here again he takes up the phrase, "the pursuit of happiness," only this time in the best American tradition, referring to it as "an inalienable right."

---

[1]Jacques Maritain. *Christianity and Democracy* (London: Geoffrey Bles, The Centenary House, 1945), p. 7. For the recent American edition see, *Christianity and Democracy* (San Francisco: Ignatius Press, 1986).

[2]*Ibid.*, p. 61. and Ignatius Press edition, pp. 79–80

[3]Jacques Maritain. *Man and the State* (Chicago: University of Chicago Press, 1951). French translation, *L'homme et l'état* (Paris: Presses Universitaries de France, 1953).

Speaking of human rights, he maintains that they have an "inalienable character."

> Some of them, like the right to existence or to the pursuit of happiness, are of such a nature that the common good would be jeopardized if the body politic could restrict in any measure the possession that men naturally have of them. Let us say that they are absolutely inalienable.[4]

While Maritain continues by distinguishing between the *possession* of "inalienable rights" and the *exercise* of them, the indispensable "open sesame" for immediate entry into the American heart has been uttered. Every American feels sure that he and Maritain cannot be all that far from one another; that here indeed at last is a Frenchman who understands America and Americans since he speaks of "the inalienable right to the pursuit of happiness." Could Maritain's long honeymoon with the United States not indeed be related to his willingness to articulate the great American shibboleth in such serious contexts?

II

As a student of French literature I have always been fascinated by the spiritual witness of French Christians, beginning with Maritain, long before I had even heard of Claudel, Péguy or Bernanos. Over the years I have observed repeatedly that a deep sense of the believer's becoming a participant in the sufferings of Christ is, in fact, a feature of that spirituality, whether in a popular modern saint, such as Thérèse of Lisieux, or in that most French of French women, Joan of Arc, who so graphically incarnates redemptive suffering, and whose strange and wonderful story bears so many marks of the Passion of Jesus Christ.

Curiously, Rome's canonization of Joan of Arc in 1920, or of Thérèse of Lisieux in 1925, did not seem to have much impact on Jacques and Raïssa Maritain. This curious fact, coupled with Maritain's embracing American idealism as expressed in the phrase "the inalienable right to the pursuit of happiness" therefore has puzzled me when trying to integrate Maritain's own intellectual faith into what I believe to be France's traditional Christianity.

Catapulted into Catholicism by Léon Bloy, Maritain shortly thereafter discovered Thomas Aquinas through Raïssa. Never again was he

---

[4]*Ibid.*, p. 101.

to look back, intellectually confident as he was in the Angelic Doctor's primacy. And, though he and Raïssa and Vera all became Benedictine Oblates, Maritain still went his own way to such an extent that when he finally attached himself to a Christian community at the end of his life, it was not to the Benedictines that he turned.

One thing that Maritain was ever mindful of, however, was the power of Rome, probably because of an early experience. Under Bloy's impact he had written a volume on Mélanie, visionairy of La Salette to whom secrets had been entrusted in her visions. With the naive good faith of a convert, Maritain, recently given the title of "Doctor" by Rome, wished to seek Vatican approval for his potentially explosive volume.[5] His and Raïssa's pilgrimage to Rome in early 1918 while war was still raging, hoping to pilot this precious volume through Vatican red tape, proved a bitter experience. Undoubtedly, it sharpened Maritain's sensitivity to Rome's arbitrary power, making him aware of how the Vatican might react to works he would later publish in the two literary series he directed in Paris.

Thus, Maritain's neutral reaction to Rome's canonization of a Joan of Arc or a Thérèse of Lisieux seems somewhat paradoxical. Still, his experience with Roman bureaucracy does make it easier for us to understand why he contested the spirituality of Bernanos's first novel, *Under the Sun of Satan*, published in his *Roseau d'or* series in 1926. By effecting a veritable theological censoring of the text, Maritain probably wished to avoid Roman censure, even though it did throw Bernanos's creative vision as a Christian completely off axis.[6]

But then was it really fear of Rome that prompted Maritain to find Charles Péguy's poetry irreverent in regard to the most holy Virgin? Fortunately, Péguy did not depend on Maritain to get his work published. Claudel, of course, escaped critical assaults from Maritain

---

[5]Jacques Maritain. *Carnet de Notes* (Paris: Desclée de Brouwer, 1965), Chapter III, "*Notre premier voyage à Rome*," pp. 113–138. For the English edition see *Notebooks* (Albany, New York: Magi Books, 1984).

[6]On this thorny question see my "Avant-Propos" in Georges Bernanos, *Sous le soleil de Satan: Première édition conforme au manuscrit original* (Paris: Plon, 1982) pp. 9–23; see also my: "Jacques Maritain and Georges Bernanos on the Problem of Evil in *Sous le soleil de Satan*," in *Notes et Documents* 4 (october-décembre 1983), pp. 91–105; plus my highly specialized scholarly volume on the question: *Genèse et structures de <Sous le soleil de satan> d'après le manuscrit Bodmer: scrupules de Maritain et autocensure de Bernanos* (Paris: Archives des Lettres Modernes 1988).

who published a volume of Claudel's correspondence in his *Roseau d'or* series. Yet when texts were chosen for *Creative Intuition in Art and Poetry* it would not be the Christian verses of either Claudel or Péguy which would exactly overwhelm the reader.

Certainly, none of our three French literary giants ressembled Maritain in flirting with the United States. Claudel, French ambassador to Washington, was never seduced by American ideals. Bernanos, I was told in 1957 by his widow, refused to set foot in the United States, something she herself lamented, though Bernanos did address a letter to Roosevelt and the Americans in his war-time volume, "*Letter to the English.*" And as for Péguy, one wonders if he even allowed that the United States existed, so terribly focused was he on the implications of France having once been saved by God Himself from a future of English Protestantism through the miracle of Joan of Arc.

Péguy's obsession with the mystery of Joan of Arc apparently left Maritain unscathed. Did she and her voices smack a trifle too much of royalist fervor to fit into the humanist philosopher's cool, republican vision of a modern, democratic world? Claudel and Bernanos, however, like Péguy, both wrestled with the mystery of Joan of Arc and of her divine significance for France. Bernanos would even marry a descendent of the saint's brother.

III

Though so very different on the surface, our three literary giants are bound by a deep and common French spirituality rooted in the glorification of that most noble, yet most mysterious reality of human existence, taught in the Gospels, incarnate by the Old Testament prophets as well as by the chosen people themselves; then taken up by St. Paul and all the Apostles, martyrs, and confessors who, throughout two thousand years, until our own time, have perpetuated it through their incarnation of the life of Christ in His Church: redemptive suffering. Put into a French Christian context, "the pursuit of happiness" could refer to nothing less than an ascetic pursuit of God in whom true and final happiness can alone be found.

But is an ascetic pursuit of God in the style of the desert fathers what the founding fathers of the American Republic had in mind in the seventeenth-century when they spoke of the pursuit of happiness? Such a possibility is preposterous, for the concept of the pursuit of happiness is, whether we like it or not, necessarily rooted in a basic, inveterate humanism where man feels he is free to pursue his "inalienable right" quite apart from the saving action of God. In such an orientation, Christian practice can be nothing more than a slightly affected, slightly suspect embellishment, an option for those weak enough to feel the need of it. Never, however, can God's revelation of Himself in Jesus Christ be envisaged as constituting the one essential and indispensable element of human life. That, as every red-blooded American is taught, is found in the Creator-endowed inalienable right to pursue happiness. Man's utter dependence upon God not only for life itself, but for the very breath he draws, for his every heartbeat, cannot but be eclipsed by the idea of the pursuit of happiness. Equally eclipsed is Christian man's vast potential, that is his whole vocation to become, on this planet earth, a little incarnation of his God, Jesus Christ, through freely accepted redemptive suffering. Indeed, could a more subtly demonic toxin be injected into the psyche of a Christian than that of the concept that he is endowed by his Creator with the inalienable right to the pursuit of happiness?

IV

For a very strong dose of French anti-toxin, I have chosen to begin with the most senior of our three twentieth-century Christian giants, Paul Claudel. At the end of his sprawling fifteenth-century medieval play, translated as *The Tidings Brought to Mary* (*L'annonce faite à Marie*), the father of the play's heroine, Violaine, lays his daughter's unconscious body on the family table so that she, devoured by leprosy, may die in their midst. At that point, just before the final curtain falls, he enunciates what he, through his daughter's sufferings, has come to see as the purpose of life.

Violaine had assumed her suffering eight years before. Out of compassion for Pierre de Craon, master architect and builder of churches, as well as a secret leper, Violaine had knowingly kissed him on the mouth after he had revealed to her that the first mark of the disease had appeared under his clothing the day after he tried to rape her during his last stay at their country estate.

Violaine's kiss thus concludes the drama's all-important prologue where we have seen Pierre, obliged to return to the estate for masonry on the neighboring monastery, vainly trying to slip away at dawn without confronting her. She, however, has arisen early to open the door for him, wishing him to share in her joy on the eve of her engagement to her true love, Jacques Hury.

Pierre explains to Violaine that he has ecclesiastical dispensations to remain in society to build a church dedicated to St. Justice, a child virgin-martyr whose relics had been unearthed. Touched by the story of the child martyr, Violaine takes off an antique pagan gold ring given her in love by Jacques Hury. Passing it to Pierre, she says it is to buy a tiny stone for his edifice to God's justice. Then, anxious that Pierre be spared to complete this church to Justice, she lucidly opts to assume his illness, sacrificing her happiness with Jacques Hury through her symbolic kiss to the leper, Pierre. Kissing him she knows will make it impossible for her ever to marry Jacques Hury. Jacques, of course, will be quickly snapped up by Violaine's younger, black-hearted sister, Mara, bitterly jealous of Jacques's love for her older sister.

Eight years later, on Christmas eve, Mara journeys to the lepers's woods to visit Violaine, bearing in her arms the little dead body of the infant daughter finally born to her and Jacques. She has hidden this loss from Jacques, fearing to lose his love, for she knows he has never ceased loving Violaine. Therefore, hate her sister though she does, Mara desperately asks her help.

In her heart Mara admits that Violaine is holy and has never ceased glorifying God's justice, even as a blind leper, and even though deprived of the esteem of the only man she has ever loved. For Violaine has willingly allowed Jacques to believe, as Mara had told him, that she betrayed him with Pierre de Craon.

Mara, bearing her pathetic little bundle, says she has come to ask that she too be enabled to praise that God who had made her sister a leper. Her joy in possessing Jacques is great, she says, but she knows that her leper sister's joy with God is greater, even in her pain. Violaine answers:

> The pain was caused by love, and love by pain.
> Lighted wood yields not just ashes, but flame.[7]

To Mara's cynical question about what light or warmth she could possibly communicate to others in her blinded, exiled state in the leper's woods, Violaine answers:

> God is a miser allowing no creature to be consumed
> Without a little impurity's being devoured,

---

[7]Paul Claudel. *L'annonce faite à Marie* (Paris: Collection Folio, Gallimard, 1975), p. 165. This is translated from the French by the author, as are all the quotes coming from French sources in this article.

be it the creature's own, or that around him. . . .
Oh certainly, unhappiness is great at this hour. . . .
That is why my body is at work here in place of disintegrating
Christianity.
How powerful is suffering when it is as voluntary as sin!
You saw me kiss that leper, Mara? Well, the chalice of suffering is
deep, and whosoever touches it once with his lips will not willingly
take them away again![8]

Thereupon, the bells for the midnight mass of Christmas ring out; the sound of trumpets announces the procession of Joan of Arc leading the dauphin to nearby Rheims for anointing as France's Most Christian King; and Violaine restores the infant to life.

True to her bitter name, Mara rewards Violaine for the miracle by pushing her into a sandpit to die. There, three days later and at death's door, she is found by their father, Anne Vercors, as he returns home from his eight-year pilgrimage to Jerusalem, undertaken just as Violaine was undertaking her mission. He had told his wife of more than thirty years that he must leave for Jerusalem because he was too happy: he needed to put his hand in the hole made in the earth by the cross of Christ. The parallel with Violaine is strong, therefore, since she too, eight years before, at the moment of her formal engagement, had told Jacques Hury, that she too was too happy.

Thus, when he finds his leper daughter's dying body as he returns from Jerusalem, Violaine's father suddenly grasps that by her acceptance of what God had offered her, she, rather than he, had succeeded in putting her hand into the hole made in the earth by the cross of Christ. In climactic lines typifying Claudel's French spirituality, Anne Vercors says:

> I wanted once again to press myself against the empty tomb, to thrust my hand into the holes made by the cross, as did that apostle into the holes made in the hands and feet and heart.
>
> But wiser was Violaine, my own little girl! Is living the goal of life? Are the hands and feet of God's children attached to this wretched earth? The goal is not living, but dying! Not constructing a cross, but getting up on it and giving what one has with a laugh.[9]

---

[8]*Ibid.*, p. 166.
[9]*Ibid.*, p. 204.

V

Our second example of French spirituality comes from Georges Bernanos's third novel, *Joy*,[10] where Bernanos deliberately made Thérèse of Lisieux's spirituality that of his heroine, Chantal de Clergerie. Characterized by a profound sense of man's utter helplessness before God, this spirituality is succinctly enunciated in Thérèse of Lisieux's "*Act of Consecration as a Victim of Holocaust to the Holy Trinity*,"[11] where she states that she feels infinite desires in her, wanting to be a saint, but, knowing her impotence, can only ask God Himself to be her sanctity.

Joy, therefore, is not found in being happy, but, having discovered that we love God and that we are absolutely impotent before Him, joy is found in trusting Him to supply what is lacking in us. Just as the child can offer no present to his father without the father's first giving him the money to buy it, Thérèse recognized that she had nothing to offer God without His first giving it her. The "infinite longings" God put into her soul to be a saint were thus His gift, His own longings in her, as were also the often painful circumstances He provided her in which to bring these longings to fruition.

In *Joy* Bernanos's heroine, Chantal, constantly struggles, therefore, whether with her learned but *arriviste* father, or with her mad grandmother, or with a twisted psychiatrist friend of her father's, or with her father's drug-addicted Russian chauffeur, or, worst of all, with her father's learned imposter-priest friend for whom she will offer herself. Prior to her final sacrifice Chantal comes to understand that the whole dazzling center of her joy, lies in the absolute certainty of her own helplessness before God to win in her struggles. Only by accepting her helplessness can she know joy.

No inalienable right to pursue happiness is allowed for here. The drug-addicted Russian chauffeur assassinates Chantal, and her martyred body, with the chauffeur's, is discovered by the cook, a good simple woman, and the imposter-priest. Upon seeing the sorry spectacle before him, the imposter-priest, a celebrated writer on saints and

---

[10]*La Joie*, published by Plon in Paris in 1929, was awarded the *Prix Femina* that year. It is a sequel to Bernanos's second novel, *L'imposture*, published in 1928. The conversion of the imposter-priest hero of *L'imposture* terminates *La Joie*.

[11]Thérèse of Lisieux. *Manuscrits autobiographiques* (Carmel de Lisieux: 1957), p. 318.

mysticism, realizes that the sacrifice has been made for him, for he had once unwittingly confided the secret of his loss of faith to Chantal.

Turning to the cook he asks if she is able to say the "Our Father." When she has finished the prayer once, he orders her to repeat it again. Then, suddenly he himself, with great effort, cries out *"Pater noster!"* and falls senseless to the floor. He, whose whole life had been devoted to putting spirituality and mysticism into words, can find but two when faced with the sanctity and justice of God in his own life: "Our Father." We are told he died without ever recovering his reason.

That such a tale should be entitled *"Joy,"* indicates the extraordinary scope of Bernanos's spirituality. He, like Claudel, remembered that the Lord had said to Angela of Foligno, "it's not for laughs that I suffered."

VI

Péguy was ten years older than Maritain and knew him intimately. Péguy's lofty and noble effort to better the world through his prestigious but ever-financially-strapped pro-socialist review, *Les Cahiers de la Quinzaine*, prior to World War I attracted many French intellectuals with socialist sympathies, among whom was not only Jacques Maritain himself, but also his sister, Jeanne. Both worked for Péguy's review, long before any of them even dreamed of converting to Catholicism. At one time Péguy even viewed the young Maritain as his successor.

Through her chidren's ties with Péguy, Geneviève Favre, ex-Madame Paul Maritain, republican and anti-Catholic divorcée though she was, became Péguy's most intimate friend. Virtually daily she received the outpouring of the secret sorrows of Péguy's great and irreparably wounded noble heart. His sufferings stemmed from his very pure love for a young Jewish girl, Blanche Raphaël, whom, to get out of harm's way, he encourged to marry. This she did and had a daughter by her husband. Péguy himself was already the father of three children, none of whom, out of respect for his wife's family's republican heritage, had been baptized. Indeed, no child had been baptized in her family since the Revolution. Péguy had, after all, married Charlotte Beaudoin as a committed socialist in a civil ceremony.

Péguy's moral—and I would myself be tempted to say even "spiritual"— suffering gradually brought him to the conclusion that he was not fit to plan the coming of the "harmonious city" of the future, if he could not keep harmony in his own rebellious heart in the present.

Thus, did he come to sense man's utter dependence upon God to save him. However great his throbbing heart's love for Blanche Raphaël might have been, Péguy found in his morally strict upbringing by his widowed peasant mother the ballast needed in his great hour of need. He came to view himself as the prodigal son, who had so self-confidently forsaken the father's house as to wind up eating with the swine—just as Péguy as a youth had self-confidently abandoned the practice of the Christian faith for socialism. Péguy discovered not only a need but a desire to return to the Father's house as the lowest of servants.

To this highly charged drama of Péguy's, Maritain's mother was not only privy, but determined to assume an active role in its resolution. Early in this affair and prior to Blanche's marriage, Péguy's widowed mother had made the trip to Paris from Orléans, dressed in her peasant-best with starched white *coiffe* and apron. Geneviève Favre received her at her splendid Parisian apartment on the rue de Rennes, and had the temerity to suggest that with Péguy so unhappy, perhaps he should divorce his wife and marry Blanche. Pounding the table, the old Madame Péguy retorted that he already had a wife and three children. That was that.

Indeed, republican liberalism left the stoic rigidity of this remarkable old lady unscathed, she who, with the support of her own illiterate mother—of whom she was the illegitimate offspring—had reared Péguy as a widow, utterly dependent upon her own very humble craft of caning chairs to feed and clothe the three of them. How, then, had she swelled with pride at the extraordinary academic honors showered on her only child by the remarkable education system of France's Third Republic! She saw him, her little boy, catapulted from one elite school to one still more elite, then dispatched to Paris to be tutored for entrance to the most elite of all: the Ecole Normale Supérieure in Paris. To her dismay Péguy abandoned the Ecole Normale, as well as the university career it promised, in order to marry Charlotte Beaudoin. This had entailed a previous trip to Paris by the old Madame Péguy in her peasant-best, where she actually slapped her son in anger in a Paris street, so great was her disappointment at his giving up the security of a brilliant academic future of which she, quite justly, would have been so proud.

Maritain, thus, was aware of Péguy's painfully throbbing heart. Ironically, it was when they once both found themselves confessing to one another that they had discovered Catholicism that Maritain's intimacy with Péguy took on its most volatile dimensions. For Péguy, unlike Maritain, had been reared Catholic but had abandoned his faith. Being civilly married to an unbaptized woman with three unbaptized children meant that Péguy had no choice but to die outside the communion of the Roman Catholic Church. Paradoxically, however, Péguy was also destined to raise the cult of the virgin Birthgiver of God to heights never before attained in French literature, attaching it, through his very personal sorrow, to his abiding devotion to the Virgin's powerful presence at the Cathedral of Our Lady of Chartres, the great high holy place of the Beauce where Péguy was born.

As Maritain's intimate Péguy suffered from Maritain's inability to grasp the very delicate situation with his wife. Maritain's self-appointed personal mission to get Madame Péguy to allow her children to be baptized resulted in disaster on all sides and Maritain's estrangement from Péguy himself, plus the fury of Maritain's mother, distraught in seeing Péguy upset.

That Péguy begat another child, and that that child was baptized after his death at the beginning of the first World War, and that Madame Péguy herself and the other children were also eventually baptized, need not concern us here. It does concern us, however, to remember that in Péguy we see a remarkable, living example of the renunciation of what Péguy himself called *"the young man, Happiness"* in favor of *"the old man Honour,"* immortalized in Péguy's long outpourings in his all-but-suppressed *Quatrains.*[12]

We shall not dwell upon the heart-rending conflict between happiness and honor in the *Quatrains*, but rather take one brief example from Péguy's very personal living out of unhappiness enunciated in his *Five Prayers in the Cathedral of Our Lady of Chartres.*[13] In those

---

[12]Charles Péguy. *Oeuvres poétiques complètes* (Paris: Gallimard, Bibliothèque de la Pléiade, 1957), pp. 1265–1388. Marcel Péguy, the poet's son, who prepared the notes for this prestigious edition, offers no comment whatsoever either on the origin or the significance of these searing *Quatrains*, where *"Old man honour"* and *"Young man happiness"* so contend. He did not, in fact, even include them in the main body of the book. As might be some minor, unfinished, and unimportant text, these more than one-hundred pages of quatrains are stuck, totally without comment, in an Appendix at the end of the volume. Madame Charles Péguy was in fact adamant in regard to the drama of her husband's suffering heart. During her life time she forbade the name of Blanche Raphaël to appear in print, regardless of whatever other candid details scholars might give regarding the strange origin of this noble poetry paying such high honor to Péguy's fidelity to his spouse.

[13]*Ibid.*, pp. 908–924.

five short poems Péguy lays bare his very unhappy soul to Our Lady of Chartres, praying for his children along with Blanche's child. He tells the all-powerful Virgin that when the moment came of finding himself at the crossroads, where one path led down toward happiness, while the other led toward unhappiness, she, the holy virgin Birthgiver of God, knew which path he had chosen. And she knew he had not chosen it out of duty, which he could not stand. Nor had he chosen it out of goodness, for he had none of which to boast. Rather, he had deliberately placed himself at the point of the crossing where the pain was greatest, freely renouncing life with Blanche out of honor, and yet never loving her any less. He had, thus, lucidly fixed himself at the very heart of his pain and in the midst of the cause of his distress. His only prayer to the holy virgin Birthgiver of God, therefore, was not that he be happy, nor even that he suffer less, but that she, his mighty protectress, might help him keep intact that deep and cherished tenderness he had genuinely felt for honor in opting for unhappiness.

Through this devastating affair of the heart at a mature age, Péguy discovered that fundamental conflict with the basic conditions of life which every spiritual man discovers sooner or later during his earthly pilgrimage. It is, therefore, all the more astounding to see that Georges Bernanos at age 18 had already grasped this truth and in a political context rather than in a personal affair of the heart.

In a letter written to a young priest friend, the youthful Bernanos mockingly opposed the Christian democrats since, in order to believe in Christian democracy, he observed:

> You have to believe in the indefinite perfectibility of the human race, you have to skip over original sin and the common dilemma in which man finds himself.[14]

Man's "common dilemma" is indeed the key issue. Anyone determined to be Christian and, at the same time, to believe in "the pursuit of happiness" must sweep that dilemma under the carpet, trusting in an out-of-sight, out-of-mind orientation to life. The trouble is that the carpet of life will always be peeled back for each of us, sooner or later, by the hand of Death, revealing, sometimes repeatedly through the loss of those we love, all our vain illusions concerning man's

---

[14]Georges Bernanos, *Oeuvres romanesques* (Paris: Gallimard, Bibliotheque de la Pleiade, 1974), p. 1736.

immortality. Only in such God-filled and privileged moments of pain do we finally grasp what we have been told so many times by the holy ones of God: all in this world is utterly dependent upon God for meaning. The empty boast of being endowed by our Creator with an inalienable right to pursue happiness is then revealed for what it is: an unclean demonic illusion.

VII

But let us conclude with a return to the theme of redemptive and expiatory suffering. Of course, this was hardly a foreign topic in the little community of the three Benedictine oblates who together formed the Maritain household where Raïssa was supposed to carry out that very special and exalted function. Everyone in the Maritain circle, including Jacques and Vera themselves, recognized Raïssa as being, by vocation apparently, "the contemplative," who was shielded from the troublesome matters of running the household, or from typing Jacques's manuscripts, which the ever-valiant Vera took upon herself to do.

What marks for me the great turning point in Maritain's own spiritual evolution, since it seems to bring him more into a typically French pattern, would occur only some four years after Raïssa's death. In 1964, when writing his chapter on Vera[15] in his *Carnet de Notes*, we find Maritain noting that Raïssa's designation as "contemplative," however well-founded it might be, still should not exclude Vera who, he insists, was *equally* contemplative. Yes, Vera, who was ever so popularly regarded—and even regarded by herself—as the "Martha" of the household! Let's listen to Maritain:

> It is easy to imagine Raïssa as a Mary devoted to contemplation, and Vera as a Martha, devoted to the active life, a super Sister of Charity. . . .
> But Vera lived from prayer as did Raïssa, she too knew that one had to *give everything* to Jesus, *everything, absolutely everything*; she too had achieved unity within herself in that peace which God gives.[16]

Maritain states that he is actually quoting from Vera's own notebooks in underscoring that one has to give *"everything, absolutely everything"* to Jesus.[17]

15Jacques Maritain, *Carnet de notes*, p. 8.
16*Ibid.*, p. 260.
17*Ibid.*, note 2.

This late insistence upon the high state of Vera's spirituality has always seemed to me an integral part of what I believe to be that other preoccupation of Maritain's in those years he survived Raïssa and wrote *The Peasant of the Garonne*. And I am still convinced of what I wrote in 1985 when I observed that

> no aspect of Raïssa's Christian thought actually took on more importance for Jacques at the end than did her reflections on coredemption. Indeed, after he had devoted a dozen pages to it with substantial quotes from Raïssa in *Le paysan*, he came back the following year and, still quoting Raïssa, took up this question again in *De la grâce et de l'humanité de Jésus*.[18]

Thus, as profoundly certain as I am that at the end Maritain did come to what I would call a very French orientation in his spirituality, where co-redemption becomes the great theme, he had indeed pursued a very long and rather liberal, humanist, slightly modernist, and completely unorthodox route to arrive there, including his flirtation with the whole American concept of the Creator-endowed right to the pursuit of happiness. On this liberal and so humanist route, the philosopher had opposed both Péguy and Bernanos on matters which confirmed their, and not his, theological rectitude, and which set both writers's artistic genius against Maritain's aesthetic reservations.

But by the time Maritain arrived at that point, all three giants had long since left this world. Péguy was killed at age 41 at the very beginning of World War I. Bernanos died of cancer of the liver at age 60, in 1948. Claudel, born in 1869 before both of them, outlived them and, after having achieved an illustrious diplomatic career and the literary status of an "immortal" of the French Academy, died as recently as 1955 at age 86.

VIII

Each of our three French literary giants did, in fact, discover that the dilemma of man's fallen state can shatter the confident pride of the self-sufficient and haughty human heart. Yet—sweet miracle of grace!—it is from such broken and lacerated human hearts that the

---

[18]William Bush. "Raïssa Maritain . . . et Jacques," in Deal W. Hudson and Matthew J. Mancini. *Understanding Maritain: Friend and Philosopher* (Macon, Georgia: Mercer University Press, 1987), p. 68.

most wondrously authentic artistic expression emerges, as well as the greatest manifestations of holiness. "*A broken and contrite heart, O God, thou wilt not despise,*" a broken King David cried out to God in the *Psalms*. Only after more than fifty years of marriage and only after he had suffered the loss of first Vera and then of Raïssa, did Maritain finally arrive at such a point. As he himself wrote in *The Peasant of the Garonne* speaking of Raïssa and Vera:

> They taught me what contemplation in the world is. As for me, I was a dawdler, a worker with the intellect, and thereby likely to believe that I was living out certain things because my head understood them a little, and that my philosophy discoursed about them. But through experience I was instructed, and well instructed, in the suffering and light of these two faithful souls. That's what gives me the courage to try to bear witness to them in speaking here of things which are above me, even though I know very well that being instructed through example, and while working side by side, does not make it any easier—far from it—to translate into ideas and words what I learned through them.[19]

Time proves relevant only for those of us allowing ourselves to be bound by its illusions and refusing to look beyond its apparent limits. What difference, then, if Maritain only got there at the end, and long after his three contemporaries were dead? The important thing for me as a student of French literature is that for Maritain at that point, the great French tradition suddenly, and almost supernaturally, seemed to well up from the depths to sustain a disheartened and very lonely Jacques as he gradually grasped what St. Thomas Aquinas had grasped before him. Whatever might be the intellectual games played by a Christian philosopher, all that is but a heap of straw unless the redemptive suffering of Jesus Christ has been assumed personally by the believer whom God Himself has stooped to create in His own image, redeem with His own blood, and heal by His stripes.

---

[19]Jacques Maritain. *Le paysan de la Garonne* (Paris: Desclée de Brouwer, 1966), p. 286. English edition, *The Peasant of the Garonne*, trans. Michael Cuddihy and Elizabeth Hughes (London: Godfrey Chapman, 1968), p. 196.

Are the Poor Blessed?
On Happiness and Beatitude

Deal W. Hudson

Happiness has been so degraded by its identification with "well-feeling" that one can appear spiritually callous in rising to its defense. The prophets who have warned against the pursuit of a subjective happiness have been made welcome, even if their warnings have not been heeded. One only has to draw a line from Augustine through Luther and Pascal, to Kant and Kierkegaard, to Reinhold Neibuhr and Karl Barth to be reminded of how much respect the rejection of happiness has been afforded. Figures such as these are heralded for their tough stance against worldliness, for their unwillingness to conform with the spirit of the age, and for their refusal to compromise with exigencies of temporal fulfillment.

However, the prophetic critique of happiness as an earthly aim can be taken seriously without concluding that what parades under the banner of "the pursuit of happiness" is necessarily self-absorbing. The prophet's warning can renew our thinking about human happiness by supplying a shift of contexts: from the maintenance of well-feeling to the struggle of forging well-being. Rather than expecting a happy life to offer freedom from suffering and disturbance, we not only accept our vulnerability to misfortune but anticipate the difficulties of seeking order in a disordered world. In short, happiness is seen not primarily as a subjective state of feeling, satisfaction, or consciousness, but an activity of seeking to realize the whole human good. It is the ancient eudaemonistic link of happiness in human life with the best, or most choiceworthy, that prophets goad us to rediscover.

At the heart of this retrieval of happiness is the willingness to view pain and suffering from a new vantage point. The advocates of subjective well-feeling regard so-called negative affections as destructive of the fragile psychological economy they deem happiness. Those who pursue happiness in its ancient meaning as *eudaimonia* are disposed to accept some obstacles and suffering as constitutive of seeking the good itself. Moral heroism is often met with scorn and misunderstanding. At the same time, moral failure and disappointment can return us to the spiritual sources we have come to ignore. The loss of external goods, even goods of the body, can do the same. Finally, those who seek happiness in human realization also understand that every aspect of the temporal good contains its tragic pitfalls: we can lose wealth, health, friendship, and even moral virtue against our will.

However, to view suffering as constitutive of happiness raises another danger: the danger of pessimism subverting our concern for the *whole* human good. The restoration of happiness as a worthy aim begins by exposing its desire for a bubble of immediacy which protects the self from itself and from suffering of others. But this recommendation, which seems like such good sense, can be distorted. It can result in wishes that run contrary to the fundamental principle of friendship and neighborly love, wishing the good for others.

While it is also obvious to anyone that suffering can and really does cripple us, it is not always instructive or redemptive. Consider the import of the Beatitudes: we are told that the poor, the hungry, and the persecuted are "blessed" (*Matthew* 5:1–11). These passages appear to ratify the connection between suffering and the final end of life. How could such wisdom invite distortion? The reason is that to say "Blessed are the poor" outside the theological context of grace and repentance is to state a maxim with cruel social implications. What results when this principle is applied in the political sphere? Should we be less disturbed by presence of an economic underclass, taking consolation from the fact that their poverty blesses them? Is it one thing to maintain that suffering is constitutive of a happy life, yet quite another to say that all suffering is a blessing, even in view of eternal happiness. This line of reasoning, it will be argued, ignores the distinction between ends of this life and the next, as well as the tragic dimension of both.

II

It seems strange, in the first place, to mention happiness and suffering in the same breath. We all know that suffering comes regardless of what we think about it, or what framework we place it in. Even those possessed of the prophetic spirit about these matters must admit that the idea of happiness naturally aligns itself with pleasure and other states of well-feeling, not pain. This association is not a philosophical or a theological mistake; it does not necessarily lead to hedonism or utilitarianism. The enjoyment of pleasure, as Aristotle has said, is necessary for the virtues to be deeply embedded.[1] Given ordinate desires, pleasure and enjoyment can indicate the possession of something good. The mistake, according to Aristotle, comes when we ignore the object of pleasure and the activities giving rise to pleasure, and treat pleasure as a value in itself.[2] As Callicles reminded Socrates, enjoyments can arise from the grain of any character: it is getting what one wants that reaps the reward of satisfaction.[3]

Now although pleasure more quickly comes to mind when we imagine happiness, once we turn our attention to the question of the objects and activities constitutive of a happy life, distress comes into view. Socrates himself left a powerful image of this association with his image of the leaky jars.[4] A good life holds on to its satisfactions because they share in the durability of virtue; a bad life enjoys its conquests, but not for very long. But it was Augustine who, in the *City of God*, challenges the entire tradition of classical eudaemonism by arguing that pagans sought the happy life as an idol to be worshipped in the place of God.[5] His own prophetic critique of happiness arises out of a meditation on his life, as he says in the *Confessions*: "I loved the happy life, *but I feared to find it in your abode*, and I fled from it, even as I sought it."[6] For him, a basic human infirmity subverts all human attempts to follow the simple and the wise injunction to seek happiness without idolatry.[7]

---

[1] *Nicomachean Ethics*, 1099a12–21.

[2] *Nicomachean Ethics*, 1174a14–1174b.

[3] *Gorgias*, 491e5–492c.

[4] *Gorgias*, 493d5–494a5.

[5] *City of God*, 19.1.

[6] *Confessions*, 6.11 (Ryan translation).

[7] In "The Happy Life" Augustine asks if "Everyone who possesses what he wants is happy?" His mother Monica answers, "If he wishes and possesses good things, he is happy; if he desires

The substance of his critique, then, has two poles: not only are we wrong about the object of our happiness, but we are also naturally disposed, because of original sin, toward embracing something less and treating it as final. Ordinate desire, therefore, requires both an appropriate object and a will to suffer the loss of familiar delectations. While we are in the habit of seeking to satisfy an infinite desire with finite objects, we are cut off from anything that Augustine, or any Christian in the pre-modern tradition, would call true happiness.

Since imperfection is unavoidable, no aspect of our terrestrial journey to that blessedness can be called happy, with the exception of our hope.[8] The suffering of the present life makes it impossible for any life to fulfill the eudaemonistic criteria of completeness and self-sufficiency. Augustine's religious reconsideration of *beatitudo* and *felicitas* lead him to add spiritual distress to the suffering of misfortune. This is due to four factors: 1) resistance to relinquishing entrenched delights; 2) guilty awareness of falling short, i.e., sin; 3) imperfection attendant even to the most sanctified life; and 4) the "undergoing," or suffering, of divine help. This is a far cry from the happy life free from all regret and repentance found in Cicero.[9] What these meanings of suffering have in common is a description of disproportion in an individual's being and the self-awareness often belonging to those states. Suffering, therefore, can be for good or ill, depending on the nature of the disproportion. If persons suffer by receiving from another an ability beyond their own power, then the suffering is beneficial. If the suffering evinces a diminished potency, as in blindness or deafness, it is destructive.

Augustine's one qualification in his rejection of earthly happiness—that one can participate in happiness in this world through the virtue of hope—might seem to have foreshadowed the emergence of psychological happiness. Hope, for him, is not simply an unfounded attitude; hope is a belief, is a knowledge of sorts, that good will lie in the future. So, from an Augustinian point of view, subjective adjustment is not enough for happiness. His suggestion that hope is the last vestige of happiness, once its object has been transposed to

---

evil things— no matter if he possesses them—he is wretched"; see, translation by Ludwig Schopp (St. Louis, Missouri: B. Herder Book Co., 1974), p. 56.

[8]*City of God*, 19.20.

[9]*Tusculan Disputation*, 5.18.

eternity, can be misconstrued as an invitation to pursue happiness as a matter of psychological training. Augustine rejects pagan eudaemonism as idolatry, but he retains its conception of happiness as well-being.

It is easy to see that with the object of happiness, God, being placed out of reach in this life, human self-consciousness would offer itself as the last domain for the possession of a good which could be called happiness.[10] Augustine's critique of happiness has been described as the problem of consciousness and satisfaction, in particular, as the inability to achieve an integration of satisfactions in this life. In short, the inability of terrestrial experience to satisfy the eudaemonistic criterion of wholeness. Thus, Augustine, it can be said, unintentionally set the scene for the dominant value of well-feeling in modernity by eliminating all the other options.

The idea of earthly happiness at the end of the Patristic period was rejected in favor of a belief in a transcendent object and the obstacle of informed desire. Helped by its strong ratification in Boethius's *Consolation of Philosophy*, this rejection stood unchallenged until the twelfth-century when discussions of "imperfect happiness" began to appear, probably in response to the earliest Latin translations of Aristotle's *Nicomachean Ethics*.[11]

III

For Aquinas human imperfection became a qualifier of happiness, not a destroyer. This challenge to Augustine's other-worldliness, made possible by the Aristotelian revival, was inspired in Aquinas by his teacher Albertus Magnus who commented on the whole of the *Ethics*. The admittedly modest notion of earthly happiness found in Aquinas's

---

[10]Charles Norris Cochrane, *Christianity and Classical Culture: A Study of Thought from Augustus to Augustine* (New York: Oxford University Press, 1944), pp. 389–92.

[11]See the series of articles by Antony J. Celano: "The Concept of Worldly Beatitude in the Writings of Thomas Aquinas," *Journal of the History of Philosophy* 25 (1987), pp. 215–226; "Act of the Intellect or Act of the Will: The Critical Reception of Aristotle's Idea of Human Perfection in the 13th and Early 14th Centuries," *Archives d'histoire doctrinale et littéraire du moyen age* 65 (1990), pp. 93–119; "The Understanding of the Concept of Felicitas in the Pre-1250 Commentaries on the *Ethica Nicomachea*," *Medioevo* 12 (1986), pp. 29–53; "Peter of Auvergne's Questions on Books I and II of his *Ethica Nicomachea: A Study*, "The <<Finis Hominis>> in the Thirteenth-Century Commentaries on Aristotle's Nicomachean Ethics," *Archives d'histoire doctrinale et littéraire de moyen age* (1986), pp. 23–53.

writings comes as a much-needed counterbalance to the Augustinian dualism, especially in the realm of politics. Though in his treatments of happiness Aquinas cites Augustine and Boethius on the lack of earthly happiness, he proceeds in an almost off-handed way with his proposal of a *beatitudo imperfecta*, seemingly unaware of the significance of his distinction.

Fully aware of the tendency to idolize temporal goods, Aquinas nonetheless includes them in earthly happiness, without any of the dramatic warnings typical of Augustine. For Aquinas the wholeness of the human good remains what it is, even in the face of possible idolatry. Aristotelian external goods and bodily goods, the subject of so much controversy among the classical schools, are reinstated as necessary to earthly happiness.[12] Their necessity as instrumental goods, serving the goods of the soul, is not treated as optional. Health, for example, helps secure higher goods in life, such as knowledge. His treatment of temporal happiness as a mixed concept, i.e, different goods, is always carefully subsumed to eternal beatitude. There are not two final ends, but one. Even with an explicit alternative of the true *summum bonum*, Aquinas shapes his account of earthly happiness with an integrity of its own.

It is legitimate to question whether turning the spotlight on this theme accords with Aquinas's intentions. After all, he directly alludes to the Augustinian rejection of pagan eudaemonism. So any reconstruction of *beatitudo imperfecta* must be carried out in the shadow of the prophetic critique, or it ignores Aquinas's own use of Augustine's authority.

To accomplish this it is not enough to interpret just the relevant texts. They must be enriched by related themes in Aquinas's thought itself and in the work of his later interpreters. There are important aspects of Aquinas's view of earthly happiness that are not developed; they must be drawn out. Aquinas thought that he was reserving a place in his ethics for Aristotle's *eudaimonia* while he was obviously superseding it with the beatitude of the beatific vision. It seems that Aquinas' attention was so strongly focused on shaping the immeasurably larger context of happiness that he did not notice the extent to which it was reshaping the Aristotelian nucleus.

---

[12]*ST.*, I-II, 4, 5 & 7.

Aquinas's use of the concept "imperfect happiness" is a deliberately minimal notion set beneath the maximal conception of the beatific vision. It is minimal in the sense that Aquinas is willing to predicate happiness of a life less than perfectly actualized in the presence of God, a happiness that can be gained and lost. Since pagans are capable of it, imperfect happiness can be acquired through the exercise of natural powers, unaided by divine grace.[13] It is based mainly on the exercise of practical reason but at its most perfect it is contemplative.[14] The classical primacy of contemplation in happiness remains but in a qualified way.

Most startling, however, is that Aquinas predicates happiness of lives perhaps destined for eternal damnation. This fact reveals the distance that Aquinas has moved away from the theories of the classical eudaemonists and their criteria of completeness, self-sufficiency, and choiceworthiness. Rather than an all-or-nothing state, Aquinas conceives happiness across a sliding scale of act and potency: "a thing is perfect in so far as it is actual."[15] Earthly happiness can be called "the happiness of the journey" toward the human good. The operation or activity which is a happy life exists in tensive relation to the end being sought.

Aquinas considers the ends of human life as twofold. To say that the human end is twofold is not to say that these are separate; they are related as last to proximate. It is crucial to notice that the two types of happiness differ in species: imperfect happiness is an imperfect operation subject to man's natural power taking its species from its object which is an imperfect good.[16] The difference between the perfect good (God) and the imperfect good (the universal good) also distinguishes the ends of human law and divine law.[17] But it remains what Aquinas calls a *participation* in the sovereign good which does not destroy the nature of temporal happiness. The notion

---

[13]*ST.*, I-II, 5, 5c.

[14]*ST.*, I-II, 3, 5c.

[15]*ST.*, I-II, 3, 2c. Also, "Since happiness signifies some final perfection; according as various things capable of happiness can attain to various degrees of perfection, so there be various meanings applied to happiness" (*ST.*, I-II, 3, 2, ad 4); "Because when a man begins to make progress in the acts of the virtues and gifts, it is hoped that he will arrive at perfection, both as a wayfarer, and as a citizen of the heavenly kingdom" (*ST.*, I-II, 69, 2c).

[16]*ST.*, I-II, 5, ad 3.

[17]*ST.*, I-II, 98, 1c.

of participation, therefore, insures the connections of the proximate to the final end.[18]

Given these distinctions, temporal happiness can consist of roughly four kinds: the active and contemplative pagan type and the active and contemplative Christian type: the former measured by prudence, the latter by charity. What complicates any kind of division is that any typology can be subdivided in terms of act and potency, as the life of charity can be enriched even further by the infused gifts and beatitudes. The diversity of the happy life on earth resembles the degrees of beatitude of the blessed in heaven.

The most significant aspect of imperfect happiness to be underscored is that it is primarily an act of willing, or love, rather than an act of knowing. The reasons given explicitly by Aquinas for this are two: 1) imperfect happiness consists first and principally as an operation of the practical intellect directing human actions and passion;[19] and 2) in this life the will can gain a closer relation to the good than the intellect.[20] Although the presence of the other virtues is necessary to support the activity of contemplation, the summit of imperfect happiness, this role is not solely instrumental. The virtues establish an ordinate relation of all human desires to the good.

Still, there is a tension between loving and knowing in earthly happiness. Aquinas and other medievals addressed this issue under the rubric of whether or not happiness consists in an act of the intellect or of the will. Aquinas uses this debate to show that terrestrial happiness is a kind of loving, but not one that rejects the demands of finality in the name of individual freedom. Aquinas's view of imperfect happiness, in spite of his claims about contemplation, can also explain how the happy life remains *in via* and in a tensive passion toward the final end.

---

[18]*ST.*, I-II, 5, 3, ad 2. For the same reason he calls the act of wisdom is a beginning or participation of future happiness (I-II. 66, 5, ad 2).

[19]"Therefore the last and perfect happiness, which we await in the life to come, consists entirely in contemplation. But imperfect happiness, such as can be had here, consists first and principally, in an operation of the practical intellect directing human actions and passions, as stated in *Ethics*. x 7, 8" (*ST.*, I-II, 3, 5c). This argument is to be distinguished from the highest form of imperfect happiness which is contemplation (*ST.*, I-II, 3, 5c).

[20]"Love ranks above knowledge in moving, but knowledge precedes love in attaining" (*ST.*, I-II, 3, 4, ad 4). The final end is present to us, as in Augustine, through the infused virtue of hope: "But sometimes it is possible to attain it, yet it is raised above the capacity of the attainer, so that he cannot have it forthwith; and this is the relation of one that hopes, to that which he hopes for, and this relation alone causes a search for the end" (*ST.*, I-II, 4, 3c).

There is no doubt, however, that Aquinas would claim the "intellectualism" that is so often laid at his feet. If we look at the insistence of Aquinas on the importance of the intellect in happiness, we notice not only his insistence on a human fulfillment that must somehow satisfy our rational nature as *homo sapiens* but also that the intellect guides the will to a happiness that is true rather than false. The will moves toward an end presented to by the intellect. The intellect is present to the will in all its willing, supplying a vision for the will to love. Aquinas repeatedly argued that the will's object, as supplied by the intellect, is naturally prior to its act.[21] Thus, his explanations of happiness usually begin with the particular need of a rational nature to know and moves to a consideration of the relation of the will to the intellect, emphasizing the role of the intellect in discriminating between the will's choices.

As Thomas argues in the *Summa Contra Gentiles*, all forms of happiness from the perspective of the will alone look identical.[22] Like Aristotle, Boethius, and Augustine before him, Thomas recognizes that competing forms of happiness bear a strong resemblance when regarded only in respect to the passions and to the delights each elicits. The will moves toward the absent good or rejoices in present, whether the good is apparent or real. But Aquinas holds the intellect responsible for distinguishing between true and false happiness, which the will is not equipped to do. It is precisely the dynamism of the moving toward the "absent good" that gives happiness in this life its special character.

However, the intellect can claim a superior mode of possessing its object, knowledge. The will must go outside itself for what it does not yet have, while the knower contains the known within himself. And, so, for Aquinas this more intimate mode of possession—actual subjective attainment—qualifies intellection as the primary activity of happiness. The will cannot possess anything on its own: in Pascal's terms it is the power that hunts rather than captures. Thus, when St. Thomas says that "happiness is in the one who is happy," his intent was not to make happiness wholly subjective, but to stress that only through rationally directed activity can we find a place of happy rest.[23]

---

[21]*ST.*, I-II, 3, 4, ad 3.
[22]*Summa Contra Gentiles*, 3. 2. 105.
[23]*ST.*, I-II, 2, 2, sed contra.

In this life the intellect cannot fully possess the only object that can satisfy its natural desire, God.[24]

For all his intellectualism Aquinas was extremely careful in not claiming more for human knowledge in this life than could be maintained in the light of sin, grace, and our need for the theological virtues. In fact, it is under the force of these theological considerations that Aquinas gives his account of earthly happiness a strong amorous tinge. Here he diverges significantly with Aristotle because the object of eternal happiness, God Himself, cannot be found within the realization of any human potency but beyond it. The reason for this follows directly from his own dictum that in this life love can attain a closer relation to a higher good than the intellect. Thus, it is in terms of the loving and of the partial realizing of the absent good that the activity of earthly happiness must be described.

IV

With this more dynamic characterization of earthly happiness, Aquinas's turn toward modernity is obvious. He moves beyond the Augustinian happiness in hope. He also moves within range of the prophetic critique. It could now be asked whether Aquinas is tempting the moral fates by reintroducing earthly happiness? In response it can be said that he surely knew its temptations, its utter centrality. After all, he depicted the fall of Lucifer as a willful choice of happiness

---

[24]Although intellect is essentially superior to will, it is not superior in relation to God, particularly in this life since we lack the "light of glory" through which we can gain knowledge of God in eternity. Intellectual apprehension of God necessarily scales Him down, while the approach of love working outwardly from our intellectual appetite preserves the nobility of his Being. Thus Aquinas could also argue that the love of God is better than knowledge of God," [*ST.*, I-II, 82, a. 3] explaining that it better to love higher things but better to know the things which are lower.

This does not present a problem in understanding Thomas's repeated insistence on the primacy of the intellect in the Beatific Vision. The emphasis on the intellectual act of seeing God affirms grace meeting the inclination of rational human nature through God's own illumination of the mind by the lumen gloriae. By His act of love God relieves human love of its task of outstripping the limited intellect. In making Himself immediately known through His essence, not by any likeness of an intelligible species, God rescinds a portion of the primacy that love enjoys in imperfect happiness. God's accommodation of Himself to the rational creature He has enable the mind to satisfy its hunger for vision and knowledge of the first cause (*ST.*, I, 12, 2 & 5). Love and joy are each perfected as a result of what God has accomplished for the human mind (*ST.*, I-II, 11, 2, ad 3).

before God.[25] In the prologue to the *Prima Secundae*, he argued that the deviation from eternal life with God is nothing less than a rejection of the object of happiness.[26]

From an Augustinian viewpoint Aquinas seems to be setting up an idol with his view of imperfect happiness. Is Aquinas guilty? This question gets us closer to the point of the prophet's critique. We have already seen that Augustine himself would predicate happiness of Christians in terms of their hope. It can be inferred from this that he, and the other prophets, would not object to Aquinas calling Christians "happy" if they participate in God by the bond of charity. After all, Catholics come to the altar at every Mass upon hearing the words "Happy are those who are called to His Supper." It goes without saying, of course, that we are far away from the common parlance of happiness which concerns itself only with measuring the degree of subjective well-feeling.

What about Aquinas's imperfect pagan happiness? At its best it is the Aristotelian life of moral virtue supported by the basic goods of the body and fortune. How could we call a life happy which may never know and love its true final end? At such an assertion the prophet must object that we only encourage the making of idols—whether virtue itself, even worse the infused gift of charity, or the more likely candidates of wealth, power, and pleasure.

And it can be said on behalf of the prophet that the entire history of happiness supports his critique—the gradual elimination of virtue from the equation and, as a consequence, the ordering of goods without reference to the genuine final end. In the place of God various candidates have emerged to claim the title of *summum bonum*: freedom, power, wealth, psychological satisfaction. All of these idols have come to inhabit the American pursuit of happiness and its imitators. Given this historical perspective, perhaps Augustine, not Aquinas, was right.

Jacques Maritain, and other contemporary Thomists like Yves R. Simon, drew upon Aquinas to construct a political theory in which the right to the pursuit of happiness is seen as integral to the political order.

---

[25]"But he [Lucifer] desired resemblance with God in this respect,—by desiring, as his last end of beatitude, something which he could attain by the virtue of his own nature, turning his appetite away from supernatural beatitude, which is attained by God's grace" (*ST.*, I, 63, 3c).

[26]*ST.*, I-II, prologus.

When you know that we are all made for blessedness, death no longer holds any terror; but you cannot become resigned to the oppression and enslavement of your brothers, and you aspire, for the earthly life of humanity, to a state of emancipation consonant with the dignity of this life.[27]

Is this perspective vulnerable to a powerful rebuttal? Since we are obliged to pursue happiness as the fulfillment of human nature, should it either be banished from the city and saved for what is truly ultimate? From the prophet's perspective any worthy pursuit of happiness entails a life of suffering love, a life that places the well-being of others first, since the word "happiness" has precisely the opposite effect and connotation. Such a life, it is argued, is made possible when people no longer place their sights upon success in this world.

Thus, the prophet here has much in common with conservative religious thinkers who have objected to the political association of Catholicism with democracy and, by implication, with the "pursuit of happiness."[28] Happiness, they argue, as total human fulfillment, promises too much in the political order. For example, it stimulates an invasion of privacy and gives government too much power, too much of a mandate, and leads to utopianism. Indeed, the prophet can remind us of how it helped justify a theocracy; now it can lead to different forms of ideological domination, all in the name of promoting human happiness.

So, the prophet and the politician can each denounce happiness: the former because it sets our sights too low; the latter because it sets the sights of government too high. It is thus no surprise that these prophets and these politicians have often been allies and have even belonged to the same church and to the same political party.

Although one can sympathize with elements of both the religious and the political critique, a moderate account of earthly happiness

---

[27]Jacques Maritain, *Christianity and Democracy* , trans. Doris C. Anson (London: Geoffrey Bles, 1945), pp. 35–36. See also the 1986 San Francisco, Ignatius Press edition of this book, p. 44. Readers of Maritain will recognize this remark as typical of his social thought. See also Yves R. Simon, "The Pursuit of Happiness and the Lust for Power" in *Philosophy of Democratic Government*, Revised edition (Notre Dame, Indiana: University of Notre Dame Press, 1993), pp. 288–296.

[28]For example, critics of Maritain's program of *Integral Humanism* and his political legacy; see Gerry Lessard, "The Critics of Integral Humanism: A Survey" in Thomistic Papers, vol. 3, ed. Leonard Kennedy (Houston, Texas: Center for Thomistic Studies, 1987), pp. 117–140.

must be defended. First, it challenges the dualistic separation of the cities of God and man by viewing human beings, as Aquinas does, as being wayfarers, from the beginning of life on a journey to God. For the *homo viator*, happiness or unhappiness is always in process of becoming. The happiness sought in this life, through the exercise of reason and the guide of virtue, is a participation in perfect happiness. This distinction is not a contemporary twist, nor an attempt to force Aquinas to speak in a more modern idiom. This is Aquinas's own image employed to describe both pagan and Christian happiness in this life, a continuity upheld by the notion of the resurrected body.

Secondly, the love of neighbor or friendship requires our wishing the whole good for others.[29] This wish includes goods of the soul, goods of fortune, goods of the body—in short, all aspects of our well-being encompassed by political happiness, i.e., earthly life. To wish someone to lack any aspect of that well-being falls short of love's full obligation. Aquinas's emphasis on the nature of earthly happiness as loving and achieving the real human good opposes the tendency of the well-intentioned prophets to misapply "blessed are the poor" to the political sphere.

However, before moving to the next point, it is necessary to look at an objection from Aquinas himself. He says that we are bound by charity to hate sin;[30] that the love of neighbor does not extend to sin and lack of justice; and that hatred of fault is equivalent to desire for good.[31] Hatred of what is evil is simply the flipside of loving the good; it indicates a desire to remove impediments to a good life. The question then becomes what if those impediments are external goods of various forms: wealth, honor, and so forth.

This issue arises in another context where Aquinas asks, "whether the Church should receive those who revert from heresy?" His answer poses a serious problem. He argues that the Church extends its charity to all, including its enemies, by wishing and working for their good. The good is twofold: spiritual and temporal. According to the spiritual good, the Church can receive them—for their salvation. We are not required by charity to will the temporal goods

---

[29]*ST.*, I-II, 26, 4c.
[30]*ST.*, II-II, 25. 11c.
[31]*ST.*, II-II, 34. 3c.

except in relation to the eternal salvation of them and others. Hence if the presence of one of these goods in one individual might be an obstacle to eternal salvation in many, we are not bound out of charity to wish such a good to that person, rather should we desire him to be without it, both because eternal salvation takes precedence of temporal good, and because the good of the many is to be preferred to the good one."[32]

The only way to meet this objection directly is to point out that this comment, and others like it, are made within a theological context. They belong to judgments made with the benefit of charity. Thus, they are not suitable as recommendations in the political sphere, in the domain of earthly happiness. In other words, Aquinas's words do not warrant our wishing that the mass of humanity remain in poverty so that they can avoid the temptation to greed.

Such judgments in charity are far too difficult to make, much like judgments about happiness, to be the province of the philosopher and the citizen. They require greater intimacy than that of acquaintances and fellow citizens. Most importantly, employing such a maxim politically ignores the distinction between the end of natural law and the end of divine law.[33] The Beatitudes are instituted, according to Aquinas, for removing the obstacle of "sensual happiness"—excess riches and bodily pleasure, inordinate passions[34]—but these are blessings that are in part voluntary, not imposed, as a spiritual poverty is voluntary.[35]

The third reason for defending imperfect happiness is the meaning of political friendship; it demands that we wish for prosperity, not suffering. While we know from experience that suffering may lead to God, we should also remember that it leads to despair and cynicism: suffering can break and cripple as well as redeem. There is no way to say in advance what will cripple any more than we can predict what will redeem. Too often, however, prospective wishes are being made on the basis of a retrospective appraisal. In other words, we see that suffering has reoriented our life in the past, so we wish suffering for someone who we think needs a similar reorientation. Such wishes can

---

[32]ST., II-II, 34, 3c.
[33]ST., I-II, 98, 1c.
[34]ST., I-II, 69, 3, ad 6.
[35]ST., I-II, 69, 3, ad 6.

become formulated into informal principles about the various lessons that suffering can teach.

Boethius makes this point when Lady Philosophy states that God imparts suffering and joy in the degree that most benefits each.[36] The way any individual is going to respond to good or bad fortune is a matter of mystery. Because of this unpredictability, joy must be seen as the better bet for leading people to their proper end. After all, human beings were made for joy, the fruit of the beatific vision. Our wishes should be for a reorientation to what is good, and leave the choice of means to a greater wisdom.

It is easy for those inspired by the religious vision of providentially ordered suffering to assume the place of active agents in the divine economy. The argument that punishment makes a wicked person happier goes back to Socrates.[37] The coherence of the position depends upon the identification of the human good, and therefore of happiness, with virtue alone. Boethius employs the same argument but broadens its implications to include the whole of our lives with God, applying the paddle, as it were, when needed.[38] Like those of Socrates, his claims are large: the wicked are happier when punished, the victims are happier than the criminals, and the actions of evil people actually made all people better.

Do such theological convictions provide license for any kind of intentional participation at a political level in such an economy? In other words, does a confidence in the outcome of punishment provide us free hand in handing out some of our own to those we think deserving? It is not my intention to address the issue of those sought by society in punishing lawbreakers, in spite of the fact that rehabilitation is still one of those stated outcomes. However, the manifest danger of bringing the weight of religious authority to our attitudes toward punishment as well as suffering must be recognized. Certainly, Lady Philosophy is correct to instruct the despairing Boethius that there is something to be learned from his suffering,[39] but to turn this bit of common sense into a generalized attitude toward the material goods

---

[36]*The Consolation of Philosophy*, 4, prose 6.
[37]*Gorgias*, 476–478.
[38]*The Consolation of Philosophy*, 4, prose 4.
[39]*The Consolation of Philosophy*, 2, prose 6.

of life is to mistake the political order for the religious, and to mistake human agency for God's.

Thus, fourthly, a revealed knowledge of original and actual sin, or even our common sense knowledge of human weakness, should not make us wish for suffering, e.g., poverty, in order to compensate for the inability of the city to teach virtue. Again, to build one's case on the cases of a few individuals who have responded heroically to misfortune is to ignore the tragedies of ordinary life. Once again, friendship does not counsel short-cuts, especially those based upon the efforts of an extraordinary few.

Neither should such a knowledge narrow the heart against sinners, which, of course, includes ourselves. One prophetic spirit has criticized the increased social involvement of the Church, as reflected in Maritain's *Peasant of the Garonne*, saying that we have "to choose between the politics of our religion or the religion of our politics."[40] This statement betrays a misunderstanding of the *politics* of his religion which calls for a full recognition of the relation of all goods to their originating source. Indeed, the advantage of the Catholic tradition over the dissenting traditions is legacy of philosophy which provides a way of mediating the claims of the political and spiritual orders while preserving their integrity. Catholics can, therefore, have a philosophy of politics that does not seek its warrant in the spiritual severity of the proof text.

Fifthly, the fundamental danger of viewing earthly happiness— regarding external goods, bodily goods, and acquired virtues—as irrelevant to Christian happiness is an indifference to real suffering and a retreat into subjective well-feeling, whether religious enthusiasms or bourgeois pig-happiness. The happiness of well-feeling is one that many of us can afford to extol precisely because we belong to a class that already claims a good share of the material goods that we think *other* people do not really need because of *our* religious beliefs.

This is the danger of using an ascetic model of spirituality to inform our criticisms of attempts at, for example, financial success, one instance of the struggle to attend to real needs, to the built-in teleologies of human nature. To think the poor blessed in this manner is precisely what Maritain warns against when he says that the Christian

---

[40]Thomas Molnar, "Seed and Harvest," *Modern Age* (Summer, 1968), p. 319.

must not "take for his pillow the very love which he has received."[41] The divide separating political happiness and earthly infused happiness is huge compared to that which distinguishes the latter and eternal happiness. Since the difference is one of species, the political realm does not have to be treated as if it were *only* the staging area of eternal salvation.

As Maritain writes, in his own reflections on the eighth beatitude, the saints know why they suffer; "they know that persecution is good for them."[42] There are those persons, however, for whom persecution follows in the pursuit of earthly justice. He sees a common purpose uniting them:

> The latter threatens to drive a man out of his mind unless it is accompanied by the former; the former requires and awakens and sanctifies the latter. How could men who daily ask that the will of the Father be done on earth as it is in heaven, not thirst after justice on earth and within the human community?. . . . So long as abysmal poverty and slavery and injustice exist in the lives of men and in their mortal societies, there will be no rest for the Christian.[43]

Maritain recognizes that there is some reorienting purpose to suffering of this kind. Turning to the example of the Jewish Holocaust and other atrocities, he writes, "Blessed are they that suffer persecution . . . these words are not for them. . . ."[44] This is not the suffering, in short, recommended by the Beatitudes; this is blind, inarticulate, and involuntary suffering. Although it can be said in faith that this suffering forecasts God's mercy, who can say that this experience does not break the spirit?

> In the throes of death, in the moment when they pass to the other side of the veil and the soul is on the point of leaving a flesh for which the world had no use, is there not yet time enough to say to them: Thou shalt

---

[41]Jacques Maritain, *Intergal Humanism: Temporal and Spiritual Problems of a New Christendom*, trans. Joseph W. Evans (New York: Charles Schribner's Sons, 1968), p. 44.

[42]"That Suffer Persecution," in *A Maritain Reader*, Donald and Idella Gallagher, eds. (Garden City, New York: Image Books, 1966), pp. 315–325. First published in *The Commonweal*, 44:26, October 11, 1946, pp. 619–622.

[43]*Ibid.*, pp. 320–321.

[44]*Ibid.*, p. 323. Maritain continues, "They did not give up their lives, their lives were taken from them, and under the shadow of horror. They suffered with having wanted to suffer. They did not know they died. Those who know why they die are greatly privileged."

be with Me in paradise? For them there are no signs, for them hope is stripped bare as they are themselves, for them, to the bitter end, nothing, even from the direction of God, has shone forth in men's eyes.[45]

The beneficence of suffering love is the innermost gesture of our happiness with God, but it is a gesture that also encompasses our neighbors and their desire for happiness both in this world and the next. Thus to defend an ordinate understanding of earthly happiness is no less spiritually earnest than to prophetically denounce it. When the prophet turns away from the miseries of the world to proclaim the eternal vision of God, heed should be paid to Maritain's warning that God can be seen, or not seen, in the face of their neighbors. Indeed, those who wish the whole happiness of their neighbor may be casting their own net of suffering much wider than those who minister solely to the inner spirit.

---

[45]*Ibid.*, p. 324.

The Book of Wisdom as a Biblical Approach to Natural Law

Joseph Koterski

That there is a crisis in moral wisdom today is beyond doubt. During a crisis the believer always has something to rely on—faith—for Bible, tradition, and church have seen crises come and go. Biblical theology, for example, works by reflection on pressing problems with scriptural eyes. But the sources from which to draw one's own answers are not always the ones most immediately helpful for others, a point to be kept in mind by those who would reach out to persons without faith during the present crisis in moral wisdom. It is a point often made in Maritain's *Moral Philosophy*,[1] and, in fact, the need for a source other than faith is one of the central reasons for the regular appeal to nature by philosophers in the Christian tradition. The ideal of "natural law" expresses a hope for objectivity and universality in morals.

Does biblical theology ever make such an appeal? Another way to raise the question is to ask whether there is a biblical version of natural law. Except for the famous (and hotly debated) case of *Romans*, chapter 2, the very suggestion of a "biblical philosophy" seems to be a contradiction in terms, or perhaps just a poorly phrased attempt to speak of the valid approaches that go under the name of "religious philosophy." Yet there is an entire part of the Bible that is quite philosophical: the books that constitute sapiential literature,

---

[1]Jacques Maritain, *Moral Philosophy: An Historical and Critical Survey of the Great Systems* (New York: Charles Scribner's Sons, 1964), e.g. pp. 458–462.

253

some of which do not even mention God or the faith of Israel, but argue entirely from common sense and the store of human experience. One of them, *The Wisdom of Solomon*, appeals in my judgment to a type of natural law argument.

Since the Enlightenment, theories of natural law have tended to take their point of departure from abstract visions of the nature of the human being, usually expressed in rights-claims.[2] Even the most formalistic systems of ethics, e.g., Kant's deontology, hold that objectivity can be provided for ethics by recourse to the natural structures of reason as regulative for human conduct, while less formalistic systems have tried to appeal by various strategies to nature as normative. However, these latter systems sometimes find their way blocked by G. E. Moore and the accusation of the naturalistic fallacy.

By contrast, earlier versions of natural law theory tended to give greater prominence to the religious origins of natural law rather than to abstract pictures of human nature. Whether we consider the Stoic originators of natural law theory or its Christian advocates, God is regarded as the author of all nature, including the human, and thus there is a divine source for the universality and teleology of moral claims. Even so, the type of demonstrations they offer tend to accentuate the discovery of natural norms by inspection of the patterns of fulfillment or frustration of human desires rather than to emphasize expressions of divine will. In fact, right relation to God is often subsumed under the general heading of justice rather than considered to be the wellspring of morality, even though the divine origin of human nature (and of all nature) remains the ultimate guarantee of moral objectivity in these systems.

In contrast to predominantly philosophical theories of natural law, biblical forays like that of St. Paul in *Romans* take a different starting-point, the accessibility of knowledge of God to human beings and an appreciation of the destiny God has planned for human nature. They then work toward the articulation of a morality appropriate to human nature so conceived. Instead of treating suitable worship of the true god as a subset of justice-relationships, biblical ethics tends to see this duty as the primary obligation from which all the rest derive.

---

[2]There is an astute analysis of this phenomenon in *'Nonsense upon Stilts': Bentham, Burke and Marx on the Rights of Man*, ed. with introductory and concluding essays by Jeremy Waldron (London and New York: Methuen, 1987).

Yet these texts still do seem to me to operate within the natural law tradition in that they insist upon reflection on human nature in due course for proper expression of the balance of this religiously based morality.[3]

The contention of the present article is that there is a certain form of natural law argumentation that is helpful in answering a rather different question, one in which biblical scholars have more interest, the very unity of the book of *Wisdom*. This book is a Greek language portion of inter-testamental biblical literature and has been generally recognized to contain a fair amount of Hellenistic thinking as well as a share of wisdom literature native to the Hebrew Bible.[4] There are a number of fine studies on the likely sources in Greek philosophy for specific passages[5] and on the structure of the book,[6] but none to my knowledge that focus on the type of argument-pattern to help establish the book's unity.

From the perspective of the development of Israel's scriptures, what is new and significant about the *Wisdom of Solomon* is a theological development of a classical position within Israel's thinking. It is often said in the Psalms and elsewhere that all nations should believe and praise God from his works, and there are a number of condemnations of idolatry (e.g., in *Isaiah*). In *Wisdom* the author develops the universalist argument a bit further, maintaining, that from nature even the pagans ought to worship this God, and that they are culpable for failing to do so.[7]

---

[3]In his article on "Old Testament Ethics" in *The Westminster Dictionary of Christian Ethics* (Philadelphia: Westminster Press, 1986), pp. 433–437, Henry McKeating observes that Old Testament literature draws no sharp distinction between ethics and religion, between right moral conduct and right religious conduct. But to my mind it is worth investigating whether this is just an "indiscriminate mixture of commands on moral and religious matters" (p. 433) or whether it would not be better to say that biblical writers tend to incorporate morality within the confines of religion and religious duties.

[4]See especially Maurice Gilbert, S.J., *La Critique des dieux dans le Livre de la Sagesse* (Sg 13–15) (Rome: Biblical Institute Press, 1973).

[5]For instance, James M. Reese, *Hellenistic Influence on the Book of Wisdom and Its Consequences*. Analecta Biblica 41. (Rome: Biblical Institute Press, 1969).

[6]Dieter Georgi, "Der vorpaulinische Hymnus Phil 2,6–11" in *Zeit und Geschichte Danksgabe an Rudolph Bultmann zum 80. Geburtstag*, ed. E. Dinkler (Tubingen: J.C.B. Mohr, 1964), pp. 263–293; and George Nickelsburg, *Resurrection, Immortality and Eternal Life in Intertestamental Judaism*. Harvard Theological Studies 26. (Cambridge, Massachusetts: Harvard University Press, 1972).

[7]See Gilbert, pp. 48–49 on the possible meanings for *physis* within *Wisdom*.

But the problem of understanding the book of *Wisdom* as a whole remains. It is here that mindfulness of the patterns of thought typical of natural law can help us to understand better the flow of thought and the internal logic of the book of *Wisdom*. Moreover, perhaps we can better see its usefulness for the present moral crisis, especially when we want to speak from faith to those who do not share our faith.

The Problem of the Unity of the Book

One aspect of the project of showing that *The Wisdom of Solomon* offers a religious understanding of natural law involves demonstrating that the book, in fact, contains a sustained, unified argument and is not just a patchwork of discrete parts.[8] Its main sections are three: 1) a vindication of some unnamed people who have been persecuted for their righteous Torah observance by the gifts of immortality (*athanasia*) and incorruptibility (*aphtharsia*) (chapters 1–6); 2) Solomon's address to the kings of the earth on the nature of Wisdom (chapters 6–10); and 3) an interpretation of some events recognizable from the Exodus story (chapters 11–19). It is not immediately obvious how these three rather different topics are related to one another.

My contention is that there is a distinctive pattern of argument common to all three sections. Displaying the structure of this reasoning both helps to make the case for holding the book to be a unity with a consistent inner logic and teaches a useful way to make a natural law ethic. The basic argument here proceeds from the link between recognition of the one true God and observance of authentic morality. Conversely, the book of *Wisdom* regularly connects a faulty idea of God with unacceptable moral behavior and its invariable punishment. Still, the pattern of argument is more sophisticated than the simple law of retribution (the correlation of acts and consequences) operating, for instance, in *Genesis* prior to the flood story, or earlier in wisdom literature (especially as *Proverbs*, *Job*, *Qoheleth*, and *Sirach* debate the right approach to the theodicy question). It is different precisely by virtue of

---

[8]In his review of the literature in the Anchor Bible volume on *The Wisdom of Solomon* (Garden City, New York: Doubleday, 1979) David Winston notes (pp. 9–14) that early modern biblical scholarship tended to find "a confusing disarray of units" and then proceeded to "carve up the book" in support of a theory of compound authorship. Among more recent commentators Reese has argued for the book's unity from the recurrence of certain terminology and the presence of such rhetorical devices as the *inclusio*.

the extension of an insight voiced only occasionally elsewhere in the Bible (e.g., *Psalms* 115:4–8; 135:13–18; *Isaiah* 40:18–20; 44:9–20) that not just Israel but all nations should be able to recognize the one true God from his works, and that all other worship is culpable idolatry (*Wisdom* 13:1–15:17). As wrongdoing this activity will invariably bring its just return upon any practitioners, in a way appropriate to the deed, even if this requires retribution beyond the grave.

The argument common to all three parts of the book[9] has three basic parts: a) recognition of the true God is a mark of wisdom; b) getting the knowledge of God right will bring knowledge of authentic morality; and c) moral living, even in the face of persecution, will bring a reward (conceived as incorruption, immortality, life). Relying on a strong sense of the consequences inherent in one's action, the author illustrates various failures to respect these conditions by some imaginative story-telling. Chapters 2–4, for instance, portray former persecutors in the after-life as now under the judgment of those they oppressed; the story illustrates the downfall of those whose haughty and imperious behavior had stemmed from their arrogance toward the true God and the elevation of those who had humbly recognized the true God even though it meant persecution. Chapters 11–12 and 16–19 consist mainly of an historical retelling of the story of the plagues mentioned in *Exodus*, with a certain stress placed on seeing how the very same natural element brings a curse on Egypt and a blessing on Israel. The vindication thus worked is parallel to the delivery of the group in the early chapters, but this time it takes place for the people as a whole and occurs in this life. Even so, the author preserves an eschatological focus on eternal life by symbolic uses of "manna," "land," and "peace" to discuss the incorruptibility and immortality of the "life" which God wants to bestow on the faithful.

In addition to these moral lessons, there is a strong moral psychology operating throughout. For instance, in the section on the critique of the gods (chapters 13–15) the author satirizes the notion of polytheism by picturing craftsmen at work on their idols. Any plurality of gods (especially when they are idols made by human hands, but even when it is various forces of nature that are worshipped) brings morality into contempt. The artisans know the artificiality of these gods, and their

---

[9]My point is not that this argument-pattern is the only one operative in the book, but simply a concentration on the recurrence of this particular pattern as a helpful tool to understand the whole.

own fearless conduct brings disrespect for any moral claims associated with the gods they have made as merely the imposition of the will and power of some upon others. As a point of moral psychology, it is the equivalent of what any high-school teacher knows about giving a mixed message. Students can be brought to accept the content of a moral claim, but they put a tremendous value on consistency, whether in seeing that the teacher follow his own rules or in apprehending that the message is coherent. To take a contemporary moral issue as an example, the current campaign to make condoms available in school health offices quickly runs afoul of this sort of mixed message when proponents tell their charges that they should not be sexually active, but, if they are, they should know how to protect themselves. What gets communicated in a mixed message is precisely a sense of something mixed up and confused, and thus something one can ignore.

The lively presence of practical moral psychology within the whole tradition of wisdom literature (for instance, the juxtaposition of the charms of Lady Wisdom and Lady Folly in *Proverbs* 1–9) thus finds a ready home in *The Wisdom of Solomon*. Here it serves to support the basic argument about the need for worshipping the true God and living a life consistent with that worship. That this argument-type recurs in various forms chapter after chapter seems to me an extremely potent reason for holding for the unity of the book.

The Recurrent Argument-Pattern

If the analysis I have attempted elsewhere[10] bears out the claim that this is a recurrent argument-pattern unifying the book, it seems to be legitimate to argue that this pattern represents a specifically biblical approach to natural law thinking. Clearly, there are broader and narrower views of what natural law is, ranging from attempts such as those by Grisez, Finnis, and Boyle to derive precepts from self-evident basic human goods, through the virtue-ethics approach of MacIntyre, Hauerwas, and Pincoffs, who want to argue from the narratival unity of the self as a source of moral character, to the

---

[10]A careful analysis of the reasoning used, section by section, is beyond the scope of this paper, but I have tried to make this sort of study in my S.T.L. thesis at the Weston School of Theology, *A Biblical Vision of Natural Law in The Book of Wisdom* (Cambridge, Massachusetts, 1992). Let me here express my gratitude to Richard Clifford, S.J. for his inspiring direction.

more traditional views of Aquinas who unite precept and virtue by a philosophy of nature and a telic analysis of human perfection.

What is required for an approach to be included in the scope of the natural law tradition is a basic respect for nature as the source of law for human conduct. The form taken here uses a decidedly more pro-active god than, say, the Stoic orderer of the universe or the Deist god of the founders of the American Republic. Yet it is still very much an attempt to relate three crucial terms: God, nature, and human nature. Though a biblical book, *Wisdom* takes the source of our moral knowledge to be natural rather than dependent on specific revelation, for instance, the divine gift of the decalogue. It is not as heavily charged as other sources of ethical teaching in the Old Testament with the specific covenant-history of Israel. In fact, it prefers to allude to important biblical figures as types rather than to refer to them by name. At *Wisdom* 10:4, for instance, we might recognize the story of Noah, but the figure is a sort of "everyman," designed to convince the reader as a "likely story" rather than as an accurate retelling of the story in *Genesis*. *The Wisdom of Solomon* stands, rather, in the universalist tradition of *Isaiah* 44.

If this book were a philosophical tome strictly speaking, the strategy we might expect would be to argue for the natural knowledge of God by moving, for instance, from effect back to cause. That is the procedure often adopted later in the history of natural theology, but it is not generally the case here. Perhaps the fact that there were few or no atheists in the ancient world explains the lack of felt need to prove the existence of God (see, for instance, *Wisdom* 9:13–16). The burden falls instead on discerning the true God and on establishing the right relationship to this God.

Likewise, Solomon's prayer (chapters 7–8) is both an actual prayer (directed to God, asking for the spirit of Wisdom) and an example of how to pray directed to his fellow kings, urging that no king can escape death. We are all mortal, all in need of wisdom, and we must all pray for wisdom with the same sort of humility Solomon is here embodying. For any king there is a special need to establish the right relationship with God because so much of the welfare of his country depends on his conduct. Solomon's long praises of the spirit of Wisdom is tightly connected to the basic argument pattern, for his listing of the gifts which this spirit brings is as much an incentive to other kings to behave and share in these same gifts as it is an act of right relationship to God, whose praises are sung by the very act of recounting these gifts.

We could just as easily consider the prolonged account of nature's decisive interventions during the Exodus (*Exodus* 11–19). The events are presented without emphasis on Moses or the covenant relationship. Rather, the whole stress is on the complicity of nature in saving those who have acted on the morality that follows from worship of the true god and in punishing those who have acted arrogantly and oppressively out of their defiance of the true god. The fancy footwork it takes to correlate each plague with a blessing worked through the same element of nature shows a tremendous confidence in the natural order to teach morality by drawing out the consequences of one's pattern of action. All the while the author keeps returning to the basic culpability argument. People should have known better, hence they are culpable. There is personal moral responsibility for living according to the ways pleasing to God, and it is within the scope of humankind to recognize divine sovereignty.

The Current Crisis in Moral Wisdom

One lesson I think we can draw from the discovery of a certain natural law argument within a biblical text is that there is an advantage, and perhaps even a certain necessity, in rooting natural law arguments in a religious framework. It may not be possible to presume that those whom we are trying to convince on some topic in morals share the precise tenets of our faith, any more than Solomon can presume that the other kings are observers of revealed Torah. Yet he manifests a confidence that they will be able to understand and recognize the truth of being humble before God, whoever God is, once they admit that they have the limitations any human being has. He can summon them to pray for the gift of Wisdom, and he expects that this will make them well-disposed to learn what God is trying to teach them through the natural order even where there has been no special revelation.

Whether one needs to advert to God in laying out an ethics or working out ethical problems is a question of enormous importance, and one on which I can foresee many good reasons supporting both sides. Some argue persuasively that there cannot in principle be any difference between religious and non-religious ethics in regard to content, for what ethics concerns is our common human nature; the turn in much of recent theology toward anthropology (such as in Karl Rahner) reflects and confirms this line of argument. Others point to the problems of objectivity and motivation. Even if they do not go so far as Sartre to suggest that in the absence of God everything is permitted, and nothing required or forbidden, they raise questions about how any ethical claim could be regarded as genuinely normative if human reason is its whole source. At most, any such claim would be culturally and temporally relative, the best a given individual in a given culture can recommend for advantageous personal and social relations. As such it is only admonition and exhortation. What we need, if we are to have anything genuinely normative, is a source beyond human reason, namely God. Religious ethics is then different in kind from any non-religious version by being normative and not merely suggestive. Going this route, however, makes it hard to see how the non-religious person would look upon religious ethics as making claims interesting to anyone outside the fold.

What seems most attractive to me about the former alternative is how well designed it is for keeping open the discussion between those whose beliefs differ. It keeps the focus on nature and human nature, reserving the question about the reason why nature and human nature are the way they are for discussion some other time. This interest in what is accessible to human reason in general is clearly among the reasons why "natural law" arguments have been a mainstay of Catholic moral theology and why this tradition has such a respectable place in the entire history of moral thinking.

The particular approach to natural law discoverable in the book of *Wisdom* reminds us that it is sometimes culturally important to return the discussion to the question about the hand that guides nature and human purposes, especially when human power and rational autonomy make us forgetful of natural creaturely dependence and when that forgetfulness allows moral discourse to disintegrate into irreconcilable opinions. Nature can, in some ages and cultures, serve as plinth for ethical discourse sufficient for grasping what is normative (short of recourse to questions about ultimate reality), but when the idea of nature is redefined in terms of utter pliability as the technological perspective culturally prominent today tends to do, it cannot easily fill the role of a plinth. To restore the reverence needed for treating nature as normative, there may be need to return the general discussion to the question of how one is related to ultimate reality, or more simply, to get people to focus on whether they are related to God aright. The more complicated ethical questions that depend on seeing nature aright will follow.

Whether because of the technological power we so easily command, the therapeutic mentality which reduces the search for truth about the nature of things to restoring an equilibrium that is out of balance, or the depths to which the rhetoric of individualism has penetrated our entire way of thinking,[11] it is hard to make a natural law case today. We cherish the hope that this kind of argument could settle some of our problems, but the assumptions it makes about human purposes and destiny are simply not widely shared. On the contrary, the confidence which our magnificent technological developments have given for the achievement of individual self-sufficiency and for the realization of "self-actualizing" ends has cast a shadow over claims that there is any natural destiny common to all humanity. Likewise, the communitarian notion of ordered liberty as part of the necessarily social nature of human beings is under tremendous strain. When these assumptions are shared, they do not always have to be stated, but when they are not shared, we either have to decide on a strategy of starting over with a lower common denominator that is shared, or we have to devise a strategy that will set about restoring the context in which the teleology of human nature will again be appreciated.[12]

How effective is natural law argumentation that disregards or de-emphasizes any theological perspective? As philosophers we want to say that if there is a good argument, it ought to be compelling just as it is and apart from whether there is a divine basis. But I wonder if that is not to take philosophical argument in a vacuum. Natural law thinking, in particular, seems to require some rather sizable cultural assumptions, so that a culture that has truly made certain kinds of progress could assume things for moral argument which a regressive

---

[11]There is a fine analysis of this trend in Mary Ann Glendon's, *Rights Talk: The Impoverishment of Political Discourse* (New York: Macmillan, 1991).

[12]The components of an effective strategy will necessarily be numerous. Without developing the point, let me simply suggest that an extremely important aspect of bringing people to grasp nature-arguments will be cultivating habits of contemplation. Given the dominance of technology even in our everyday epistemology (both the pragmatist thesis that things are "true" because they "work" and the nominalist propensity to treat all concepts as the products of our own minds, constructed for some purpose and alterable at need), there are special difficulties for seeing anything "natural" as "normative."

A limited amount of experience in teaching grade-school religion leads me to believe that schools which have a greater focus on art, on appreciating really beautiful things, tends to foster this sort of contemplation. Whatever the method, the goal must be to encourage receptivity and alertness to the contours of being, that is, a sensitivity to divine providence and stirrings of grace as well as a humility before the forms and limits of nature (one's own nature, human nature in general, and the nature of which we are stewards). There will then be much encouragement to the active and constructive side of the mind.

culture is unable to presume and which must be re-stated and argued for quite explicitly. In our own day, the attempt to do ethics without reference to God has produced manifold diversity, both in the academy and in the marketplace. There are occasional atheists and agnostics who defend what the strongest theists hold in morality (for instance, Max Hentoff or Baruch Brody), and some have even been led to faith. But the general state of moral discussion is in a state of crisis, and I think the solution will have to be a culture-wide religious renewal.

The value of story-telling is incalculable, if we choose to employ this strategy. It has always been a central piece of Christian evangelization, and I suspect that its strategic function has much to do with the approach we are pondering in the book of *Wisdom*. Philosophers, of course, want argument-trails, not beautiful tales, but ordinary moral discourse often works more effectively when we do not shy away from stories. Admittedly, the "whole story" has to rest ultimately on solid argument, but sometimes it is precisely a story which spurs interest in the question we want to raise.

At the beginning of *Wisdom*, it is precisely the story about vindication in the after-life that links this book most directly to the rest of the Wisdom literature tradition. The debate between the optimistic expectations of *Proverbs* and *Sirach* that virtue will be rewarded in this life and the pessimistic (or at least agnostic) interpretations of *Job* and *Ecclesiastes*, which point out that the unjust often prosper at the expense of the just, here finds biblical resolution in the necessity of an after-life to ensure the justice of God toward all parties. The argument is not rehearsed here, but only a story about a reversal of victim and oppressor in the after-life is provided; yet the allusions to earlier parts of the Wisdom literature tradition assure us that this book is a deliberate participation in that long-standing debate as well as an exhortation to those outside the debate who are simply looking for wisdom. The stories, then, focus our attention on the argument for moral responsibility (the connection of acts and consequences that flow from one's stance toward God) with the added motivation that comes from divine assurance about rewards and punishments. Here too is a lesson to be learned as we ponder strategy for the current crisis in moral wisdom.

Morality and Christian Morality

Joseph M. de Torre

In his recent work *Das Natürlische und das Vernünftige*, Robert Spae-
mann has drawn attention to the famous questions of Kant: the metaphysical, what can we know? the ethical, what should we do? and the
religious, what can we hope for? In his *Logik*, Kant formulates a fourth
question taken from *Psalm* 8: what is man? This is how metaphysics,
ethics, and religion lead to anthropology. Feuerbach was not the first
to point out that all theology is but anthropology. But in trying to
answer the anthropological question, Kant came to the conclusion
that there is no answer to it. The dualism of the "physiological" and
"pragmatic" views of man make it impossible to have a unified vision
of man, thus going back to the Cartesian dualism of *res extensa* and
res cogitans.

For his part, Alasdair MacIntyre, in *After Virtue*, and later in *Whose
Justice? Which Rationality?*, has made a remarkable effort to recover
the metaphysical ground of morality by showing the implausibility of
both Nietzsche's and Marx's attempts to start a new anthropology, as
well as the equally unsuccessful and inadequate attempts of Weber,
Dilthey, and Heidegger. A similar attempt was made by the present
writer in *The Roots of Society: The Metaphysical Background of Social
Ethics* (first ed., 1977; second, 1984).

Allan Bloom, in *The Closing of The American Mind*, has made a
similar attempt, but by falling back into the shallows of the Enlightenment he has offered a rather anti-climactic solution to the problem
he has so brilliantly diagnosed, as Mortimer J. Adler has noted. The
contributions of John Finnis, William May, and Germain Grisez are
also worth noting.

We can easily detect in these writers and other essayists human-kind's perennial overriding interest in morality. But we can also some-times detect the equally perennial tendency of thinkers to entangle themselves in subtle complications which obscure, rather than clarify, the issues through the fear of being labelled "simplistic." It is true that there is always a risk of oversimplifying, but it is also true that wisdom possesses simplicity as well as depth and is definitely not complicated.

Volumes have been written on moral philosophy over the centuries, but we cannot say that the majority of them qualify as wisdom. Jacques Maritain's contribution, however, does qualify, as is evident in such works as *The Degrees of Knowledge*, *The Range of Reason*, and *Moral Philosophy*. Drawing a powerful force from the Thomist conception of knowledge by connaturality, he has applied this notion brilliantly to the fields of metaphysics, ethics, aesthetics, and mysticism. He deals with these subjects with greater success than Kant. In providing a basis for a clarification of moral philosophy, Maritain avoids the pitfalls of Nietzsche's nihilism, as well as all forms of moral relativism. These virtues appear especially in *An Introduction to The Basic Problems of Moral Philosophy*.

The purpose of this paper, adapted from my book *Christ and The Moral Life* (1983), is to attempt a further clarification and simplifica-tion (but not an oversimplification) of the perennial ethical questions by considering them in the context of biblical theology. Jesus was once approached by a young man who wanted to know what he should do "to have eternal life."[1] Jesus answered him in no uncertain terms: "Keep the commandments." And when the young man asked for a clarification, Jesus gave him a summarized list of the moral commandments as they were taught to the Jews ever since the times of Moses. The Ten Commandments given to Moses[2] were nothing but the explicit declaration (what is called divine-positive law) by God himself of the eternal moral laws (the natural law), inscribed in every man's heart but often difficult to recognize by man in practice, due to the weakness of his fallen nature.[3] In fact, it was this plight of man that, according to the First Vatican Council, moved God's mercy to

---

[1]*Matthew*, 19:16.
[2]*Exodus*, 20:1–17 and *Deuteronomy*, 5:6–21.
[3]*Romans*, 2:15.

explicitly reveal the natural moral law, a revelation which reached its final and perfect form in Christ.[4] In this regard, the Second Vatican Council states the following:

> Although he was made by God in a state of holiness, from the very dawn of history man abused his liberty, at the urging of personified evil. Man set himself against God and sought to find fulfillment apart from God. Although he knew God, he did not glorify Him as God, but his senseless mind was darkened and he served the creature rather than the Creator (cf., *Romans* 1:21–25). What divine revelation makes known to us agrees with experience. Examining his heart, man finds that he has inclinations toward evil too, and is engulfed by manifold ills which cannot come from his good Creator. Often refusing to acknowledge God as his beginning, man has disrupted also his proper relationship to his own intimate goal. At the same time he became out of harmony with himself, with others, and with all created things. Therefore man is split within himself. As a result, all of human life, whether individual or collective, shows itself to be a dramatic struggle between good and evil, between light and darkness. Indeed, man finds that by himself he is incapable of battling the assaults of evil successfully, so that everyone feels as though he is bound by chains. But the Lord himself came to free and strengthen man, renewing him inwardly and casting out that prince of this world (cf. *John* 8:34). For sin has diminished man, blocking his path to fulfillment. The call to grandeur and the depths of misery are both a part of human experience. They find their ultimate and simultaneous explanation in the light of God's revelation.[5]

Two questions in this regard have always in one way or another stirred the human heart, but they have acquired peculiar features in our age: an age that tends to pitch chance against permanence; the physical against the moral; the temporal against the eternal; facts against values; with a bewildering display of complex combinations which often erupt into personal and social crises and upheavals.

The first of these questions asks: what is the relationship between the moral laws as applicable to all men, if there is such a thing, and the moral law given by Christ to his disciples? This question involves

---

[4]Denzinger edition, *Enchiridion Symbolorum*, 1785–1786.
[5]Pastoral Constitution, *Gaudium et Spes*, no. 13 (Abbott Edition of Vatican II Documents. All subsequent quotations from Vatican II are from this Edition).

the issue of the dialogue of the Church and the world, which the Second Vatican Council tackled extensively in its Pastoral Constitution, *Gaudium et Spes*. The second question asks whether the moral law, either natural or Christian, is subject to change in any sense?

What follows is an attempt to discuss these two questions in the light of what the Church has always taught about the moral law, especially following the Second Vatican Council. But it is a matter of justice to acknowledge my debt to the teachings of the Blessed Josemaría Escrivá. The official decree (February 19, 1981)[6] advocating his beatification and canonization called him the forerunner of the Second Vatican Council for having proclaimed loudly and clearly the evangelical call of all men and women to holiness, i.e., to the continuous progress in the moral life, and for having instituted suitable means—the sanctification of everyday work[7]—for the attainment of this goal by ordinary people in the world.

Another characteristic of our age is the lack of time and leisure for unhurried reading, heightened by the growing competition for attention from the mass media. To condense ideas thus becomes a necessity, while providing references for further information and reflection. This is the approach I have tried to follow, keeping the text as short as possible without sacrificing substance.

1. *Morality and Christian Morality*

A few years ago I wrote an essay entitled "Education and Christian Education,"[8] in which I tried to show the essential link between humanity and Christianity along the line of the well-known principle that divine grace does not suppress human nature but brings it to perfection.

Likewise, Christian morality is not cut off from natural morality, although, since divine grace is an entirely gratuitous gift from God to man to which the latter has no right, we cannot say that human nature strictly needs divine grace for its completion, or that natural

---

[6]*Rivista Diocesana di Roma*, March-April, 1981.

[7]J. L. Illanes, *On the Theology of Work. Aspects of the Teaching of the Founder of Opus Dei* (Dublin: Four Courts Press, 1982).

[8]Published by Catholic Position Papers, Ashiya, Japan, October, 1975, and reprinted as a chapter of my book, *The Leaven of the Gospel of Secular Society* (Manila: Vera-Reyes, 1983).

morality is incomplete without the Gospel. However, we can say that, since human nature is a damaged nature, it needs outside assistance for its healing, the source of which only comes as a non-obligatory merciful condescension from the only being who is above man. And in like manner can a divinely-revealed (Christian) morality come to heal, or to fill in the gaps of natural morality, without changing its fundamental orientation?

What is the link between morality and Christian morality? The term "morality" has three analogical meanings: a) the factual status of moral standards in a given social milieu; b) the science of morals or ethics which studies the principles and rules of human behavior as human; and c) the quality peculiar to human acts whereby they are intrinsically related to moral standards. This last captures the primary meaning of the term "morality," and must be carefully scrutinized in order to understand the other two properly. It shows the characteristic transcendence of human nature, which is the basis of the unique dignity of every human being and of his or her inalienable rights.

Man's Transcendence

Man transcends or goes beyond himself, and hence beyond temporal society precisely through the ethical dimension of his being, whereby he subordinates his temporal existence to an eternal set of values deriving from an eternal source. This eternal source is seen as both origin and end of man, and indeed of all beings.[9]

When man acts with that freedom proper to him, which consists in the power of directing his own acts to their end with personal responsibility and with no outside coercion, his acts have a moral quality inhering in them and hence in the human person who performs them.[10] This moral quality is measured not quantitatively but by its intensity of goodness, i.e., by its degree of approximation to the right end.[11] And since God is the last end (the infinite good) of man, the morality of human acts is measured by their conformity to the eternal law of God, which is called natural law when discovered by human reason as the law governing man's free decisions.

---

[9]Joseph M. de Torre, *The Roots of Society* (Manila: Sinag-tala, 1977), ch. I.

[10]As distinct from the divine freedom, which is equivalent to divine omnipotence.

[11]Joseph M. de Torre, *Christian Philosophy* (Manila: Vera-Reyes, 2nd ed., 1981), ch. 23, d.

Moral Values

This is the natural morality guiding every single human being in every sociological setting. It is learned gradually as human reason grows which evidences the paramount importance of parental education for moral awareness: for values to be assimilated they must be first inculcated in a living experience of communication.

At first human reason is simply a power or faculty waiting to be actuated. This actuation happens when, confronted with reality, reason asks the first two original questions: what is it? and what is it for? The first aims to know and the second to do; the first is speculative or theoretical, the second active or practical; the first is answered with a first concept ("being") and a first judgment ("to be and not to be are incompatible"), both in the speculative order; the second is answered with another first concept ("good") and another first judgment ("good should be done and evil avoided"), both in the practical order.[12]

With this first principle of practical reason, which the Greeks called *synderesis*, man possesses the tool for discovering the precepts of the natural law. "Good" is the perfection of being. Man has a power (reason or intelligence) to know being and a power (will) to act in order to perfect his own being, which are both without limits: only the infinite being or infinite good can satisfy them. Man's thirst for perfection is as insatiable as is his frustration unrequitable when he sets his ultimate goals on finite goods and thus falls into sin, the only real evil.

Thus breaks into light the first precept of the natural law: "Love God above all things." And the second follows from the first: "Love other beings as creatures of God," i.e., bearing in mind their relationship to God.[13]

Natural Law and Civilization

From the first of these two fundamental precepts derives that of worshipping God with adoration, thanksgiving, atonement, and petition (religion). From the second derives that of loving humanity as the point of confluence of creatures and Creator, as the reflection of God in his creation; and from this, that of loving other human beings

---

[12]*Ibid.*, ch 38, f.
[13]Joseph M. de Torre, *The Roots of Society* (Manila: Sinag-tala, 1977), note 43.

as much as one ought to love one's own humanity; out of this love emerges self-esteem; social and personal love and justice; respect and honor for sex as the God-given source of human life; and commitment to truth. The Biblical Ten Commandments spell out these imperatives of the natural law.

All cultures and civilizations have in varying degrees attained this understanding of the natural law, with recurring relapses into barbarism and savagery. Indeed, sometimes in an institutionalized fashion, and most often in the individual behavior of their people, they have fallen into distortions and outright errors, both theoretical and practical, due to the patent damage of human nature revealed in the tendency to *rationalize*, i.e., to surrender reason to selfish emotion.

Divine Revelation

God's pity for man's plight has been manifested in the Judeo-Christian revelation, wherein God, speaking through a living tradition enshrined in the Bible and sustained by God's own authority, has actually told man how he should live in order to attain his last end. This end he has communicated in a twofold way: by disclosing this goal as being above human nature (as being supernatural, depending, in fact, on a free divine decision) and by bringing it wondrously closer to man by taking on himself a damaged human nature, thus radically healing it by raising it to his own divine level.

This divine revelation has shed powerful light on man's understanding of the natural law without in any way supplanting it, just as grace does not suppress nature but brings it to its perfection. The Ten Commandments (divine-positive law) given to Moses do not promulgate a new law, but only specify the two fundamental precepts of the natural law (love of God and neighbor): the first three commandments capture the former precept; the remaining seven, the latter.[14] But The Ten Commandments are then summarized in these two: love the Lord your God with all your heart, and with all your soul, and with all your strength,[15] and love your neighbor as yourself.[16] Thus, Jesus would answer the question from the Doctor of the Law: "Master, which is the

---

[14]*Exodus*, 20:1–17; *Deuteronomy*, 5:6–21.
[15]*Deuteronomy*, 6:5, 10–12, 11–13.
[16]*Leviticus*, 19:18.

great commandment of the Law?"[17] And that is why he said that he had not come "to destroy the Law or the Prophets" but "to fulfill."[18]

The New Commandment

In what way did Jesus bring natural morality to its perfection, transfiguring it, so to speak, without changing its substance? The answer is found in the *Mandatum Novum*: "A new commandment I give you, that you love one another: that, as I have loved you, you also love one another. By this will all know that you are my disciples, if you have love for one another."[19]

This commandment is new, not in the sense that it abolishes the old commandments, but in the sense that it raises their standard to the summit of perfection. This is the love which is distinctively Christian, and a distinctive mark of Christians. Besides, Christians are provided with the means to attain that kind of love, namely a communion of life with Christ himself: a life of faith in Christ, hope in Christ, and love in Christ through the sacraments instituted by him and left to his Church.

Christ has transformed the meaning of love by enriching it, expanding it, heightening it, and making it surpass itself, but without changing it altogether. This can be seen by comparing the evangelical *agape* expressed in the New Commandment with both the Platonic *eros* and the Aristotelian *philia*.[20]

First, love is a passion: an inclination toward what appears to be good or an abhorrence of what appears to be bad. For animals "good" is what is pleasant and "bad" is what is unpleasant; this is not quite the case with rationally intelligent beings as these can perceive the real value of things regardless of their feelings about them. If men are inclined to possess the good, it is because they do not yet possess it. This is a manifestation of both the imperfection and the potential of man. The inclination to possess the good absent from the lover Plato calls *eros*. It is good in itself, and shows both the wealth and the indigence of man; it is the attraction to what is good in order to perfect oneself.

---

[17]*Matthew*, 22:35–40; cf. *Mark*, 12:28–34; *Luke*, 10:25–28.

[18]*Matthew*, 5:17; cf. *Luke*, 16:17.

[19]*John*, 13:34–35.

[20]Joseph M. de Torre, *The Roots of Society* (Manila: Sinag-tala, 1977), p. 5.

A second meaning of love is the inclination to share what one already possesses. The discovery of other beings with the same nature and goals creates fellowship, friendship, and sharing. It implies "give and take," but not so much *acquiring* in the Platonic sense. Aristotle calls this love *philia*, and considers social friendship as the indispensable force to preserve society.

What about the love that God has for his creatures? It cannot be *eros* because there is nothing that he does not possess. Nor can it be *philia* since God has no need to share in order to attain a greater good by giving and taking. Not surprisingly, neither Plato nor Aristotle ever thought of a God who loves his creatures. Only the Bible reveals this love.

God is Love

Agape means pure and total giving, without sharing or any inclination to anything in return: sheer benevolence.[21] God gives without losing. He loves his creatures by wanting them *to be*. He gives them a created participation of being and goodness.[22] This is why God is called "love," because in him goodness overflows in creation: *bonum diffusivum sui*.[23] "The Lord is good to all and compassionate toward all his works."[24] The Book of *Wisdom* expresses the point admirably:

> For you love all things that are and loathe nothing that you have made; for what you hated, you would not have fashioned. And how could a thing remain, unless you willed it; or be preserved, had it not been called forth by you? But you spare all things, because they are yours. O Lord and lover of souls, for your imperishable spirit is in all things![25]

This creation involves not only making things be, but also *preserving* them in being, leading them to their end and *providing* for them; and in the case of man re-creating him by *redeeming* him through an elevation to the supernatural life of faith, hope, and love.

---

[21]St. Francis de Sales deals with this subject in a classical fashion in his *Treatise on the Love of God*. Benevolence is incidentally, the basic human virtue for Confucius.

[22]Creatures are not "pieces" of God (pantheism) but created beings which are not fullness of being, since what they actually are is limited by what they can be (actuality limited by potentiality).

[23]*I John*, 4:8 and 16.

[24]*Psalms*, 144:9.

[25]*Wisdom*, 11:24–26.

The redemption of man is achieved through the incarnation of the Son of God, which is a convergence of the love of God, i.e., the Holy Spirit, and of perfect humanity, i.e., the Virgin Mary.[26] God thus re-creates humanity through the incarnation and the redemption which is accomplished by the perfect priest or mediator between God and man,[27] with the perfect sacrifice and atonement.[28] This is why we say that in Christ is found both the love of God for man and the love of man for God. Christ is thus the Pontifex or "bridge-man."

The actual sacrifice of Christ, his most humiliating and sorrowful passion and cross, perpetuated and made present in the Holy Mass, is the true *agape* of God overflowing with generosity, teaching men that they should love without limits.[29] "No one has ever seen God. If we should love one another, God abides in us. In this we know we abide in him and he in us, because he has given us of his spirit. We have seen and do testify that the Father has sent his Son to be savior of the world. Whoever confesses that Jesus is the Son of God, God abides in him and he in God."[30] This kind of love does not contradict *eros* nor *philia* but empowers them beyond themselves; hence the unique originality of Christian morals.

The pre-Christian philosophers could not even catch a faint glimpse of that love of God revealed in Jesus Christ. Of them, the Fathers and Doctors of the Church, from Justin to Aquinas, would say that, while they did discover the goal, they never knew the way.[31]

2. Christian Morality as Revealed by God

Christian morality does not contradict natural morality, as we have seen, but neither is it a logical consequence of it; that is to say, neither

---

[26]*Luke*, 1:28–35. "At the message of the Angel, the Virgin Mary received the Word of God in her heart and in her body, and gave Life to the world. Hence she is acknowledged and honored as being truly the Mother of God. As a result she is also the favorite daughter of the Father and the temple of the Holy Spirit." (Second Vatican Council, Dogm. Const., *Lumen Gentium*, no 53).

[27]*I Timothy*, 2:5.

[28]*Hebrews*, 9:11–26.

[29]*Matthew*, 5:38–48; 18:21–22.

[30]*I John*, 4:12–15.

[31]The present Pope has been driving home precisely this point: the attainment of a real humanism, that is, a full Christianity that raises what is best in humanity by means of communion with God. See particularly his first three Encyclicals, *Redemptor Hominis*, *Dives in Misericordia*, and *Laborem Exercens*.

is it a morality that man could discover by his own reasoning alone. Both faith in the divinity of Christ and the morality that derives from it are a gift from God, not a product of "flesh and blood."[32] Thus was it defined by the First Vatican Council.[33]

Christian morality is the ethical aspect of the divine revelation made by God through the prophets and brought to a climax in Christ,[34] who entrusted it to the Apostles,[35] giving them the authority to transmit it to all generations by the power of the Holy Spirit.[36] This is what we call the Magisterium, the teaching office of the Church.[37] The Church cannot change the content of this revelation but only interpret it.[38] This also applies to Christian morality and to natural law brought to perfection by it.[39]

---

[32]See Peter's confession of faith in the divinity of Jesus, and the latter's reply to it: Matthew 16:16–17.

[33]"Faith is a supernatural virtue whereby under God's inspiration and with the help of his grace, we believe that the things revealed by him are true, not on account of the intrinsic truth of those things perceived by the natural light of reason, but on account of the authority of God himself who reveals, who can neither deceive nor be deceived." (Const., *Dei Filius*, ch. 3: Denzinger, 1789).

[34]"After speaking in many places and varied ways through the prophets, God 'last of all in these days has spoken to us by his son' (Heb. 1:1–2). For he sent his Son, the eternal Word, who enlightens all men, so that he might dwell among men and tell them the innermost realities about God (cf. Jn. 1:1–18)." (Second Vatican Council, Const., *Dei Verbum*, 4).

[35]"Christ the Lord, in whom the full revelation of the supreme God is brought to completion (cf. *II Corinthians*, 1:20; 3:16; 4:6), commissioned the apostles to preach to all men that gospel which is the source of all saving truth and moral teaching" (cf. *Matthew*, 28:19–20, and *Mark*, 16:15; Council of Trent, session IV, Decree on Scriptural Cannons: Denzinger, 783 (1501). (*Ibid.*, 7).

[36]*John*, 16:14. "And so the apostolic preaching, which is expressed in a special way by a continuous succession of preachers until the end of time. . . . This tradition which comes from the apostles develops in the Church with the help of the Holy Spirit (cf. First Vatican Council, Dogm. Const., ch. 4, 'On Faith and Reason': Denzinger, 1800 (3020)." (Second Vatican Council, Const., *Dei Verbum*, no. 8).

[37]"The task of authentically interpreting the word of God, whether written or handed on (cf. I Vatican Council, Dogm. Const. on the Catholic Faith, ch. 3 'On Faith': Denzinger, 1792 [3011]), has been entrusted exclusively to the living teaching office of the Church (cf. Pius XII, enc. *Humani Generis*, Aug. 12, 1950: AAS 42 [1950], pp. 568–569: Denzinger, 2314 [3886], whose authority is exercised in the name of Jesus Christ." (*Dei Verbum*, no 10).

[38]"This teaching office is not above the word of God, but serves it, teaching only what has been handed on, listening to it devoutly, guarding it scrupulously, and explaining it faithfully by divine commission and with the help of the Holy Spirit." (*Dei Verbum*, no. 10).

[39]"No believer will wish to deny that the teaching authority of the Church is competent to interpret even the natural moral law. It is, in fact, indisputable, as Our Predecessors have many times declared, that Jesus Christ, when communicating to Peter and the Apostles His

Can Morality Change?

No human activity can change Christian morality or natural morality. What does change, however, is the actual manner in which man understands it. The Sacred Congregation for the Doctrine of the Faith has expressed it well:

> There can be no true promotion of man's dignity unless the essential order of his nature is respected. Of course, in the history of civilization many of the concrete conditions and needs of human life have changed and will continue to change. But all evolution of morals and every type of life must be kept within the limits imposed by the immutable principles based upon every human person's constitutive elements and essential relations— elements and relations which transcend historical contingency.[40]

There are two main reasons for the fluctuations of man's understanding of the natural law:

(a) The weakness of man: his tendency to rationalize his emotional attachments by appealing to cultural factors, or to economic or social conditions, in short, factors extrinsic to him, conditions which are often used as scapegoats: "Hence, those many people are in error who today assert that one can find neither in human nature nor in the revealed law any absolute and immutable norm to serve for particular actions other than the one which expresses itself in the general law of charity and respect for human dignity. As a proof of their assertions they put forward the view that so-called norms of the natural law or precepts of sacred scripture are to be regarded only as given expressions of a form of particular culture at a certain moment of history."[41]

(b) The wealth of divine revelation: the enormous demands of the moral life that may require a gradual acceptance on the

---

divine authority and sending them to teach all nations His commandments, constituted them as guardians and authentic interpreters of all moral law, not only, that is, of the law of the gospel, but also of the natural law, which is also an expression of the will of God, the faithful fulfillment of which is equally necessary for salvation." (Paul VI, *Humanae Vitae*, July 25, 1968, no. 4).

[40]Sacred Congregation for the Doctrine of the Faith, Declaration on Sexual Ethics, 29 December, 1975, no. 3.

[41]*Ibid.*, no. 4.

part of man, God leading him with a wise pedagogy along a gently upward slope.

This is why, for example, polygamy and divorce were tolerated among God's chosen people until Christ came and told them that it was not so "from the beginning";[42] it was a concession allowed or tolerated by God, although it indeed was a backward step on man's part. In other words, it was a concession "by reason of the hardness of your hearts."[43] But this type of concession is not possible now that the fullness of divine revelation has been made in Christ: no lowering of moral standards is henceforth logically possible.[44] Christ never condones or "permits" sin. What he does is always to forgive the sins of those who are repentant. The Church founded by Christ follows the same line: she cannot condone, permit, or "legalize" sins; through her ordained ministers, however, she can always forgive sins confessed in the sacrament of penance with true repentance.

The Beatific Vision

Christ reveals the last end of man most explicitly by identifying it with the beatific vision, which is the indescribable enjoyment of the possession of God by facial vision and love: "we shall see him just as he is";[45] "we see now through a mirror in an obscure manner, but then face to face."[46]

This supernatural destiny of man is communicated to us through grace,[47] and Christ reveals himself as the way to that end.[48] In this life, it is through grace—a created participation in the divine life itself[49]— that man is able to attain an imperfect though real union with the Blessed Trinity. It is a true enlightenment that would have baffled Plato and Aristotle, for whom man, when facing God, is like an owl facing the sun. This is indeed true on account of both the wealth of the object and the weakness of the subject. But God's revelation in Christ

---

[42]*Matthew*, 19:3–9.
[43]*Matthew*, 19:8.
[44]Cf. note 35.
[45]*I John*, 3:2.
[46]*I Corinthians*, 13–12.
[47]*John*, 1:17; *Romans*, 6:23; 7:25; 11:6; *Titus*, 2:11; *Ephesians*, 2:7.
[48]*John*, 1:14–18; 14:6.
[49]*John*, 4:14; 15:5; *Ephesians*, 4:15; *II Peter*, 1:4.

so empowers man's capacity that he is raised to the understanding of divine mysteries, as the First Vatican Council states.[50]

Grace comes to man as the light of faith in this life, and the light of glory after this life: "Now I know in part, but then I shall know even as I have been known. So there abide faith, hope, and charity, these three: but the greatest of these is charity,"[51] when faith will become vision.

The Enlightenment of Faith

Thus faith is both darkness and light. It is darkness in relation to God because, if we look at him directly, we are dazzled by the excess of light, like an owl facing the sun. God reveals himself to us through the twilight of analogy.[52] He remains incomprehensible to us in himself, since the infinite cannot be encompassed by the finite. God "dwells in light inaccessible, whom no man has seen or can see."[53] But faith is light in relation to man because when we look at the things of the world bathed in light that shines from divine revelation, we understand them in their true meaning and value: we see them in their true light. "For with you is the fountain of life, and in your light we see light."[54]

What then does grace do to man? Since man's natural powers are inadequate to attain a supernatural end, he needs to be given (though God is not thereby obliged to do so) a new set of powers which are supernatural and wherewith he can reach the supernatural end. These powers or abilities have to be communicated or infused into man from outside himself: they cannot come from within man because then they would be merely natural powers.

Supernatural Life

These infused powers come in the form of habits or virtues called supernatural virtues. There are two sets of them: one concerned with God himself, namely the theological virtues of faith, hope, and charity;

---

[50]Denzinger, 1796.

[51]*I Corinthians*, 13:12–13.

[52]"For from the greatness and beauty of created things their original author, by analogy is seen." (*Wisdom*, 13:5).

[53]*I Timothy*, 6:16.

[54]*Psalms*, 35:10.

and the other with human conduct in general, namely the cardinal virtues of prudence, justice, fortitude, and temperance. To these are added the gifts of the Holy Spirit,[55] whom we have received along with "the charity of God":[56] the gifts of wisdom, understanding, knowledge, counsel, fortitude, piety, and fear of the Lord. These gifts are not stable dispositions, like the virtues, but rather are like flashes of divine power that enhance human acts depending on the intensity of man's love of God.

This is then how grace raises nature, thus healing it and saving it. Man is neither totally innocent and in no need of grace, nor totally corrupt and incapable of being saved. He has no natural ability for self-salvation, but he has the obediential capacity to be raised to the supernatural level by grace and thus be saved. In other words, he can only obey or respond to the healing action of grace and cooperate with it.[57]

Faith and Reason

The relationship of Christian morality to natural morality is parallel to that of grace to nature, to that of faith to reason, and to that of theology to philosophy. This was St. Thomas's idea in writing the *Summa Contra Gentiles*, a book addressed to those outside Christianity. There he presented the natural moral law as common ground for Christian and non-Christian alike, showing the latter that Christian revelation contains the answers to the deepest questions of philosophy. Not only is there no conflict between reason and faith, but in fact there is a marvelous continuity and harmony between both.

Two conclusions follow therefrom, as a summary of this article:

- (a) that Christians must be the strongest defenders of the natural law, for the love of humanity;
- (b) that the Church, as recipient of divine revelation, has in her Magisterium the authority to explain and interpret the natural law.[58]

---

[55]*Isaiah*, 11:2–3.

[56]*Romans*, 5:5.

[57]All this doctrine on justification was elucidated and authoritatively defined by the Council of Trent, in response to the Protestant belief in the "total" corruption of human nature which would make the latter incurable.

[58]Cf. note 39.

PART III

The Moral Agent and the Common Good

The Self, Intersubjectivity, and the Common Good

Joseph J. Califano

In an earlier article on human suffering, I tried to reveal the intrinsic objective goodness of the "being" of all persons[1] and the positive notion of justice that follows from this objectively demonstrable truth. There I attempted to demonstrate that justice is not merely a negative notion prohibiting certain actions but primarily a positive notion requiring that we act in a way that views the existence of other persons as a good to be preserved. Acts of omission, also, can be real acts of injustice. I also affirmed that any *bona fide* moral philosophy requires a knowledge of God derived from some version of St. Thomas Aquinas's fourth way of proving God's existence. Such a proof discovers God's existence from our experience of the gradation of pure perfections in finite things. This is evident in our experience, for example, of life, unity, goodness, truth, and beauty. These pure perfections are also discovered by means of this proof to be identical with the *esse* of things, a metaphysical truth also necessary to understand the intrinsic goodness of the human person, whether suffering or not. I also demonstrated how the postmodern mind transfers the evil of the affliction of the suffering person to the very existence of the suffering person herself, who thus becomes an evil to be destroyed.[2]

---

[1]The intrinsic goodness of each and every person from the moment of conception to the moment of a natural death.

[2]"Human Suffering and Our Post-Civilized Cultural Mind: A Maritainian Analysis," *The Twilight of Civilization* ed. Peter Redpath (Notre Dame, Indiana: American Maritain Association/University of Notre Dame Press, 1990), pp. 201–214.

Nevertheless, while I am confident that I justified these various claims, my earlier article has been the object of certain criticisms. These criticisms fall into two groups. The protest of the first group is that I confuse justice, friendship, faith, and charity and thereby distort the philosophical notion of the common good. This group also charges that I have distorted what the moral law and/or the positive law should require of us—an objection that appears to be rooted in the view that the common good is merely a collection of private goods. This objection in the end claims that I have confused faith with philosophy and thereby have warped both. A corollary of this is that my argument is fideistic and Augustinian, but certainly not Thomistic—a very odd objection since St. Thomas's natural law ethics is heavily influenced by St. Augustine. This view seems to hold that a knowledge of the common good is possible without affirming the existence of God or the positive relationships that exist between persons. However, as I have already demonstrated, to grasp the realities of human relationships, one must know that God exists and that God has created all persons, both men and women. Whatever notion of the common good is at play within the view from which the above objections arise, it is definitely not a notion of the common good that could stand up to rational examination, nor could it in any way be attributed to Thomas Aquinas, Yves R. Simon, or Jacques Maritain.

The second group's criticism is that I assume that from conception to death humans are actual persons, in spite of the fact that an embryo or even a newborn suffering human being may not have all the specifying activities of an adult of our species. Thus, it was asserted that I misused the principle of *operatio sequitur esse* and that I ignored the popular opinion that the embryo is not a person until it is viable at a time late in pregnancy. Judith Jarvis Thomson's argument that an embryo is a mere parasite has been proposed as a refutation of my position.[3]

These objections can be met, provided that we examine the notions of the self, intersubjectivity, and the common good. It is the absence of a genuine understanding of these three principles that may be at the root of these objections. The intensity with which these realities

---

[3]J.J. Thomson, "A Defense of Abortion," *Philosophy & Public Affairs*, Vol 1, Fall (1971), pp. 47–66.

are denied or distorted today is a serious threat to the very survival of our humanity. A proper understanding of these truths is essential to the foundation of our moral life and the sustaining of a civilized society; however, one should not be surprised that the negation of these basic truths has become a fact of everyday experience. We live in an age permeated by myths and distortions exemplified by the fact that there has been an attempt to discuss justice in a way disconnected from reality and any substantive knowledge of self, other persons, and intersubjectivity.

This is clearly evident by the prominence of a distracted surrealist discussion of justice in our century in terms of Robert Nozick's[4] crude radical individualism and John Rawls's[5] argument from a veil of ignorance. One would have us blindly affirm the *status quo* as just, irrespective of what means were used to create the *status quo*. The latter would have our sense of justice and our relationship to others be rooted in self-interest which puts us into a condition not unlike Avicenna's "suspended man" in our attempt to discern justice. Neither Nozick nor Rawls can give us an intelligible reason for accepting his position as a foundation for justice. Neither view of justice has any relationship to the real; instead each would have us consent to an arbitrary construct. Harsher criticisms are possible given the absence of reality in their definitions of justice. There is no conformity of intellect to what is—neither in their concepts of a human being nor in their explanations of human interpersonal relationships; nor, consequently, in their notions of justice. The failure of contemporary philosophical movements (exemplified by the Anglo-American analytical movement)[6] to understand that the intellect can grasp real being has rendered the current philosophical fashions impotent in addressing important moral issues.

The point here is that both in modern psychology and philosophy the self has disappeared from the realm of substantive realities, and along with the self, all social awareness of our social and interpersonal life. It is clear that we have entered into a Tower of Babel built

---

[4]Robert Nozick, *Anarchy, State and Utopia* (New York: Basic Books, 1974).

[5]John Rawls, *A Theory of Justice* (Cambridge, Massachusetts: Harvard University Press, 1971).

[6]See the writings of Richard Rorty and Kai Nielsen in *After the Demise of the Tradition* (Boulder, Colorado: Westview Press, 1991).

by a deconstruction of the transsubjective nature of both man and God and we have opted for individualistic loneliness over the reality of community life. Others would have us opt for a vague distracted sentimental notion of our social nature. These views do such violence to our understanding of the reality of persons as knowing and loving beings that the very notion of personhood has lost its meaning today. In psychology we have the strange phenomenon of theories of personality without admitting the existence of persons. When John Locke said that "substance is and I know not what," and Hume followed with "I am and I know not what: I am a mere bundle of perceptions," they were predicting the disappearance of the reality of the self, the reality of other persons, and the reality of the common good in the consciousness of twentieth-century modernity.

With the disappearance of the self and of the intellect's contact with reality, the possibility of obtaining truthful answers to the following questions also disappears: What is it to be a person or a human being? Who are to be identified as persons? Who are said to have rights? What is the nature of our interpersonal relationships? and What is the nature of justice? Any attempt to explicate and answer any of these questions becomes fruitless. Without a knowledge of how to answer these questions in terms of what is, one must depend on arbitrary answers and definitions that one somehow hopes others will accept. If they are accepted, they may become conventions. One hopes that they will be accepted willingly; if not, political force may be necessary. In such a context, any answer to the above questions is as good as any other; accordingly, no one can say that anyone's definitions are true or false, or that moral judgments are right or wrong.

For example, the definition of an embryo as an indeterminate clump of cells, a parasite, claims equal consideration with any other definition. Nor is any criterion admitted to discern the truth of any proposition. A woman can claim that an embryo is part of her body, to be disposed of as she wishes, because of a conventional arbitrary definition of who is a person and a distorted notion of the right to privacy. The fact that the embryo is never part of her body is not important. The fact that, if this were the case, the woman would lose her organic integrity after giving birth (one of the parts of her body or an organ of her body would be missing) does not matter. Nor can we consider the fact that histologists can identify human development in an embryo within the first three days after conception and possibly treat genetic diseases at this stage of development.

The right to privacy cannot be invoked to grant one person the power to destroy another simply because one regards another as unwanted or an inconvenience. A private matter is one that only involves oneself as an individual. If there are two persons involved in any situation, the right to privacy cannot be invoked to deny the rights of either. This must be understood if the right to privacy is to have any intelligible meaning at all.

Scientific, philosophical, and moral facts have become irrelevant to our contemporary post-civilized cultured minds, for such minds live only in a world of their own making, a world where only "conventions" give it a veneer of moral objectivity and permanence. The facts are not relevant since what does not fit into one's subjective, conventional world view simply does not have to be affirmed as real. The majesty of God and the goodness of other persons do not have to be affirmed because the individual becomes his own god. To sustain this view, a person must shut out of his world all other persons, including the real God.

Self-esteem, in this context, is something one can only shout about and wish for but it is difficult to obtain. The hope is that others will not question the arbitrariness of one's foundation for self-esteem. However, contemporary history teaches us that there are those in the world who will reject human dignity, if its foundations are not clearly preserved. It is precisely because our postmodern world has failed to be able to preserve the genuine foundations of self-worth, that self-esteem has become elusive.

Two very important distinctions have been lost by the postmodern mind. The first is the distinction within beings between potency and act; the second is the distinction within beings between substance, power, and activity. The loss of the first distinction—between potency and act—causes one to conclude that potency is not a real, discoverable part of a being. However, the distinction between potency and act, as revealing that which is an intrinsic principle of a thing, is employed every day when one chooses what to eat. For example, if one asks why one prefers chicken and broccoli to sand and rocks, the answer is simply that the former has the potency to be genuine food, a source of real nourishment, whereas the latter, of course, does not. The potency of chicken and broccoli to become real food is an actual defining part of their natures. Thus, we say chicken and broccoli are foods and sand and rocks are not.

A germinating seed includes within its being the nature of a plant, the principles that enable it to actually develop into a fully mature plant. The human embryo also possesses within its being the nature of a human person, the principles of *essence* and *esse*, potency and act. These principles, in turn, enable it to develop into a man or a woman. No substantial change occurs within the life of a human being between the moment of conception and the moment of death. Therefore, at any stage of human life, from the moment of conception to the moment of death, if one asks, "what is it?," the truthful answer would have to be, it is a human being with all the rights that follow from this truth. In fact, all development in an embryo is from within, and specific activities manifest themselves as the organs necessary to perform these activities develop. However, all these activities, from the moment of conception, have a specifically human genetic code and characteristics that require a human life principle to be present. Any notion of a succession of forms has no place in contemporary genetic science.

In conjunction with the loss of the understanding of the realities of potency and act, there is a loss of the second distinction between substance, power, and activity. The absence of this distinction causes the postmodern mind to confuse the identification of substance and activity in a somewhat Cartesian manner. This error fosters the conclusion that a being must be actually performing all the activities of an adult of the species to have the specific nature of that species. According to this view, for example, if one were to stop thinking, one would stop existing as a human being. Thus, the modern mind distorts the principle of *operatio sequitur esse* by not understanding the nature of *ens* as manifesting within itself the distinctions between potency and act and the distinctions between substance, power, and activity. Once these genuine distinctions are recognized, one is able to understand and unite sound philosophical judgments with what contemporary histology and genetics have discovered. To perform any of the activities of a species in a way that is species-specific, one must have the nature of a member of that species. One must have the essence and *esse* of that species.

In our postmodern world, the absence of a recognition of the truth in conjunction with a blind commitment to a world of moral inventions has resulted in an absurd notion of justice. Here, justice becomes a mere word, a rhetorical clique, appealing to "individualism" and "privacy" as institutionalized isolationism. What has resulted is a visionless mass of lonely unhappy people who do not know who they are, why they are, where they are, and what they are supposed to do. Hell is other people! Hate becomes the only real human emotion. Disengagement of the self from all other persons, whether human or divine, as unknown and unknowable unrealities, has become the only course of action. The conclusion is accepted that even though conventional morality and law are constructed on the flimsiest of foundations, they must be affirmed anyway. Law must merely be a call to non-action, leaving me alone to be alone, and act in whatever distorted view of self-interest I may happen to entertain for the moment.

The goal is to make law conform to my enclosed perspective through the art of rhetorical persuasion, a skill the Sophists mastered. Hereby, one convinces others to accept one's own egocentric preferences. This is Nietzsche's will to power in operation: the polytheism of human *egotheism*, the false gods of our present age. This effort presumably makes the best of an impossible situation, one which is, in reality, without meaning. In the absence of a notion of being and goodness, we are left only to muddle about within the parameters of evil. Without a perception of light, we only have darkness. As darkness is only known by reason of our knowledge of light, and evil is known by reason of our knowledge of the good, the absence of a knowledge of light and the objective knowledge of the goodness of being—in this case, the goodness of other persons—brings about the most profound kind of ignorance: willed ignorance of what it is to be and a willed ignorance of good and evil. This becomes a world where there exists, instead of a love of being (life, unity, goodness, and beauty), a love of nothingness: death (suicide, abortion, and euthanasia), disunion (disorder, disintegration), and the morally ugly (the grotesque). Nothing can be recognized as really good and nothing can be recognized as really evil. "Where there is no vision the people shall perish" *Proverbs*, 29:18. The result is the shrinking of the human life to the pathetic dimensions of the amoral.

The reason the self has disappeared is that it has no place in the various materialistic, deterministic philosophies of human knowledge and action that are prevalent today: philosophies that search for an empirical, purely physicalist notion of the self,[7] an impossible quest which of necessity must conclude, as does Stephen Priest in his *Theories of the Mind*,[8] that there are neither selves nor minds. One no longer sees oneself as a self among others; as the reality of the other

---

[7]Cf. Daniel Dennett, *Consciousness Explained* (New York: Little, Brown and Company, 1991). For an anthology of contemporary views see: *Self & Identity: Contemporary Philosophical Issues*, ed. Kolak & Martin Raymond (New York: Macmillan, 1991).

[8]*Theories of the Mind* (Boston, Massachusetts: Houghton Mifflin, 1991).

disappears, so does the reality of oneself. What disappears along with the self is all those communicable goods which become our common goods. The only notion of the common good possible in this enclosed view is a mutilated one, a dismemberment of the common good into a mere collection of individual private goods, or perhaps to some quantifiable notion of individual preferences—and this notwithstanding the fact that no material thing can be a common good.

In such a context, a community of persons is only an illusion of the mind without any substantive foundation. We are left with only "possessive individualism," or "political atomism." This is why in our postmodern age family life and, indeed, all forms of community life, break down. Today even religious life is threatened by corrosive philosophies and theologies that misunderstand the nature of "self" and "other" as the foundations of community life. Therefore, even many religious communities are experiencing numerous difficulties which threaten their very survival.

Human individuality and selfhood are not grasped through the image of material individuation, a principle of separation of one being from another in time and place. The self is only properly understood in light of the fact that, as persons, we can transcend our material individuation through transobjective, transsubjective acts of knowledge and love. Thus, we discover the spiritual principle of our individuality, a unitive principle, as I have previously demonstrated.[9] It is precisely because a person's individuality can be shared through knowledge and love that persons can concretize the common communicable goods at the foundation of social life.

The difficulty here is that there is no direct knowledge of the self nor is there any possibility of forming a material image of the self. Further, knowledge of the self as singular goes against the grain of the ordinary way in which our intellect operates. For the intellect ordinarily seeks to know the other *as other* by means of abstracting concepts from phantasms. The intellect forms universal concepts by prescinding from existence and singular characteristics. This is why God's knowledge of us is perfect: He does not have to abstract His knowledge from

---

[9]Joseph Califano, "Maritain's Philosophy of the Person and the Individual," *Notes et Documents* (Rome), vol. 12, July-September, 1978. pp. 19–22, and "Maritain's Democracy of the Human Person and Man as a Moral Agent," *Jacques Maritain: A Philosopher in the World*, ed. Jean-Louis Allard (Ottawa: University of Ottawa Press, 1985), pp. 303–311.

phantasms. He knows things directly in their singularity. God is not rational in a discursive sense. He knows the individual soul directly and completely. His whole being is, as Yves R. Simon stated, His transsubjectivity.[10] There are, accordingly, no real distinctions to be made within the reality of God. There is no distinction between His knowledge and His love. He is simple.

We are like God insofar as we are centers of liberty and the author of our actions. It is through reflection on our actions that we become aware of ourselves as ourselves. This is especially the case when a person takes herself in hand and gives her life a fundamental direction by virtue of interiorizing a law. This crossing of the threshold into moral life—which comes from free commitment and the exercise of self-mastery—is how we come to know ourselves, a truth Kierkegaard understood so well. These primal acts of freedom determine what I live for, what I hold to be good, what I ultimately love.[11] These free acts enable one to define and discover what she is, whereby she interiorizes a law, either given by God and rooted in reality, or a law of her own invention. This law will reflect the absolute love which one will live by: whether it be love of money, power, things, the body beautiful, novelties of one's own mind and will; or the love of objective truth, in and through God, which is the only authentic foundation of human life.

The degree to which self-revelatory choices commit us to virtue, in light of one's existential ultimate end, reveals to us the degree to which we achieve genuine selfhood and genuine self-knowledge. The degree they commit us to vice and move us away from existential truths and reality is, of course, the degree to which we fail to become an authentic self. In such a condition we withdraw from life into a world of *ens rationes*, a world which is indistinguishable from nothing. Without God and His truth, we can do nothing and be nothing. We can only come to self-awareness through a realization of the transsubjectivity of our nature as described above. A genuine grasp of ourselves and of our intersubjectivity only results from the recognition of the existence of God, the goodness of being, and the goodness of other persons. Only a positive commitment to the above makes us aware that interpersonal

---

[10]Yves R. Simon, *An Introduction to Metaphysics of Knowledge* trans. by Vukan Kuic and Richard J. Thompson (New York: Fordham University Press, 1990).

[11]*Ibid.* See also Jacques Maritain, *The Range of Reason* (New York: Charles Scribner's Sons, 1942), ch. 6.

relationships are existential relationships that make community life a natural part of our being.

It is only in this context that the unanswerable questions of the postmodern mind, cited above, become answerable. Who am I ? A word spoken by God in love, (although, not The Word Who is Christ). Where do I come from? From God. Where am I going? To God. How do I get there? Through love, through a love of God and the realities of His creation.

Parenthetically, it should be noted, that the root of the postmodern mind is a rejection of the authority of reality or of what exists: that is, God and nature as the epistemological ground of our judgments. This has occurred because postmodern men and women confuse a desire to be free from the various abuses and distortions of authority by oppressive governments, including religious institutions of the past, with a freedom from the authority of reality. Thus, freedom of thought becomes a separation from what exists, a freedom of the intellect and will from truth and goodness. Another way of saying this is that it becomes freedom from my nature, the nature of God, and the nature of other persons. For to give truth a place in our lives is to accept a self-discipline in respect to the real that the postmodern mind finds intolerable. Thus, to preserve my absolute independence from a relationship to anything other than myself, I must make the reality of God irrelevant. To preserve this absolute autonomy of the self, one must also make all human interpersonal relationships meaningless. All of these negations enable one to deny or ignore the goodness of what exists—for example, other persons and our interpersonal relationships. The result of these negative principles is that the common good becomes an unintelligible and irrelevant concept, except in the sense of an idolatrous separateness, which declares "leave me alone to do my own thing."

On this view, I am free to give full authority to the products of my disassociated mind. I am free to view my self as a god, the absolute judge of what is true and false, good and evil. In this way, the world of the postmodern mind is invented by a human self and gives a distorted priority to individual rights, whereby one may readily rationalize the witholding of goods to others. At the root of it all, one usurps God for oneself. For if one were to admit the truth of the existence of God, then one could no longer claim to be free to do whatever one wanted. If God is allowed in the process of my own self-development, I could not claim to be the cause of myself and the sole truth for myself. The fact that this pretense at human *aseity* is absurd, an impossible illusion, a result of a delusion of grandeur, has not deterred the postmodern mind at all. God, reality, and other persons cannot really be admitted into the postmodern metaphysics without destroying this exaggerated and arrogant individualism and without constraining and correcting its moral license. Therefore, God, real knowledge, and other persons must be rejected so that an "ethics" of the absolute autonomy of the self can be postulated, and they are all rejected in the name of freedom, of course. Egotheism wins the day. The irony of the postmodern mind is that, only by the recognition of that which it has rejected (namely, self, freedom, and the common good), can it find what it wishes: meaning in this ambiguous world.

As to the objection that I have confused charity, friendship, and justice, I offer the following for your consideration. If one affirms the existence of God, the goodness of being, and the existence of other persons, then one must also affirm that some level of friendship is a part of justice. If appreciating this point means that there is a philosophical analogue to supernatural charity in the natural order, then there is some kind of analogue of charity to be found in the natural law. For charity completes and perfects nature in its full amplitude; it does not replace nature nor does it destroy nature.

The great danger is to take an atheistic or secular model of what can be known naturally or as a standard for what can be philosophically discovered. Equally great is the danger of taking Aristotle's secular, incomplete, exclusivist notion of justice as our model. A view that excludes women, artisans, and slaves from consideration in respect to justice is philosophically abhorrent. (Still further, it is an error to conclude that every moral teaching in Scripture cannot be discovered by reason.) St. Thomas, it so happens, follows St. Augustine, rather than Aristotle, in accepting an all-inclusive notion of justice, recognizing that all persons are children of God and somehow our brothers. In this respect as well as many others, St. Thomas is not an Aristotelian.

Personality, selfhood, is not a static material given, but a spiritual reality to be achieved through the conquest of our freedom and the discovery and realization of the intersubjectivity of our being. The person discovers community with God and other persons as necessary conditions for becoming an authentic self. Authenticity, then, becomes an activity of integrating the manifold aspects of the self by directing our freedom toward the goods of the existential order: God, being, and other persons.

All of this bears directly on a philosophy of the common good, which is a communicable, interpersonal good. The first universal common good is God, whose whole being is to be found in His communication of His goodness to us, for He has created us as actual beings out of love. The common natural law is also part of the common communicable good. These universal formal aspects of the common good must be known and willed for the possibility of any genuine notions of the material common good to be actualized through meaningful choices.

Society today seems to be collapsing because *de facto* people in general and specifically those who have the responsibility for directing society toward a material realization of the common good are not willing the common good, either formally or materially. Thus, the very foundations of civilized life are eroding before our eyes. Civilized society, even in the order of intention, is ceasing to exist. This is true both for the public and private sector of our contemporary world.

Yves R. Simon[12] has accurately pointed out that the proper functioning of society, and especially a democratic society, presupposes that all should intend the common good formally and that those in authority and public office must intend it both formally and materially. This is a necessary prerequisite for the survival of community life.

However, if the common good is neither intended formally by all, nor materially by those who are in authority in public life, then the common good ceases to be. In such a context, because there is no admitting of a common life, but only the positing of an invented, contractual notion of public good as a collection of individual private goods, then virtues, and especially, the virtue of justice, lose their meaning. Since virtue implies a love of the common good, and there is no common good to be loved, then virtue (especially the virtue of justice) has no implied object. Justice can have no place in our lives. A disinclination away from the good is instilled rather than a right inclination toward the good. The vice of injustice becomes *de facto* the rule. As a result, the disintegration of the self, intersubjectivity, and the common good become a traumatic fact of human life.

---

[12]Yves R. Simon, *Philosophy of Democratic Government* (Notre Dame, Indiana: University of Notre Dame Press, 1993), Revised edition.

The Good Citizen and the Demands of Democracy: An Application of the Political Philosophy Of Yves R. Simon

Diane Caplin

Introduction

Democratic government, like any human institution, is not perfect. It is by all accounts in recent history, however, the form of government preferred by most of the people in the world. There are good reasons for this preference, not the least of which is that democracy by definition entails an essential respect for human freedom. Humans, being what they are, cherish their freedom. For this reason and others, there is a natural affinity between human beings and democratic government.

Granted that democratic government respects human freedom, it is of the utmost importance that the free citizens of democratic nations understand the true meaning of human freedom and that they be prepared to accept the responsibilities and obligations of citizenship in such nations. If freedom is merely understood to be the absence of constraint or the abundance of choice, its essential meaning is lost. Full human freedom in a democratic society requires government of the citizens by the citizens themselves. So clear was this to Yves R. Simon that he defined democratic government in terms of the self-government of the people. "When the political idea assumes the democratic form, the people asserts, over and above its freedom *from* abusive power, its freedom *to* govern itself. Keeping the government confined within a definite field is no longer held sufficient; the government has been taken over by the people. Such is democratic freedom, the defining feature of democracy."[1]

By further exploration of the political philosophy of Yves R. Simon, I will show in this paper that the defining feature of democracy, this self-government of the people, is linked to a distinct understanding of human nature. I do this first by showing that for Simon, democratic freedom has the character of an end for which free choice is the means. Secondly, I explore Simon's definition of virtue and show how prudence functions in Simon's thought as the human disposition that perfects human choosing in order that it achieve its end. Finally, I show why Simon insists on the interdependence of prudence with the moral virtues and what the consequences of this interdependence are for the democratic citizen. These three moves in the argument provide the structure for my paper: Part I, "Democratic Freedom as Human Achievement"; Part II, "Prudence: Freedom's Virtue"; and Part III, "Justice and the Common Good." I conclude that if democratic government is blessed with virtuous citizens of good character, it is never an accident. Such a blessing is not a luxury of democracy; it is essential to it. Government may be many things without virtuous citizens but it cannot properly be called democratic. If Simon is right, his political philosophy has much to offer to the democracy we claim in the United States today.

Democratic Freedom as Human Achievement

The relation of choice to full democratic freedom is a relation of means to end. Simon understands means/end relations in terms of the Aristotelian language of causality.

> Let the formal cause be defined as that by reason of which a thing is *what* it is. In the relation to the composite, matter is describable as that *out of which* a thing is made; but in relation to the form itself, matter should be described as that *in which* the form resides and that which owes its own determination, its own being such and such, its own whatness, to the form. Clearly, a relation of matter to form obtains within the order

---

[1] Yves R. Simon, *Philosophy of Democratic Government* (Chicago: The University of Chicago Press, 1951, 1961, 1977), p. 76. Revised edition (Notre Dame, Indiana: University of Notre Dame Press, 1993), detailed subject index added.

of final causality, between the means and the end. Every means, as such, derives from the end its being what it is, its desirability, its goodness, its intelligibility as a thing in the order of final causality.[2]

In other words, means is to end as matter is to form. Just as matter owes its determination, its "whatness" to the form, so too does the means owe its own determination to the end for which it acts. This is no small point in Simon's argument. The end of an action *defines* the means, making the means be what it is. Only those means that achieve their ends, then, can properly be called means at all. If a means to a particular end was chosen and the means failed, then its character as means was mere illusion.

Some ends function as means when they are intended to achieve an ulterior purpose. "The end is the form of the means; the ulterior end, which is more of an end, is the form of the inferior end, which is more of a means."[3] Calling the concepts of "means" and "end" "opposite and related concepts," Simon reminds us that they "admit of combination in all degrees."[4]

> Let us never think that whatever is a means is thereby entirely denied the character of an end, or that whatever has the character of an end is thereby denied the character of a means. A pure means is a thing that has absolutely no desirability of its own and cannot be desired except as a way leading to a thing desirable.[5]

The end of one action, therefore, may take on the character of the means for another.

To illustrate, let us say that a citizen supports the election of a particular person to public office. Certain actions lead to the desired end of victory on polling night: door-to-door campaigning, fund-raising activities, and participation in public rallies all help the cause. This election result, though the end of the political activism, itself becomes the means to some other end. For what was this person elected? For the purpose of having a friend in an influential position who will return the good favors from the campaign? Or, for the purpose of serving the

---

[2]Yves R. Simon, *Freedom of Choice*, ed. Peter Wolff (New York: Fordham University Press, 1969, 1987, 1992), pp. 61–62.

[3]*Ibid.*, p. 62.

[4]*Ibid.*, p. 59.

[5]*Ibid.*

common good of the entire community, whatever personal sacrifices that may entail on the part of the campaign worker? This difference in motive is significant because the goal of electing a particular person now takes on the character of the means to achieving some other end. The process goes on until the ultimate end is reached. No means employed in the achievement of any intermediary end can properly be called a means if it interferes with the ultimate end of the political order. Any choice can be illusory.

Choice need not be mistaken, however. To avoid illusory choice, one needs only to behave according to the law of human nature. "The basic statement that every nature is the realization of an idea implies that every nature has within itself a law of activity which is its own law."[6] Simon accepts, with St. Thomas, that any being, simply because it exists, enjoys some degree of autonomy because of its law of activity. Further, the more a thing participates in the idea of being, the greater its autonomy. How is human autonomy, then, related to human being? "Autonomy is the glory, the splendor of being. Now terminal freedom, since it is both freedom of choice and autonomy, is the kind of autonomy which properly fits the rational nature as such. Terminal liberty is the glory of the rational nature."[7]

Maritain scholars will recognize the term "terminal liberty" from the first chapter of *Freedom in the Modern World*.[8] In this work Maritain distinguished between the initial freedom that human beings inherit with their rational nature, and terminal freedom, which is an achievement of that nature. "We are called upon," Maritain says, "to become in action what we already are in the metaphysical order: a person (an individual substance of rational nature)."[9] The freedom to choose, then, is not its own end. Initial freedom is *for* terminal freedom: that which we are by nature called to be. Initial freedom is for the achievement of rational personhood, the glory of our being. For that reason, human choosing that fails to achieve terminal freedom is not properly called free choice.[10]

---

[6]Yves R. Simon, *Nature and Functions of Authority* (Milwaukee: Marquette University Press, 1940, 1948), p. 42.

[7]*Ibid.*

[8]Jacques Maritain, *Freedom in the Modern World*, trans. Richard O'Sullivan (New York: Charles Scribner's Sons, 1938).

[9]*Ibid.*, p. 30.

[10]Simon adopted Maritain's terms "initial" and "terminal" freedom in most of his writings on the subject. In 1958 in a lecture at the University of New Mexico, however, he distinguished

Simon recognizes that the *terminus* about which Maritain spoke is achieved by a human mastery over all the possible ways of acting:

> [F]reedom proceeds not from any weakness, any imperfection, any feature of potentiality on the part of the agent but, on the contrary, from a particular excellence in power, from a plentitude of being and an abundance of determination, from an ability to achieve mastery over diverse possibilities, from a strength of constitution which makes it possible to attain one's end in a variety of ways.[11]

Further, it is something at which human action *must* aim. The last end of being human is not a matter of choice. This object of human action is "the spontaneous, natural, necessary, and involuntary adherence of the will to the comprehensive good; it is the natural desire for happiness; it is the necessary volition of the last end."[12]

Using the Aristotelian metaphysics of causality, Simon has shown that the final end ultimately conditions and defines all means. Now he asserts that the final end is something to which the will adheres spontaneously and naturally. Human beings necessarily will the last end understood to be the comprehensive good. Given these two premisses, Simon is justified in the claim that choices which lead away from, rather than toward, true freedom, are not free choices. The task is to understand that "freedom of choice, as freedom of choice, calls for the elimination of the power of making wrong choices."[13]

In contrast to what Yves R. Simon has offered as definitive of democratic freedom, the images of democratic freedom that prevail in the United States today make choice alone the ultimate value. To suggest that the range of choices available to U.S. citizens be limited is tantamount in some circles to an assault on human freedom itself. There is little consciousness in the slogans of either the political right or left of this society that the power to choose can be used for bad as well as good ends. The human power to reason among a myriad

---

initial freedom from "mature" freedom. His notes for the lecture entitled "Free Choice and Its Relation to Law" (July 8, 1958) include the following: "The maturation of freedom is one with the interiorization of the law, and this is one with the acquiring of the virtues." Jacques Maritain Center, University of Notre Dame; see the file on "Newman Lecture Series: On Authority and Liberty."

[11] Yves R. Simon, *Freedom of Choice*, p. 153.

[12] *Ibid.*, p. 103.

[13] Yves R. Simon, "On the Foreseeability of Free Acts," *The New Scholasticism* 22, No. 4, (October, 1948), p. 359.

of alternatives for action is not alone a guarantee of human glory. If Simon is right, something else is needed: the power of making wrong choices must be eliminated.

Prudence: Freedom's Virtue

By *nature* reason makes choice among alternative courses of action possible. That same rational nature, however, is the very one that entails the possibility of making wrong choices. The predicament suggests that another nature would be preferable. That is, it would be easier for human beings to achieve their comprehensive good if the possibility of error could be eliminated. The difficulty is that neither first nature nor final end are objects of choice for human beings. It is within the power of human nature, however, to cultivate a second nature. The character and disposition of human nature can be shaped so that error and illusion in human choosing are all but eliminated.

Simon's answer to how citizens can eliminate the power of making wrong choices requires an examination of virtue, "a quality that renders the will good and consequently less and less capable of making wrong choices."[14] Simon defines virtue as follows: "a *habitus*, that is, a disposition stable or steady by essence, like science and art, not uncertain by essence, like opinion; and which guarantees not only the perfection of a power, but also that of its use. (A quality of which no one makes a wrong use.)"[15]

A disposition is an arrangement of the parts of something "with a view to an effect pertaining to the whole."[16] When the "whole" in question is a human being, Simon says this about disposition:

> By a man's disposition we mean precisely the unique arrangement of all his moral traits. And when his arrangement makes him totally reliable and dependable in human affairs, we call both the man and his disposition virtuous. . . . This . . . has always been the common understanding of the

---

[14]The first explicit connection between free choice and virtue that I found in Simon's work was in some notes from the spring semester of 1948 at the University of Chicago. The course was entitled, "Freedom of Choice and the Ethics of Liberty." of Simon's papers at the Jacques Maritain Center at the University of Notre Dame Hesburgh library.

[15]Simon from the course notes, "Freedom of Choice and the Ethics of Liberty."

[16]Yves R. Simon, *The Definition of Moral Virtue*, ed. Vukan Kuic (New York: Fordham University Press, 1986, 1989), p. 79.

meaning of virtue: dependability in matters pertaining to the good of man as man.[17]

Still, for people to be considered virtuous, it is not enough for them to be dependable. A person who seems to be programmed to behave in certain ways can be reliable enough but this kind of dependability does not really capture the meaning of virtue. For this reason, Simon distinguishes *habitus* from habit. *Habitus* is grounded in objective necessity and allows for free choice and intention. Mere habit is something else: its character more resembles that of stubborn opinion, having a mechanical nature. This is why a disposition to act that is mere habit cannot characterize virtuous action. "Truly moral action," says Simon, "is never involuntary. In virtuous action we do precisely what we want to do."[18] Further, the disposition that is *habitus* is vital, thinking, and creative, always mindful of the objective necessity for which it acts. "Habit relieves us of the need to think; but *habitus* makes us think creatively."[19]

Something is still missing. Full virtue must be put to good use. In Simon's definition of virtue its stable essence was both related to science and art and distinguished from them. The distinction rests on how the particular disposition is used. Science, art, and virtue all possess what Simon calls a "qualitative readiness." The scientist who is highly skilled in syllogistic reasoning and the artist who is a talented painter are both prepared enough, in the qualitative sense, to put their skills to good use. But will they achieve the potential that their talents promise? Only those who possess an "existential readiness," in addition to their qualitative abilities can achieve the ends for which their talents are useful.[20] An intelligent but lazy scientist, for example, is not likely to make any new discoveries. It is only those whose dispositions are both qualitatively talented and existentially ready who are properly called virtuous.[21]

---

[17]*Ibid.*, p. 84.

[18]*Ibid.*, p. 55.

[19]*Ibid.*, p. 60.

[20]*Ibid.*, p. 71.

[21]The phrase, "existential readiness," is roughly synonymous with finality, ("the good or goodness of a process"). Simon saw the need to coin this new phrase because "finality" is so laden with difficulties not only in discussions among philosophers of different schools, but also between philosophers and scientists. Though biologists, for example, often scoff at the

From the refinements in Simon's original definition of virtue, the following can be said about persons with virtuous dispositions: their moral traits are ordered in a way that makes them dependable in matters pertaining to human goodness. The steady disposition of the virtuous person is not merely the repetition of habit; it is a disposition characterized by free action and mindful of the objective necessity which guides its action. Finally, virtuous persons exhibit, along with the qualitative ability to perform certain acts, an existential readiness to put their skills and talents to good use. It remains to be seen how a virtuous disposition is related to the achievement of democratic freedom.

"Among virtue," Simon says, "there is one which is principally the virtue of freedom. It is the virtue which concerns choice: prudence."[22] Prudence is concerned with choice because it means "wisdom in acting, wisdom in practice, wisdom in what we have referred to as human use."[23] Though choices about the best way to act are certainly subject to the unpredictable and uncontrollable contingencies of life, judgments about how to act do enjoy a truth. The truth that is appropriate to practical judgments enjoys a steadiness that can be assured in the employment of free choice toward the achievement of its natural end.

> Speaking of the truth of the practical judgment, we do not refer to its conformity to the reality of things—this conformity cannot be perfectly ascertained—we refer to its conformity with the requirements of a will which is supposed to be sound, healthy, honest. According to the so enlightened view of Aristotle, the certain truth of which the practical judgment is capable is no theoretical but a practical truth; it is not the truth of a cognition but the truth of a direction; it does not consist of a relation of conformity between the mind and things, but in a relation of conformity between the judgment of the mind and the requirements of a right appetite of the end to be pursued.[24]

---

notion of a teleology in nature, it is considered perfectly reasonable to discuss the function of a particular organ. Simon recognizes that to discuss the function of something is essentially the same as asking: what is it good for? The problem is that we do not always know the good for which certain natural processes act. For these reasons it makes more sense to speak of "existential readiness" than of finality when discussing the purpose, function or good of a particular disposition. Yves R. Simon, *Definition of Moral Virtue*, p. 71.

[22]From the course notes, "Freedom of Choice and the Ethics of Liberty."

[23]Yves R. Simon, *Definition of Moral Virtue*, p. 96.

[24]Yves R. Simon, *Nature and Functions of Authority*, p. 24.

Any choice for action will be subject to the contingent circumstances of life over which no citizen has control or foreknowledge. In that theoretical sense, actions can only be engaged with a probable certainty of what the outcome will be. In a practical sense, though, a steady principle of truth is assured: the prudential judgment is a "rule of direction" and as such "enjoys an absolute certainty."[25]

Even though a moral science can be syllogistic when the reasoning is about general or hypothetical moral dilemmas, something more is needed to guide the good person in choosing when the circumstances are concrete and particular. The judgment of *what* to do is certainly an affair of the intellect and in that sense, prudence is an intellectual virtue. Because its judgment is concerned with what to *do*, however, it is also concerned with the will. The intellect relies on right reason for sound judgment. The will, on the other hand, relies on right inclination. This dual vision of prudence toward the intellect and will in human judgment, justifies Simon's contention that, though moral science can be helpful in guiding concrete moral action, no dependable formula for good action is available for the particularities of our lives. The only dependable indicator, therefore, of the truth of practical judgments is the correct disposition of the person acting.

Simon's discussion of the prudential judgment makes it clear that its truth lies in the truth of a direction. Such a premise betrays the assumption that there is a best place to go. According to this assumption, prudence shares with freedom the distinction of being misunderstood in our democracy. To be prudent in the United States of the twentieth-century is to protect one's own self-interest. When President Bush insisted that a course of action "wouldn't be prudent," he clearly meant that it would not be in our national *self*-interest. Non-tenured faculty members know that to be prudent, they ought not to be too daring in their criticisms of unjust university policies. The risk is of their job security and their reputations in the academy. Members of the AARP protect their entitlements by threatening to turn from office those public servants who dare to talk of personal sacrifice for the sake of the common interest of the country. It is not "prudent," therefore, to speak this truth if one's own elected office is at stake. These examples and others indicate that it is, all too often, not the "truth of a direction"

---

[25]*Ibid.*, p. 25.

that defines prudential judgment in our democracy. Rather, it is the truth of individual self-interest that gives meaning to "being prudent." In the political philosophy of Yves R. Simon, individual self-interest is not the goal that shapes human freedom. The indissoluble relationship among prudence and the moral virtues reveals that "the best place to go" in the political order is toward the good of the whole human community.

Justice and the Common Good

Democratic citizens are no different from all other human beings in these ways: they share with everyone the rational nature that entails the possibility of error and illusion; they are destined to will a comprehensive good; they have the ability to cultivate a second nature that makes right choice easy and dependable. Imbedded in this notion of dependability, however, is the mindfulness of the objective necessity which shapes human choice. In the political order this object takes the form of justice, the virtue concerned with human relationships and the good end at which all human choice must aim.

It takes some care to define justice because, though it is the perfected ability to give consistently to "others" that which is their due, the "other" that is the object of this virtue may be either another individual or communal.[26] The subject or moral agent of justice can also be an individual or the community representing the person of one. It is because of the multiple ways in which the subjects and objects of just actions can be understood that the virtue itself is necessarily explained in three modes: commutative, legal, and distributive.[27]

The commutative mode governs the relationships between strictly equal individuals who enter into contractual agreements with one another. If all goes well, what is "due" is clearly defined by the terms of the contract and any arbiter can adjudicate disputes about who owes what to whom. The legal mode of justice is concerned with the relation of individuals to the whole community, what is owed by the parts to the whole, and this too is regulated by law. It is this kind of justice that

---

[26]Yves R. Simon, *Definition of Moral Virtue*, p. 98.

[27]The division is Aristotle's and Aquinas's and explained very well by Simon in *Definition of Moral Virtue*, pp. 98–100.

is concerned with a tax code, for example, giving all citizens the terms according to which they must contribute their individual earnings to the commonwealth. Finally, distributive justice is concerned with how that commonwealth is redistributed to the citizens; its relation is of the whole to its parts. But strict equality is not the standard according to which the redistribution is completed. Citizens who are victims of a natural disaster, for example, are distinguished by their hardship and may enjoy some financial relief from the federal government. That distribution would not, however, entitle citizens without the hardship to an equal share of that money in the mode of distributive justice.[28]

The question of how to secure distributive justice for a society returns us to a consideration of the virtue of prudence. The law or general principles that govern the distributive relationship in the community must always be applied to the particular and contingent circumstances of life. How does government decide, for example, whether sufficient need exists to distribute precious resources to the victims of a hurricane or an earthquake? Do the victims of a riot deserve similar consideration? If citizens insist on the right to rebuild on a vulnerable beach, should the government continue to finance this kind of risk? The point is that in every application of the principles that are designed to insure justice in the human community, some prudential judgment is required and this judgment cannot be a technological or scientific calculation. The common good is the only standard by which to judge the practical judgments of those whose duty it is to protect the whole community. The predicament of the democratic citizen is that those responsible for distributive justice are the people themselves.

The dependence of justice on prudence is not a one-way street. In fact, Simon tells us that making any prudential judgment requires all of the other virtues.

> And that is the whole story: all moral virtues are knotted together in prudence. In any moral situation, we need prudence in order to find the mean, that is, the right answer. But prudence cannot determine this mean by logical derivation from general principles. To know what is the right thing to do in this unique existential situation, the prudent man relies on

---

[28]*Ibid.*

inclination which, in order to be reliable, must be sound not just in some but in all respects.[29]

Simon's definition of virtue emphasizes the dependability required of the virtuous person. At first it might seem as though a person could lack one virtue yet still be generally dependable. But Simon insists that such people cannot properly be called virtuous. "The good qualities of people who lack one virtue are *hypothetical*, which does not mean that they are not valuable. A good disposition which is hypothetical is not a virtue, it is not even a *habitus*."[30] The example Simon uses is that of the just man who breaks a contract under pressure because of his cowardliness. The dependability of this otherwise just man is threatened by his inability to do the just act when faced with his fear of some loss or suffering. So, his justice is undermined by his lack of courage. So, too, it can be said that a person's prudence suffers if temperance is lacking. Recall the activities of the marine embassy guards whose duty to national security was readily exchanged for time with Soviet prostitutes. It is important to note that claiming that a person cannot have one virtue without having all of them is not the same as claiming that all virtues must be equally developed in the person of good character. In the absence of any one virtue, though, all may be threatened, and this threat undermines the steadiness that is characteristic of virtue itself.

Citizens of democratic governments are uniquely situated when it comes to the development of their virtue and the ends for which their choices are implemented. In contractual arrangements in the commutative relationship, the necessity for which choices are made is merely that of the formal agreement. One citizen agrees to sell a house for a price that another agrees is fair. The steadiness of disposition that is required is that of keeping one's word and of being attentive to both the spirit and the letter of the contract. Each party to the contract negotiates the terms with an eye toward his or her own best interest. But the relationship of the democratic citizen to the distributive mode of justice is something else altogether. When citizens make decisions on the best way to govern, on whom to elect to represent them, the good intended must be that of the whole nation. Such citizens, when

---

[29]*Ibid.*, 127.

[30]From the course notes, "Freedom of Choice and the Ethics of Liberty."

acting as the self-governing people of a sound democracy, see their individual self-interest taken up in the common good. And this is what makes democratic citizenship unique and challenging. Sometimes responsible citizenship requires the vigorous pursuit of self-interest and sometimes the goal is the good of the whole. A self-governing people needs the wisdom to know the difference.

Conclusion

In this paper, I have drawn out from the thought of Yves R. Simon the following: a) democratic freedom has the character of an end for which free choice is the means; b) insofar as any choice that fails to achieve its end is empty and illusory, an ability to perfect human choosing, the virtue of prudence, is required; and c) prudence is so intertwined with the moral virtues of justice, fortitude, and temperance that their relationship is one of complete interdependence.

Emerging from Simon's definition of democratic freedom as self-government, there is a distinct understanding of human nature that invites attention. Democratic citizens understand themselves to be acting for ends. They know that with the rational nature that makes choice possible, they also inherit the possibility of making bad choices. To be self-governing is to understand that human beings have the power to shape a second nature that reduces the possibility of error in choice. It is to recognize and honor a destiny in the political order that makes the common good the legitimate end for which they choose. When the government has been taken over by the people, the objective of choice is the nation's good, and the assurance of truth in those choices is the dependable disposition of its citizens. Citizens without virtuous dispositions are incapable of self-government.

Thus, Simon's definition of democratic freedom, the relationship of free choice to the virtue of prudence, and the interdependence of prudence with the other moral virtues, reveals something essential about democratic citizenship. I stand by the claim that government is not properly called democratic if the citizens of that government lack a virtuous character.

As I look around our country today and listen to the political rhetoric, it is precisely this understanding of the citizen that is lacking. "Pro-choice" has become the slogan not only of those who believe that it is up to pregnant women alone to decide whether to carry a pregnancy to term, but also of those who believe that public monies ought to be used to fund school choices whether they be public or private. When the U.S. citizen "takes over" the government, what ought to be the objective of decision-making in these cases? The answer is, of course, the common good. Yet, I have never heard an argument that it is in the *nation's* interest to allow abortions on demand or to forbid them. Nor have I heard anyone argue the merits or drawbacks of a federal voucher system for education based on what is in the country's best interest in forming the young.

Another example: faced as we are with a huge federal budget deficit, some admit that taxes must be raised or that entitlements must be cut as long as those sacrifices are not requested of them. And many of those who have suggested that individual sacrifices will be required of all if we are to restore our nation's financial integrity have either been voted from office or driven from public service in frustration. Yet when we vote as the governing people in a democracy, it is precisely our vision of the common good that is supposed to shape our decision-making. It is this vision and our responsibility to it that has all but left the consciousness of American citizens.

This brief exploration and application of Simon's moral and political philosophy reveals that there are actually two possible outcomes: we can either stop claiming that our form of government is in any legitimate sense a democratic one, or we can begin attending to what is truly the obligation of democratic citizenship, the formation of a national character that makes self-government possible. To accept the first option is to resign ourselves to enslavement. To commit to the second one is truly to choose for freedom.

Beyond Ideology in Christian Economic Thought: Yves R. Simon and Recent Debates

Clarke E. Cochran & Thomas Rourke

Introduction: Debates over Catholic Social Thought

Catholic social doctrine has long been the subject of controversy. The debates can be broadly categorized into two areas. First, there are questions over the foundations of the doctrine. One argument rejects the very notion of an ethical social doctrine because such a doctrine can only be based upon the kind of logical demonstrations foreign to the practical reasoning that governs policy choices.[1] Another argument contends that the doctrine is not specific enough to state a coherent plan for social change.[2] Another line of attack, dating back to Niebuhr's criticism of *Pacem in Terris*, states that the Church's teaching bypasses the real world of conflict in its discussion of a harmonious ethical universe.[3] Finally, some reject Catholic teaching because they believe that morality is as separate from the laws of

---

[1]Shirley Letwin, "The Pope, Liberty and Capitalism: Essays on Centesimus Annus," *The National Review: Special Supplement*, June 24, 1991, p. 7.

[2]Mary Hobgood, *Catholic Social Teaching and Economic Theory* (Philadelphia, Pennsylvania: Temple University Press, 1991).

[3]Shirley Letwin and Jacob Neusner lean in this direction in their essays in "The Pope, Liberty and Capitalism: Essays on Centesimus Annus," *The National Review: Special Supplement,* June 24, 1991, pp. 7, 9–10.

economics as it is from the laws of physics.[4] Hence, it is futile to discuss economics from a moral perspective.

In addition to these fundamental questions over the viability of Catholic social teaching, there are vigorous debates over its content. In particular the related issues of private property and capitalism have been the source of vigorous dispute. On the one hand, Michael Novak believes that the Church's teaching essentially affirms global capitalism and the economic system in the United States.[5] On the other, there is within American conservatism a trend of longstanding suspicion, even downright hostility, toward the Church's criticism of existing capitalism.[6] Each side in this dispute selectively quotes the parts of the encyclicals which they see as confirming their respective positions.

The range of responses to the encyclicals clearly reflects ideological commitments. Liberals, conservatives, neo-conservatives, and radicals all have claimed to find support for their beliefs in official Catholic social thought. Moreover, they diminish the force of those points which challenge their respective views. The question which remains is whether or not it is possible to get beyond ideology both in interpreting these texts and, more significantly, in theorizing about economics itself. Normative approaches to economics tend to be captured by the various ideologies. The problem, then, is to develop an ethical approach that both goes beyond ideology and has the capacity to resist ideological capture.

In striving to get beyond ideology, we reject two false paths. The first treats economics as a pure (neutral, objective) science. This path's costs are too high; separating economics from ideology in this way severs it also from moral norms. The second false path divorces Church teaching from specific policy questions. The Church, it is argued, should address only the fundamental moral principles that endure through space and time. Such a position avoids ideology, but it also avoids the real world of political, economic, and moral conflict in which the faithful must live.

---

[4]Ernest van den Haag, "The Pope, Liberty and Capitalism: Essays on Centesimus Annus," *The National Review: Special Supplement*, June 24, 1991, pp. 14–15.

[5]Michael Novak, "The Pope, Liberty and Capitalism: Essays on Centesimus Annus," *The National Review: Special Supplement*, June 24, 1991, pp. 11–12.

[6]Francis Canavan, "The Popes and the Economy," *First Things* 16 (1991), pp. 35–41.

We argue, contrary to these paths, that the Church usually should avoid specific policy recommendations, but this does not entail avoiding "middle principles" that have a bearing on policy issues. The political philosophy of Yves R. Simon outlines an ethical approach to economics that avoids ideological capture, "objective" economism, and detached moralism. We shall say something, first, about Simon's view of ideology. Then we shall address his ethical approach to economic justice according to the principles of natural law. Finally, from the perspective thus developed, we will critique current reactions to John Paul II's encyclical, *Centesimus Annus*.

Simon on Ideology, Natural Law
and Virtue Philosophy and Ideology

Simon insists upon a fundamental distinction between ideology and philosophy.[7] Ideology, Simon contends, is characterized by the way it reduces truth to the utilitarian, the sociological or the evolutionistic (or "timely"). In the simplest terms, what Simon means by this tripartite characterization is that ideology is a body of claims, expressed in universal moral terms, which are useful for a particular group of people in their efforts to attain their social, political or economic goals, at a particular point in time. The quintessential example of ideology for Simon was the justification of slavery espoused by John C. Calhoun in the Nineteenth Century. Calhoun saw the Southern landowners' way of life threatened by opposition to slavery. In response Calhoun argued that the labor of the slaves was necessary to the maintenance of the landowners. In all societies, he contended, one group depended upon the labor of another. It had always been that way. Therefore, the principle was universal. Here we have an obvious example of the elements of an ideology: a particular group of people, in this case Southern landowners, who had a particular aspiration, namely, to preserve their form of life; they advanced an argument which took on a universal and moral form; yet it fit the requirements of their aspirations at a particular point in time.[8]

---

[7]Yves R. Simon, *The Tradition of Natural Law*, Revised edition, Introduction by Russell Hittinger (New York: Fordham University Press, 1992), pp. 16–27.

[8]*Ibid.*, pp. 17–18.

For Simon the most important distinction between ideology and philosophy is that ideology is essentially related to the fulfillment of aspirations, while philosophy strives to be free of such aspirations. Ideological approaches to political life do not treat society and its various segments purely as objects to be studied, but also as ends to be obtained. For example, the classical Marxist does not study the owners of the means of production merely to advance the state of knowledge concerning them, but as a class whose power is to be eliminated by revolutionary action. Similarly, the classical liberal economist does not look upon the impacts of government regulation on the economy only in the manner of a physicist observing the properties of freely falling bodies, but as something which is to be limited as far as possible. It is precisely this element of aspiration that the philosopher must seek to avoid. In philosophy, the object of study must not be an end but a "pure object."[9] In *An Introduction to Metaphysics of Knowledge* Simon goes so far as to say that the character of the object of knowledge as a pure object is the defining characteristic of cognition.

> We are looking at the relation of the object of knowledge to the faculty of knowing. What kind of relation is it? Well, it is a relation of pure qualitative determination, innocent of everything involved in the order of movement, effectuation, or desire. . . . Knowing is not making, creating, or transforming; we could say that in knowing we touch the object, but we never interfere with it. . . . Indeed, to conceive knowledge either as some sort of making or as the result of some sort of desire is to misconstrue its nature. . . . [10]

Virtue and Natural Law

In addition to the renunciation of ends chosen *a priori*, the philosopher needs concepts and approaches that go beyond ideology. Drawing on his extensive knowledge of the history of philosophy, Simon found that the concepts of virtue, particularly practical wisdom (*phronesis*), and natural law, when properly understood and properly employed, were perennially viable, indeed necessary. His understanding of virtue and natural law is quite rich and a valuable corrective to much of what

---

[9]Yves R. Simon, *An Introduction to Metaphysics of Knowledge* (New York: Fordham University Press, 1990), p. 8.

[10]*Ibid.*, p. 8.

is wrong on both the left and the right of the contemporary political spectrum.

In order to get a handle on Simon's understanding of these two concepts, let us consider first that, even for one who would take both concepts seriously, the relationship between them is not obvious. More specifically, with reference to the practical moral judgments over which economic policies would be best for a particular society at a given time, it is not immediately clear the extent to which practical wisdom and/or natural law should be appealed to.

Broadly speaking, two approaches suggest themselves. The first perspective emphasizes practical wisdom and holds that when deliberating actual moral practice natural law is epistemologically not significant. This position would not necessarily renounce the proposition that nature has some contribution to make to moral orientation. It would, however, contend that nature orients humanity toward the broadest of ethical principles, such as, do good and avoid evil, and therefore contributes no concrete moral guidelines. At best natural law might have some limited role to play with respect to explaining why certain actions contribute to the moral good. Nevertheless, natural law does not supply either the ends or the means for practical moral decision-making. What natural law theories cannot and do not provide for the realm of action is precisely the role of virtue. Virtue is the set of stable dispositions that directs people to morally good choices. Virtue is not obtained by the mere following of the precepts of deductive reasoning from natural law principles. It is virtue itself which provides the practical moral direction. Thus, virtue is about both the selection of ends and the selection of means. The source of the virtues is not found in nature but in reason drawing upon the tried and tested traditions of a community. If one wishes to know what morally good actions or policies are, the answer is to be found by observing what the good person or the good statesman does. In other words, the answer is found uniquely in the realm of action and experience.

The second of our prototypical approaches would emphasize the role of natural law in determining the moral content of practical moral choices. In its strongest form such an approach would treat the moral universe as a biologist treats the universe of living organisms; all moral actions are identifiable according to species identifiable by readily discernible characteristics. One need only learn the various species and their respective characteristics to recognize those species in the "field" of real moral choices. In this view, moral reasoning has a deductive quality: actions of species A are immoral; action B is a member of species A; therefore, action B is immoral. When natural law is seen as capable of doing all this in the realm of moral choice, it follows that virtue will not play a decisive role in the process of moral deliberation itself. Rather, virtue is the strength of character permitting the will to pursue those actions which the intellect has discerned to be right. A less rigid form of this view would allow virtue a broader realm of action. Such an approach would concede that natural law is somewhat limited in its capacity to determine practical moral choices; therefore, virtue would be relied upon to choose the means to the ends determined by natural law. In both the more rigid and less rigid forms, natural law is the primary determinant of moral choice with the role of virtue limited to giving "moral support," so to speak, to the conclusions that follow from natural law.

With these prototypes in mind, we are ready to get a handle on Simon's view of the relationship between the virtue of practical wisdom and natural law. We will approach the relationship by explaining Simon's broad understanding of virtue. According to Simon virtue is characterized by three essential traits: objective necessity, vitality, and freedom. In order to understand what is meant by these, it is useful to begin by following Simon and see how he contrasts virtue with habits. Simon argues forcefully and persuasively against the equation of virtue with what is commonly called "habit." Habits, Simon contends, are acts the necessity of which is subjective and which exclude voluntariness.[11] Perhaps the best illustration of this is to consider the habitual smoker or drinker. There is a certain necessity attached to their acts of smoking and drinking, but the origin of the necessity is within the person as affected by previous patterns of action. The necessity to continue chain smoking is not a product of the requirements of the person's relationships, health, occupation or any other personal good.

A second characteristic of virtue as opposed to habit is that the former is characterized by vitality and the latter by mechanical repetition.[12] Habits are formed by repeated actions and generally absolve us of the necessity to think and judge. Consider the pronunciation of words in one's native tongue. Regardless of the creative and vital ways

---

[11]Yves R. Simon, *The Definition of Moral Virtue* (New York: Fordham University Press, 1986, 1989), pp. 51, 54.
[12]*Ibid.*, p. 60.

in which we might employ such words, no one will want to say that the pronunciation of the words themselves involves anything more than the mechanical repetition characteristic of habit. However, the patterns of behavior of the virtuous person bear little resemblance to such a conditioned pattern of behavior. As will be elaborated more fully later, virtue for Simon does not involve subjectively predetermined behaviors. Virtue is creative, involving a vital involvement with the world around us.[13] The person of fortitude, for example, is not one whose behaviors are predictable in all circumstances. The person of fortitude is the most likely to come up with fresh, original responses to the most trying circumstances. Consider the behavior of someone such as Dorothy Day. Her life was replete with creative confrontations with injustices. This is a true mark of virtue.

Virtue is further distinguished from habit in that the former involves the highest uses of human freedom, while the latter excludes voluntariness.[14] In order to clarify this point, it is essential to grasp Simon's understanding of freedom. Simon's central theoretical contribution is that human freedom is incorrectly identified with indetermination. Freedom is, rather, a form of "superdetermination," by which he means that the truly free person is the one who, through the disciplined exercise of her faculties, has "determined" her character to be reliable under even the most trying circumstances.

> Few thinkers ever awoke to the theory that freedom is superdetermination rather than indetermination and that its principle is more highly and more certainly formed than that of determinate causality; freedom proceeds, not from any weakness, any imperfection, any feature of potentiality on the part of the agent but, on the contrary, from a particular excellence in power, from a plenitude of being and an abundance of determination, from an ability to achieve mastery over diverse possibilities, from a strength of constitution which makes it possible to attain one's ends in a variety of ways. In short, freedom is an active and dominating indifference.[15]

Since virtue is characterized by objective necessity, vitality and the highest use of human freedom, it would seem that virtue has a

---

[13]*Ibid.*

[14]*Ibid.*, p. 78.

[15]Yves R. Simon, *Freedom of Choice*, Foreword by Mortimer J. Adler (New York: Fordham University Press, 1969, 1987, 1992), pp. 152–153.

great deal to do with determining the content of moral action. This is surely the case for Simon, who places particular importance on practical wisdom or prudence. Following Aristotle and Saint Thomas, Simon understands prudence to be, broadly speaking, the virtue that directs us in the choice of which human goods to pursue in particular circumstances.[16] The qualifying phrase, "in particular circumstances," is crucial because "the specific duty of prudence is to tell me what to do no matter how unprecedented the circumstances, no matter how unique the situation."[17] In other words, a judgment must be made in particular circumstances as to which goods will be pursued in the midst of any number of contingencies, which cannot be known with certainty. Prudence must take into account the full range of contingencies to the extent practicable. What determines the choice to be made? Simon is clear that the judgment to be made is ultimately determined not by intellectual cognition but by the inclination of the will.[18]

This is in no way to imply that moral deliberation is anything other than a reasoned deliberation. It is to say, however, that in practical matters, where there are questions not only about the nature of things but of the use of things, and where such use takes place in the context of contingency, judgment by inclination takes precedence over cognition by way of intellect.[19] This is because the truths involved in practical judgments are truths of direction and not of cognition.[20] What Simon argues is that in the realm of human action, when there are many contingencies, the action to be chosen cannot be the result of the kind of thinking taking place outside the realm of action and contingency. The difference between the deliberation involved in making difficult moral choices and that involved in doing philosophy is one of kind. Moreover, it is precisely the role of the virtues, particularly prudence, to provide the direction in action that conceptual thinking cannot provide.

Considering what we have gathered from Simon's understanding of virtue up to this point, in tandem with the prototypical approaches to virtue and natural law outlined at the outset of this section, it might

---

[16]Yves R. Simon, *The Definition of Moral Virtue*, pp. 96–97.

[17]*Ibid.*, p. 96.

[18]Yves R. Simon, *Practical Knowledge* (New York: Fordham University Press, 1991), pp. 17–23.

[19]*Ibid.*, pp. 61–66.

[20]*Ibid.*, p. 13.

well appear that Simon strikes a blow at natural law and leans in favor of the first of the perspectives outlined above. Virtue appears to supply the content of moral decision-making, providing the direction for the will which no moral philosophy can give. However, once we gain an understanding of Simon's theory of natural law, we will realize that he sees no incompatibility between virtue and natural law.

In order to grasp Simon's understanding of natural law, it is necessary to unpack some of the implications of the term "nature." First, nature implies teleology, or "direction toward a state of accomplishment."[21] As a philosopher of the first rank, Simon is aware that teleology is not exactly "in" in the most influential sector of contemporary thought, science. Nonetheless, Simon forcefully defends the notion of teleology implied in the concept of nature.

> It would be exceedingly difficult to speak of acorns and oak trees, infants and adults without assuming . . . the proposition that such things as acorns or infants are essentially related to a state of accomplishment to be achieved through progression.[22]

Simon is similarly emphatic about the source of the philosophical difficulties at the root of the rejection of teleology: the influence of mathematics on our view of nature. In mathematics, there are no natures or final causes.[23] Whenever we observe mathematical entities such as equations or geometrical entities in the development of their properties, we are aware that there is no progression toward an end involved. In fact, the development of the equation or geometric figure "takes place in our mind."[24] This is to say that no final causes are involved. Thus, Simon concludes, "The exclusion of final causes from every science where mathematical forms predominate follows upon the laws of mathematical abstraction and intelligibility."[25] Therefore, if we approach the study of human nature and society in a manner similar to the way we consider equations and geometric entities, we will assume that the development of our understanding of moral essences is reducible to what takes place within our minds.

---

[21]Yves R. Simon, *The Tradition of Natural Law*, pp. 45, 47.
[22]*Ibid.*, p. 47.
[23]Yves R. Simon, *Practical Knowledge*, p. 122.
[24]Yves R. Simon, *The Tradition of Natural Law*, p. 48.
[25]*Ibid.*

In opposition to the mathematical approach, which Simon sees as inconsistent with our experience and actions, Simon adheres to the proposition that teleology is inherent in nature and thus in natural law. However, how are we to square this with what Simon has told us about virtue? If, in matters of practical moral choice, judgment has priority over concept, how can natural law, which emphasizes the universal validity of concepts, be salvaged? Simon finds the answer in the concept of "natural finality." In order to see how natural finality reconciles natural law with the proposition that judgment has priority over concept in moral choice where contingency is involved, Simon invites us to consider the genesis of our ethical concepts.[26] Take, for example, the concepts of economic justice and economic injustice which have been so frequently discussed in recent years. The concept of economic justice is informed by a judgment that certain uses of material goods are morally right, while economic injustice is rooted in a judgment that certain other uses of material goods are wrong. But we need to ask the further question: on what basis are these judgments made? They are judgments about use, that is, practical judgments. Yet, Simon continues:

> these practical judgments were born of judgments about natural finalities, in which the law of concept over judgment fully obtains, for it is by the understanding of nature, by an exact expression of what a nature is and of what it tends to be, that we are led to judgments of finality. All we have to say, in terms of use, about the excellence of intellectual life derives from theoretical judgments of finality concerning human nature and its powers and functions. Clearly, these judgments of finality are themselves derived from apprehensions of natures, of essences, of whatnesses and of the corresponding tendencies.[27]

What Simon is implies here is that, even in a realm as highly contingent as the practical choice of economic policies, where judgment has priority over concept, sound judgments ultimately rest on a foundation of natural finalities. To clarify, we can say that, in deciding what tax policy is best at a certain point in time, the choice of policy will not be a deduction from an assertion of natural finality. However, whatever

---

[26]Yves R. Simon, *Practical Knowledge*, p. 67.
[27]*Ibid.*

moral "truth of direction" is embodied in the policy ultimately rests on a truth of natural finality.

It is precisely in these natural finalities that we have the basis for natural law, as Simon understands the term, and that we can grasp the relationship between judgment and natural law. The ground of natural law is nature itself. Nature provides the natural finalities which permit us to formulate propositions. The propositions, of course, are the work of the mind, but this is to be sharply distinguished from the role of the mind as the creator of values. In the former case the final word belongs to nature, in the latter with the mind itself.

> [N]atural law, in the very meaning of that expression, exists ontologically before it exists rationally in our minds; it is embodied in things before it is thought out, thought through, understood, intellectually grasped. . . . [I]t is a work of the reason. But notice that it is a reason measured by things, which bows before things. . . . The natural law exists in nature before it exists in our judgment, and it enjoys the latter existence . . . by reason of what the nature of things is.[28]

In conclusion it is clear that the kind of opposition suggested by the two prototypical views outlined at the outset does not exist for Simon. Rather, virtue and natural law coexist in fundamental unity, the former directing human will to the enactment of the finalities determined by the latter, and yet in a manner that goes beyond merely applying conclusions reached by the latter. In matters where there is contingency, the judgments proceeding from a virtuous disposition will have priority over concepts derived from natural law. On the other hand, virtuous disposition implies the existence of natural finalities the knowledge of which is governed by the priority of concept over judgment. When properly understood, there is no ontological tension between virtue and natural law. Simon neatly sums up the interrelationship between the respective roles of law and judgment as follows:

> The genuineness of a rule of action is its conformity to intention, provided, of course, that intention itself is genuine, that is, relative to a proper end. Posit the intention of the proper end and posit, in relation to the means, a judgment in unqualified agreement with the genuine intention. This judgment is the true rule of action. . . . Again, the rightness of desire

---

[28]Yves R. Simon, *The Tradition of Natural Law*, p. 137.

is in no case compatible with indifference to the real condition of the factors involved in the bringing about of the intended good.... [T]he probable agreement of the practical conclusion with what does exist is something that right desire necessarily demands.[29]

A good deal of confusion can be avoided if we consider the distinction between two related uses of the term "natural law." As we have seen, Simon holds that nature has finality and contributes guidance to moral decision-making. Simon is of the opinion that the guidance nature offers can and frequently is known through inclination. For example, a simple, uneducated person may perceive quite clearly that to lie or steal is wrong without being able to explain why in philosophical terms. Even in less obvious cases, Simon thinks that we can correctly come to a conclusion about an ethical matter without being able to give a fully satisfactory explanation.[30] Even without an explanation, we would still have in such a case an assertion of natural law in the primary meaning of the term, that is, the law which is embodied in nature, whether it be known through inclination or cognition. Secondarily, we have natural law as a system of explanations of the law of nature. This latter meaning is frequently what philosophers refer to when they use the term. But it is important to remember that the existence of natural law in the primary sense is in no way contingent upon the existence of the second. Moreover, natural law in the sense of natural law philosophy is contingent upon the first but never identical with it. This is because natural law as a system of explaining natural finalities is always in an ongoing stage of development and clarification.[31] Development is possible in two senses. We can move from the wrong conclusion to the correct one. Perhaps our understanding of slavery would be an example of this. Or we can move from grasping by inclination an unexplicated moral truth to understanding that same moral truth according to progressively better explanations. This is important because it implies that rejection of particular natural law formulations in no way implies the rejection of natural law itself.

---

[29]Yves R. Simon, *Practical Knowledge*, p. 13.
[30]*Ibid.*, p. 33.
[31]*Ibid.*, pp. 34–35.

Natural Finalities in Economics

In the preceding section we saw Simon's approach to natural law and virtue. We saw how Simon affirmed the importance of both natural law and virtue without seeing an inherent tension between the two. Natural law in its primary sense refers to finalities (teleology) which exist in nature itself. In this section we wish to discuss natural finalities in economics. Simon does not codify or systematize his ideas on this subject. However, from his discussions of work and his frequent references to problems of economic justice, we can pull together a series of propositions expressing natural economic finalities.[32]

First, with respect to that most fundamental economic principle, ownership, Simon belongs to the Thomistic tradition, which asserts that the ownership of property should be private while the use of goods should be common. With respect to the first half of the formulation, Saint Thomas argued that it was proper for people to possess goods as their own for three reasons. First, people are naturally more careful to procure what is for themselves alone as opposed to what is for many; labor done on behalf of the community is likely to be shirked. Secondly, private ownership leads to a better ordering of affairs; if everyone were to be in charge of everything, much confusion would result. Thirdly, there is more civil peace if goods are properly divided among private owners; more discord arises when there is no clear delineation of ownership.[33] However, with respect to the use of goods, Saint Thomas argued that goods should be possessed as common, so that one who has goods in abundance will share them with the needy.[34]

Two important implications flow from this principle. First, a system of state socialism would be unethical. The state does not have the authority to terminate the private right to own. Secondly, the demand

---

[32]Due to limitations of space and the desire to maintain a focus on the *approach to* economic justice, we present Simon's principles in sketch form. We have discussed these matters at greater length elsewhere. See Thomas R. Rourke and Clarke E. Cochran, "The Common Good and Economic Justice: Reflections on the Thought of Yves R. Simon," *The Review of Politics* 54, No. 2 (Spring 1992), pp. 231–252.

[33]William Baumgarth and Richard Regan, *Saint Thomas Aquinas: On Law, Morality, and Politics* (Indianapolis, Indiana: Hackett Publishing, 1988), pp. 178–179.

[34]*Ibid.*, p. 179.

for the distribution of goods to the needy is not a request of charity but a demand of justice. The economic system is part of society's comprehensive common good and therefore demands real participation on the part of all who are able.[35] It is insufficient to argue that a given economic system allows people to compete for the opportunities to support themselves. The principle of common use must be concretized in real policies.

The second principle states that the primary purpose of the production of goods and services is the fulfillment of human needs. Although this may seem obvious at first glance, Simon points out that this imperative is compromised by the profit motive in two ways. First, the profit motive leads to the proliferation of unnecessary goods and the absence of needed goods. Resources and labor are employed to produce luxury goods while many lack decent housing or even any housing at all. The reason is that there is a profit to be made in the luxury goods sector and not in the production of basic goods. Simon is aware that the dominant forms of economic thinking do not recognize the validity of the concept "unnecessary goods." In economics demand exists when there is purchasing power. No distinction can be made in such an approach between the hungry person purchasing a loaf of bread and the compulsive drinker purchasing his seventeenth beer. Simon insists that here is another example of a principle that cannot be consistently employed in daily life. In fact, we do distinguish among claims of human need; we acknowledge that there are many purchases for which there is no genuine need. Our economic thinking should recognize the validity of principles exercised in daily life.[36]

Need, however, is not the only principle of distributive justice. Merit and free distribution also have important roles. Obviously, there is room for quite a bit of debate as to what constitutes merit. Though Simon does not specify how merit is to be calculated, it would seem that merit would be calculated with respect to contribution to the common good. The notion of free distribution is, according to Simon, widely, even universally practiced. Again, Simon is aware that the concept is not recognized by economists. Nonetheless, it is necessary

---

[35]Rourke and Cochran, "The Common Good and Economic Justice."

[36]Yves R. Simon, *Work, Society and Culture*, ed. Vukan Kuic (New York: Fordham University Press, 1971, 1986), pp. 38–39, 126–142.

because distribution by exchange alone is insufficient to insure an adequate distribution of needed goods.[37]

Principles two and three have important implications for the American "free market" economy as it confronts "social market" economies in the European nations. Social market economies assume that everyone has an important place in the economy, and government has a responsibility to see that everyone is equipped with the job skills, health care, child care, and other supports and opportunities needed to fulfill that place.[38] Such economies are at least as robust as the American individualist notion of the market, and they come closer to fulfilling the kinds of principles developed by Simon.

A fourth principle treats human work. The organization and condition of workers was a constant preoccupation of Simon's. Simon contended that, since work is a distinctively human act, work should involve the exercise and development of human freedom. Moreover, since human freedom involves the choice of direction, it follows that workers must be allowed to participate in the direction of work. Work cannot be reduced to mere execution, for work too is a participation in the common good. Therefore, the worker must have something to say about the goal and purpose of production as well as how work is to be organized. Simon was under the impression that new institutional forms would be necessary to realize the workers' proper place in industrial society. He refers to the following kinds of institutions as desirable: mutual assistance societies, consumers' cooperatives, institutes for popular education, factory committees and autonomous workshops.[39] Today, we might appropriately add the importance of education and re-education for more challenging job skills, apprenticeship programs, and (possibly) workfare and guaranteed jobs for welfare recipients.

The activity of work should draw workers into a sense of community which is experienced as such. Simon recognized forty years ago that modern industrial life tends to produce a heavy and unwelcome sense of isolation. Moreover, it tends to deprive the worker of a sense of service, which "gives man a chance to enter into communication

---

[37]*Ibid.*, p. 141.

[38]Lester Thurow, "Communitarian vs. Individualistic Capitalism," *The Responsive Community* 2 (Fall, 1992): 24–30.

[39]Yves R. Simon, *Work, Society and Culture*, p. 149.

and communion with his fellow men."[40] This stems from the fact that the worker does not normally have contact with the one who consumes what he produces. Simon adds here a unique insight. He says that the "sentiments which cause the most painful restlessness when they are frustrated are not the most selfish ones. Generous sentiments, if denied opportunity, grow rebellious."[41] Therefore, it is essential that workers experience a sense of service and membership in community through their work.

The fifth principle is that economic relations are to be governed by equality of exchange. Again we have a proposition that seems superficial until its implications are unpacked. We are not accustomed to a great deal of reflection on equality of exchange because of the assumption that the market determines equality of exchange. Simon rejects that assumption and invites us to consider the existence of "one-way exchanges" and "illusory services."[42] One-way exchanges occur whenever someone derives income from a change in price without contributing either production or service. Simon is quick to acknowledge that such transactions may be rare in pure form, which is to say that many exchanges contain elements of both income for service and one-way exchange. Speculative economic activities top the list of one-way exchanges for Simon.

Illusory services constitute another category for which there is no place in economic theory. Nevertheless, Simon insists that one cannot consistently deny the existence of such a category. Society does not permit the sale of placebos as a cure for cancer, for example. What is needed is to take the common sense insight and apply it more broadly to our thinking about economic justice. Simon refers to the sales effort as one area worth particular focus.[43] We would include advertising as another. In each case what frequently occurs is people deriving income from the attempt to convince people to purchase things they do not need and which frequently they cannot afford. We would hardly say that the person who, through calculated psychological tactics,

---

[40]Yves R. Simon, *Philosophy of Democratic Government* (Chicago: University of Chicago Press, 1951), p. 310. Revised edition (Notre Dame, Indiana: University of Notre Dame Press, 1993).

[41]*Ibid.*, p. 310.

[42]Yves R. Simon, *Work, Society and Culture*, pp. 37–39, 122–126.

[43]*Ibid.*, p. 123.

convinced someone to purchase a more expensive car than he or she could afford, which drove that person's family into debt and eventual bankruptcy, had performed a "service" for the purchaser. Similarly, one would have to question, from the standpoint of equality of exchange, the profits advertising firms derive from the attempt to imbue their products with any number of mythical qualities.

Modern forms of "social" and "economic" public regulation of free enterprise are means of preventing or limiting such one-way exchanges and illusory services. Regulations that ensure quality products, that force disclosure of interest rates, or that protect workers and nearby residents from dangerous chemicals in manufacturing processes would be specific examples.

The sixth principle is that the economic organization of society must acknowledge the complementarity of authority and freedom. Ideological thinking on the left and the right has so deformed our understanding of both freedom and authority that we have particular difficulty seeing the validity of this principle. Ideology has accustomed us to setting freedom and authority in opposition. The Left tells us that freedom is a mere cover for the freedom of the owners of wealth; the Right tells us that government has little or no essential role to play in economics.

The problem with freedom has been discussed previously. So long as freedom is reduced to freedom from authority, it is reduced to an ideological shibboleth. However, when we continue to regard freedom as superdetermination, we can begin to shed some genuine light on the issue. Surely, a healthy economic system must allow for initiative and creativity, as conservatives tend to suggest. However, the rich sense of freedom discussed by Simon has interesting implications for the conditions of the worker as well. Specific contemporary examples might be the now-familiar Japanese practices of guaranteeing workers lifetime employment and a rich network of mutually supportive relationships between major corporations and their suppliers.[44] American discussions of "industrial policy" draw upon this example to some extent.

Work must contribute to the development of free persons. Surely, this does not imply that work will not be experienced as irksome on occasion. However, this irksomeness should not result from the fact

---

[44]Lester Thurow, "Communitarian vs. Individualistic Capitalism."

that the work is habitually characterized by either of the following: the worker plays no role in determining the end or purpose of the work; the work does not contribute to, or even detracts from, the development of character. In neither case would the worker be free in the sense that Simon understands freedom. Unfortunately, too much of our attention is focused on the issue of wages for workers. Surely, wages are important. But far more attention needs to be paid to the destructive effects of modern working conditions insofar as these frustrate the development of freedom and hence human character.

The concept of authority has been similarly deformed by ideology. This time, we can point the finger somewhat more at the Left. Simon criticizes what he calls "deficiency theories of authority," which locate the origin of the need for authority in some type of human deficiency.[45] Moreover, authority has in modern times increasingly been portrayed as disruptive of freedom and in conflict with the search for truth and justice. Simon contends that authority is essentially positive and would be necessary even if human beings were without deficiencies. Authority is needed to make the choice of means to social ends when the means are not unique. For example, authority is necessary to determine the forms which social insurance, unemployment insurance, and income maintenance programs are to take. Beyond this, what Simon calls the most essential function of authority is "the issuance and carrying out of rules expressing the common good considered materially."[46] In any community, the pursuit of the common good requires that fundamental choices be made as to how that common good can be concretized. Authority must direct the community to the realization of its capabilities at the individual and collective levels.

We have discussed the role of Simon's concept of authority with respect to economic life elsewhere.[47] Let it suffice to say here that authority has a necessary role to play to insure that the economic system is inclusive of all the able-bodied with respect to participation in the production of goods and services and inclusive of all with respect to the distribution of those goods. To leave the issues of production and

---

[45]Yves R. Simon, *A General Theory of Authority* (Notre Dame, Indiana: University of Notre Dame Press, 1962, 1980, 1990), pp. 13–18.

[46]*Ibid.*, p. 57.

[47]Rourke and Cochran, "The Common Good and Economic Justice."

distribution only to private hands, particularly in times of widespread unemployment, underemployment, and need, is unethical. The essence of the moral issue here is that the community may not leave to chance what is part of its responsibility.

Finally, Simon affirms the long-held principle of Catholic social thought, the principle of subsidiarity, which is concerned with the proper development of human freedom and responsibility. Subsidiarity asserts that problems of economic life should be solved at the lowest possible level. For example, if a factory is capable of solving its own problems, government should not intervene so as to deprive the factory of its right to do so. Or, if local government can solve a problem, it should not be subsumed by state or federal government. When the opposite holds, when smaller and more localized organizations cannot cope with a problem, then responsibility transfers to the next highest level capable of resolving the problem.

The principle of subsidiarity helps us to clarify our thinking about authority. Free market ideology has conditioned us to think negatively about the role of government in economic affairs. Therefore, when the quite valid point is made about the essential role of authority in economic organization, there will always be those who will insist that such a statement is ideological in nature. Perhaps there is a tendency for liberal society to assume that government involvement in economic organization implies socialism or welfare state liberalism. The principle of subsidiarity shows that such assumptions are not the case. One can defend government's essential role while protecting the essential role of private initiative. Moreover, opponents of government involvement need to take more seriously that the absence of government intervention may be the cause of the absence of initiative they deplore. Capitalism exhibits a tendency toward concentration of ownership when unregulated. Conditions for small business become very precarious. Many people are forced into low level service sector jobs or clerical jobs, as they were in the 1980s, and this is hardly a victory for human freedom and initiative. The moral point here is that insistence on an essential role for public authority with respect to economic life is not at all a call to stifle individual and local-level initiative.

Another example of subsidiarity that has economic implications is the American constitutional principle of federalism. Local zoning codes and building codes are specific examples, but some economists are now proposing that some government activities supportive of economic development be allocated more systematically among local, state, and national government.[48]

Implications of Simon's Thought

Simon's thought has important implications for the way we appropriate Catholic social teaching. First and foremost, Simon demonstrates convincingly the importance of the struggle, no matter how difficult in practice, to get beyond ideology to the ethical core of various issues. This is not to say that one will expect agreement on which policies will be chosen once the ethical criteria are established; Simon would deny in most cases that there are unique solutions to economic problems. Nevertheless, it is necessary to refute the cynical view that any purported attempt to discuss economic issues from an ethical approach is merely "political." Moreover, Simon argues that it is possible to identify the ethical problems and insists that public policy address them, even if sincere people might disagree over the best means to implement them. Furthermore, with Simon as a guide, we have a basis for identifying what are clearly ideological as opposed to ethical approaches to economic problems.

A second implication of Simon's thought, which is clearly echoed in Catholic social teaching itself, is that it is neither possible nor desirable to separate economics from moral norms. Economic issues have to do with the maintenance and advancement of human life. They affect the kinds of choices people make with their lives, including whether they will live at all. In addition, economic issues are central to the common life of any political community. To argue that morality is separate from economics is tantamount to arguing that morality is separable from shared life, which would clearly be a contradiction in terms.

A third implication of Simon's thought is that it refutes the assertion that a discussion of natural finalities in the context of natural order culpably bypasses the conflicts of the real world. From Simon's standpoint this would be an unnecessary and even frightening diminution of human reason. The beauty of Simon's approach is that it preserves the role of reason and natural law, never slighting the importance and

---

[48]Alice M. Rivlin, "Making Responsibilities Clearer: A New Federal/Local Division of Labor and Resources," *The Responsive Community* 2 (Fall, 1992), pp. 17–23.

difficulties of judgments to be made in the myriad of contingencies involved in the real world of economics. In fact, precisely because Simon sees the difference between that use of reason permitting us to assert natural finalities and that use forcing us to make practical judgments, he insists upon the limits of natural law philosophy in the formulation of real policies. As a philosophy natural law cannot go beyond the explanation of finalities existing in nature. That is why those who wish the Church to be more specific in its statements err. There is nothing more destructive to the natural law approach than when its practitioners attempt to make natural law prove more than it can. Such an approach would undermine natural law by transforming it into an ideology, something which Simon himself feared.[49]

With respect to debates over the relationship between Catholic social teaching and capitalism, a grasp of Simon should lead one to the conclusion that a great deal of the argument here is ideological in nature. Simon was quite clear about the limitations of natural law with respect to the issue of property.

> Circumstances are conceivable in which doing without private property is the thing good and desirable and right, for the obvious reason that the common forms of civilization which make private property desirable are not realized. Wherever the normal conditions of civilized existence are realized it is right by nature ... that there be some sort of private ownership. Do not try to obtain more precision ... by way of logical connection. It will not work. ... The issue is not one of logic but of prudential determination.[50]

A properly ethical approach to economic justice, therefore, cannot really conclude that American capitalism, the global free market, or any other contingent arrangement is the one best following from ethical principles, because such statements confuse contingent judgments with natural finalities. The cause of ethics in economics is poorly served by statements identifying the Church's teaching with contingent arrangements.

Although natural law cannot tell us which means is best to a given end, this does not make natural law irrelevant to discussions of economic policy. Even the recognition of valid finalities can help

---

[49]Yves R. Simon, *The Tradition of Natural Law*, p. 16.
[50]*Ibid.*, p. 154.

to point us in the right direction. With respect to free distribution and aid to those unable to support themselves for instance, Simon is quite clear that such help should be institutionalized as opposed to being left to purely private initiative.[51] Many people might at first glance suspect that such a conclusion cannot be made from natural law, that Simon has gone out on a limb. It is clear, however, that when the political community chooses to leave something to private initiative, it refuses to accept responsibility for it. Natural law, as Simon argues, does assert a realm of responsibility for political authority with respect to the production and distribution of wealth.

Ideology Right and Left

The 1980s witnessed the conscious effort by some Catholic writers and business persons to "relegitimate" capitalism within the Church.[52] "Relegitimation" seemed needed because a constant theme within the encyclical tradition has been criticism of the liberal individualism and materialism of which capitalism is a part. Papal encyclicals, therefore, had to be confronted. This happened in two ways. First, the unbridled liberalism and capitalism criticized by the popes was distinguished from actual late twentieth-century capitalism, especially that practiced in the United States. Secondly, a new theory of capitalism drawing on roots deeper than its historical liberal origins was constructed in order to show capitalism's essential conformity with traditional Catholic social theory. The publication of *Centesimus Annus* in 1991 provided some neo-conservatives with ammunition in both respects. They read in it a distinct softening of the papal position on capitalism. Some indeed found it putting the Vatican wholeheartedly in the capitalist camp. John Paul II's supposed rejection of a Catholic "third way" between capitalism and communism could only mean, in the context of the collapse of communism, a decision for free market economics.[53]

---

[51]*Ibid.*, pp. 165–166.

[52]Michael L. Budde, *The Two Churches: Catholicism and Capitalism in the World System* (Durham, North Carolina: Duke University Press, 1992), and "The Religious Relegitimation of Capitalism," paper presented at the 1992 Annual Meeting of The American Political Science Association, Chicago.

[53]William McGurn, "A Challenge to the American Catholic Establishment," in *A New Worldly Order: John Paul II and Human Freedom: A Centesimus Annus Reader*, George Weigel, ed. (Washington, D.C.: Ethics and Public Policy Center, 1991), pp. 111–117.

Two elements of the attempt to rehabilitate capitalism within the Church illustrate well the direction of conservative thinking and its limits. A key theme, most fully articulated by Michael Novak, is that capitalism both depends upon and is an expression of fundamental Christian virtues. Capitalism grows and produces its abundance with a moral-cultural system fundamentally Christian. Capitalism needs and reinforces order and stability, social cooperation, willingness to defer gratification, hard work, and careful stewardship of resources. Where these are present, capitalism creates unparalleled economic progress for whole societies. It is a social good. Where these are not present, economic development is unlikely to occur.[54] Although there is a truth to this argument, it overlooks something else at least equally profound in the Christian tradition. Novak's argument subtly suggests that successful entrepreneurs, wealth creators for society, possess (by definition, must possess) the Christian virtues. Non-entrepreneurs and unsuccessful persons, particularly the poor, therefore, must lack these virtues.

A second key theme in the conservative rehabilitation of capitalism is that Catholic thought, particularly in papal encyclicals before *Centesimus Annus* and in statements of the American bishops, has focused too heavily on distribution of wealth, ignoring the prior necessity of wealth creation. Capitalism does better attacking poverty than other economic systems because it knows the secret of creating the wealth that is necessary to provide a decent standard of living for all. Again, there is some truth to this argument. Nevertheless, capitalism as production of wealth still is subject to the criticism that it must do more than produce riches; it must also (either by itself or in conjunction with political or social mechanisms) distribute resources in such a way as to provide a sufficiency for all persons, both domestically and globally. Otherwise, it remains subject to the justice-critique from the Left and from official Church statements. Yet pure free market theory accepts whatever distribution happens to result from free capitalist transactions. Moreover, actual resource distributions in capitalist nations are not noticeably more just, by standards independent of capitalist theory, than those in other systems.

---

[54]Michael Novak, *The Spirit of Democratic Capitalism* (New York: Simon and Schuster, 1982).

Finally, capitalism continues to be characterized by profound moral ambiguities, particularly its instrumentalization of most areas of life and its destruction of rich social, religious, and political traditions.[55] When university presidents begin to import into campus life the business concepts of "customer service" and "total quality management," it is not difficult to hear echoes of Marx and Engel's charge that capitalism reduces all of life to a naked cash nexus.

Since the Left's reaction to official Church teaching mirrors the Right's, that reaction can be considered more briefly. "Capitalism" is also the liberal or radical Catholic's key word. Commentators on the Left do not look to papal and episcopal documents for praise of socialism in its various forms, clearly a futile endeavor, though some go so far as to find a "modified socialism" in recent encyclicals.[56] Rather, they look for criticisms of capitalism and make sure to highlight them. They trumpet phrases and passages of anti-capitalist bent, particularly those critical of private property, markets, and unlimited acquisition.[57]

Liberal response to *Centesimus Annus*, then, is just as predictable as responses on the right. The Left points out the many passages that continue to be critical of capitalism, that focus on global justice in distribution, and that mandate a strong juridical framework within which the Pope believes a limited capitalism or a "business economy" must be contained. In short, they emphasize the great continuity between *Centesimus Annus* and its predecessors.[58]

In words critical of the neo-conservative Catholic writers, David L. Schindler points out the fundamental danger of ideological capture in

---

[55]David L. Schindler, "The Church's Worldly Mission: Neoconservatism and American Culture," *Communio* 18 (1991), pp. 365–397. For a more in-depth criticism of neoconservative political economy from a perspective informed by Simon, see Thomas R. Rourke, *Yves R. Simon and Contemporary Catholic Neoconservatism*. Dissertation: Texas Tech University, 1994.

[56]George E. McCarthy and Royal W. Rhodes, *Eclipse of Justice: Ethics, Economics and the Lost Traditions of American Catholicism* (Maryknoll, New York: Orbis Books, 1992), pp. 175, 181, 183. John J. Mitchell, Jr., "Embracing a Socialist Vision: The Evolution of Catholic Social Thought, Leo XIII to John Paul II," *Journal of Church and State* 27 (1985), pp. 465–481.

[57]See, for example, McCarthy and Rhodes, *Eclipse of Justice*, p. 164, and Charles K. Wilber, "Incentives and the Organization of Work: Moral Hazards and Trust," in John A. Coleman, S.J., ed. *One Hundred Years of Catholic Social Thought: Celebration and Challenge* (Maryknoll, New York: Orbis Books, 1991), pp. 212–223.

[58]See J. Brian Hehir, "Reordering the World," in George Weigel, ed. *New Worldly Order*, pp. 85–89, and Charles K. Wilber, "Argument that Pope 'Baptized' Capitalism Holds no Water," *National Catholic Reporter*, May 24, 1991, pp. 8, 10.

either direction. Commenting on the work of Novak and Weigel, he writes:

> The new spirituality which these men are calling for . . . appears already to have its own *a priori* form built into it: a form which is given in and by these assumptions of the modern Western world. The risk, then, is that these latter assumptions will already be functioning normatively when one turns to the gospel-and this is something quite different from having one's assumptions *first judged by the gospel.*[59]

From the perspective of Simon's natural law philosophy, the danger is almost precisely the same. Instead of probing the fundamental principles of natural law for critical perspectives on contemporary economic reality, the ideologue reads fundamental principles from the standpoint of transient economic theories. One of the great values of Yves R. Simon's political philosophy is that it points toward sound theoretical ways of understanding these matters and of tying them to the specific conflicts of economic life in the late twentieth-century.

---

[59]David L. Schindler, "Church's Worldly Mission," p. 381. Emphasis in original.

Private Morality and
Public Enforcement

Peter Redpath

In his "Foreword" to Michael Novak's groundbreaking work on political economy, *The Spirit of Democratic Capitalism*, Alan Peacock
makes the following claim: "Democratic capitalism," he asserts, "rests
on the supposition that public enforcement of virtue is neither desirable
nor possible. Diffused power and liberty of conscience," he adds, "may
be conferred in a capitalist system on mean-minded individuals with
what David Hume called 'a narrowness of soul,' but as Novak points
out: 'it is the structure of business activities, and not the intentions
of businessmen, that are favorable to rule by law, to liberty, to habits
of regularity and moderation, to healthy realism and to demonstrated
social progress—demonstrably more favorable than the structures of
churchly, aristocratic, or military activities'."[1]

In a somewhat similar vein, in his book *Six Great Ideas*, Mortimer
J. Adler distinguishes among three types of freedom (natural freedom,
moral freedom, and circumstantial freedom); and he asserts that the
domain of public enforcement is limited to the last of these—that is,
to circumstantial freedom. As Adler puts it:

> There would be no sense at all in saying that we are entitled to have a free
> will or freedom of choice. That is a good conferred on us by nature—or
> by God. The lower animals are deprived of it, but we cannot say that they

---

[1] Michael Novak, *The Spirit of Democratic Capitalism* (Lanham, Maryland: Madison Books,
1991), p. 91.

are deprived of something they are entitled to. It would be equally devoid of sense to say that we are entitled to the moral freedom that consists in being able to will as we ought and to refrain from willing as we ought. We either acquire or fail to acquire such freedom through the choices we have ourselves freely made. It is entirely within our power to form or to fail to form the virtuous disposition to will as one ought that constitutes an individual's moral freedom. No other human being can confer such liberty on us or withhold it from us. According to Christian dogmas concerning man's original sin and man's redemption through Christ's saving grace, fallen man cannot, without God's help, acquire the moral virtue required for moral liberty. That is why Christian theologians refer to moral freedom as the God-given liberty enjoyed only by those whom God has elected for salvation. On the secular plane of our social lives, it remains the case that we can make no rightful claim upon others or upon society to grant us a freedom that is entirely within our power to possess or to lack. The only liberties to which we can make a claim upon society are the freedom to do as we please within the limits imposed by justice and that variant of circumstantial freedom that is the political liberty enjoyed by enfranchised citizens of a republic.[2]

The above positions adopted by Novak and Adler are intriguing for a number of reasons. One of these is because of the political liberalism which both views advocate. For while both Novak and Adler might consider themselves to be proponents of some sort of political liberalism (at the very least of the often referred to "Madisonian principle" of limited government), in many more progressive political circles their reputations would place them in the political camp of right wing fanatics and other political neanderthals. It is somewhat odd, then, that two such thinkers, both of whom are Thomistic sympathizers, would be adopting what appears to be an archetypal liberal position about the domain of public enforcement of what in popular parlance today is called "private morality." Seemingly, according to Novak, the intentions of businessmen (and one would presume of other human beings as well) "are not favorable to rule by law." Rather, it is "the structure of business activities" to which the rule of law applies. Similarly, for Adler, it is not to moral freedom that the rule

---

[2]Mortimer J. Adler, *Six Great Ideas* (New York: Macmillan Publishing Company, Inc., 1981), pp. 149–150.

of legal enforcement applies. Rather, legal enforcement is restricted to the domain of "circumstantial freedom," which for Adler means to the realm of enabling means of action. That is, public enforcement has authority to exercise restraints upon freedom of opportunity and freedom of conditions, and to influence human freedom through these, but, strictly speaking, it must remain mute and immobile before the domain of moral freedom.

I do not know about others, but I find these positions of Novak and of Adler somewhat odd, to say the least; yet, at the same time I think they are in a way expressing truths about the nature of political government which are traceable to St. Thomas, and which, if framed in a slightly different fashion, can throw a great deal of light upon the obfuscated "private morality" and "public enforcement" distinction which has become such a popular foil for use by nominal Catholic politicians in the latter part of the twentieth-century.

The purpose of this article is to take a somewhat detailed look at this issue of private morality and public enforcement against the background of certain Maritain sympathizers, principally Novak and Adler, and against the background of the writings of St. Thomas himself. In the writings of the latter one can find the deeper roots out of which this contemporary moral and political "real distinction" has been able to sprout.

In order to begin this investigation, let me turn again to Michael Novak. In his fairly recent book, *Free Persons and the Common Good*, he refers approvingly to Lord Acton's quip that St. Thomas was "the first Whig."[3] Now, I am not sure whether or not St. Thomas was the first "Whig"; and I think the case can be made for a number of other likely candidates— such as St. Augustine, or Our Lord, or, as some of my Jewish friends might argue, Moses himself. Nonetheless, I think Novak's reference to Lord Acton provides a helpful reminder about the proximate roots of contemporary liberalism within the Catholic theological tradition. The question, however, which needs to be considered is what more precisely are these roots and how closely does the fruit which has grown from the seed resemble its source.

Taking the latter question first, it seems incredible to someone in any way familiar with the moral and political teaching of St. Thomas

---

[3]Michael Novak, *Free Persons and the Common Good*, (Lanham, Maryland: Madison Books, 1989), p. 80 and p. 201, n. 5.

to think that he would agree with Alan Peacock's assertion that "public enforcement of virtue is neither desirable nor possible." Similarly, it seems unlikely that, without serious qualification, St. Thomas would agree with the position attributed to Novak that it is not the intentions of people, but only the structures of their activities which are favorable to rule by law. Without even probing very deeply into St. Thomas's work itself, one might simply ask how the activities of people can be divorced from their intentions; since is it not through their intentions that acts of human choice receive their identity? Furthermore, according to Adler, the domain of public enforcement is not the domain of moral freedom; yet, at the same time, for him, the realm of public enforcement is the dimension of human freedom regulated by justice. Now, one might wonder, how can this be? Unless the moral domain has been ceded to the likes of Callicles, how can it be that the realm of freedom regulated by justice—one of the four cardinal moral virtues— is not within the moral order?

In making these criticisms I do not for an instant think Michael Novak actually accepts the view attributed to him by Alan Peacock that "democratic capitalism, rests on the supposition that public enforcement of virtue is neither desirable nor possible." Indeed, I would contend that Novak holds just the opposite: namely, that within democratic capitalism public enforcement of virtue is not only possible and desirable, it is even necessary. In his view, however, there is within democratic capitalism a public enforcement of virtue that is intentionally limited, decentralized, and diffused through various systems of behavioral control. In a similar vein, Novak is not arguing that within the context of democratic capitalism it is impossible, undesirable, or unjust for the governmental bureaucracies to regulate the intentions of people. Rather, he is saying that personal intentions are not favorable to such regulation, especially if such regulation is attempted directly rather than through subsidiary agencies.[4]

In the above respects Novak's views are quite similar to those of Mortimer J. Adler, who argues that the domain of public enforcement is the dimension of circumstantial liberty. Yet I do not think Novak would assert that the domain of public enforcement does not touch the area of moral freedom. In fact, I do not think that Adler himself can

---

[4]Michael Novak, *The Spirit of Democratic Capitalism*, p. 31–95.

be accused of seriously making such a claim. No, what Adler seems to mean when he says that only circumstantial freedom of action, rather than moral liberty, is amenable to being joined with the political liberty of enfranchised citizens under constitutional government is not that the domain of circumstantial freedom is outside the moral order.[5] For, if this were what he meant, it would make no sense for him to assert that our natural right to circumstantial freedom of action

> flows from our natural possession of a free will and a power of free choice, which we exercise in making the decisions that we must make, either rightly or wrongly, in our pursuit of happiness. What good would it do us to make decisions that we cannot carry out? Without liberty of action, our freedom of choice would be rendered totally ineffective. We would be exercising it without achieving the ultimate good we are under an obligation to seek, if our freedom of choice is thwarted by unjust limitations on our liberty of action, or is nullified by the deprivation of such freedom. Lacking free will and freedom of choice, the lower animals have no rightful claim on liberty of action. Zoos do not exist in violation of rights. However much we may sympathize with caged or confined animals, we are not moved by a sense of injustice done them.[6]

Indeed, Adler's words themselves give the firmest evidence that his intention is actually to include the realm of public enforcement within the moral order. Otherwise the above-cited passage would be incoherent. Furthermore, he says:

> It would be equally devoid of sense to say that we are entitled to the moral freedom that consists in being able to will as we ought and to refrain from willing as we ought not. We either acquire or fail to acquire such freedom through the choices we have ourselves freely made. It is entirely within our power to form or to fail to form the virtuous disposition to will as one ought that constitutes an individual's freedom. No other human being can confer such liberty on us or withhold it form us.[7]

His claim is true only up to a point—as he himself recognizes. For whether we acquire or fail to acquire such moral freedom depends upon our having access to the essential enabling means of action

---

[5]Mortimer J. Adler, *Six Great Ideas*, p. 150.
[6]*Ibid.*, p. 152.
[7]*Ibid.*, p. 149.

through which good habits of action can be formed. Thus, it is entirely within our power to form or not to form the power to will as we ought only up to the point that we are allowed the possession of essential enabling means of so willing and only to the extent that included among the moral virtues of prudence, temperance, and courage, we are allowed to exercise, and have exercised upon us, the virtue of justice.

However, once this relationship between circumstantial freedom of action and the moral order is recognized, Adler's examination of the nature of justice and its relation to human freedom throws a tremendous amount of light not only upon the domain of private morality and public enforcement but also upon the whole private morality/public morality debate and its provenance in traditional Catholic thought. In particular, the following remark from Adler is quite telling regarding these matters: "Whether we have political liberty or not and the extent to which we have a limited freedom to do as we please depend largely, if not entirely, on the society in which we live—its institutions and arrangements, its forms of government and its laws."[8]

What I find most revealing about this comment is Adler's reference to *doing as one pleases* within the limits of *justice*; and, secondly, the dependence of *doing as one pleases* within the limits of *justice* upon forms of political arrangement—in particular, upon forms of law. I find these two assertions noteworthy because, for me at least, they indicate the extent to which the Madisonian principle of limited government is rooted in the classical cardinal moral virtues themselves, inasmuch as these are conjoined with and synthesized through St. Thomas's treatment of the variety of law in the *Summa Theologiae* I-II, Q. 91.

Specifically, in article four under this question St. Thomas examines whether a divine law is necessary beyond natural law and human law. In his reply he asserts that such a law is necessary for four reasons: a) because law directs human beings to actions proportionate to their end; b) because of the uncertainty of human judgment, especially regarding contingent and particular matters, which results in the passage of diverse and conflicting laws; c) because people are competent to make laws concerning what they are able to judge, but they are not able to judge interior human acts but only exterior movements—while full virtue requires that a person be right in each area; and d) because,

---

[8]*Ibid.*, p. 150.

as Augustine says, human law is not able to prohibit and to punish all evil.[9]

Now, if not all evil is able to be prohibited and to be punished, and simultaneously if the moral order is the domain of the possible (because it deals with human choice, which, as Aristotle states, is always of the actual, and must therefore be of the possible),[10] then the domain of human law, as well as of just civil government, must be limited.

The question, however, remains whether all vice is to be prohibited by civil law; and if so, two other questions follow: specifically, which vices lie within the domain of civil law? and practically, how are they effectively to be limited? Put in another way, to how much freedom *to do as one pleases* is one entitled?

Again, the answer to this question lies within the recognition that the domain of civil governmental authority lies within the domain of the humanly possible. No one, not even civil governments, can be obliged, nor have they the authority to do the impossible. What, however, lies within the domain of governmental possibility within the civic order? According to St. Thomas, and as Novak and Adler have rightly observed, just governments are limited to regulating human choice through outward and observable behavior (what Adler calls circumstantial freedom). Why? Because, as St. Thomas has explained well, human beings can only rightly make laws on matters upon which they are competent to judge (because, once again, since they deal with human choice, laws are of the possible), and the interior judgments of human beings are not readily apparent to, nor regulable by, external judgment. Consequently, neither are the cardinal moral vices of intemperance, cowardice, and foolishness. Thus, when asked the question: "To how much freedom to do as one pleases is an ordinary human being entitled by just government?," it seems reasonable to conclude, as Adler has done, that a human being is entitled to the circumstantial freedom to do as one pleases within the bounds of justice.

In other words, to put the discussion within the context of contemporary political parlance, the domain of private morality is the domain of the cardinal moral virtues of prudence, courage, and temperance, and, to certain lesser extent, of the virtue of justice, along with

---

[9]Aristotle, *Nicomachean Ethics*, 112b–113a.
[10]St. Thomas Aquinas, *ST.*, I-II, 96, 3, Respondeo.

their attendant vices. Within the boundaries of these human actions, a person can be authoritatively regulated by civil government only through the virtue of justice and through institutions of justice and only when the circumstantial freedom of a person in the exercise of a vice actually begins to exert an unjust limitation upon another. Such injustice consists in impeding access to the essential enabling means of opportunity to exercise circumstantial freedom within the bounds of justice. Thus, even with respect to just and unjust actions as they bear upon circumstantial freedom, civil government cannot be expected to regulate every aspect of human behavior. Consequently, St. Thomas wisely observes that human law does not prescribe all acts of virtue but only those which, in some way, either immediately or remotely, have a bearing upon the common good, as, for example, when some way of behaving has been commanded by a lawmaker related to the character formation of good citizens so that the common good of justice and peace may be maintained.[11] This being the case, even acts of injustice, such as those committed by one family member against another, are not the proper subjects for rule by civil government, unless and until they begin to intrude upon the domain of those enabling means which are essential for the exercise of the justly regulated choice of another, such as the natural rights to life, freedom of association, of speech, of the press, and so on.

Thus, from the standpoint of just civil government, people are entitled to be as foolish, or as cowardly, or as intemperate as they want until they exceed the bounds of justice in the exercise of their external acts—a boundary beyond which these acts interfere with access of another to the essential enabling means of exercising just choice. When this occurs, people enter the domain of *public morality, which is that part of the domain of circumstantial freedom of action regulable by justice*; and their entitlement to circumstantial freedom to exercise their vices becomes justifiably impaired without any loss of their political freedom.

Now aware of the classical source of the contemporary domains of private morality and public enforcement, one can accept these domains as more intelligible. Beyond this, however, and in conclusion, something else becomes even more intelligible—namely, the extent

---

to which the private and public morality distinction, as framed by politicians such as Governor Mario M. Cuomo, has divorced both the domain of private morality and of public morality from the moral order of vice and virtue. In substitution for the order of private and public virtues and vices (that is, the virtues of prudence, courage, temperance, and justice, and their corresponding vices), they have placed group rules arbitrarily made by the vote of group wills; and in the place of the order of circumstantial freedom regulated by the cardinal moral virtue of justice, they have put the will of consensus—a specter from the irrationalism of Rousseau.

By so doing, some contemporary politicians have made the domain of private morality an area of concern solely between individuals and factional groups within the political body—in particular, a church of one denomination or another. Now, of course, given the roots of the domain of private morality in the private judgments of individuals, there is some truth to this position. Indeed, St. Thomas makes a similar point to indicate the need for divine law to supplement human law; and, in fact, were some such form of regulation absent from a political order, beyond regulation by civil government, the body politic would suffer; for, without certain restraints on those more interior areas of human behavior, institutions of civil justice would be severely damaged. It is ludicrous to conclude, however, that, because there exists an area of private morality which, strictly speaking, is not directly susceptible in itself to regulation by the civil state, that private morality cannot be regulated by the civil state at all. Furthermore, it is even more ludicrous to contend that actions better regulated by churches because of the ability of religion to influence the interior decisions of people are in no way within the domain of civil government—especially, when these decisions have an influence upon the just exercise of circumstantial freedom by another. Consequently, even those actions expressly forbidden by the members of a religion are matters of public morality when they relate to matters of the just exercise of the essential enabling means of circumstantial freedom; all members of the body-politic have a moral and political right to object to the exercise of free choice when it exceeds the bounds of justice. After all, the right to choose and the political right to choose are not the same. One possesses the right to choose by nature, but the political right to choose is an entitlement regulated not by consensus but by just compatibility with the circumstantial freedom of others. Because they fail to keep this distinction in mind, is it any wonder that not only in their pronouncements but also in their other forms of political behavior so many contemporary American Catholic politicians seem more to reflect the moral views of Thrasymachus and Callicles than those of Thomas More, Thomas Aquinas, or Jacques Maritain?

The Scope of Justice

Ralph Nelson

An attentive reader of *The Italian Campaign and French Political Thought*[1] and later *The Road to Vichy*[2] cannot fail to notice Yves Simon's passionate and pervasive concern for justice. While the former book is directly concerned with the question of whether the Italian attack on Ethiopia was a just war, the latter study not only deals with the issue of the just war but that of the just price and just wage as well. By explaining in concrete terms how France developed politically in the inter-war period, Simon constantly evaluates what was thought and done in terms of its justice. There is no doubt in Simon's mind about the iniquity of the war in Ethiopia—"this obviously unjust and cruel war"[3]—and he is worried about Catholic opinion. He refers to the position taken by many Catholics during the Dreyfus affair: "With very few exceptions French Catholics committed themselves unreservedly in the anti-Dreyfus campaign and against justice".[4] He notes the suffering brought on the Church subsequently through the anti-clerical legislation of a vengeful kind at the turn of the century.

Three times in *The Road to Vichy* he invokes the principle of equal justice: first, as part of the ideology of the French Revolution; secondly, as a foundation for the League of Nations; and thirdly, as

---

[1] Yves R. Simon, *La campagne d'Ethiopie et la pensée politique Française*, 2nd edition (Paris, Desclée de Brouwer, 1936).

[2] Yves R. Simon, *The Road to Vichy: 1918–1938*, Revised Edition with an Introduction by John Hellman (Lanham, Maryland: University Press of America, 1988, 1990).

[3] *Ibid.*, p. 112.

[4] *Ibid.*, p. 70.

an aim "to evolve a world where the principle of equal justice for all will prevail. . . ."[5]

But having said this about his concern for justice, we must note how unfortunate it is that Simon did not devote an entire essay, much less a monograph, to the subject. It would have facilitated the task of grasping what his systematic views on the subject were. In the absence of such a treatise, the interpreter must piece together a considerable number of references to justice throughout the Simonian corpus and attempt to present a more or less systematic account of what I call the scope or extent of the concept of justice as he saw it.

The most reasonable and faithful beginning, I presume, would be to examine several of his pre-war essays on Pierre-Joseph Proudhon. Going back to these comparatively early considerations of the notion of justice should not, however, give the impression that a purely chronological order will be followed. Rather, once having identified a suitable starting point, the inquiry will then proceed from a general consideration of justice to an examination of its specific forms and, in regard to the specific forms, to issues of context, rules, and criteria.

At one stage in his career Simon had envisaged a general study of Proudhon's political philosophy. He had done a great deal of research on the subject, had published several articles, but he abandoned the project when Henri de Lubac's work appeared in 1945.[6] There has been a good deal of interest in Proudhon by French scholars and there remains a wide latitude of interpretation, whether one stresses the moral side, the political idea of federation, the theory of mutualism, or Proudhon's version of anarchism.[7]

Simon describes Proudhon's great *opus* on justice[8] as "a veritable summa, indeed a classic statement of Proudhon's ethics."[9] And in spite

---

[5]*Ibid.*, p. 204

[6]Paule Yves Simon informed me of this in October, 1988. Henri de Lubac, *Proudhon et le Christianisme* (Paris: Editions du Seuil, 1945), translated as *The Un-Marxian Socialist* (New York: Sheed and Ward, 1948). Simon's extensive Proudhon manuscripts and notes are housed at the Maritain Center, Hesburgh Library, University of Notre Dame, Indiana.

[7]See Robert L. Hoffmann, *Revolutionary Justice: The Social and Political Theory of P.-J. Proudhon* (Urbana, Illinois: University of Illinois Press, 1972).

[8]Pierre-Joseph Proudhon, *De la justice dans la révolution et dans l'église* (Paris: M. Rivière, 1930–1935) 4 volumes.

[9]Yves R. Simon, "The Problem of Transcendence and Proudhon's Challenge," *Thought*, Vol. LIV, No. 213, June, 1979, p. 176.

of the rather disorganized manner in which Proudhon's ideas are presented, "as soon as the emotional intuition which animated Proudhon, that is, the idea of commutative justice with its requirement of strict equality is disengaged from his thought, one sees that a profound logic controlled the seeming chaos of his thinking."[10] While Proudhon correctly saw that strict equality, or some would say equivalence,[11] is "the law of commutative justice and the law of honest exchange,"[12] this intuition was conceptualized in an erroneous way, "for it introduced unity at the cost of utterly neglecting the complexities of realities and values."[13] What are these complexities? The Proudhonian reductionist conception of justice "absorbed every other kind of justice. It got rid of the notions of distributive and legal justice with their laws of proportion rather than of strict equality."[14] In other words, the triadic relationships of justice in the classical or Aristotelian scheme disappear and we are left with the justice of exchange. The political implications of the Proudhonian theory of justice are examined in Simon's "A Note on Proudhon's Federalism."[15]

Alan Ritter in his excellent study of Proudhon's political thought gives credit to Simon since he "is the only critic, so far as I know, who remarks on Proudhon's total hostility to distributive justice."[16] Ritter incidentally discusses the difficulties Proudhon would have to face if his conception of mutualism were to completely dispense with any concept of distribution whatsoever.[17] Although the social ideal of mutualism may seem different from the political notion of federation, Simon suggested at one point that Proudhon wanted to eliminate any distinction between the two, holding a thorough-going anarchism that effectively implies the end of politics. However, this reduction never occurred. Thus, the question of the interaction between the mutualist

---

[10]*Ibid.*, p. 177.

[11]Vladimir Jankélévitch, *Traité des vertus* (Paris: Bordas, 1949) p. 378.

[12]Yves R. Simon, "The Problem of Transcendence and Proudhon's Challenge," p. 177.

[13]*Ibid.*

[14]*Ibid.*

[15]Yves R. Simon, "A Note on Proudhon's Federalism," in *Federalism as Grand Design: Political Philosophers and the Federal Principle* ed. Daniel J. Elazar (Lanham, Maryland: University Press of America, 1987), pp. 223–234.

[16]Alan Ritter, *The Political Thought of Pierre-Joseph Proudhon* (Princeton, New Jersey: Princeton University Press, 1969), p. 99 note 15.

[17]*Ibid.*, p. 137.

society, or social economy, and the federative political system must be posed.

According to Proudhon, then, the notion of commutative justice may operate at the socio-economic level and at the political level. So if the concern is primarily with the socio-economic aspect, it is evident that Simon endorses the Proudhonian objection to wealth "leaking out" of society (a concern at the heart of Proudhonian socialism) along with traditional Thomistic concerns with prices and wages. A significant instance of such a leakage would be windfall profits on land. Libertarian proponents of the spontaneous market order argue against the relevance of such moral conceptions and against the idea of distributive justice as appropriate to organization but not to the spontaneous market order.[18] Proudhon, in contrast to the libertarians, supported a substantive, not just a procedural, conception of commutative justice, and for that reason his theory has a strong resemblance to the Thomistic one.

The rejection of any conception of distributive justice by Proudhon is based on the rejection of any hierarchical relationship in the structure of the society or in the polity. Because Simon's conception of economic distribution has been adequately dealt with elsewhere,[19] I will concentrate on the political side of the problem. According to Simon, in Proudhon's political theory "federal society is not hierarchical."[20] This means that there can be no whole-part or subordinative relationship. In the presence of horizontal relations alone, there are only the criteria of equality and equilibrium. In such a view the central level of government only plays a coordinating role. Having rejected any hierarchy, Proudhon would have to look upon a federation as a system in which the constituent units are bargaining with each other or maintaining exchange relations. Simon, on the contrary, believes that hierarchy is inevitable in a political organization, particularly one based on the division of power and authority.

To illustrate the issue I shall briefly refer to the Canadian federal system. One interpretation of the Canadian federation, a rather

---

[18]See F.A. von Hayek , *Law, Legislation and Liberty* (London: Routledge, Vol. 2, 1976).

[19]Thomas R. Rourke and Clarke E. Cochran, "The Common Good and Economic Justice: Reflections on the Thought of Yves R. Simon," *The Review of Politics*, 54, 2, Spring 1990, pp. 231–252.

[20]Yves R. Simon, "A Note on Proudhon's Federalism," p. 230.

widespread one in fact, resembles to a great extent the Proudhonian system of political exchange. The federal-provincial conferences have become over the years the characteristic federal forum in which the Canadian prime minister and the provincial premiers periodically assemble, debate the agenda, bargain, and, hopefully, arrive at a consensus—a deal, if you will; if that deal were a constitutional change, it would then be subject to the rules of ratification. This looks very much like the Proudhonian idea of a federation. Yet what was evident on several occasions when serious constitutional change has been at stake, and consensus has been difficult to achieve, has been the threat by the central government to act unilaterally, thus emphasizing the hierarchical order of the whole and the parts. That the threat was not eventually carried out is beside the point. The fact is that the central government may properly act unilaterally on such questions, even if the practice has been one of bargaining.

Thus, the main shortcomings of this interpretation or ideology of federalism as a bargaining system à la Proudhon is that it does not pay attention to the conditions of political foundation, and it does not clearly distinguish between a federal system in which no unit is really sovereign and a confederation in which each and every unit is. Despite the fact that Canada was called a confederation in 1867, it emerged at first as a federal state with a strong centralist bias. At any rate, the bargaining conception of federation illustrates the manner in which the Proudhonian notion of exchange might relate to an actual political system.

Having shown why Proudhon rejected any conception of justice other than commutative justice, Simon then goes on to argue for a broad notion of justice that includes commutative and distributive as well as legal or general justice. Simon, unlike Proudhon, having described social and political organization as hierarchical, would seem to oppose not only the anarchist perspective but other contemporary ideological currents as well. The radical attacks the social hierarchy; the liberal favors the conception of a political society based on a contract.

If the political order, and at least segments of the social order, are hierarchical, that is, involve relations of the whole to the parts, then commutative justice cannot be the whole of justice. There are two vectors: the whole to the parts (distribute justice), the parts to the whole (general or legal justice). Simon shows a preference for the term "legal justice," although it too may be misleading in that legal may seem to contrast with natural. On balance Thomas Aquinas uses the term general justice more frequently than he does legal justice, even if the two are taken to be synonyms.[21]

Now, the emphasis on the relationships involved in the different kinds of justice is not intended to obscure the fact that justice for Simon is a virtue, a stable disposition, a *habitus*. There is a temptation in much of the contemporary writing on justice to speak of it solely in terms of a state of affairs or in terms of a social configuration. The primary meaning, it is clear, is that justice is a *habitus* and that the state of affairs or social configuration is a consequence of the presence or absence of the requisite virtues.

A recent study of social justice is based on the notion that there are three criteria of social justice.[22] Furthermore, the emphasis on one or the other of these three criteria rests on a certain conception of society. Thus, there is a correspondence between an ethical theory of justice and an account of a certain kind of society. There are in fact two agencies involved in distributive justice: social and political. While Aristotle was solely concerned with the distribution of political offices, the current literature on distributive justice mainly concerns economic distribution, whether or not the state is directly involved. It would seem that social distribution must be pluralistic. Simon focuses on political distribution, though he does mention the way in which the non-public agencies are involved. The three criteria of distributive justice, mentioned above, are needs, desert, and rights. I take the last named first.

Simon accepts the idea that there are three criteria and finds a place for each of them in his writings. It is apparent that he placed much less emphasis on a human rights approach than does Jacques Maritain, for instance. However, the concern is still there. Let us say that Simon is primarily preoccupied with the foundation of human or natural rights, and is inspired to show that a consistently nominalistic philosophy undercuts any notion of natural rights simply because it undermines the

---

[21]Thomas Aquinas, *ST.*, II-II, 58, 5c.

[22]David Miller uses rights, deserts, and need in *Social Justice* (Oxford: Clarendon Press, 1976). The three paradigm cases are the rights theory of David Hume, the desert theory of Herbert Spencer, and the needs theory of Prince Peter Kropotkin.

concept of human nature itself.[23] He doubts, however, that important political philosophers so inclined—Locke, for instance—were consistent nominalists.[24] So the discussion of distributive justice in Simon will concentrate on needs and deserts rather than on the distribution of, that is, the protection of, human or natural rights.

A comparison between Mortimer Adler and Simon on the use of the criteria is instructive. In his most complete examination of justice in *The Time of Our Lives*,[25] Adler mentions needs alone as a criterion of distributive justice in a teleological context of self-fulfillment and then proceeds to identify needs and rights, so we may speak, I think, of needs-rights. (There is even a passage in his little book on Aristotle in which he attributes such a theory to that philosopher which seems anachronistic, to say the least.)[26] Nowhere in this central book on ethics is there any reference whatsoever to the idea of desert or merit. However, when Adler comes to deal with the problems of justice in *Six Great Ideas*,[27] his theory broadens. While stressing natural equality in both the political and social setting, he now refers to admissible forms of inequality based primarily on "unequal contributions to the welfare of the community."[28] Where there are "unequal contributions . . . [there is] inequality of results in the rewards they receive."[29] Unfortunately, Adler uses the term "equalities of condition" in a somewhat misleading way.[30]

As to "circumstantial equality . . . with respect to economic status, treatment and opportunity", Adler wants to endorse a kind of socialism.[31] This is based on the questionable assumption that present day socialists or egalitarians would accept the notion of desert. R. H. Tawney did so, but, if John Rawls is taken as an example of the egalitarian liberal, the fact is that he specifically rejects the idea that

---

[23]Yves R. Simon, *Philosophy of Democratic Government* (Chicago: University of Chicago Press, 1951, 1961, 1977), p. 201. Revised edition (Notre Dame, Indiana: University of Notre Dame Press, 1993).

[24]*Ibid.*

[25]Mortimer J. Adler, *The Time of Our Lives: The Ethics of Common Sense* (New York: Holt, Rinehart and Winston, 1970).

[26]Mortimer J. Adler, *Aristotle for Everybody* (Toronto: Bantam, 1978), pp. 84–91.

[27]Mortimer J. Adler, *Six Great Ideas* (New York: Macmillan Publishing Co., 1981).

[28]*Ibid.*, p. 138.

[29]*Ibid.*, p. 161.

[30]*Ibid.*, p. 139 and p. 165.

[31]*Ibid.*, p. 181 and p. 195.

anyone is meritorious or that anything anyone does is a basis for distribution by merit.[32] In this regard it is interesting to note the evolution of "liberal" (social democrat) thought beginning with J. S. Mill, continuing through Dewey and Hobhouse, and terminating in Rawls.[33] If Adler is capable of calling the mixed economy "socialized capitalism,"[34] I suppose he has no difficulty in calling a system that uses both needs and deserts as criteria or distribution as socialism. I would maintain that both identifications are unwarranted and that to describe his theory as "socialism" is a misnomer, more prone to confuse than enlighten the reader.[35]

Now one can read some of Simon's works, such as *Work, Society, and Culture*, and draw the conclusion that he is primarily, if not exclusively, taken up with the problem of needs and their satisfaction. Yet the impression of reductionism is scotched in *Philosophy of Democratic Government* where he offers a more balanced account of the criteria of distribution. In that work Simon does discuss the three criteria, but in varying and uneven ways. There is no doubt that, leaving rights aside, there are two main reasons for distribution: needs and deserts.[36]

Moreover, there is no doubt that Simon is quite aware of the complexity of allocations in terms of needs, for there are different kinds of need. In *Philosophy of Democratic Government* there is a distinction made between biologically determined and sociologically determined needs.[37] Speaking of what he calls "a philosophy of human needs," he identifies *capitalization* and *free distribution* as two social needs.[38] Furthermore, he refers to elementary, real, and genuine

---

[32]This interpretation has been made by a number of commentators. For a succinct statement, see D.D. Raphael, "John Rawl's Theory of Justice" in *Justice and Liberty* (London: Athlone Press, 1980) pp. 102–114. For an argument that there is a place for desert in Rawls's theory, see Thomas W. Pogge, *Realizing Rawls* (Ithaca, New York: Cornell University Press, 1989), pp. 81–86.

[33]John Stuart Mill, *Principles of Political Economy* (Toronto: University of Toronto Press, 1965), p. 202. John Dewey and James H. Tufts *Ethics* (New York: Henry Holt and Co., 1913) p. 546. Leonard Hobhouse, *The Elements of Social Justice* (London: Allen and Unwin, 1922), pp. 97–101.

[34]Mortimer J. Adler, *Six Great Ideas*, p. 181.

[35]*Ibid.*, p. 180.

[36]Yves R. Simon, *Philosophy of Democratic Government*, pp. 230–241.

[37]*Ibid.*, p. 242.

[38]*Ibid.*, p. 245.

human needs.[39] So initially, at least, he is concerned primarily with determining significant social needs. For a more developed treatment of the complexity of the conception of needs, we turn to the essay "Common Good and Common Action"[40] that can be taken as a further elaboration of some of the themes incompletely explored in *Philosophy of Democratic Government*. Here one finds a new distinction and a somewhat different approach to the concept of social needs. It would be a mistake, he argues, to confine the notion of needs to biological, physical, and material requirements, in short, to physical goods, and ignore "goods of the spirit" and the "service that society renders to individuals in intellectual, esthetic, moral, and spiritual life."[41] He then proceeds to question the assumption "that a need is necessarily self-centered."[42] In fact, the notion of need expresses merely the state of a tendency not yet satisfied with ultimate accomplishment."[43] So while there is a need to have or take, there is also a need to give. Such a need is clearly other-centered, generous. It seems to me that what Simon articulates here connects with the anthropological study of the gift by Marcel Mauss and the social service idea of the gift-relationship examined by Richard Titmuss in regard to blood donors.[44] In such instances, two needs are satisfied: the need to have or take and the need to give. The need to give is surely related to what in other contexts is called free distribution by Simon.

Ethical concerns for need-satisfaction normally developed within a larger theory of a teleological kind. One such theory is the widely known conception of higher and lower order needs of Abraham Maslow, tied to "the fostering of universal self-actualization."[45] Maslow combines the ethical and the psychological by referring to "a good and healthy man." The theory is controversial in that it

---

[39]*Ibid.*, "elementary" p. 291, "real" and "genuine" p. 300.

[40]Yves R. Simon, *A General Theory of Authority* (Notre Dame, Indiana: University of Notre Dame Press, 1962, 1980, 1990), pp. 23–79.

[41]*Ibid.*, p. 24.

[42]*Ibid.*

[43]*Ibid.*

[44]Marcel Mauss, "Essai sur le don," *L'année sociologique*, Seconde série 1923–1924 and Richard Titmuss, *The Gift Relationship* (London: Penguin, 1970).

[45]Abraham H. Maslow, ed. "Psychological Data and Value Theory" in *New Knowledge in Human Values* (New York: Harper and Row, 1959), p. 129.

stipulates that "these needs or values are related to each other in a hierarchical developmental way, in an order of strength and priority."[46] The objection to it is that the idea of the end is vague, or merely formal; and, secondly, any sort of hierarchy presupposes an assertion about human excellence and such a notion is unlikely to gain wide assent given the character of ethical discourse today. The second objection is characteristic of the moral pluralist or the liberal political philosopher who seeks a moral consensus and argues that no such agreement is possible concerning the *telos* or ultimate end.[47] (In a sense this is a political approach to ethics since the primary objective is not to develop a moral theory, defensible in its own right, but always to keep in mind the fact that only some minimal principles will garner the desired consensus.) Rawls is one of the most prominent, but surely not the only, political philosopher to pursue a liberal consensus. The general pattern is to endorse a deontological solution and reject a teleological one, usually vaguely expressed as a theory of flourishing.

I think the rejoinder to the moral pluralist in regards to need is to make a distinction. Granted that any agreement among moral philosophers concerning an ultimate end (or conception of the good-as-end) is extremely remote. But surely there can be agreement on a number of intermediate ends, on provision of food, clothing, shelter, and on health and education (at least to a certain level). Once one goes beyond that list, disagreement will obviously be significant.

Once one has elaborated a schedule of needs, the logical or inevitable question bears on who will provide these needs. It would be an erroneous interpretation of Simon's theory, I think, to believe that the state would be responsible for the satisfaction of all of these needs. (In some instances, like free distribution, it could not be the state.) Given Simon's concern for autonomy, there would be a number of distributing agencies, so to speak, from the family to voluntary associations, from benevolent associations to public bodies. He does refer to the French system of family allowances as a means of providing "distribution according to needs."[48] That does not mean that

---

[46]*Ibid.*, p. 123.

[47]Raymond Plant, *Modern Political Thought* (Oxford: Basil Blackwell, 1991), Chapter 5.

[48]Yves R. Simon, *Work, Society, and Culture* (New York: Fordham University Press, 1971, 1986), pp. 133–135.

the state becomes the "supreme dispensator."[49] The plurality of distributors in regard to needs and other criteria may be implied more than may be patent in Simon's account. The plurality of distributors has been properly noted in other accounts of distributive justice, and it indicates one of the lacunae of Simon's often schematic treatment of justice.[50]

I noted earlier that there was a long period in the English-speaking liberal tradition in which both needs and merit or desert were recognized as criteria of justice. Common or basic needs had to be satisfied and individual differences taken into account, recognized, and individual performances rewarded. Rawls's *A Theory of Justice* broke with that tradition or line in endorsing need alone as a criterion of distributive justice, but rejecting desert or merit in any form. The personal characteristics of individual members of the society became resources deployed for the society. This is a sort of communism of attributes. In fact, Rawls's theory reflected a split between egalitarian liberals who stressed need alone and libertarian liberals, like John Hospers,[51] who selected desert alone. Since Simon believes that the principal question concerning distributive justice is to discern "in what respects are men equal and in what respects are they not equal,"[52] a defensible account of justice cannot ignore characteristics that persons as persons possess and the use that is made of those characteristics (or properties, if you will). It seems that he combines two considerations when he speaks of merit: that excellence should be recognized and regarded and that unless it is given appropriate weight, society will not be "properly served by its best members."[53] The second consideration taken out of context and treated in non-moral terms would be the familiar incentive argument in economics.

---

[49]This is my translation of the French original in a treatise by Bertrand de Jouvenel. The strength of the original is lost when the translator uses "a supreme legislator" instead. The English version is *Sovereignty: An Inquiry into the Political Good* (Chicago: University of Chicago Press, 1957), p. 164.

[50]*Ibid.* See also Michael Walzer, *Spheres of Justice: A Defense of Pluralism and Equality* (New York: Basic Books, 1983).

[51]I use a distinction made by Michael Sandel, ed. "Introduction," *Liberalism and Its Critics* (New York: New York University Press, 1984) p. 4. John Hospers, *Human Conduct: Problems of Ethics* (New York: Harcourt, Brace and Jovanovich, 1972), pp. 433–467.

[52]Yves R. Simon, *Philosophy of Democratic Government*, p. 197.

[53]*Ibid.*, 94.

The position defended is that, while there are common needs based on common human nature, there are individual characteristics, individuated traits, that when properly used constitute a claim for meritorious distribution. "Distributive justice is the rule by which the community renders their due to each and every one of its parts," and "the relation of the whole to the parts is covered by the rules of distributive justice, by which the community renders their due to its members according to merit and need."[54] The plurality of distributive agencies, corresponding to different kinds of community, would seem relevant to distributive justice as in the case of promotions in the armed forces, in business enterprises, or in educational institutions. Simon's reference to the common good, rather than to the social product, reiterates once more his primary focus on the political aspects of distribution, at least in *Philosophy of Democratic Government*.[55]

To return once again to a comparison of Simon and Adler, let us note that both of them are critical of the concept of quotas in regard to distributive justice. Adler's arguments imply a rejection of quotas as they are presently employed.

> Difference in gender is a totally irrelevant consideration, as is difference in skin color, difference in ethnic origin, difference in religion. These differences being irrelevant, the persons involved are equal.[56]

This presumably implies that being irrelevant to justice, these differences may neither count against nor for someone; they are neither disadvantages nor advantages. Simon refers to "such contingencies as color or other so-called 'race' features" as not being pertinent to distribution.[57] But a stronger argument is explicitly mounted against the use of quotas in a wartime book that investigated the support for the use of quotas in Nazi Germany. He notes the reasons why such quotas are popular: they eliminate competitors. (He refers specifically to the professions, education, medicine and law.) Once established, the next step will be a proliferation of quotas. There will be "a quota for every group which persistently preserves its identity within the community

---

[54]Yves R. Simon, *The Definition of Moral Virtue* (New York: Fordham University Press, 1986, 1989), p. 99.

[55]*Ibid.*

[56]Mortimer J. Adler, *Six Great Ideas*, pp. 189–190.

[57]Yves R. Simon, *Philosophy of Democratic Government*, p. 203.

and refuses to let itself be assimilated. There follows a multiplication of quotas."[58] His final statement on the consequences of the practice of quotas not only reflects on a historical situation, but is, I fear, unfortunately prophetic: "With the consistent application of the quota principle we see a savage struggle take shape, a merciless war between hardened and irreconcilable groups, a delirium of discord which no community could possibly resist."[59] It may be observed that the acquiescence of liberal-minded people in our day to the practice of quotas marks a shift from the former liberal stress on achievement to the conservative conception of ascription and status. And since the conservatism alluded to is closer to the old regime than it is to the open society, liberals may be returning to notions they once fiercely opposed.

No account of distributive justice would be complete without some reference to the notion of social justice, often used interchangeably with it. There are at least two instances in which Simon employs the term, the first being a discussion about its ambiguity, the second being an attempt to give it some kind of precision. In the first instance in which he calls social justice "an extremely ambiguous expression"[60] he reminds us that in most of the current literature on the subject, the term social justice is taken as a synonym for distributive justice. On the other hand, Roman Catholic writers use the term as a synonym for general or legal justice. If the first identification is about pattern theories of justice, the second summons the Christian to duties in regard to the common good. Then again the term is often used in a vague way without any specification of other usages. In order to enter into a discourse from which the Roman Catholic view is excluded, it would be important to employ a more common vocabulary, or at least one free from ambiguity.

In his book, *The Definition of Moral Virtue*, Simon uses the term to refer to the whole of justice of which general and particular justice are parts. "And that leaves us with just three kinds of what we may call social justice: general, distributive and, corrective (or commutative) justice."[61] So, Simon avoids both the contemporary tendency to equate distributive with social justice and the Roman Catholic practice of

---

[58]*Ibid.*, p. 49.

[59]*Ibid.*, p. 50.

[60]Yves R. Simon, *Work, Society, and Culture*, p. 138. Cf. Bertrand de Jouvenel, *Sovereignty: An Inquiry into the Political Good*, p. 139.

[61]Yves R. Simon, *The Definition of Moral Virtue*, p. 100.

using the term to designate legal or general justice. An objection to the first use is that it is too narrow and does not specifically include political distribution. In the second case, the term is not preferable to the terms legal or general justice and, in fact, may be misleading.

We finally come to the third form, of justice, legal or general justice, "ruling the relations of the parts of the community to the community itself."[62] If we are speaking of the political community, as Simon usually is, the issue at hand is the conception of good citizenship and the responsibility of political leaders. Although he does not explicitly say that he is examining aspects of legal or general justice in the passages I shall use to illustrate this form of justice, there seems little doubt that the issues are pertinent to the rule of legal or general justice, and that rule, or "law," as Simon prefers to say, is one of proportion just as is the case with distributive justice, its converse, so to speak.

In the first instance, the intention of the common good by the citizen is examined. Simon takes the case of the wife of a convicted murderer. If she is to be a good citizen, should her intention be that her husband be severely punished? As a private person "as far as content and matter is concerned" her "business is to will and intend private goods."[63] To demand that a private citizen will or intend the common good both formally and materially would be to eradicate the distinction between the private and public person. Of course, some tension between these two *personae* might arise in a direct democracy, for instance, in which the citizen "is the bearer of two capacities—the public and the private."[64] In that situation a proprietor of land may have to suffer some disadvantage if the common good requires the appropriation or use of some of his terrain.

In the second instance, Simon examines the political party and the danger that once in power it will substitute its own interests for that of the whole community. Simon refers to "the formal identification of the party with the whole of the state" in the totalitarian one-party state.[65] Yet the modern notion of party politics in a non-totalitarian setting, if

---

[62]*Ibid.*

[63]Yves R. Simon, *A General Theory of Authority* (Notre Dame, Indiana: University of Notre Dame Press, 1962, 1980, 1990), p. 55 and *Philosophy of Democratic Government*, pp. 41–42.

[64]*Ibid.*, 54.

[65]Yves R. Simon, "Thomism and Democracy," in *Science, Philosophy and Religion* ed. Lyman Bryson and Louis Finkelstein (New York: The Conference on Science, Philosophy and Religion in Their Relation to the Democratic Way of Life, Inc., 1942), Vol. 2, p. 259.

it is not to become "a permanent threat against the common good,"[66] must recognize that the power it exercises through the electoral process is a power to serve the community as a whole and not simply its own supporters. The leaders of a governing party in a democracy, just as the medieval kings, only act justly to the extent that they intend the common good. If legislative acts benefit some portion of the population, the rationale for that legislation has to be in terms of the good of the community as a whole.

The eclipse of the concept of political community and the good of that community may mean that the sole legitimacy and foundation of the exercise of power is deemed to be its origin in an electoral contest. Henceforth, it becomes just a matter of our turn, our turn to use the public power for the benefits of our partisans. And when the other party or parties get into power, they will act in like manner. It is not difficult to surmise how this would breed conflict of interest. This would make democracy a perpetual alienation of the public good for the benefit of a temporary majority.

In a modification of Lincoln's famous formulation of the democratic ideal, Simon says that "the essence of democracy is a government for the people, for the whole of the people, for the common good of the people."[67] This is not, of course, to deny that political authority is transmitted from the people to those who exercise it. It is to point out that it does not suffice that party government has been established by a legitimate constitutional process; it must also subscribe to the ethics of the common good.[68]

Evident even in his earliest reflections on justice, Simon emphasized the importance of the political context. Not satisfied with purely abstract considerations of distributive justice, unlike a number of our contemporaries, he spoke of the agency or agencies of distribution in a particular political community. Now, there are exponents of a cosmopolitan morality inspired by John Rawls's theory of justice as fairness who question whether any country owns its own resources—because, after all, no individual does either—and who will impose on

---

[66]*Ibid.*

[67]*Ibid.*, p. 260.

[68]Raymond Aron comments that for Max Weber "it is as if the catholic notion of the common good of the polity were not valid, or in any case could not be rigorously defined." *Main Currents in Sociological Thought* (Harmondsworth: Penguin, 1967), Vol. 2, p. 214.

richer countries heavy responsibilities while ignoring the real conditions of interstate relations and the meaning and limitations of political community. If their prescriptions were followed, there would be a massive redistribution of wealth and countless interventions.[69]

The difficulties of distributing goods to assuage basic human necessities for those who lack them in Africa, in Ethiopia, in Somalia, and in the Sudan, to mention but three cases, has centered around the obstacles placed in the way of various relief agencies. Aid has been confiscated, and aid has been used as a weapon to force a regime's enemies to capitulate; aid is siphoned off by various competing bands in a condition of civil anarchy. States unable to provide or secure the basic material needs for their people resort to the concept of state or national sovereignty in order to thwart humanitarian aid from getting to its destined recipients.

So, I think that Simon's reflections on justice are a corrective to the political shortcomings of this conception of "duties beyond borders" (to use Stanley Hoffmann's phrase).[70] We not only need to understand the scope of justice, the kinds of justice, the criteria of justice, but also, where relevant, the agents of effecting justice, whether it concerns the duties of leaders and citizens under general justice or the responsibility of those who are in charge of the distribution of the goods of the whole to the parts of the political community.

I think Simon's theory and application of the various forms of justice includes both universal and particular factors. Such particular factors include the world of the city-state, the medieval monarchies, and the modern nation-states. Maybe the attention to the particular circumstances at stake here is another way of connecting the sense of justice to political prudence. Maybe it is another way of saying that a distinction should be made between what is permanent and what is transitory in a theory of justice.

---

[69]I refer particularly to Charles R. Beitz, *Political Theory and International Relations* (Princeton, New Jersey, Princeton University Press, 1979). In a similar vein, see James P. Sterba, *The Demands of Justice* (Notre Dame, Indiana: University of Notre Dame Press, 1980).

[70]Stanley Hoffmann, *Duties Beyond Borders: On the Limits and Possibilities of International Relations* (Syracuse, New York: Syracuse University Press, 1981). Hoffmann, like Beitz and Sterba, relies on certain Rawlsian notions.

Epilogue

Michael Novak

Not a few of the essays in *Freedom, Virtue, and The Common Good* open with an allusion to the moral "crisis" of our time, and even more, by the time they reach their final lines, express a certain dismay at the "malaise" and infirmity of the moral life—and moral thinking—of our society. Well they should.

The reader notes, too, the immense learning reflected in these pages. How many hours, days, years went into the reading of and reflection on documents ancient and new in order to produce these essays.

Still, arduous efforts yet await us before we can make our work as a philosophical society bite into the realities of our current civilization as the work of our models, Jacques Maritain and Yves R. Simon, altered the realities of theirs. Consider the role of Maritain in inspiring the worldwide movement of Christian Democratic parties and in helping to found UNESCO, as well as to formulate the Universal Declaration of Human Rights. The work of Simon was, perhaps, more purely philosophical and yet it, too, was directed toward expounding the moral foundations of democracy, the common good, authority, and moral liberty, in preparation for the new world order that both of them, and their colleagues, hoped would follow on the successful conclusion of World War II. Both thinkers took controversial positions on hotly contested issues of their generation, such as opposition to the Vichy government of France, the role and limits of existentialism, the Civil War in Spain, and the character of "real existing Socialism."

Both of these masters understood quite well the nobility and limits of the philosophical vocation, its "poverty and misery," and its high moral demands. But they also knew themselves to be incarnated historical creatures, called to master the maelstrom of their

358

own time (surely even more confusing and desperate than our own) and responsible in their time and place for speaking to the needs of their fellow voyagers through that time. Indeed, it is not possible to read their work without seeing how many of their keenest insights arose from the pressure—necessity even—to find ways out of the sharpest contemporary perplexities. Far from being disengaged, they were—Maritain, in particular, was—on the front line of social disputes and creative (that is to say, bitterly contested) practical arguments about the shape of postwar institutions. They were philosophers first, but also philosophers of the concrete and the practical. (Again, this is more true of Maritain than of Simon; yet even the latter had a sharper prudential eye than he is often given credit for even by his followers.) When historical duty called, they did not hesitate to become publicly committed—to choose *this* course rather than *that*, and to accept responsibility for the "ideology" implied by such practical action.

Thus, in reading through this book I asked myself: What comes next? What would Maritain and Simon have us do now? The example of what they did offers clues.

Now that the two great totalitarianisms that dominated their lifetimes—Fascism and Communism—have been defeated, we need an equivalent to Maritain's *True Humanism*, a statement of a proximate practical ideal for the civilization to come. We need an analysis of the great philosophical-cultural forces at play on the stage of our era, and an inspiring statement of the best practical response to them. That we *ought* to produce such a response may be taken for granted, since we are bound by the example of those whom we have chosen to be our masters. *Freedom, Virtue and The Common Good* does not take this last step, but it does suggest some steps that need to be taken *before* that vision can be set forth.

In "Private Morality and Public Enforcement," for example, Peter Redpath takes one such step and points the way to further necessary steps. He takes up "two positions" on the limits of government enforcement of private morality, Mortimer Adler's and mine, that appear to him, on first glance, as he puts it, "somewhat odd, to say the least; yet at the same time I think they are in a way expressing truths about the nature of political government which are traceable to St. Thomas, and which, if framed in a slightly different fashion, can throw a great deal of light." In other words, he finds in Adler and myself a distinction about governmental enforcement of morality that, on the face of it, seems "liberal," not Thomist, and yet it evokes in his memory an oddly Thomistic echo. He then explores this hunch and validates it.

This first experience of oddity and then, on reflection and in a slightly different frame of reference, of recognition of something familiar, is altogether common among those brought up in the tradition of natural law, practical wisdom the virtues, and the philosophy of being, as they begin to explore the roots and intellectual grounding of the Madisonian "commercial republic." This sense of oddity, indeed, lends some real credence to an observation made by the followers of Leo Strauss, *viz.*, that a decisive rupture yawns between the ancient (including early medieval) world and the modern world. Words and concepts no longer mean the same thing. Starting points are quite different. From the ancient and medieval point of view, modern thinking is off-kilter, inefficacious. Every time one tries to mediate between the one and the other, the Straussians say, the rupture between these two incompatible intellectual horizons causes dissonance and shock.

Politically speaking, of course, large stretches of today's world still live under authoritarian systems of the type known to the ancients and medievals—under sheiks, ayatollahs, and kings; under dictators and authoritarian presidents; under party chiefs and ruling committees. Paternalistically, whether with benevolence or with indifference, such rulers still have autocratic sway over the common good; and the personal rights of their subjects have only so much freedom of exercise as their rulers permit. Quite often, this is not much. Unique in world history, and now established in only a few places, is a regime of the Madisonian type, whose *government* is limited, constitutionally confined, and self-confessedly incompetent ("shall make no law") concerning the free exercise of religon (conscience), nor restricting the freedom of the press and speech; and whose *economy* is to an unprecedented degree free of state management and control. In such regimes the people are sovereign, and governments are not exactly democratic (under unchecked majority rule)—since everyone fears tyranny by a majority—but more precisely of a type called the democratic republic, charactrized by constitutional limits, the rule of law, checks and balances, and representative government. The economic order of such regimes, unlike those in ancient, medieval, or other modern states, is not controlled, managed, and directed by government officials. Rather, it is organized to offer social supports to the economic creativity, initiative, and enterprise of individuals (working, mostly, in free associations and linked cooperatively by a desire to conclude multiple and long-term acts of mutual consent).

The intellectual roots of such a novel type of human polity—a kind of *novus ordo seclorum*, to use the motto chosen by its founders— reach back through medieval thinkers to ancient times, and not last to the Jewish and Christian scriptures, it is true. Nonetheless, it must be confessed that many of the insights making such a system practical awaited modern discovery. Further, these new insights ("the new science of politics") require modes of reasoning that extend ancient and medieval thinking in new ways. Neither ancient nor medieval modes of thinking, not those, at least, of the *philosophia perennis*, are stationary, closed, fixed, and nonhistorical. The *philosophia perennis*, is, in principle, open to development. From systems that are in accord with the truth about human nature and human liberty, it not only can learn but it must learn. Its vocation is to follow truth where it leads, through following evidence.

In *The Tradition of Natural Law*, Yves R. Simon makes a distinction between the objective, eternal realities that are the object of philosophy, properly so-called, and the historical, contingent events that are suffused with aspiration, vision, and dream that are proper to ideology.

Regimes of the Madisonian type are, today, both a historical reality and systems in pursuit of a dream. They claim to represent, to some unpretentious and determinable degree, "the system of natural liberty," that is, a systemic representation of what the truth about human liberty in society demands. This is a claim about truth. "We hold these truths," the Continental Congress declared on July 4, 1776.

Of course, July 4 was an event in history, one pregnant with "aspiration" rather than with fulfillment. To this extent, one must confess, in the distinction drawn by Yves R. Simon, "We hold these truths" is an expression of "ideology" rather than of merely objective, detached, nonhistorical philosophy. As Simon points out, however, an ideology of this sort is not necessarily lacking in philosophical truth about human nature. Hear him out:

> In spite of all the dangers of error to which every ideological belief is exposed, let it be repeated that the content of an ideology is not necessarily at variance with the truth of philosophy. . . . What expresses the aspirations of a society may also express a real state of affairs. *That society is blessed whose aspirations coincide with truth.* No doubt something can be done to promote such happy coincidence. (*The Tradition of Natural Law*, p. 24, italics added.)

To promote the coincidence between ideology and truth is, of course, one historical mission of the philosopher. There are many accidental reasons why the philosopher *qua* philosopher is not likely to have the practical experience and the resulting prudence necessary for guiding concrete action. Philosophy, in Simon's view, is strictly about the universal eternal truth in things, and not about the historical visions to which humans aspire. But regarding national aspirations, the philosopher can contribute some distinctions and some standards by which to measure their degree of truth. "The need for such an ability is obvious when there is a question of contributing as much truth as possible to the visions which animate a community, to its role in mankind and history—to its ideology, if this word could be freed from all bad connotations" (*ibid.*, p. 26.) In short, the term ideology does have a good use, related to the degree of truth it attains.

"Without a vision, the people perish," *Proverbs* admonishes us. Simon has no hesitation in praising the visions which express the concrete vocation of particular peoples. "It is too bad," he complains, "that philosophers should generally be so ill-prepared to understand the contingencies of political history, for their help is certainly needed to formulate, in a spirit of uncompromising objectivity, the visions which express and inspire the vocation of a people." He commends Jacques Maritain for formulating a good phrase for this necessary and useful kind of ideology, as Maritain did in *True Humanism*: "a concrete historical ideal."

Like other philosophers, Thomists too may be "ill-prepared to understand the contingencies of political history," through not having mastered the philosophical underpinnings of the modern Madisonian republic, with its novel capitalist economy. Even if in the end one rejects such a philosophy, the mastering of a dozen or so basic concepts is required, just to understand it well. It is necessary to test each of its basic philosophical propositions, such as those about the nature of human action (e.g., von Mises), the tacit tradition of experience (e.g., Hayek), catallaxy (a process quite different from what Professors Cochran and Rourke, *supra*, call "chance"), and the organizing cooperative function of markets as a computer-like instrument of human order. Traditionalists are often especially weak in their grasp of the logic of the commercial side of the commercial republic. Many are content merely to reject ideological slogans with which they do not agree, without looking into the empirical arguments that are far more complicated, and have more lasting value, than the slogans.

To some extent, the regime of self-government of the Madisonian type came into existence by historical trial and error and sometimes through tacit rather than explicit modes of understanding. But to a certain extent, in addition, its coming into existence also depended upon explicit intellectual argument. In fact, arguments were made for it well before its historical triumph. One small example, of which Madison himself was extraordinarily proud: It had been believed at least since the time of Aristotle that for a democracy to succeed, it had to be practiced in a very small area, no larger than one that could be reached by a single human voice in a democratic forum. In small city states like Athens or early Rome, with a very small circle of free men, this could be accomplished. But the young Madison himself saw that, in historical practice, the small-sized democracy was often in fact subject to the mischief of factionalism, including "the superior force of an interested and overbearing majority" (*Federalist* 10). Therefore, he proposed a new theory, also based upon his own historical observation: *viz.*, the principle of "the enlargement of the orbit" (*Federalist* 9). His new hypothesis was that the republican regime is safer in a larger territory (such as that of the federation of all the States of the eastern seaboard in 1787) than it would be in any single smaller state. His reasoning was that in separation each single state could too easily be governed by a majority organized by a single clique of powerful families disdainful of "the rights of the minor party" (*Federalist* 10). In the larger orbit, however, he reasoned, each of these power centers would be balanced by the many others thriving in the other thirteen states. Thus, those whose rights were being violated could make appeal to the body of the whole. Therefore, in the larger orbit, the rights of individuals and minorities would be better defended than in the small jurisdiction.

Madison's argument, of course, was crucial in the ratification debates, state by suspenseful state, for the new Constitution of 1787. In *Federalist* 14, the young Madison boasted of the historical originality of the American conception, against the revered background of the long history of political philosophy. Indeed, this originality is celebrated in the motto chosen by the founders for the Seal of the United States: *novus ordo seclorum*, with its striking emphasis on *novus*.

Another difficult conceptual breakthrough is visible in *Federalist* 10 and 51, in the theory of factions. Against the notion that a Union will require the topdown imposition of a conceptual order—i.e., what Friedrich Hayek calls "the rationalistic fallacy"—Madison argues that the mischief of faction cannot be prevented by removing the causes of factions. He further argues that relief from the mischief of factions is to be sought by means of controlling their effects by the "extent and proper structure of the Union," providing "a republican remedy for the diseases most incident to republican government" (*Federalist* 10). An order produced in this way has the added advantage of protecting a free people from the tyranny of a majority. Here, in making sure that there are many factions, and that the very multiplicity of these factions works in a mysterious, counter-intuitive way toward order, Madison draws on insights of Hume, Montesquieu, and Adam Smith.

For more than a generation before Madison, both in France and in Scotland, there had been sustained reflection on the problem of liberty and order. Such thinkers as Montesquieu and Smith had formulated two novel modern insights. First, they discerned and formulated the principle of unintended consequences, especially the unintended consequences of the social decisions taken by kings or other authorities in every polity. Unlike God, the human being is finite, and particularly so in insight into the future, including the future consequences of present large-scale actions. Whereas God's mind is able to have a simultaneous and perfect insight into every single detail in every moment in history (even the number of hairs on a human head or the condition of each lily of the field), no human mind is of comparable power. Therefore, actual consequences are always working out quite differently from the intentions of human rulers. These rulers do not—they cannot—know the full concrete panoply of the consequences that flow from their decisions. As Reinhold Niebuhr loved to put it, irony is the primary characteristic of human politics.

Secondly, Montesquieu and Smith (the latter drawing on the historical essays of David Hume, as well as on such great predecessors as Adam Ferguson, Francis Hutcheson, and the Salamanca School in Spain) began to look at commercial societies in a way very unprecedented in the tradition of the ancient and the medieval writers. Most of the ancients and medievals (but not all the fathers of the church) had disdained commerce as an inferior human activity. Most had a preference for the aristocratic way of life and some form or other of an aristocratic regime ("the rule of the best"). In historical fact, of course, aristocratic regimes had led a long and most unnecessary series of wars and military campaigns, based upon the pursuit of glory, riches, and pride of arms. Throughout history, the condition of the lower classes— the large majority—remained that of *les miserables* (Victor Hugo). By contrast, the motto of the port city of Amsterdam was Commercium et Pax. There is something about commerce that tames the heroic, warlike virtues and instructs men to prudence, relative gentleness, farsightedness, respect for the rule of law, and a preference for peace rather than annual war. Montesquieu, Adam Smith, and others came to think that the dynamic core of ancient and medieval regimes—the pursuit of power—should give way to a new dynamic core for modern regimes: the pursuit of plenty. This would be, they argued, better for the large majority of the "subjects" of these regimes.

The first liberals argued that under new modern regimes, built on a different sociological basis, "subjects" should become "citizens." The principle of republican self-government—of government of the people, by the people, and for the people—should become the new concrete historical ideal. To be successful in practice, however, such an experiment would have to be based on some other elite than the three classical elites: the aristocracy, the clergy, and the military. Although ancient and medieval writers had despised commerce, the liberals argued, a regime whose most significant social class was the new commercial and industrial class, the growing middle class, would be more inclined to be peaceful, law-abiding, concerned to maintain a prosperous and progresive social order, inclusive, open, prudent, virtuous, and less vain-glorious, idle, and self-destructive. Such were, as Albert O. Hirschman (who does not approve of them) puts it, "the arguments for capitalism before its triumph."

Although I have not mentioned all the crucial arguments, only a small sample of them, it is obvious that most of these new arguments flew in the face of the received and conventional wisdom of the ancient and medieval tradition. Furthermore, most of these new insights are counter-intuitive. They do not spring from premises by logical deduction. On the contrary, they arise out of careful observation of the way history has actually worked, combined with strikingly fresh hypotheses about how to escape from the constant repetition of historical mistakes. The emphasis is on finding a "breakthrough." The preferred method is inductive.

Even in the seventeenth or eighteenth century, the social condition of the large majority had not been substantially changed since the time of Christ. Indeed, the politics of the past had kept the large majority of human beings in varying degrees of misery and subjection. Therefore, it was incumbent on philosophers and practical statesmen to find "a new science of politics" and even to invent a new science altogether, that of "political economy." The accomplishment of the latter would entail new and sustained reflection on how the economic world actually works, as distinct from how the conventional wisdom of the past pictured its working.

To recount even the highlights of this intellectual and practical history would take us too far afield. But perhaps I have said enough to conclude on three points. First, most of us (I include myself) have not yet paid enough attention to the rupture between the modern and the ancient/medieval traditions, and particularly to placing in appropriate order the large number of original modern insights into political and economic realities. Secondly, we have not carefully diagnosed the inadequacies of those modern philosophies that attempt to articulate the philosophy of liberty. The latter, after all, develop only weak, hesitant, and self-admittedly anti-intellectual defenses (Rorty) of the fundamental ideas of free societies. Thirdly, we have yet to provide an alternative statement of the intellectual foundations of the free society. Such a statement would both draw upon and add to the tradition of the *philosophia perennis* and the Jewish/Christian anthropology with which it has been in many-centuried dialogue. Maritain and Simon began this task, but they did not complete it.

The present volume, for all its many and varied small contributions to the overall design, still falls short of presenting such a statement. It does not yet present a formidable "concrete historical ideal" for societies that now try, however inadequately, to represent "liberty, virtue, and the common good." In that larger task, however, if this volume is not yet the beginning of the end, it may well mark the end of the beginning. As God is in the details, so larger visions always depend upon many well-done smaller pieces of work. Conscious of working toward greater things to come, that is the contribution appropriate to our generation and to this volume.

Contributors

Don T. Asselin, an Associate Professor of Philosophy at Hillsdale College in Michigan, has written several reviews and scholarly articles on Maritain. He is the author of the book *Human Nature and Eudaimonia in Aristotle.* He also has published in the areas of ethics, medical ethics, and the philosophy of religion.

William Bush is Professor of French at the University of Western Ontario, known primarily for his work on Georges Bernanos. In 1993 his critical edition of Marie de l'Incarnation's *La Relation du martyre des seize Carmélites de Compiègne* was published in Paris by Les Editions du Cerf. His forthcoming English volume on that martyrdom, *To Quell the Terror: The Mystery of the Vocation of the Sixteen Carmelite Martyrs of Compiègne,* is being published by the Institute of Carmelite Studies in Washington, D.C.

Joseph J. Califano is Professor of Philosophy at Saint John's University (Jamaica, New York). He has published articles in *The Thomist, Divus Thomas,* and in past publications of the *American Maritain Association.* His article, "Human Suffering and Our Post-Civilized Cultural Mind: A Maritainian Analysis," appeared in *From Twilight To Dawn* (Notre Dame, Indiana: Notre Dame University Press, 1990). He has presented papers internationally under the auspices of the International Association of Energy Use Management and the International Association of Hydrogen Energy.

Diane M. Caplin is Associate Director of the Mount Saint Agnes Theological Center for Women, Baltimore, Maryland. In addition, she teaches professional ethics at the College of Notre Dame of Maryland. Her doctoral dissertation was entitled *Essentially Human: Democracy in the Thought of Yves R. Simon* (Marquette University, 1993).

367

Clarke E. Cochran is Professor of Political Science and Adjunct Professor, Department of Health Organization Management at Texas Tech University. He received his Ph.D. from Duke University in 1971. Professor Cochran's primary fields of teaching and research are religion and politics, political philosophy, and health care policy. He is the author of three books, including *Religion in Public and Private Life* (Routledge, 1990), seventeen articles and book chapters, and numerous reviews and conference papers.

Donald DeMarco is an Associate Professor of Philosophy at the University of St. Jerome's College in Waterloo, Ontario. He is the author of eleven books, including *Biotechnology and the Assault on Parenthood*. His twelfth book, *The Heart of Virtue*, is in the process of being published. He is an Associate Editor of *Child and Family Quarterly* and an advisory editor for *Social Justice Review*. An extensive lecturer, he also has numerous publications in a variety of scholarly journals.

Joseph M. de Torre is Social Ethics Professor and Chair of the department of philosophy at the Center for Research and Communications in Manila, Phillipines. Father de Torre is the author of several books, including *Social Morals: The Church Speaks on Society*, *The Metaphysical Ground of Social Ethics: The Roots of Social Order*, and *Christian Philosophy*.

Roger Duncan, Ph.D., Yale, 1969, teaches philosophy at the University of Connecticut, Hartford Campus; moderates three ongoing Thomist study groups which meet in Connecticut; consults Philosophy for Children Program at the Patton School of Montessori in Bridgewater, Connecticut; authors numerous articles on philosophical and theological subjects.

Curtis L. Hancock is Associate Professor of Philosophy at Rockhurst College, Kansas City, Missouri. With Randolph M. Feezell he co-authored *How Should I Live*, a book on ethics. He has published several articles and book reviews on ancient and medieval philosophy, political philosophy, and ethics. He has served as an officer of the Executive Committee of the *American Maritain Association*, and is currently associate editor of *Contemporary Philosophy*.

Thomas Hibbs is Associate Professor of Philosophy at Boston College. He earned a B.A. at the University of Dallas in 1982, and a year later was awarded the M.A. He received his Ph.D. from Notre

Dame in 1987. He is the author of a book forthcoming from the University of Notre Dame Press: *Dialectic and Narrative in Aquinas: An Interpretation of the Summa Contra Gentiles.*

Deal W. Hudson is Professor of Philosophy at Fordham University and presently serves as managing editor of *Crisis.* He is co-editor of *Understanding Maritain: Philosopher and Friend,* and is the current President of the *American Maritain Association.* He is author of a forthcoming book on happiness.

John Killoran teaches Philosophy at King's College in the University of Western Ontario. He has a B.A. from Northeastern University in Boston and an M.A. and a Ph.D. from the University of Western Ontario. His interests focus on Aquinas's moral philosophy and natural law ethics in general.

Joseph Koterski, S.J. teaches in the philosophy department at Fordham University and is the editor of *International Philosophical Quarterly.*

Wilfred L. LaCroix, S.J. is Professor of Philosophy at Rockhurst College. He has published several books on ethics and political philosophy, including *International Ethics and The Just War* (Washington, D.C.: University Press of America, 1988).

Thomas Joseph Loughran received a B.S. In Chemistry (1980) and a Ph.D. in Philosophy (1986) from the University of Notre Dame. He has held faculty appointments at the University of Notre Dame and the University of Portland, and is currently a member of the Center for Christian Studies in South Bend, Indiana and Visiting Scholar at the University of Notre Dame. He recently authored "Freedom and Good in the Thomistic Tradition," *Faith and Philosophy*, Vol. 11, No. 3 (July, 1994).

Mark McGovern is currently Associate Pastor of St. Patrick's Church in Anamosa, Iowa. He has taught at Loras College, Dubuque, Iowa, Cardinal Newman College, St. Louis, Missouri, and Rockhurst College, Kansas City, Missouri. He has presented many papers at national organizations, including the American Catholic Philosophical Association.

Ralph McInerny is Professor of Philosophy at Notre Dame Universi and Director of the Jacques Maritain Center there. He was for ye editor of *The New Scholasticism.* He is the author of such deligh reads as *Ethica Thomistica* and the Father Dowling mysteries. He has long worked in the thought of Maritain and Simon, having published, for example, *Art and Prudence: Studies in the Thought of Jacques Maritain* and having translated Simon's *Critique of Moral Knowledge*.

Ralph Nelson teaches in the department of political science in the University of Windsor, Ontario. He has written numerous articles on the moral and political philosophy of Jacques Maritain. He is currently working on a translation of Yves R. Simon's treatise on the philosophy of science, *Prévoir et savoir*, the tentative English title being *Foresight and Knowledge*.

Michael Novak is George F. Jewett Scholar in Religion, Philosophy, and Public Policy at the American Enterprise Institute, Washington, D.C. In 1987 and 1988 he was Professor of American Studies at the University of Notre Dame. He is author of *Free Persons and the Common Good*, and *The Catholic Ethic and the Spirit of Capitalism*. He is recent winner of the Templeton Prize.

Joseph L. Pappin III is Dean of the University of South Carolina at Lancaster and Professor of Philosophy. His work on *the Metaphysics of Edmund Burke* was published by Fordham University Press in 1993. He has previously published articles on Sartre, Karol Cardinal Wojtyla, Kierkegaard, Maritain, Rahner, and Burke in such journals as *Philosophy Today*, *ACPA Proceedings*, *The Thomist*, and *Modern Age*.

Alice Ramos is Associate Professor of Philosophy at St. John's University in Jamiaca, New York. She has published articles in such areas as the Christian anthroplogy of Pope John Paul II, Thomistic metaphysics, and Kant's ethical theology. Her main interests lie in 'losophy of religion and in metaphysics.

' **A. Redpath** is currently Professor of Philosophy at St. John's ;ity in Staten Island, New York. He is the author of several ımerous articles and book reviews related to Thomas Aquinas s Maritain. He is currently Vice President of the *American ʾociation* and a member of the Advisory Board of the *Institute*. He edited *From Twilight to Dawn: The Cul-ʾacques Maritain* (Notre Dame, Indiana: University of 1990). He is also associate editor of *Contemporary*

Mary Carmen Rose is Professor Emeritus of Philosophy and also presently Adjunct Professor of Philosophy at Goucher College, Baltimore, Maryland. Her philosophical interests are in aesthetics, the relations between philosophy and theology, the present-day need for the development of a world philosophical community, and the issues of ontological, epistemological, and moral realism. She has published nearly 160 articles and most recently her work has appeared in *Priests and People*, *The Month*, *The Journal of the British Society for Aesthetics*, *World Order*, and *Between the Species*.

Thomas R. Rourke is Visiting Assistant Professor of Political Science at Florida International University, Miami, Florida. He has published on the political and economic thought of Yves R. Simon. His dissertation at Texas Tech University, 1994, compared Simon's thought with that of contemporary Catholic neoconservatism.

Anthony O. Simon is director of the *Yves R. Simon Institute* and secretary-treasurer of the *American Maritain Association*, and he serves as general editor of the Association's publications. With Ralph Nelson he edited Yves R. Simon's *Foresight and Knowledge* and was editor of *Jacques Maritain: Homage in Words and Picture* by John Howard Griffin and Yves R. Simon.

Brendan Sweetman is Assistant Professor of Philosophy at Rockhurst College, Kansas City, Missouri. He is a native of Ireland and was educated at University College, Dublin, and at the University of Southern California, where he obtained his Ph.D. He is co-editor of an anthology in the philosophy of religion, *Contemporary Perspectives on Religious Epistemology* (Oxford University Press, 1992). He has published and presented several papers on the philosophy of Gabriel Marcel, and on recent Continental Philosophy.

John G. Trapani, Jr. is a Professor of Philosophy at Walsh University in North Canton, Ohio, where he has taught for twenty years. He has a B.A. from Boston College and a Ph.D. from St. John's University in Jamaica, New York. His dissertation, *The Interrelation of Poetry, Beauty, and Contemplation in the Philosophy of Jacques Maritain*, heads a list of published articles on Maritain's philosophy.

Index